BETWEEN MARX AND MUHAMMAD

Born in the Indian sub-continent, Dilip Hiro was educated in India, Britain and America. He has been living in London since the mid-1960s, and is a full-time writer and journalist, and a frequent commentator on Middle Eastern, Islamic and Central Asian affairs on radio and television in Britain and North America. His articles have appeared in the *Observer, Sunday Times, Independent, Guardian, Washington Post, Wall Street Journal, Toronto Star* and *International Herald Tribune*. His books include *Inside the Middle East, The Longest War: The Iran–Iraq Military Conflict* and *Desert Shield to Desert Storm: The Second Gulf War*.

From the reviews of *Between Marx and Muhammad*:

'Dilip Hiro has produced the first and only book to summarize Central Asian history following the collapse of the Soviet Union . . . Hiro sensibly includes parallel surveys of related developments in neighbouring Muslim states such as Iran, Turkey and Afghanistan . . . The strength of Hiro's book is the effort he has spent on tracking down hard-to-find elements of the region's history: the book will be invaluable to businessmen, diplomats or journalists as a reference work on political events.'

HUGH POPE, *Independent*

'This intelligent and lucid book . . . Dilip Hiro's scholarly and readable *Between Marx and Muhammad* does an excellent job of chronicling the attempts of Azerbaijan and the republics of Central Asia to deal with the consequence of their new independence from Moscow. A series of maps and a first-rate glossary and chronology provide invaluable reference points . . . A fascinating account.' TIRA SHUBART, *Daily Telegraph*

'Dilip Hiro . . . uses his deep knowledge of the Islamic world to record the USSR's rise and fall as seen from Tashkent, Samarkand, Alma Ata, Dushanbe, Tehran and Ankara . . . The Western reader of this valuable book sees the world from an unfamiliar perspective . . . Hiro uncovers an intricate mesh of interconnections between them all, and his judgements carry authority.' WILLIAM MILLINSHIP, *Observer*

'A thought-provoking book . . . Thanks to his meticulous reporting of domestic politics, Mr Hiro is able to explain why each new state is engaged in different kinds of nation-building.'
Economist

'Indispensable as an historical summary and a source of basic information . . . sober and objective . . . Dilip Hiro's book will remain the best there is on the subject.'
ANATOL LIEVEN, *Tablet*

'Chronicles Soviet involvement in Central Asia since the Russian Revolution with impressive attention to the twists and turns of policy.' MALISE RUTHVEN, *Times Literary Supplement*

'For the growing throng of diplomats and businessmen with an interest in the region – not least in Caspian oil – *Between Marx and Muhammad* must surely be required reading.'
CHRISTIAN TYLER, *Financial Times*

'A useful guide to those trying to make sense of a vital region at a time when the US State Department has announced its resolve to stop focusing post-Soviet foreign policy solely on Russia.'
CHRISTIAN CARYL, *Wall Street Journal Europe*

Between Marx and Muhammad

Non-Fiction

Lebanon, Fire and Embers: A History of the Lebanese Civil War (1993)
Desert Shield to Desert Storm: The Second Gulf War (1992)
Black British, White British: A History of Race Relations in Britain (1991)
The Longest War: The Iran–Iraq Military Conflict (1989)
Islamic Fundamentalism (1988)
Iran: The Revolution Within (1988)
Iran Under the Ayatollahs (1985)
Inside the Middle East (1982)
Inside India Today (1976)
The Untouchables of India (1975)
Black British, White British (1971)
The Indian Family in Britain (1969)

Fiction

Three Plays (1987)
Interior, Exchange, Exterior (poems, 1980)
Apply, Apply, No Reply *and* A Clean Break (two plays, 1978)
To Anchor a Cloud (play, 1972)
A Triangular View (novel, 1969)

DILIP HIRO

Between Marx and Muhammad

The Changing Face of Central Asia

HarperCollins*Publishers*

HarperCollins*Publishers*
77–85 Fulham Palace Road,
Hammersmith, London W6 8JB

This paperback edition 1995
1 3 5 7 9 8 6 4 2

First published in Great Britain by
HarperCollins*Publishers* 1994

Copyright © Dilip Hiro 1994

The Author asserts the moral right to
be identified as the author of this work

ISBN 0 00 638367 X

Set in Linotron Bembo

Printed in Great Britain by
HarperCollinsManufacturing Glasgow

CONTENTS

ILLUSTRATIONS

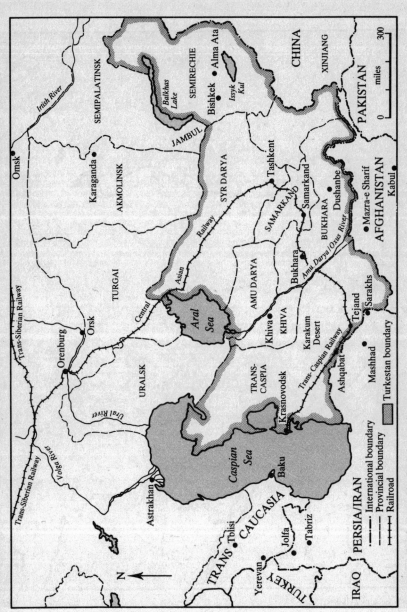

Central Asia before the 1917 Bolshevik revolution

The Soviet Union (1918–91)

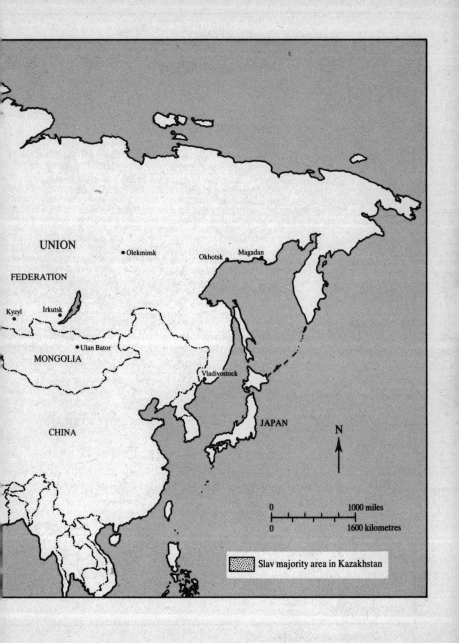

UNION

FEDERATION

Kyzyl Irkutsk

● Olekminsk   Okhotsk ● Magadan

● Ulan Bator

MONGOLIA

Vladivostock

CHINA

JAPAN

N

| | 0 | | | | 1000 miles |
| 0 | | | | 1600 kilometres |

Slav majority area in Kazakhstan

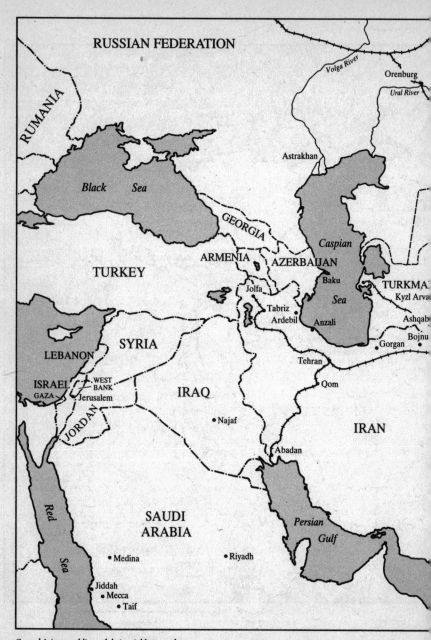

Central Asian republics and their neighbours today

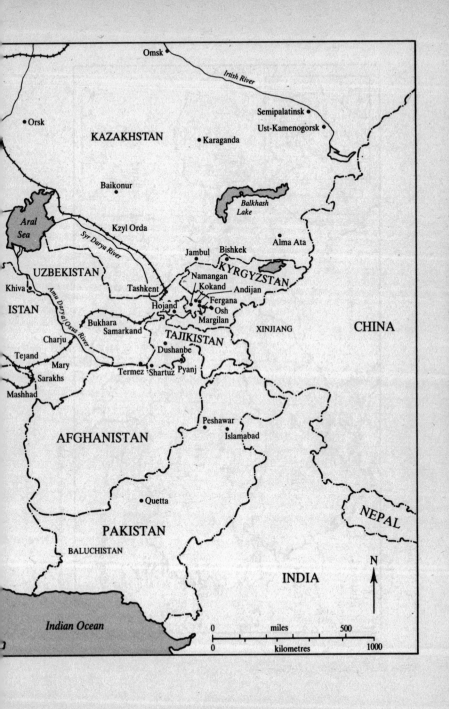

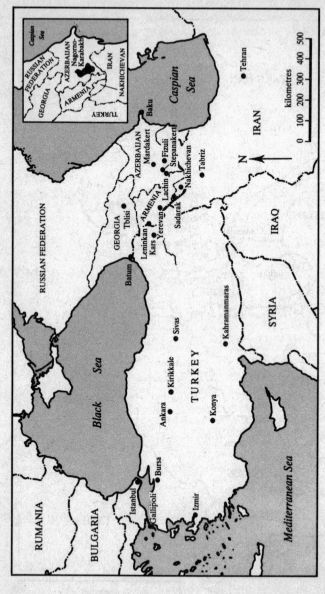

Trans-Caucasian republics and their neighbours today

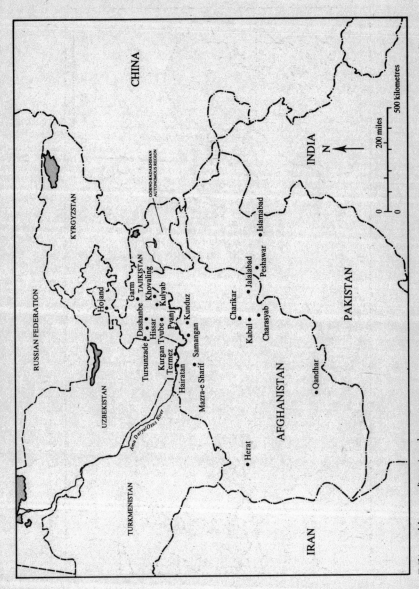

Tajikistan and the surrounding region today

LIST OF ABBREVIATIONS

ASEAN	Association of South-Eastern Asian Nations
ASSR	Autonomous Soviet Socialist Republic
AUNP	Armenian United National Party
BSCC	Black Sea Cooperation Council
CBMO	Central Bureau of Muslim Organizations
CDT	Collective Defence Treaty
CEC	Central Executive Committee
CIA	Central Intelligence Agency
CIS	Commonwealth of Independent States
CPA	Communist Party of Azerbaijan
CPD	Congress of People's Deputies
CPK	Communist Party of Kazakhstan
CPKz	Communist Party of Kyrgyzstan
CPSU	Communist Party of the Soviet Union
CPT	Communist Party of Tajikistan
CPTu	Communist Party of Turkmenistan
CPU	Communist Party of Uzbekistan
CSCE	Conference on Security and Cooperation in Europe
CYL	Communist Youth League
DFRTC	Democratic Federative Republic of Trans-Caucasia
DGRA	Directorate General of Religious Affairs
DISK	*Devrinci Isci Sendikalari Konfedasyony* (Confederation of Revolutionary Workers' Unions)
DKM	Democratic Kyrgyzstan Movement
DP	Democratic Party
DRA	Democratic Republic of Azerbaijan
EC	European Community
ECO	Economic Cooperation Organization
EEC	European Economic Community
GDP	Gross Domestic Product
GNA	Grand National Assembly
HIC	Higher Islamic Council
ICO	Islamic Conference Organization

IMF	International Monetary Fund
IPP	Islamic Progress Party
IRGC	Islamic Revolutionary Guards Corps
ISI	Inter Services Intelligence
JP	Justice Party
KGB	*Komitet Gosudarstvennoy Bezopasnosti* (Committee for State Security)
Khad	*Khidmat-e amniyat-e dawlati* (Service of State Security)
KNB	*Komitet Natsionalnoy Bezopasnosti* (Committee for National Security)
Komsomol	*Kommunisticheskiyo soyuz molodyezhy* (Communist Youth League)
NAP	National Action Party
NATO	North Atlantic Treaty Organization
NIM	National Islamic Movement
NKVD	*Narodnyi Kommissariat Vnutrennikh Del* (People's Commissariat of Internal Affairs)
NLFA	National Liberation Front of Afghanistan
NLP	Nationalist Labour Party
NOP	National Order Party
NSC	National Security Council
NSF	National Salvation Front
Omon	*Otryady militsiy osobovo naznachenia* (Special Purpose Militia Units)
PDA	People's Democratic Army
PDP	People's Democratic Party
PDPA	People's Democratic Party of Afghanistan
PF	Popular Front
PLO	Palestine Liberation Organization
PVC	People's Volunteer Corps
RCP	Russian Communist Party
RDC	Regional Development Council
RPMC	Russian Party of Muslim Communists
RPP	Republican People's Party
RSFSR	Russian Soviet Federated Socialist Republic
SDPP	Social Democratic Populist Party
SSR	Soviet Socialist Republic
UN	United Nations
UNHCR	United Nations High Commissioner for Refugees
US	United States (of America)
USSR	Union of Soviet Socialist Republics

GLOSSARY OF FOREIGN TERMS

(NR = Non-Russian*; R = Russian)

adalat (NR)	justice
Adat (NR)	customary
akbar(NR)	great
al/el/ol/ul (NR)	the
Allah (NR)	God
ashura (NR)	(lit.) tenth; (fig.) tenth of Muharram
ayatollah (NR)	sign or token of Allah
azam (NR)	big; great
azat (NR)	free
bai (NR)	notable
basmachi (NR)	bandit
beg (NR)	landlord
bek (NR)	servant of ruler or chieftain
birlik (NR)	unity
commissar (komissar in Russian)	head of government ministry (1917–46)
cumhuriyet (NR)	republic
din (NR)	faith
-e (NR)	of
emir/amir (NR)	one who gives *amr* (command); commander
erk (NR)	freedom
erkin (NR)	free
faqih (NR)	religious jurist
gazeta (R)	gazette; newspaper
hadith (NR)	action or speech of Prophet Muhammad or an imam

* Non-Russian languages include Arabic, Persian, Tajik, Turkish and Uzbek.

haji (NR)	one who has performed the hajj
hajj (NR)	pilgrimage to Mecca
halk (NR)	people; popular
haq (NR)	truth
harakiti (NR)	front; alliance
hazrat (NR)	title for prophet or imam
himmat (NR)	endeavour
hizb (NR)	party
Hizbollah (NR)	Party of God
i (R)	and
-i (NR)	of
ibn (NR)	son (of)
ikhwan (NR)	brotherhood; brethren
imam (NR)	(lit.) one who leads prayers in a mosque; (fig.) religious leader
ishan (NR)	(spiritual) guide
izvestia (R)	news
jadid (NR)	innovator
jammat (NR)	society; association
Jeltoksan (R)	December
jihad (NR)	(lit.) struggle in the name of Allah; (fig.) holy crusade or war
jirga (NR)	assembly
kazi/kadi (NR)	judge
khalq (NR)	people; popular
khan (NR)	chieftain; ruler
kolkhoz (R)	collective farm
kyzyl/kzyl (NR)	fort
levykh (R)	left
literaturnaya (R)	literary
madressa (NR)	religious school
majlis (NR)	assembly
marja-e mutaliq (NR)	absolute source
maslahty (NR)	council
maulavi (NR)	religious scholar
mestnichestvo (R)	local favouritism
milli/melli (NR)	national
mufti (NR)	one who delivers fatwas, religious rulings

mujahedin (NR; sing. mujahed)	(lit.) those who volunteer for jihad; (fig.) holy warriors or crusaders
mujtahid (NR)	one who practises *ijtihad*, interpretative reasoning
musavat (NR)	unity
narod (R)	people
nasr (NR)	victory
natsiya (R)	nation
nauka (R)	knowledge
nur (NR)	light
oglu (NR)	son (of)
orda (NR)	horde; group
parcham (NR)	flag
pasdran (NR)	guards
pravda (R)	truth
pravykh (R)	right
qadim (NR)	precursor
rastakhiz (NR)	resurgence
religiya (R)	religion
riba (NR)	usury
sawad (NR)	group
sayid (NR)	(lit.) lord or prince; (fig.) title applied to a male descendant of Imam Hussein ibn Ali
sazman (NR)	organization
sejah (NR)	army
shah (NR)	king
shaikh (NR)	(lit.) old man; (fig.) a title of respect accorded to a wise man
shaikh-al-Islam (NR)	wise man of Islam
Sharia (NR)	sacred law of Islam
shura (NR)	consultation
soviet (R)	council
sultan (NR)	ruler
tanzimat (NR)	reorganization
ulema/ulama (NR; sing. alim)	body of religious-legal scholars
vecherni (R)	evening
vich (R)	son (of)
vostoka (R)	east
wahadat (NR)	unity

waqf (NR)	religious endowment
watan (NR)	homeland; nation
zakat (NR)	alms; charity
zaman (NR)	present time
zvezda (R)	star

PREFACE

There is no universal agreement as to whether or not the term Central Asia includes Kazakhstan, which is twice as large as Turkmenistan, Uzbekistan, Kyrgyzstan and Tajikistan combined. Actually, there are two Kazakhstans – the Russian-dominated north, and the Kazakh-dominated south – with the latter undoubtedly part of Central Asia culturally and otherwise. During the Soviet era and its immediate aftermath, the region was officially known as 'Middle Asia and Kazakhstan'. For the sake of simplicity, I have used the term 'Central Asia' to include all of Kazakhstan.

The names of the republics have undergone changes since the Bolshevik revolution of 1917, the latest version during the Soviet period being Uzbek Soviet Socialist Republic, Kazakh Soviet Socialist Republic, and so on. But once again, to simplify matters, I have used Kazakhstan, Turkmenistan, Uzbekistan, Tajikistan and Kyrgyzstan (even though its May 1993 constitution specifies Kyrgyz Republic).

To make sense of contemporary events one needs to delve into history, all the more so in the case of the Central Asian republics. They came into being in the 1920s as a result of the policies devised mainly by Joseph V. Stalin (1878–1953). That is why my Introduction covers the period up to the death of Stalin. Since Azerbaijan, a Muslim-majority state in the Caucasus, is separated from Central Asia by the Caspian Sea, and since during the civil war that followed the Bolshevik revolution it existed as the Democratic Republic of Azerbaijan for two years, I have treated it separately within the Introduction.

As the book examines the relationship between the Central Asian republics and Azerbaijan and their immediate Muslim neighbours – Turkey, Iran and Afghanistan – I begin the main text with a history of Turkey, concentrating on the religious/secular aspects of its recent history. Due to the cultural and linguistic affinity that exists between Turkey and Azerbaijan, my next chapter deals with Azerbaijan.

Given its size, and its significant, though unstated, role as a buffer between Russia and Central Asia proper, Kazakhstan forms the subject of Chapter 3. And since Kazakhs and Kyrgyzs are kinsmen, the next chapter focuses on Kyrgyzstan.

Turkmenistan, a contrast to Kyrgyzstan in more ways than one, follows. Then comes Uzbekistan, the most populous, complex and strategic state in the region, the subject of Chapter 6. The next chapter, the last one dealing with Central Asia, outlines a history of Tajikistan, culminating in a civil war between Islamists and Communists, which raged until December 1992, and which involved Islamic forces from Afghanistan.

As a Muslim country that escaped European colonization and recently witnessed a victory of Islam over Marxism, and which before the Communist coup of 1978 resembled in many ways the Central Asia of the Tsarist era, Afghanistan deserves a fairly detailed outline of its history. I provide it in Chapter 8. Then follows an account of the Islamic revolution of 1979 in Iran, another Muslim country which was not colonized by a European power. Since the Iranian revolution involved transforming a secular society and state into a religious one, and since its strategic position gives substantial leverage to Iran in its relations with Afghanistan, Central Asia and Azerbaijan, I examine the subject at some length in Chapter 9. The book ends with a set of conclusions drawn heavily from the earlier narrative.

To assist the English-speaking reader to grapple satisfactorily with a plethora of exotic names of people, places and ethnic groups, it is necessary to set out some ground rules.

First, Turks and Turkic peoples. They can be broadly categorized as Western Turks and Eastern (or Central Asian) Turks. The term 'Western Turks' applies to Turks of Turkey as well as Azeris and (linguistically, not geographically) Turkmens; and 'Central Asian Turks' to those inhabiting the Turkestan region under the Tsars. In between come Turko-Tatars or Tatars, the inhabitants of the Volga region in the Urals and parts of the Crimea.

Turkish means the language of the Turks of Turkey; and Turkic pertains to a sub-family of Ural-Altaic languages as well as the peoples speaking these languages. In modern Turkish, written in the Roman alphabet, 'c' corresponds to 'j', 'ç' to 'ch' and 's' to 'sh'. Wherever necessary, I provide the English pronunciation of a Turkish name in parenthesis the first time it appears: e.g. Celal (Jelal).

Second, the Russian language and Russification of Muslim names.

Almost always Muslim names are rooted in Arabic, the language of the Quran, or Persian, the language of many commentaries on it. Russian is written in the Cyrillic alphabet, which lacks 'h', 'j', 'w', 'x', etc., their equivalents in Latin being respectively 'kh' or 'g', 'dzh', 'v', 'ks', etc. Also, often the vowels 'a' and 'o', and 'i' and 'y', are interchangeable. As a result 'Rahman' is Russified as 'Rakhmon', 'Tajikistan' as 'Tadzhikistan', 'Heidar' as 'Geidar/Kheydar'. Sometimes the troublesome 'h' disappears altogether, with 'Mohammed' reduced to 'Mamed', or even 'Mama'. Then there is the Russian custom of adding 'ev', 'yev' or 'ov' to the last name of a male. The metamorphosis of 'Jehangir Muhammad' into 'Dzhekhangir Mamedov' incorporates the above elements of Russification. To assist the non-Russian reader in familiarizing him/herself with a long list of Russified names of Muslim people and places, wherever necessary I have used the most current spelling of the Muslim name in its pristine form, adding the Russified version in brackets, or vice versa. Thus, Hojand (Khodzhand); Yusupov (Yusuf).

Since many of the names in the text are long and exotic, it should help to know the meanings of the most frequent suffixes: 'al Din/uddin/iddin' (Arabic; of faith); 'oglu' (Turkish; son of); 'vich' (Russian; son of); 'zade/zadeh' (Persian; son of). Also the following suffixes are used in the Turkic world to denote a person of high social status: 'bai/bayev', 'bay/bey', 'manab/manap'.

The following Arabic, Persian, Pushtun or Turkish words signify religious or secular titles: 'ayatollah', 'emir', 'haji', 'hazrat', 'imam', 'kazi', 'maulavi', 'mufti', 'sayid', 'shah', 'shaikh', 'shaikh-al-Islam' and 'sultan'.

The dates in brackets after the first mention of a monarch specify when he/she reigned. But corresponding figures for non-hereditary figures indicate their years of birth and death.

There is no standard way of transliterating Arabic and Persian names. In each case I have chosen one of most widely used spellings in the English-speaking world, and stuck to it – except when the spelling of an author is different from mine. There I have simply reproduced the published spelling.

Some of the place names were changed following the Bolshevik revolution, and then again after the break-up of the Soviet Union. Wherever possible, at the first mention of a place name I give the old version in brackets, or vice versa: thus, Leninabad (Hojand), Alma Ata (Verny), Volgograd (Stalingrad).

Finally, a key to understanding racial differences between various ethnic groups. The best way is to start with the 'primary races' of the region – Mongols, Europeans and Iranians – and then graduate to major combinations, or 'secondary races': Mongols and Europeans yielding Turks/Turko-Tatars; and Mongols and Iranians producing Tajiks. Next come the most frequent combinations of primary and secondary races: Turks and Mongols resulting in Kazakhs/Kyrgyzs; and Turks and Iranians in Uzbeks, the largest ethnic group in the region. In reality there are of course several more hybrids. But this fairly simplified formula should help the reader conjure up a mental image of a particular ethnic group and assist him/her to identify them while travelling in the region.

During the Soviet era there were three centres of power at the republican and federal levels: the Central Committee of the Communist Party (headed by the first secretary); the Presidium of the Supreme Soviet (led by the chairman, the nominal head of the republic/Union), which dealt with legislation in between the infrequent and brief sessions of the Supréme Soviet; and the Council of Ministers, called People's Commissars during the first thirty years of the Bolshevik Revolution (led by the chairman, the head of the government). Changes in the Union constitution in early 1990 created the new office of the executive president, who became the head of the Union, superseding the chairman of the Presidium of the Supreme Soviet. This job went to Mikhail Gorbachev (1931–) in March 1990. Later the constituent republics followed the same path.

The symbol used for Soviet/Russian roubles is R.

This paperback edition includes a revised Epilogue which covers events up to September 1994. I spent the best part of the period May–December 1992 travelling around the region, and revisited Turkey in September 1994.

Dilip Hiro
London, October 1994

INTRODUCTION

Former Soviet Central Asia, officially called 'Middle Asia and Kazakhstan', is a land mass east of the Caspian Sea framed by the frontiers of Iran and Afghanistan in the south, Siberia in the north, and the Xinjiang province of China to the east.

Russia's domination of the area came about in two stages: the capture of the Kazakh steppes from 1731 to 1854; and the conquest of the rest of the region during the period 1865–81. Expansion in the Trans-Volga region in the early eighteenth century by the Tsars set the scene for Russian control over the Asian steppes used for grazing by Kazakhs, the largest of the nomadic cattle-breeders, who were divided into three major groups – Hordes – often at loggerheads with one another. The Small Horde was based between the Caspian Sea and the Aral Sea, the Middle Horde in the central Hungry Steppe, and the Great Horde in the Semirechie region stretching towards the Chinese border. Through trade and diplomacy the Russians accentuated differences between the Kazakh Hordes and weakened them. The Hordes sought, and secured, agreements with the Tsar – the Small Horde signing a treaty in 1731, followed by the Middle Horde (1732) and the Great Horde (1742).

However, the Russian–Kazakh relationship proved uneasy, and led to periodic uprisings by Kazakhs, which invariably failed. Gradually tightening their grip over Kazakh land, Tsars Alexander I (1801–25) and Nicholas I (1825–55) deposed Kazakh rulers, called Khans, starting with that of the Middle Horde (1822) and ending with the Great Horde (1848).

This prepared the ground for further Russian incursions into Asia. Having staged an abortive campaign against the Khanate of Khiva in 1839, Tsar Nicholas I opted for a long-term strategy. In 1853 the Russians mounted a slow two-prong attack – marching from the west up the Syr Darya River and from the east along the lower slopes of the Tien Shan Mountains – which was to last until 1864 (during the rule of Tsar Alexander II, 1855–81), and which yielded Kzyl Orda and Alma Ata (then Verny) to them in the first two years.

Having encircled the Kazakh territory, the Russians embarked on their next stage of empire-building in Asia. They confronted the Khanates of Khiva and Kokand, and the Emirate of Bukhara, comprising a region with a long and glorious history, which was now in comparative decline. After taking Tashkent (literally City of Stones), a part of Kokand, in 1865, they defeated the Khan of Kokand the following year. In 1867 Tsar Alexander II set up the Turkestan Governor-Generalship, with Tashkent as its capital, which also included his new protectorate of Kokand under a nominally independent Khan. Next year he expanded Turkestan by incorporating the Emirate of Bukhara as a protectorate. The same fate befell the Khanate of Khiva in 1873. Three years later the Tsar annexed Kokand, thus ending its nominal independence. With the remaining area of Central Asia, known as Trans-Caspia, the land of Turkmen tribes, falling into Tsarist hands in 1881, Russia completed its control of the region. Five years later Tsar Alexander III (1881–94) renamed the enlarged Turkestan Governor-Generalship as Turkestan Territory.

To consolidate their new acquisitions the Russian authorities extended the Trans-Caspian railway to Samarkand (1888), Tashkent (1889) and Andijan in the Fergana Valley (1899). By connecting Tashkent with Orenburg by railway in 1906 the imperial government increased contacts between Central Asia and other parts of the empire.

The region was populated mainly by races that were admixtures of Europeans, Mongols and Iranians, with European-Mongol interbreeding having created Turks/Tatars, and Iranian-Mongol interbreeding Tajiks; and the admixture of Turks and Mongols having resulted in Kazakhs/Kyrgyzs, and that of Turks and Iranians in Uzbeks. While the Kazakh, Kyrgyz and Turkmen tribes were predominantly nomadic, others had a long history of sedentary life in the fertile valleys and oases.

When the Russians arrived as conquerors, they found Samarkand, Bukhara, Khiva, Kokand, Tashkent and Mary (then Merv) possessing a rich heritage of historical monuments, and functioning as eminent centres of Islamic learning. They refrained from interfering with the traditional way of life of the Muslim community, which was determined by the requirement of the Sharia, the Islamic law.

The Russian colonization centred around urban settlements, with the settlers including not merely the usual contingents of civil servants, traders and troops but also skilled and semi-skilled workers to operate the railways and industrial plants. Among local peoples, sedentary Uzbeks were foremost in supplying indigenous labour for railways and cotton-ginning factories. With this, Tashkent, hitherto a city of secondary significance, became the leading industrial, commercial and administrative hub of Central Asia.

Russian colonization imposed an alien layer on the traditional Muslim social order, noted for its close family and clan ties and strong religiosity. Indigenous society consisted chiefly of nomads and landless peasants who received their wages in kind from landlords or cattle-owners, who lived mainly in urban centres. Only a minority of peasants, tending cotton fields, received its remuneration in cash. Together, these peasants and nomads maintained not only landlords, craftsmen, civil servants, money-lenders and soldiers, but also the religious hierarchy of prayer leaders, mullahs and kazis (religious judges). Such public services as schools and post offices were scanty or non-existent.

The strong religiosity of the traditional Muslim community was well illustrated by the statistics of the nominally independent Bukhara on the eve of the First World War (1914–18). This emirate of about two million Muslims had 2600 mosques.[1] Girls aged four or more had to wear the *paranja* (veil). The clergy were in cahoots with feudal lords and impressed on their impoverished congregations the value of a spartan existence, a key to God's affection and entry into heaven.

Like the rest of their co-religionists in the Tsarist empire, especially in the Caucasus, Central Asians considered themselves as Muslims first and foremost. 'The settled peoples of Central Asia regard themselves first as Muslims and then as inhabitants of any given town or region; ethnic concepts having virtually no significance in their eyes,' noted Vasiliy V. Barthold, Russia's leading specialist on Islam.[2]

Not surprisingly, therefore, Central Asian leaders analysed the unmistakable decline of their community in a religious context, pondering also the reasons for the growing strength of Tsarist Christian Russia. Either Russians had devised a system better than Islam or their community had failed to follow true Islam. One school, to be known as Qadimian or Qadims (i.e. Precursors), much favoured by the Islamic hierarchy, advocated strict application of the Sharia, while the other, called Jadidian or Jadids (i.e. Innovators), proposed innovation in the light of a fast-changing world which they saw from a predominantly westernized perspective.

Qadims too wanted to change but within the framework of Islamic tradition and not Western thought or practice. Since their ranks were filled with clerics and *ishans* (guides) of the Sufi (i.e. mystical Islam) orders, who were scattered throughout the countryside, Qadims had a mass appeal. They were opposed to the Russian rule but refrained from confronting it, aware that the call to jihad, holy war, by a leading Sufi leader in 1861 had not led to a widespread uprising. Their caution was well advised. A jihad by the Muslims in Andijan, a Fergana Valley city, in 1898, inspired by Muhammad Ali, a local leader of the Naqshbandi Sufi order, resulted in the deportation of the participants to Siberia and the transfer of their lands to Russian settlers.

While most Jadids were graduates of Quranic schools or Islamic colleges, they were also well versed in one or more Western languages, an asset which gave them an understanding of Western political theory and practice. However, lacking political power as well as access to the faithful, who were under the sway of predominantly Qadim clergy, they focused on socio-cultural reform. They established reformed schools which offered Russian and modern sciences along with religious instruction, the standard fare at the traditional madressas (theological schools), and demanded better rights for women. They toyed with the ideas of adopting Western dress and changing the Arabic script of their languages to Latin. But because they went along with Russian dominance, describing it as nothing more than 'a necessary evil', they failed to win popularity. Their leader, Shaikh Shahabuddin Marjani (1818–89), was noted for his attacks on the practices of Bukhara's clerics. Later, another leading figure, Ismail Hasbarali (1851–1914) – better known by his Russified name, Ismail Gasprinsky – a Crimean Tatar aristocrat, encouraged the founding of reformed schools through his newspaper *Terjuman-Perevodchik* (Interpreter), established in 1893.[3]

The 1905 constitutional revolution in Russia opened up opportunities for freer political activity in the empire. Jadids took advantage of the changed situation. Their leader, Abdul Rashid Ibrahimov, secured official permission to hold a pan-Islamic conference. Surprisingly, the Qadim leadership opposed the gathering, dismissing it as a Tsarist ploy to interfere in Islamic matters. In the end, 120 Jadid delegates met aboard a yacht in Nizhniy Novgorod (later Gorkiy), 400 km east of Moscow. They established the Alliance of Muslims, and demanded popular participation in politics under a constitutional monarch, freedom of expression for Muslims, and an end to the confiscation of Muslim land and its transfer to Russian and other Slav colonizers.

There were two more such assemblies, the last one in August 1906, again in Nizhniy Novgorod, where the delegates decided to transform the Alliance of Muslims into a political organization, the Muslims Party, with its own election manifesto. As before, the conference was dominated by Volga Tatars. Eleven of the fifteen central committee members were Tatars from Volga, with the only member from Turkestan also being a Tatar.[4]

In the late 1890s, Tatar intellectuals from the Crimean and Volga regions had begun advocating pan-Turkism as an alternative to westernization and pan-Islamism. *Turk*, a periodical established in Cairo in 1902, was active in promoting pan-Turkism – political unity of all Turkish-speaking peoples from the Balkans to China. In his essay 'Three Political Systems', published in 1904, the journal's founder, Yusuf Aq Churaoglu, claimed to provide 'scientific evidence' that all Turkic peoples 'from Egypt to China' constituted a single nation. Later, Ali Husseinzade, one of Churaoglu's disciples, coined a catchy slogan: 'Turkicization, Islamicization, Modernization'. A variant of this slogan came from Ziauddin Goek-Alp. 'We belong to the Turkish nation, the Muslim religion and the European civilization,' he said.[5]

The elaboration of pan-Turkism went hand in hand with efforts to forge a common version of Turkic, a sub-family of the Ural-Altaic languages, to be used by all Muslim subjects of the Tsar. A pioneer in this field was Ismail Gasprinsky, who coined the slogan: 'Unity of language, unity of thought, unity of action'. He arrived at a suitable language by eliminating Persian and Arabic loan words from a simplified version of the Ottoman Turkish, and used it for his newspaper, *Terjuman-Perevodchik*, where he stressed politico-cultural commonality of the Turkic peoples. But his experiment failed. The reality was that various Turkic dialects had by then matured as languages in their own right, Ottoman Turkish being one; and a common language failed to take hold. He closed the newspaper in 1905.

In Central Asia, the Emirate of Bukhara was the chief battleground for the competing ideologies of pan-Turkism and pan-Islamism. To meet the growing challenge to his power from pan-Turkists, the Emir promoted the minority Tajik-speaking Shias at the expense of the Sunni[6] Uzbek and Kazakh-Kyrgyz notables. This policy led to bloodshed between Sunnis and Shias in 1910, with the latter getting the worst of it. The intra-Muslim violence reflected badly on pan-Islamic forces, and weakened the Qadims. This enabled the Jadids, who included both Sunnis and Shias, to widen their base. Their efforts led to the founding of the Association for the Education of Children, called Tarbiyat. It expanded so quickly that by 1914 it could claim the loyalty of most of the Muslim intelligentsia.

Riding a wave of popularity, the Jadid leadership formed an alliance with the heads of the Qadims and Kazakh-Kyrgyz tribes on an anti-Russian platform, and convened a clandestine congress in Samarkand in June 1916. It resolved to organize an armed insurrection against Russian rule in Turkestan. The clergy issued calls of jihad against the Tsar. Their efforts received a boost when, responding to the pressures of the First World War – fought between the Allies (Russia, France, Britain *et al.*) and the Central Powers (Germany, Austria-Hungary and Ottoman Turkey) – the Tsar signed a decree drafting Turkestani Muslims, previously exempted from military service, into non-combatant army units. The order was highly unpopular,[7] and acted as a trigger for the anti-Russian insurrection, which erupted on 13 July. But the Russian army crushed it promptly. It was all over by 20 July.

AZERBAIJAN

As in Central Asia, the social order in Muslim-dominated Azerbaijan in Trans-Caucasia in the early twentieth century was feudal, with eighty per cent of the population being peasant, five per cent merchant, and 2.5 per cent aristocrat.[8] Following the same policy as in Central Asia, the Tsars had transformed several khanates in Trans-Caucasia, including Karabakh (originally Karabagh, meaning Black Garden) and Shirvan, into protectorates by 1805. The campaign by Iran to recover Georgia from the Russians in 1804 led to the First Russo-Iranian War, which lasted nine years. According to the 1813 Treaty of Gulistan, Iran surrendered to Russia most of its territory in the Caucasus to the north of its present frontier. However, the ill-defined territorial clauses of the treaty became a source of bitter disputes between the two sides. Efforts at reconciliation failed. The result was the Second Russo-Iranian War in 1826. This too ended in an Iranian defeat. According to the Treaty of Turkmenchai in 1828, Iran surrendered to Russia all of the territory west of the Caspian

Sea and north of its present border along the Aras River (except in the east where the frontier moved southwards), including the Khanates of Yerevan and Nakhichevan.

Following this, the Tsars proceeded to incorporate the Trans-Caucasian territories into the empire. By 1883 Baku was linked to the Black Sea coast and central Russia through the Trans-Caucasian railway. The region, associated with oil and gas since ancient times, fostered the petroleum industry in the early nineteenth century with hand-dug pits. The output increased to the extent that by 1901 this region provided half of Russia's oil needs and became one of the leading industrial centres of the Tsarist empire with a growing working class.[9] Baku was a cosmopolitan city with a large population of Armenians, Russians, Jews and Poles.

In contrast the hinterland was overwhelmingly Azeri and Muslim. The hold of Islam was strong, with the clergy, often of Iranian or Turkish origin, moulding public opinion along anti-Russian lines. This was a matter of concern to the viceroy of the Caucasus, I. Vorontsov-Dashkov, who reported to the Tsar in early 1905 that though there was as yet no separatist movement among local Muslims at the popular level, a nationalist feeling was emerging within the influential Muslim intelligentsia.[10]

At about the same time, a minority of Muslim intellectuals began taking an interest in socialism. In 1904 Muhammad Amin Rasulzadeh, a journalist from Baku, the Azeri capital and a leading oil-producing centre, founded a socialist study circle. It drew such local intellectuals as Nariman Bey Narimanoglu (later Narimanov) and Ahmed Azizbekoglu. Out of this emerged the Himmat (i.e. Effort) Party, linked to the Russian Social-Democrat Labour Party (Bolshevik). By 1906 it had become a significant entity in Baku and other Trans-Caucasian cities. The government kept it under surveillance, and finally banned it in 1912.

The subsequent vacuum was filled by nationalist and pan-Islamic trends among Muslim intellectuals, the two merging into the Musavat (i.e. Equality) Party, a nationalist organization with Islamic overtones, formed in late 1912. Among its founders was Muhammad Amin Rasulzadeh, who had by then broken with the Russian Social-Democrat Labour Party (Bolshevik). Musavat called for the unity of all Muslim peoples irrespective of nationality or sect, restoration of independence to all Muslim nations, and assistance to all Muslim peoples and countries 'in offence and defence'. The vagueness of the party objectives was symptomatic of its lack of a clear political philosophy, which made it vulnerable to exploitation by opportunists.

THE FEBRUARY 1917 REVOLUTION

The protracted bloodiness of the First World War, which erupted on 1 August 1914, led to a revolution in Russia on 27 February 1917. The abdication of Tsar Nicholas II on 2 March was followed by the official inauguration of the Provisional Government under Alexander Kerensky of the Social Revolutionary Party. Kerensky declared that he would maintain Russia's territorial integrity.

Internally, the revolution produced favourable conditions for the rise of the Russian Social-Democrat Labour Party (Bolshevik) under the leadership of Vladimir I. Lenin (1870–1924), then in exile. At its seventh congress in April, the party reiterated its backing for the right of 'all nations forming part of Russia' to 'free separation and the right to form their own independent states'. At the same time, in his report on the nationality question, Joseph V. Stalin, the party's specialist on the subject since 1903, reaffirmed Lenin's position that recognizing this right did not mean the Bolsheviks would support every demand for separation.

As for Russia's Muslim citizens, their representatives met in Moscow under the aegis of the First All Muslim Conference to forge a common position. But this did not happen. The delegates from Turkestan split along the Jadid–Qadim divide, the progressive Jadids forming the Islamic Council, and the conservative Qadims the Council of Ulema (Religious-legal Scholars). The Kazakh-Kyrgyz delegates kept out of the fray, and decided to establish Alash Orda (i.e. Group), a party named after Alash, the legendary ancestor of the Kazakh-Kyrgyz people. Its main demand was that the Kazakh lands given to Slav colonizers be restored to their original possessors. In contrast, the Islamic Council backed the slogans of 'Land to the Landless' and 'Expropriate Feudalists and Capitalists' raised by the Bolsheviks. As expected, the Council of Ulema focused on religion, urging the Kerensky government to replace the Russian law with the Sharia in Turkestan.

Following the revolution, Tashkent, the administrative headquarters of Turkestan, became the scene of two competing centres of power: the Provisional Government's Turkestan Committee and the Bolshevik-dominated Soviet (i.e. Council) of Workers' and

Peasants' Deputies. Both were Russian in composition. The uneasy co-existence of the two bodies could not be sustained for long. In mid-September 1917 the Bolsheviks staged strikes and demonstrations as a prelude to capturing power, but failed.

In late September the Second All Muslim Conference, led by local intellectuals, met in Tashkent, and demanded the formation of a Muslim government and autonomy for Turkestan in a federated Republic of Russia. But nothing came of it.

In Azerbaijan, the industrial city of Baku witnessed the rise of a Soviet of Workers' Deputies, consisting of various parties, including the Musavat, within a week of the February revolution. In May the All-Caucasus Muslim Congress pledged its support to the Provisional Government. In the October election to the Baku Soviet, almost forty per cent of the vote went to the Musavat, but it did not take up its seats.

All this happened against the background of the war between the Allies and the Central Powers, which had necessitated the deployment of half a million Russian troops in the Caucasus to frustrate Turkish plans to mount an offensive.

The war had created such acute political and economic crises that the Russian government had become weak and vulnerable. Sensing this, the Bolshevik leader, Lenin, thought the time had come to deliver a fatal blow to the system.

THE BOLSHEVIK REVOLUTION OF OCTOBER 1917

According to the Julian calendar then in vogue in Russia, the Bolshevik revolution occurred on 24–25 October 1917 when the Provisional Government was overthrown by the Bolshevik forces. But with the changeover to the Gregorian calendar (on 1 February 1918), these dates were transformed into 6–7 November.[11] Within hours of the revolution, power passed to the 650 delegates to the Second All-Russian Congress of the Soviets of Workers', Peasants' and Soldiers' Deputies which assembled in St Petersburg (then Petrograd). They elected the Council of People's Commissars, the new Soviet government, headed by Lenin.

On 25 October (7 November) the Presidium of the Tashkent Soviet, which had secretly won over the loyalties of the local Russian military unit, the Siberian Second Reserve Rifle Regiment, resolved to stage an armed uprising. The commissar-general of the Provisional Government in Tashkent got wind of this. On 27 October (9 November) he declared martial law, and tried to disarm the soldiers suspected of disloyalty. Fighting broke out the next day, with a workers' combat unit of 2500 joining the mutinous troops against the Provisional Government's loyalist forces. The Bolsheviks achieved victory in Tashkent on 1 November (14 November).

The next day the Council of People's Commissars of the Russian Soviet Federated Socialist Republic (RSFSR) in St Petersburg issued a Declaration of the Rights of the Peoples of Russia. It included equal sovereignty for all the nations of the former Tsarist empire; their right to self-determination up to and including the right to secede and form independent states; an end to the privileges and limitations of a national or religious nature; and recognition of the right to development for all national and ethnic minorities.

Following the lead of the centre, the Third Regional Congress of the Soviets of Workers', Peasants' and Soldiers' Deputies assembled in Tashkent on 15 November (28 November) and declared Soviet rule in Turkestan. It elected the regional Council of People's Commissars under the chairmanship of F. I. Kolesov. On 19 November (2 December) it decided by ninety-seven votes to seventeen to give Muslims four places on the Regional Council, two on the Regional Executive Committee, but none on the Council of People's Commissars.[12]

Concurrently, the Third All Muslim Congress, led by intellectuals, gathered in another district of Tashkent. Reiterating its demand for autonomy for Turkestan, it called for the immediate formation of a Muslim administration. It came out against the Bolshevik revolution. Later it received the support of clerics when their petition to the Tashkent Soviet to base its civil administration on the Sharia was rejected.

On 25 November (8 December) 197 delegates – 150 from the Fergana region, twenty-two from the Syr Darya region, twenty-one from Samarkand and four from Bukhara – assembled in Kokand under the auspices of the Fourth Extraordinary Regional Muslim Congress. Declaring Turkestan to be autonomous, they appointed a twelve-member Kokand Autonomous Government under Mustafa Chokaioglu, a Kazakh, and elected a council of thirty-six Muslims and eighteen Russians.

The Muslim leadership saw a glimmer of hope when, on 3 December (16 December) 1917, the Council of People's Commissars of the RSFSR addressed an appeal, signed by V. I. Lenin, and J. V. Stalin, the commissar of nationalities, to 'All Muslim Toilers of Russia and the East': 'Muslims of Russia! Tatars of the Volga and the Crimea! Kyrgyzs and Sarts[13] of Siberia and of Turkestan! Turks and Tatars of Trans-Caucasia! Chechens and mountain peoples of the Caucasus! All you whose mosques and prayer houses used to be destroyed, and whose beliefs and customs were trodden underfoot by the Tsars and oppressors of Russia! From today, your beliefs and customs, and your national and cultural constitutions, are free and inviolate. Organize your national life freely and without hindrance. You are entitled to this. Know that your rights, like the rights of all the peoples of Russia [i.e. RSFSR], are protected by the whole might of the Revolution and its agencies, the Soviets of workers', soldiers' and peasants' deputies. Support, then, this Revolution and its sovereign Government . . . Comrades! Brothers! Let us march towards an honest and democratic peace. On our banners is inscribed the freedom of all oppressed peoples.'[14]

On 13 December (26 December), Prophet Muhammad's birthday, the Muslim leadership in Tashkent proclaimed Turkestan's autonomy. They backed it up by staging a big demonstration in the city, and organizing a gathering of Muslim workers and peasants in Kokand in early January 1918. On 10 January (23 January) 1918 the Kokand Autonomous Government urged the authorities in Tashkent to convene a Turkestan constituent assembly, a demand which went unnoticed.

In his speech to the Fourth Regional Congress of Soviets, F. I. Kolesov put the Kokand Autonomous Government in the same adversarial column as the troops of General A. I. Dutov – a counter-revolutionary officer then responsible for cutting communications between Central Russia and Turkestan – and promised to quash the 'counterfeit autonomy' of the Muslim nationalists. The reasoning behind his stance was that conflict between different nations had arisen on a class, not a national, basis, and that self-determination for a nation meant self-determination for its toiling masses, not its bourgeoisie. The Bolsheviks argued furthermore that their proletarian revolution had destroyed Tsarist imperialism in order to end exploitation by all national bourgeoisies, and not to create opportunities for Turkestan's national bourgeoisie to exploit Turkestani workers and peasants. The scene was thus set for an armed confrontation between the Tashkent Soviet and the Kokand Autonomous Government.

Instead of waiting for the Russian Soviet forces to attack them, some ministers of the Kokand Autonomous Government led an assault on the Kokand citadel, where their adversaries were garrisoned. The Russians repulsed the attack, and called for reinforcements from other garrisons while engaging the enemy in truce negotiations. The military commissar of the Tashkent Soviet, leading a large Russian force, arrived from Tashkent on 5 February (according to the Gregorian calendar in use since 1 February), followed by further reinforcements from the Orenburg front a week later. Backed by the local Russian Soviet detachments, the new arrivals encircled the Muslim Old City and breached its walls on 18 February. For the next three days the attackers went on a rampage, looting and massacring some 14,000 Muslims who had not managed to flee, and finally setting the settlement on fire.[15]

By then the Soviet authorities in the region had already solved another irredentist problem militarily. At the Third All Kazakh National Congress sponsored by Alash Orda, meeting in Orenburg (then in counter-revolutionary hands) from 5 to 13 December 1917, the delegates declared the Kazakh-Kyrgyz region autonomous, and elected its government, called the Provisional People's Council of Alash Orda, under the leadership of Muhammad Buyuki Khanev, a Kazakh chieftain. But the autonomy proved short-lived. On 18 January (31 January) the Bolshevik militia, the Red Guards, from St Petersburg, the Volga region and Central Asia, expelled the anti-Soviet forces from Orenburg, and dispersed the Alash Orda government.

In contrast, the developments in Trans-Caspian/Turkmenistan Oblast (i.e. Province) went against the Bolsheviks, whose Congress of Soviets had established a Council of People's Commissars in Ashqabat (then Ashkhabad) on 2 December (15 December) 1917. A nationalist movement backed by local intellectuals, and centred around Turkmen army officers, emerged under the aegis of the Regional Turkmen Congress and its National Committee, headed by Colonel Oraz Sirdar. It assigned itself the task of helping famine victims. But it overstepped its objective when one of its delegates joined the Kokand Autonomous Government. In February 1918, to improve its military preparedness, the National Committee formed the Turkmen National Army, with the existing Turkmen Cavalry Squadron forming its core. In response, the Soviet regime set up a Turkmen section within its administration, convened an All Turkmen Peasant Congress, and established the Turkmen Red Guards.

It despatched party cadres into the countryside to recruit partisans for social revolution. The Soviet of Ashqabat, a Russian majority town, appealed to F. I. Kolesov in Tashkent for military assistance. At home it ordered a census of all arms-bearing males in the town. On 17 June 1918, the scheduled date for the census, rioting broke out. It went on for two days. On 24 June an armed detachment under Commissar V. Frolov arrived from Tashkent, and disarmed the Turkmen Cavalry Squadron. But after Frolov had departed for Kyzyl Arvat in early July to suppress an uprising there, a rebellion by an anti-Soviet alliance erupted in Ashqabat on 11–12 July. It resulted in the overthrow of the local soviet, and the emergence of a nationalist government. Frolov's attempt to pacify Kyzyl Arvat failed too. The administration in Tashkent – the capital of the Turkestan Autonomous Soviet Socialist Republic (ASSR), encompassing Trans-Caspian Oblast, established in April 1918 – declared the nationalist Trans-Caspian government illegal. But that made little difference. By late July 1918, the latter had secured the assistance of General Sir W. Malleson, the British commander at Mashhad, Iran, who had been posted there to foil any Turkish-German designs to open a war front in the Middle East. In exchange for the right to destroy the usefulness of the Trans-Caspian railway, and mining the Caspian port of Krasnovodsk, to spike any plans by the Central Powers to mount an offensive in the region, Malleson despatched a detachment of Indian troops under his command to Ashqabat.

By mid-1918 Russia was in the midst of a civil war, with the Bolsheviks being opposed by regular and irregular armed men called the White Guards, local nationalist elements, and Russia's erstwhile allies in the First World War, including Britain, France, America and Japan. Prominent among those leading the White Guards were Admiral Alexander V. Kolchak, General Anton I. Denikin (1872–1947) and General A. I. Dutov, a Cossack chief. After the Bolshevik revolution, Admiral Kolchak, who commanded the Russian Black Sea fleet in the First World War, declared himself commander-in-chief of Russia, and was so recognized by the Allies. He took up arms against the Bolsheviks in Siberia. He was joined by General Dutov whose forces conquered Orenburg in November 1917. In January Rumanian troops captured Moldova (then Bessarabia). Two months later British, French and American forces seized the port of Murmansk in north-west Russia, and established the Government of Northern Russia. Soon the Japanese occupied the Russian port of Vladivostok; and the Germans occupied Kiev, and then Odessa.

France and Britain armed the Austro-Hungarian prisoners of war detained in Siberia to fight the Bolsheviks. Riding trains along the Trans-Siberian railway, they seized Samara and Kazan. Britain was also active along the southern borders of Russia. It combined the sending of Cossack troops from Bojnurd, northern Iran, to the Trans-Caspian Oblast, with the despatch of British (Indian) troops from Mashhad to Ashqabat in July to help the nationalist forces topple Soviet rule. General L. C. Dunsterville, the British commander of the Allied Supreme Command, based in Iran, led an expeditionary force to Baku in August 1918 on the pretext of safeguarding oilfields that happened to be partly owned by British capital. In the spring and summer of 1918 most of the territory in the Kazakh-Kyrgyz region fell to the anti-Soviet alliance of Kolchak's White Guards, Dutov's forces and Kazakh-Kyrgyz nationalists, resulting in the emergence of the Kazakh Autonomous Region based in Orenburg, which in early July had come under the control of Dutov, enabling him to sever Turkestan from Central Russia. Thus, within a year of the October 1917 revolution, over three-fifths of former Tsarist Russia was out of Bolshevik control.

Then the tide began to turn against the anti-Soviet camp. In November 1918, Admiral Kolchak proclaimed that he was the Supreme Regent of Russia, and repeated his vow that he would fully restore the Russian empire. He ordered the abolition of the Kazakh Autonomous Region and put Kazakh fighters under his command. This caused a split between them and the White Guards.

The repeated statements by Kolchak and other counter-revolutionary leaders that they wanted to recreate the old Tsarist empire went down badly with Russia's Muslim citizens. Such influential Muslim leaders as Sultan Galiyev threw in their lot with the Bolsheviks, since the latter had combined their promise of self-determination for all nationalities of the former empire with land to peasants and an end to the war. Soon Stalin, the head of the Commissariat of Nationalities,[16] appointed Galiyev to a high position in the Muslim section of the commissariat in Moscow – where the Soviet government had moved from St Petersburg on 12 March 1918 – and instructed him to attract Muslims to the party. Aware of the impending trend, the Fifth Regional Congress of Soviets, meeting in Tashkent in late April 1918, conducted its proceedings in Russian and Uzbek. On 30 April the assembly announced the formation of the Turkestan Autonomous Soviet Socialist Republic, incorporating Trans-Caspia/Turkmenistan Oblast – thus renaming the Turkestan Territory – within the RSFSR; and decided to nationalize land, water resources, railways, banks and industrial enterprises in the newly created ASSR.

Nationally, Galiyev was active. Starting with the founding of the Muslim Communist-Socialist Party independently of the Russian Communist Party (RCP) in March 1918, he transformed it into the Russian Party of Muslim Communists (RPMC). His move was in line with developments elsewhere, with the Russian Communist Party breaking up into smaller units based on territorial, religious or ethnic loyalties – a matter of grave concern to Stalin. He attended the First Congress of the Russian Party of Muslim Communists, held under the chairmanship of Galiyev in November 1918, as the representative of the RCP. He rejected Galiyev's proposal for autonomy for the RPMC by stressing the need for 'democratic centralism within a single united party capable of acting as the vanguard of the international proletarian revolution'. His argument won, and the delegates elected him as their representative in the Central Committee of the RCP.

This occurred against the background of growing difficulties for the Soviet authorities in Turkestan ASSR, the most populous Muslim-majority area in the RSFSR, stemming from the fact that the counter-revolutionary forces had once again severed it from the remainder of the RSFSR in July 1918. Encouraged by this, the anti-Soviet forces staged an uprising in Tashkent on 19 January 1919, killing fourteen Turkestan Soviet commissars. But they failed to overthrow the government, which crushed them in two days.

Overall, in the continuing civil war, as the Red Army, created and led by Leon Trotsky nationally, and by General Mikhail V. Frunze regionally, began gaining the upper hand, various Muslim groups abandoned the counter-revolutionary Whites and joined the Reds. By late 1918 many Uzbek, Tajik, Kazakh-Kyrgyz and Tatar units were fighting alongside Red Army contingents.

To tackle the nationality problem politically, Stalin created the Central Bureau of Muslim Organizations (CBMO) and put it in charge of party organization in the Muslim areas of the RSFSR. In Turkestan ASSR its task was to reshape the Russian-controlled party into a Muslim-dominated body. However, its fast progress along these lines was to prove problematic for Stalin. At the First Conference of the Muslim Organizations in Tashkent in May 1919, organized by the CBMO, the representatives of 108 organizations demanded the establishment of the Soviet Republic of United

Turkestan to include the Turks of Russia and the Caucasus. They thus revived the pan-Turkic scenario of the Muslim reformists of Central Asia before the Bolshevik revolution, an undesirable development from Stalin's viewpoint.

By then the CBMO's programme of indigenizing the regional Communist Party, formally founded in June 1918, had worked so well that more than half of the 248 delegates to the Third Regional Congress of the Communist Party, held in Tashkent from 1 to 15 June 1919, were natives. This boosted the confidence of the Muslim Communists. At the Second Conference of the Muslim Organizations in Tashkent in September 1919, T. Ryskulov, a forceful Muslim leader, reiterated the First Conference's proposal for a United Turkestan. When no positive response came from Moscow, the Third Conference, held a few months later, demanded that Turkestan be transformed into the Autonomous Turkish Republic and that the Turkestani Communist Party affiliated to the RCP be reconstituted as an independent Turkish Communist Party.

Much angered, Stalin dissolved the CBMO. But the central leadership in Moscow realized that there was a severe problem in the region which needed to be tackled. On 8 October 1919 the RSFSR government and the RCP's Central Committee appointed a special Commission for Turkestan Affairs, consisting of six Russians, including General Frunze, to oversee the soviets in Turkestan. Its dual mandate was to rid the soviets of 'nationalist deviants', and conciliate the Russian colonizers and Central Asians. The establishment of the Commission came soon after the units of the Turkestan front, led by General Frunze and V. V. Kuibyshev, had routed the White Guards of Kolchak in the northern and eastern parts of the Kazakh-Kyrgyz region, and linked up with the contingents of the Red Army of Turkestan ASSR at Muhajar (Mugodzhar) on 13 September. Also by then, thanks to the peasant alienation engendered by the forced requisitions of food grains by the nationalist Trans-Caspian government in the middle of a famine, and the success of the Bolsheviks in setting up underground cells in urban areas, the Red Army offensives in the Trans-Caspian region had resulted in the capture of Mary in May 1919, culminating in the expulsion of the anti-Soviet forces from Ashqabat on 9 July following the withdrawal of the British force in June.

In the autumn of 1919 the Red Army prepared to regain the rest of the Kazakh-Kyrgyz region from its adversaries. In early November the Military Revolutionary Soviet under the leadership of Frunze combined its amnesty offer for those Alash Orda partisans who detached themselves from the White Guards with open sympathy for the Kazakh-Kyrgyz aspiration for autonomy. This encouraged Alash Orda members to sever their links with the White Guards and join forces with the Red Army, now poised to retake the western part of the Kazakh-Kyrgyz region. It completed this mission in early 1920, and capped it with the recapture of the Semirechie region in March. The surrender of some 6000 White troops in early April signalled the final victory of the Reds. On 30 April the RCP's Central Committee formed the Kyrgyz[17] Regional Bureau of the Russian Communist Party, paving the way for the formation of the Kyrgyz Autonomous Soviet Socialist Republic within the RSFSR on 26 August, with its capital in Orenburg.

However, despite Moscow's improved military position and growing confidence, Muslim Communists refused to yield to its pressure to give up their Turkic aspirations. At the Fifth Regional Congress of the Turkestani Communist Party in mid-January 1920 they found themselves in a majority. Following Ryskulov's lead, the delegates changed the name of their organization to the Turkish Communist Party and called on the RCP to recognize it as such.

Moscow responded on 8 March, declaring that the only Communist Party in the area was that of Turkestan ASSR incorporated as a regional organization into the Russian Communist Party.

Its hard line stemmed partly from the fact that by now the Red Army had turned the tide decisively in the civil war in the region. Responding to a petition from the Young Khiva Movement in late January 1920, the Red Army marched into the Khanate of Khiva, which had been enfeebled by inter-tribal violence. There followed the deposition of the ruler, and the establishment of Soviet power in April in the form of the Khorezm People's Soviet Republic which, being less socialistic than a soviet socialist republic, guaranteed private ownership of land. In early February the Red Army drove out the anti-Soviet forces from Krasnovodsk, their last stronghold in Trans-Caspia; and two months later it entered Baku, another important Caspian port. In late August, responding to a call from the Young Bukhara Movement, the Fourth Army under General Frunze attacked Bukhara, much weakened by peasant revolts triggered by famine and repression, and conquered it. On 2 September Emir Said Alam Khan, the last ruler of the Mangit dynasty, fled to the eastern corner of Bukhara. As in Khiva, Soviet power was established under the aegis of the Bukhara People's Soviet Republic.

Bolshevik military and political ascendancy led to the members of the major Muslim parties, from the Himmat in Azerbaijan to Alash Orda in the Kazakh-Kyrgyz region to the Young Bukhara Movement and Young Khiva Movement, enrolling themselves into the Communist Party. Also, the Communists/Bolsheviks had gained popularity by their actions, especially in rural areas where most Central Asian Muslims lived. Contrary to the Muslim clergy's dire warnings that the Bolsheviks would introduce wife-sharing and rape women in the countryside, they had concentrated on confiscating the lands of feudal lords and distributing them to landless and poor peasants, thus swiftly fulfilling their most far-reaching promise.

Their major problem in the region now was how to tackle the continuing nationalist Basmachi (i.e. bandit, in Uzbek) movement. This armed movement had emerged in the winter of 1919–20 when, following a sixty-two per cent drop in the cultivated area of Turkestan ASSR and the government's policy of feeding the military at the expense of civilians, nearly half of the population had faced starvation. It was led by those who had been prominent in the Kokand Autonomous Government. Their partisans, operating from mountain bases, resorted to attacking Red Army supply convoys and outposts. Since the Basmachi movement drew its ideological inspiration from Islam, it succeeded, by the summer of 1920, in acquiring popular backing in a sizeable part of the Fergana Valley, a traditional bastion of Islam. Following his flight from Bukhara in September, Emir Said Alam Khan, now based in the village of Dushanbe in the mountainous eastern part of his former emirate, joined the Basmachi movement, with two of his generals raising a militia of over 30,000 men.

The authorities decided to combine their military campaign against the Basmachis with socio-economic reform to improve the condition of local peasants. A decree issued in March 1920 ordered the return to Central Asians of the agricultural land taken from them by Russian settlers. The speed and efficiency with which this fiat was implemented could be judged by the fact that some 280,000 hectares of land were redistributed to Central Asian households in little over a year.[18] Moscow despatched the powerful Commission for Turkestan Affairs to Tashkent with a mandate to tackle Russian chauvinism in the region. It repatriated to Russia those Russians who were blatant chauvinists and exponents of the superiority of the Slavic race. It actively encouraged Central Asians to join the Communist Party and government organs. The revival of private trading as part of the New Economic Policy also helped to regain Muslim confidence. Altogether these measures diminished the appeal of the Basmachi movement which had its own internal problems, the chief among them being the lack of a centralized political-military command. This enabled the Red Army to overpower the Basmachis led by the former Emir of Bukhara.

The movement was saved from extinction by the arrival in the region of General Enver Pasha, a former Turkish war minister. An exile in Moscow after the end of the First World War, he convinced the Soviet government that he could conciliate the warring parties in Turkestan. However, after his arrival in eastern Bukhara in the spring of 1921, he abandoned the task. Instead, he sought and forged an alliance of conservative and liberal Muslim leaders and mountain tribal chiefs under the twin slogans of pan-Turkism and pan-Islam with the aim of creating a single Islamic state in the region. In November 1921 he succeeded in having the former Emir of Bukhara, Said Alam Khan, appoint him commander-in-chief of the Basmachis. He transformed the poorly led Basmachi groups into a professional army of 16,000, and launched a series of campaigns that brought a considerable part of the Bukhara People's Soviet Republic under Basmachi control by early 1922.[19]

Little wonder that in October 1921 the Soviet government and the RCP's Central Committee described crushing the Basmachi rebellion as the most pressing task of the local party and soviets. They sent the commander-in-chief, S. S. Kamanev, to Tashkent to oversee the anti-Basmachi campaign. The result was a two-prong strategy: political and economic reconciliation with the indigenous people, and the use of Muslim fighters to confront Basmachi partisans. The New Economic Policy, launched in late 1921, signalled much-needed pragmatism: it alleviated the material and political situation in the region. The government returned mosques and *waqf* (i.e. religious trust) properties to Islamic authorities, and allowed religious schools and Sharia courts to re-open, thus securing the neutrality of the clergy in its anti-Basmachi campaign. It established a militia of indigent Muslim peasants, called the Red Sticks, and engaged them and regular Muslim soldiers to fight the Basmachis. So, when in May 1922 Enver Pasha issued an ultimatum to Russia to withdraw from the region, Moscow was well prepared for a confrontation.

In a battle at Kafrun the Soviet units defeated the Basmachi forces of Enver Pasha, who retreated. On his flight to Afghanistan, he was killed in an ambush on 5 August near Khovaling in the Kulyab Valley of east Bukhara. This marked a virtual end to the Basmachi movement. In late 1922 there were only about 2000 Basmachis, mainly in the Fergana Valley. Within two years the movement was to become virtually extinct in Turkestan ASSR.[20]

Addressing the Tenth All Russian Congress of Soviets on the formation of the Union of Soviet Socialist Republics (USSR) on 22 December 1922, Stalin, now the First Secretary of the RCP, pointed out that the independent soviet republics of Khorezm (previously Khiva) and Bukhara – being people's, but not socialist, republics – remained outside the framework of the USSR solely because they were not yet socialist. However, he added: 'I have no doubt . . . that, in proportion to their internal development toward socialism, they [Khorezm and Khiva] likewise will enter the structure of the Union state now being formed.'[21]

'Internal development toward socialism' meant downgrading the 'non-toiling' sections of society at the expense of workers and peasants. Much needed to be done in that direction. At the Fourth Conference of Responsible Workers of the National Republics and Regions in June 1923, Stalin noted that while Bukhara's Council of People's Commissars had eight merchants, two intellectuals and one cleric, it had no peasants.

The Communist Party in Bukhara as well as Khorezm took note. In September, the Third Congress of the Bukhara Communist Party disenfranchised the 'non-toiling' citizens in its march towards socialism. And, a year later, the next congress of the organization transformed the Bukhara People's Soviet Republic into the Bukhara Soviet Socialist Republic (SSR). In early October 1924, the Fourth Congress of the Khorezm Communist Party altered its constitution to deprive its non-toiling members of voting rights, and changed Khorezm People's Soviet Republic to Khorezm Soviet Socialist Republic. With this Bukhara and Khorezm joined the family of soviet socialist republics. However, the union was short-lived. On 27 October 1924, as part of the administrative reform coincident with promulgation of the first USSR constitution, the multi-ethnic Khorezm and Bukhara SSRs and Turkestan ASSR underwent territorial reorganization. None of them contained an ethnic group that was in a clear majority. In Bukhara, Uzbeks were forty-five per cent of the population; Tajiks, forty per cent; and Turkmen, eight per cent. In Turkestan, Uzbeks formed forty-one per cent of the population;

Kazakhs, nineteen per cent; Kyrgyzs, eleven per cent; Russians, ten per cent; and Tajiks, eight per cent.

Following the Tsarist practice of calling Kazakhs Kyrgyzs, and Kyrgyzs Kara-Kyrgyzs, the Soviet authorities named the Kyrgyz-majority areas of Turkestan the Kara-Kyrgyz Autonomous Province (later, in May 1925, the Kyrgyz Autonomous Province, subsequently renamed Kyrgyz ASSR in February 1926), and retained it within the RSFSR. Its population was just under one million. The Kazakh-majority provinces of Syr Darya and Semirechie of Turkestan were transferred to the existing Kazakh (officially called Kyrgyz) Autonomous Province within the RSFSR. It was to be given its historically correct name, Kazakh, and upgraded to the status of an ASSR in May 1925, and its capital moved from Orenburg (which went to the RSFSR) to Kzyl Orda. It had nearly 6.5 million inhabitants.

The predominantly Turkmen areas of Trans-Caspia – Ashqabat, Krasnovodsk, Tejand and Mary districts – were combined with the Turkmen-majority districts of Khorezm and Bukhara to form the Turkmenia Soviet Socialist Republic. Its population was about 950,000.

The remainder of Turkestan and parts of Bukhara and Khorezm were reconstituted as the Uzbek Soviet Socialist Republic with a population of 5.2 million. It included Tajik-majority areas – the Pamir mountainous region, eastern Bukhara and parts of the Samarkand and Fergana provinces – which were given an autonomous status as the Tajik ASSR. It had some 700,000 inhabitants.[22]

Carving up the region into separate units broadly along ethnic-linguistic lines stemmed as much from administrative as political and ideological considerations. With Stalin in the ascendancy, following the death of Lenin in January 1924, his theory on nationalities acquired an official stamp, and he now began putting it into practice.

According to Lenin, nationalism (as a form of social relations) emerged during the early period of capitalism as a response to national-social oppression caused by capitalism. However, the later period of capitalist development, dominated by monopoly capital, spawned a trend towards internationalism. With the internationalist trend in ascendancy, as late capitalism gives way to socialism, nationalism will wither away and be replaced by class loyalties under socialism. As a practical politician, Lenin came to grips with particularist nationalisms which had emerged in response to Tsarist expansion, and backed the right to national self-determination vis-à-vis Great

Russian imperialism (which he considered as 'the highest form of capitalism'), even extending its interpretation to mean 'the right to free secession'.[23] At the same time he believed that the policies designed to build a socialist society would result in the dissipation of particularist nationalisms and the rise of proletarian internationalism. Stalin, a Georgian, accepted Lenin's thesis. Within its parameters he developed his own definition of nation (*natsiya*, in Russian) which, he argued, was different from people (*narod*, in Russian). According to him, a nation was 'a stable and historically developed community' based on four criteria: a common language, a united territory, a shared economic life, and a shared psychological outlook manifested in a common culture.[24] The 'national delimitation', effected in 1924–25, signified implementation of the policy of national self-determination in Stalinist terms, providing each of the major nations with 'a united territory'.

Stalin's linguistic policy was to give each delimited Union or Autonomous Republic its own language. This was best achieved, so it was thought, by exaggerating the differences between several Central Asian languages which were written in the Arabic script and mainly rooted in Turkic. Out of this arose the three-prong process of enrichment and completion of the local language, the replacement of Arabic and Persian loan words with Russian, and the changeover from the Arabic script to the Roman (on the grounds that the Arabic script was difficult to learn). The alternative of a switch-over to the Cyrillic alphabet was considered and rejected: such a move would have smacked of Russian supremacy, vehemently decried by Lenin, being institutionalized.

Often the Soviet regime acted as a catalyst for the creation of a nation out of a group of nomadic or semi-nomadic tribes. Of the Kyrgyz-Kazakh family of tribes, Kyrgyzs, being totally nomadic, had proved immune to conscription. Therefore Moscow quickened the process of separating them from Kazakhs, partly by providing them with a written, standardized language of their own. This occurred in 1922 when the Kyrgyz dialect, belonging to the Central Turkic group, was written down in the Arabic alphabet. As for Turkmens, a largely dispersed and unassimilated ethnic group, they forged a common written language (in the Arabic script) out of two tribal dialects, belonging to the South Turkic group, in 1921. In their case the Soviet policy of nation-building coincided with the aspiration of a recently settled tribal society to differentiate itself from Azeri Turks to the west and Iranian tribes to the south.

While policy-makers in Moscow were quick to recognize Turk-mens and Kazakh-Kyrgyzs as the minorities which the ruling Uzbeks held in contempt, they took several years to define correctly the relationship between the Uzbek majority and the Tajik minority. Thus the Uzbek SSR came to accommodate sedentary and semi-nomadic Uzbeks speaking Uzbek, belonging to the East Turkic group, and Tajiks, possessing a long settled history and speaking Tajik, which is akin to Persian. This was so because until the 1917 revolution Tajik had also been the cultural and political language of Uzbeks, and Tajik and Uzbek were seen as complementary. How-ever, since they had different roots, and since the Uzbek literary language had come into vogue by the mid-1920s, it dawned increas-ingly on the authorities in Moscow that the anomaly of the two nations with distinct languages living in a single Union republic needed to be resolved.

Politically, too, the Tajik ASSR proved different from the rest of the Uzbek SSR. In early 1925 there was a revival of the Basmachi movement, whose activists managed to infiltrate the soviets in the countryside. The Red Army, assisted by the local auxiliary force, managed to suppress the movement, thus enabling the government to declare an official end to the civil war on 14 August 1926. In December, the founding Congress of the Soviets of Tajik ASSR nationalized land, forests and water resources, and freed women from the restrictions imposed on them by the Sharia. Progress towards socialism continued, as did the evolution of Tajik as a modern language containing many technical terms.

In the spring of 1929 Stalin concluded that the Tajik ASSR had progressed sufficiently along the socialist path to become a candidate for Union republic status. While it possessed the geographic and ethnic requirements – being on the periphery of the Russian Federa-tion, thus geographically capable of seceding from the Union as allowed by the constitution of 1924, and having its leading national-ity, Tajiks, form a compact majority – it lacked the population requirement of one million. The solution lay in transferring the Uzbek SSR's Leninabad (Hojand) Province to the Tajik ASSR on the ground that its 'primary population' was Tajik, thus boosting the population of the enlarged republic to just over one million.[25] In foreign policy terms, Stalin considered it politically expedient to create a socialist republic 'at the gates of Hindustan [India]' to provide a socialist model to the eastern countries. On 22 June 1929, therefore, the USSR's Central Executive Committee (CEC) decided to upgrade the Tajik ASSR to a Union republic, followed by the transfer of Leninabad to it in early October. The Third Congress of the Soviets of Tajikistan endorsed the CEC's decree on 14 October, and the final CEC approval came on 5 December 1929.

However, Kazakhs and Kyrgyzs, the two other nations of the region, had to wait until after the mass collectivization of cereal, cotton and cattle-breeding farms had been virtually completed in their autonomous republics (within the RSFSR) in 1934 to have their territories upgraded to the level of a Union republic by the new constitution promulgated in December 1936.

For Moscow the delimitation of the region along ethnic-linguistic lines had the additional merit of eroding any potential for the unification of Central Asia around the twin banners of pan-Turkism and pan-Islam, with Jagatai, a Turkic language, as the cement. With this worrisome political prospect out of the way, the planners in Moscow concentrated on effecting a rapid socio-economic transformation of this predominantly rural region heavily dependent on agriculture and cattle breeding.

The Soviet regime followed up its 1920 policy of distributing the lands of Russian colonizers to poor and landless Central Asian peasants with a programme to hand over the landholdings of local landlords and mullahs (in charge of managing the religious trust lands) above a certain ceiling to poor peasants. This plan went into effect in 1925. By early 1926 all farms above fifty-five hectares in Uzbekistan had been confiscated and redistributed. The process continued elsewhere in the region until 1929. The Communists' overall objective was to use the agrarian reform and the accompanying propaganda to emasculate landlords of their traditional political, economic and social power, and free the peasantry from the deprivations of the past. The landless, poor and middle-income peasants, forming the bulk of the population, benefited economically and politically. For instance, in the 1927–28 elections to the soviets in Tajikistan, the landless, poor and middle peasants accounted for eighty-seven per cent of the deputies.[26] They were also the primary beneficiaries of the literacy campaigns mounted by the Communists.

Alongside the drive against illiteracy went the campaign against religious superstitions and archaic customs throughout the USSR. The Communist Party decided to wage a struggle against religion through a planned reorganization of socio-economic activities of the masses, socialist re-education of peasants and workers, expansion of educational facilities, and anti-religious propaganda. During the first decade of Soviet rule the anti-religious movement was directed chiefly at the European population. At the First All Union Conference of the Atheist Movement in 1926, of the 123 Slav and non-Slav nationalities in the USSR only six non-Slav nationalities were represented.[27]

The Communists implemented the anti-religious campaign in the Muslim-majority areas with considerable caution, partly because Muslim society was largely feudal, lacking a revolutionary industrial proletariat, and partly because of the all-pervasive nature of Islam. It impinged on every facet of life, individual and social; viewed the state and mosque as two sides of the same coin; and considered the right to private property sacrosanct.

As a result, anti-religious propaganda in Central Asia was limited to verbal attacks delivered in school classrooms, and at trade union and Komsomol (*Kommunisticheskiyo soyuz molodyezhy* – Communist Youth League) meetings. The main thrust of the anti-Islamic argument was along the following lines, which took into account Islamic doctrines and practices as well as Islamic history in the region. It was argued that Islam was an alien faith which had been imposed on the local population by invading Arabs, Iranians and Ottoman Turks. Since Islam discriminated against women, upheld the power of male elders, and encouraged intolerance and fanaticism, it was conservative, even reactionary. Since it divided the world strictly into believers and infidels, it was presented as a barrier to fraternization among different peoples of the USSR. Such Islamic practices as circumcision, fasting during Ramadan and self-flagellation (by Shias during Ashura ceremonies) were portrayed as primitive, barbaric or unhealthy. Islamic art, architecture and literature were perceived as static, having failed to move with the times. The root cause of the malaise, according to party ideologues, was that Islam belonged to a feudal era and had not even caught up with the capitalist stage of human development, much less the socialist. The overall purpose of the anti-Islamic campaign was to engender a new Muslim 'Soviet man' who, having released himself from the influences of the reactionary socio-religious traditions of Islam, was ideologically and culturally ready to join forces with his Russian counterpart, freed from *his* socio-religious traditions, to construct a socialist order.

Given the paucity of literate adults and the sensitivity of the subject, much stress was laid on personal example. The party strategy was to convert a few inhabitants of a Muslim village to atheism, and let them quietly deflate the importance and relevance of Islam in modern times. While refraining from challenging Islam, these converts tried to explain natural phenomena and social problems in scientific terms with a view to undermining superstitious beliefs rooted in Islam.

Equally importantly, the takeover of religious trust properties by the state, initiated in 1925, had the effect of depriving mullahs of their income and starving mosques and theological schools of funds. This process was still in train when the socialist family code, giving equality to men and women, was promulgated in 1926 throughout the USSR. This caused much upheaval in Central Asia, Daghestan and the Muslim areas of the Caucasus, and as a result Moscow exempted the Soviet Union's Muslim regions from the socialist family code. However, this slack was promptly taken up by the governments at the republican level. In 1926–28 the authorities in the Muslim-majority Union and Autonomous republics abolished the practices of polygamy, bride purchase and veil, and closed down the Sharia and *Adat* (customary) courts. Also they forbade religious propaganda, and religious education to minors in groups larger than three. This meant the closure of the last of the 8000 Islamic schools which had functioned in Turkestan Territory before the Bolshevik revolution. A ban on the Arabic script in 1929 struck at the root of Islamic scriptures and commentaries, making clerics wholly dependent on the religious material that the Soviet authorities deemed fit to be printed in the Cyrillic or Roman alphabet. Thus what was left of the once powerful Islamic infrastructure and tradition in the late 1920s in the USSR was only a part of the 26,000 mosques and 45,000 (severely handicapped) mullahs originating in pre-revolutionary times.[28]

During the First and Second Five Year Plans (1929–38) Stalin concentrated on destroying this religious network in the course of his campaigns aimed at obliterating Islam and promoting scientific atheism. What drove him was his commitment to vest all economic power in the state, and to eliminate any creed capable of challenging Marxism-Leninism. A firm believer in historical materialism, he tackled the economic foundation of society first before dealing with its religio-cultural superstructure. In 1925, soon after he had emerged as the leading light of the USSR, he argued that the peasantry provided the main fighting force to the national movements because the 'peasant question' lay at the root of the 'national question'. Among peasants he perceived kulaks (rich farmers) as prime adversaries of Marxist-Leninist internationalism since they were not only powerful economically but were also the carriers of national consciousness. To break the power of kulaks, Stalin initiated a drive for farm collectivization on a voluntary basis in 1927, mainly in the European sector of the USSR. But he found progress patchy. So on 29 December 1929 he introduced compulsory collectivization of farms – a decision that became part of the First Five Year Plan (1929–33) which he had launched earlier in the year after discontinuing Lenin's New Economic Policy. His aim was to eliminate not only the power of kulaks – known in Central Asia as *bais*, *beks* or *manabs*, used as suffixes in names – but also the authority of tribal notables, clan chiefs and village elders, and make the Soviet system the sole guiding force in the countryside where a majority of Soviet citizens lived. Stalin operated in an environment where the authority and size of the Communist Party were on the rise. The 1924 Soviet constitution, bearing his stamp, had enabled the Russian Communist Party, renamed the Communist Party of the Soviet Union (CPSU) in 1925, to emerge as a powerful instrument of unity. The party had territorial and functional dimensions. Since it functioned in all fields of activity open to citizens it became all-pervasive. Its territorial organization ran parallel to the Soviet Union's administrative divisions, with a major exception: whereas each of the republics had its own Communist Party, the RSFSR had none. The CPSU was also the party of the RSFSR.[29] While each of the Union republics was nominally independent, with its own constitution and foreign minister, its Communist Party was not. A cross between a territorial body and an affiliate of the CPSU, a republican party was subject to the authority of the CPSU, which was committed to cementing republican divisions into an ideologically and administratively centralized Soviet Union.

One of the side-effects of the collectivization campaign was to revive the Basmachi movement, with its self-exiled leaders returning from Afghanistan and Iran to Tajikistan and Turkmenistan. However, their renewed struggle proved short-lived. It collapsed in mid-1931 in the face of the offensives by the Red Army, assisted by the Russian-dominated militia and political police. The same fate befell those who resisted farm collectivization. Some 2100 kulak households from Turkmenistan were deported to Siberia. Turkmenistan was also the scene of two major anti-collectivization uprisings: in the Karakum desert in 1931 and near Yangi-Tuar Oasis in 1932. In Tajikistan, there was resistance to collectivization even from within the Communist Party. This led to purges of the soviets in

1927–28 and the party in 1929–30. The collectivization went ahead none the less and – following its completion in 1934 – was capped with a major purge in the party, reducing its membership from 14,329 in January 1933 to 4791 two years later.[30] The purged Tajik officials were often replaced by newly arrived party activists from Russia.

The nomadic Kazakh and Kyrgyz tribes, chiefly engaged in cattle-breeding, suffered most. For them the new state policy meant both settling down and giving up their herds. Instead of letting their cattle be included in the collectives being formed, many Kyrgyzs and Kazakhs either slaughtered them or drove them into China. During the First Five Year Plan (1929–33), Kazakhstan, Kyrgyzstan and Uzbekistan experienced the loss of about half of their livestock, and migration of whole clans to Iran, Afghanistan or China. According to some specialists, between fifteen and twenty per cent of the Kazakh population of 4.5 million crossed over into the neighbouring countries, and about the same number died due to collectivization and the ensuing famine in the mid-1930s.[31] Moscow surmounted the resistance of local kulaks, peasants and livestock breeders through force, mass deportations, propaganda and the despatch of Russian-dominated Communist Party brigades from the European part of the USSR to Central Asia to provide manpower and technical and managerial skills for the newly established collective farms. These settlers were a sizeable part of the 1.7 million Russians who migrated from the European Russian Federation to Central Asia between 1926 and 1939.[32] Those who became members of a collective farm, called *kolkhoz*, signed regular contracts with the elected management to lease land and equipment belonging to the collective, which also ran schools, clubs, libraries, cinemas and agro-based industries. Though supervised by the local party's central committee, a collective farm had considerable freedom of manoeuvre. A typical collective farm in Central Asia was centred around an existing village, and had a tendency to attract extended families and even whole clans.[33] Thus the feudal relationship was transplanted into a socialist system, which over decades created its own hierarchy, and led to strange distortions – especially in the cotton-growing areas of Uzbekistan, which became a major source of revenue to the state.

Towards the end of the First Plan, Stalin mounted a concerted five-year (1932–36) anti-religious campaign. The Soviet authorities placed the control of all places of worship into the hands of the Union of Atheists, which transformed them into museums, places of entertainment or factories. They forbade the Muslim practice of going on a pilgrimage to Mecca; the collection of a religious tax, *zakat*, to provide funds to the needy and for maintaining mosques and religious monuments; and the printing and distribution of the Quran. The banning of some 3500 books on the grounds of propagation of Islamic superstition was accompanied by highly publicized burnings. Muslim women were encouraged to burn their veils in public, and did so in their thousands. When the faithful took to the streets in protest, their marches were suppressed, and their leaders, often clerics, arrested. Thousands of mullahs fled to Afghanistan and Iran.

The Communist governments in Central Asia consolidated social reform by incorporating it in the republican constitutions which were modified in the light of the new constitution for the USSR adopted on 5 December 1936, which was accompanied by the establishment of the Kazakh SSR – with its capital moved from Kzyl Orda to Alma Ata – and the Kyrgyz SSR with its capital in Bishkek (then Frunze). For instance, Article 109 of the new constitution of Tajikistan, promulgated in March 1937, explicitly forbade 'giving minors in marriage, bride purchases, resistance to women going to school or engaging in agricultural, industrial, state or other social or political activities'.[34]

In 1937 there were large-scale expulsions from the party and government in the region. These were part of the Great Purge – named *Yezhovshchina* after N. I. Yezhov, the head of the NKVD (*Narodnyi Kommissariat Vnutrennikh Del* – People's Commissariat of Internal Affairs) – directed against 'enemies of the people', which occurred throughout the Soviet Union from 1936 to 1938. The source of the purge in Central Asia was an alleged nationalist conspiracy in Uzbekistan which involved the heads of two of the three centres of Soviet power: the Communist Party, headed by the First Secretary of the party's Central Committee; the government, led by the chairman of the Council of People's Commissars; and the state, headed by the chairman of the Presidium of the Supreme Soviet, which issued legislation between the (often brief) sessions of the Supreme Soviet. Following an accusation that he had buried his brother according to Islamic custom, Faizullah Khojayev (Hojayev), the chairman of Uzbekistan's Council of People's Commissars, was dismissed at the Seventh Congress of the Communist Party of Uzbekistan (CPU) in June 1937. In September a local newspaper accused Akmal Ikramov, the party's First Secretary, of being a nationalist. Khojayev and Ikramov were arrested. In March 1938 they were tried along with twenty-one other accused, including Nikolai Bukharin, a leading Russian Communist based in Moscow, as members of the 'bloc of Rightists and Trostkyites', found guilty of various charges, and executed.

Their positions were taken over by Abdujabbar Abdurakhmanov (Abdul Jabbar Abdul Rahman), aged thirty-one, and Usman Yusupov (Yusuf), aged thirty-eight. Moulded by the Bolshevik regime, they represented that generation which had been mobilized by the Soviet system in the earlier phase of its assault on traditional society. A similar process was at work in Kazakhstan, the largest and the second most populous SSR in the region, and Kyrgyzstan. The party's membership campaigns in the 1920s had brought many young Kazakhs and Kyrgyzs into its fold, thus giving an increasing number of Kazakhs and Kyrgyzs a stake in the new system. The mortal blow that nationalization of most rural property and collectivization delivered to the power and prestige of traditional leaders opened up opportunities for young party cadres. They moved up steadily in the party and government hierarchy in a milieu where literacy campaigns, laced with ideological education and propaganda, and directed at adults, had a dramatic impact on predominantly nomadic and rural societies with literacy rates of below five per cent.[35]

In Tajikistan the disgraced Tajik leaders included the chairmen of the Council of People's Commissars and the Presidium of the Supreme Soviet. Following their expulsion from the party in 1937, the job of the First Secretary of the Communist Party was given to a Russian, Dmitri Z. Protopopov, who had initially arrived in Dushanbe, the Tajik capital, as a representative of the CPSU's Central Committee. This illustrated the failure of Moscow to implement fully its earlier policy of indigenization.

Over the years, as Stalin became more and more obsessed with the idea of creating a highly centralized Union, the party and government authorities increasingly refused to make allowances for local traditions and interests. This led them to put a high premium on unquestioned loyalty from the republican capitals. Consequently, Russian party members either domiciled in the region or sent from Moscow rose in the republican hierarchy. Lacking indigenous roots, they were not susceptible to local lobbying, and remained loyal to Moscow.

One of the major consequences of centralization was accelerated

Russification of the non-Slavic parts of the USSR. In 1938 Russian was made compulsory in all non-Russian schools in the Union. The following year the script of Azeri was changed from Latin to Cyrillic. In 1940 Kazakh, Kyrgyz, Tajik, Turkmen and Uzbek underwent the same change. The switch-over to the Cyrillic alphabet for the native languages made it easier for indigenous pupils to learn Russian, especially when the Arabic and Persian loan words in their languages had been replaced earlier by Russian grammatical forms and loan words, which were also used to build up a fresh technical vocabulary. By depriving the regional people of their ability to read foreign publications published in the Roman alphabet, the authorities were able to control further their reading material. The full impact of these changes could be gauged fully only against the backdrop of virtually universal illiteracy that prevailed. The literacy rate in Central Asia, as measured by the first post-revolution census in 1926, varied between 2.2 per cent (in Tajikistan) and 7.1 per cent (in Kazakhstan), confined almost wholly to men. The census of 1939 showed that the literacy rate had jumped to 71.7 per cent in Tajikistan, the most backward republic in the USSR.[36] The dramatic rise in literacy was accompanied by a rapid growth in the mass media, newspapers, periodicals and radio broadcasts.

By then major road and rail projects in the region, as well as the massive Fergana Canal, had been completed, enabling Moscow to tighten its grip over Central Asia as well as accelerate socio-economic development.

But the Second World War, which erupted on 1 September 1939 and gave an impetus to the Soviet conscription drive initiated a year earlier, severely interfered with Moscow's plans for building socialism. The USSR, which had concluded a non-aggression pact with Nazi Germany under Adolf Hitler in August 1939, stayed neutral until June 1941 when it was invaded by Germany. This was the beginning of the Great Patriotic War for the Soviets in which they joined Britain and France to fight the alliance of Germany and Italy.

THE GREAT PATRIOTIC WAR AND AFTER

Nazi Germany's invasion of the USSR on 23 June 1941 caused massive material damage to the country. At the same time it enabled the Soviet leadership to create a symbiotic relationship between patriotism and Marxist socialism, thus enabling the Bolshevik revolution to be absorbed into the socio-psychological fabric of the public at large a generation after it had been launched in the midst of violence and chaos.

Since the Russian Federation was at the core of the USSR – accounting for seventy-eight per cent of its area and fifty-eight per cent of its population – Stalin considered it expedient to encourage a revival of Russian nationalism to mobilize the populace to fight the powerful invader. He compared the current German aggression to the 1812 attack on Russia by France's Napoleon Bonaparte, and described the latest hostilities as 'The Great Fatherland/Patriotic War'. Shortly after the celebrations of the Bolshevik revolution on 7 November, he revived the military titles used during Tsarist times. In order to placate traditional forces in the USSR, he virtually deactivated the Union of Atheists. Ending his persecution of the Russian Orthodox Church, he co-opted it to raise patriotic feelings. In September 1943 he publicly received the Church hierarchy, and allowed it to elect a new synod and patriarch.

Stalin executed a similar about-turn in his policy towards the Islamic hierarchy, which had seen the number of functioning mosques in the USSR in late 1941 reduced to five per cent of the pre-revolution total of more than 26,000.[37] Having ordered an end to the persecution of Islamic clerics, often on charges of sabotage, spying for Germany or Japan, or counter-revolutionary activities, and the re-opening of some major mosques, Stalin permitted Muslim leaders to hold a pan-Islamic conference in Ufa, capital of the Bashkir Autonomous Region in the RSFSR, in 1942. It urged Muslims at home and abroad to back the Allies (now including America, which joined the war in December 1941) and assist the Soviet Union to overpower Nazi Germany.

The next year Shaikh Abdul Rahman Rasulayev, the Mufti of Ufa, reached an accord with Stalin similar to the one which the latter had signed earlier with the Patriarch Sergius for the Russian Orthodox Church. It marked the end of anti-Islamic propaganda and accorded a legal status to Islam along the lines followed by Tsarist Russia in the form of the Central Spiritual Muslim Directorate (*Tsentral'noe Musul'manskoe Dukhovne Upravlenie*) for European Russia and Siberia established in Orenburg in 1783. The result now was the formation on 20 October 1943 of the Official Islamic Administration divided into three Muslim Spiritual Directorates (*Musul'manskoe Dukhovne Upravlenie*) based at: Ufa (Sunni sect), for the Muslims in the European sector of the USSR; Tashkent (Sunni sect), for the Muslims of Middle Asia and Kazakhstan; and Baku (Sunni and Shia sects), for the Muslims of Trans-Caucasia. The overall function of these directorates was to manage that part of Islamic life that centred around working mosques and officially registered clerics and religious communities. In return, the leaders of the Official Islamic Administration saw to it that the mosque served the political interests of the Soviet regime at home and abroad. This concordat between mosque and state had a healing effect in the Muslim-majority region of Central Asia.

Hitler's invasion of the USSR had come at a time when Stalin had concluded that the basic economic objectives in Central Asia of increased output of cotton, cereals, fruit and animal products could be achieved without further assaults on the traditional way of life. He was therefore resigned to accepting what Donald S. Carlisle, an American academic, calls 'the continued co-existence of traditional and modern society with a semi-permeable wall separating and connecting the Central Asian and European worlds'.[38] But the pressures of war and country-wide conscription helped to erode the semi-permeable wall between the Asian and European sectors of the USSR.

The course of the war was partly determined by the efficient maintenance of the Ashqabat railway and the Caspian port of Krasnovodsk, Turkmenistan, which connected the southern fronts and the Trans-Caucasian republics with Central Russia, which fell under German occupation. It was the uninterrupted operation of this crucial transportation link during late 1941 and early 1942 that enabled the Soviet forces to expel the German troops from the Volga region and the foothills of the Caucasus, and finally break the German siege of Volgograd (then Stalingrad). Little wonder that over 19,000 soldiers from Turkmenistan, a republic with a little over one million inhabitants, received military honours. The corresponding figure was 20,000 for Azerbaijan, a Muslim-majority republic which also helped the war effort crucially by keeping open the rail link with Iran's Persian Gulf ports, where massive military supplies were unloaded by the United States for delivery to the USSR. During the war the Baku region produced seventy per cent of the total Soviet oil output.[39]

Central Asia's industrialization received a boost due to the wartime policy of transferring factories from the frontline zones in the European USSR to peripheral regions. As a result, Kyrgyzstan gained more than thirty industrial enterprises, Kazakhstan 140, and

Uzbekistan about 100, half of them pertaining to heavy industry. In addition, Uzbekistan obtained dozens of military and civilian educational and scientific institutes and hospitals. During the war, 238 new factories were opened in Uzbekistan, and seven hydro-electric plants commissioned.[40]

Equally impressively, Uzbekistan, with a population of a little over six million, contributed about a million men and women to the military and its auxiliary units. In Kazakhstan two-thirds of the members of the Communist Party (125,600) and Komsomol (347,000) joined the military. Kazakhstan and Kyrgyzstan impinged far more on the Soviet psyche because their 316th Infantry Division, commanded by I. V. Panfilov, participating in the combat near Moscow, fought bravely. Both the troops and civilians of Tajikistan also performed well, with more than 50,000 winning awards and medals. Kazakhstan received a million evacuees from the European USSR, as did Uzbekistan. The figure for the much smaller Kyrgyzstan was 139,000.[41]

The aggregate effect of these wartime developments was to unify the many nationalities living in Union republics in more ways than one. In the process of working with Russian troops, the hundreds of thousands of indigenous Central Asians improved their Russian, and this reinforced the politico-economic unity of the USSR. The transfer of hundreds of factories from European Russia to Central Asia accelerated the region's industrialization. This, and the conscripting of the local manpower, opened up unprecedented employment opportunities for women, thus furthering women's emancipation.

Victory in the Great Patriotic War, which ended in May 1945 with Soviet troops capturing Berlin, was a great boost to the Soviet system. The warfare had created a USSR more united than ever before, with its many nationalities sharing pride in their hard-earned victory which had cost them twenty-two million lives.

The task of constructing a new socialist order – rapid economic development and cultural sovietization – began in earnest since the two preconditions for its success had now been satisfied. The masses had been exposed to political education, and the leading party cadres had been properly trained ideologically as a means of creating organic unity between the Russian core and the non-Slavic periphery – as well as professionally to perform managerial and executive jobs in the economic and administrative spheres. Indeed, a new generation of such Soviet-educated, war-hardened party cadres, totally loyal to the regime, had begun rising up the hierarchical ladder in the Central Asian republics.

To the economic planners in Moscow, a special feature of Central Asia was its cotton, the leading raw material for clothing, a basic need of any society; and all efforts were made to increase its output. In Uzbekistan and Tajikistan, irrigation and switch-over to cotton cultivation had emerged as complementary aspects of collectiviz-ation, an all-pervasive achievement of the Communists in the countryside. The central government in Moscow had a special minis-ter for cotton, a job to which Usman Yusupov was promoted in April 1950. Following the transfer of Yusupov and Abdurakhmanov from Tashkent to Moscow, Amin Niyazov, aged forty-seven, was elected First Secretary of the CPU, and Sharaf Rashidov (1917–83), who had been a journalist before the Great Patriotic War, elected chairman of the Presidium of the Supreme Soviet. In April 1951, Nuritdin Mukhitdinov (Nuruddin Muhyiddin), aged thirty-three, became the chairman of the Council of People's Commissars. Thus, in the trio of party chief, prime minister and head of state, two were in their early thirties.

This set of new regional leaders had to establish their credentials as party loyalists by carrying out purges which, though not on the same scale as the 1930s, occurred in 1951 and 1952, and were coordinated with similar moves by Moscow. The victims in Central Asia were those party activists who had been found to have displayed one or more of the failings of 'local favouritism' (*mestnichestvo*), 'bourgeois nationalism' and 'archaic customs' (meaning Islamic rituals or practices).

The end to these intermittent purges came only when Stalin died on 5 March 1953.

AZERBAIJAN

Following the Bolshevik revolution, the Baku Soviet called upon the people of Azerbaijan to support the new regime. The Musavat Party did so, but did not extend its backing to the Baku Soviet which, it pointed out, had not been elected on a democratic basis. In late December 1917, a conference of Trans-Caucasian Muslims decided to convene a constituent assembly of Azeris and Caucasian Mountaineers, a step which soured relations between the Musavat and the Baku Soviet.

Tension between the two sides built up in March 1918 when the Azeri Savage Division, controlled by the Musavat, arrived in Baku from the hinterland. Faced with an ultimatum by the Baku Soviet, the Musavat leadership agreed to withdraw its force by the deadline of 1 April. But from a practical viewpoint it was too late. Its fighters and their adversaries had taken up positions in the streets. In the subsequent violence, which lasted three weeks and involved 20,000 men, the Dashnaktsutiun, an Armenian nationalist group, sided with the local Soviet, and transformed the struggle into a series of attacks on Muslims irrespective of their political loyalties or social standing. Thousands of people perished, with both camps being guilty of massacres. In the end the Baku Soviet emerged as the most powerful force, absorbing part of the Armenian National Council's army into its own military. The local Council of People's Commissars, formed on 25 April, claimed sole authority in the Baku region, containing more than a million peasants, and nationalized the vital oil industry.

However, elsewhere in the Caucasus developments went against the Bolsheviks. Fearing a takeover by the powerful Ottoman Turkish empire, the Trans-Caucasian Assembly (Sejim) decided on 22 April 1918 by a majority vote to establish an independent Democratic Federative Republic of Trans-Caucasia (DFRTC). On 26 April a government of twelve ministers, four each from Azerbaijan, Armenia and Georgia, was formed. To its relief, the new republic, which excluded the oil-rich Baku region, found itself recognized by Ottoman Turkey on 28 April.

But the DFRTC lasted only a month. Angrily pointing out that Trans-Caucasian Muslims had welcomed the Turkish invaders, the Georgian Assembly declared Georgia independent on 26 May. Two days later the Azeri members of the Trans-Caucasian Assembly and the members of the Muslim National Council declared Azerbaijan independent, and named Fatah Ali Khoiskiy as the premier of the Democratic Republic of Azerbaijan (DRA) with its capital in Ganja. The new republic signed a treaty with Turkey, hoping to capture Baku with its assistance.

At the end of July, DRA and Turkish forces reached the outskirts of Baku, compelling the leaders of the Baku Soviet to flee along with their weapons by ship. But they were intercepted and thrown into jail. Responding to the pleas of the Armenian and Russian residents of Baku, who were afraid of the advancing Turks, General L. C. Duntersville, the British head of the Allied Supreme Command based in Iran, arrived in Baku with a force of 1400 on 17 August.

But when the Turks managed to break the city's main defence line on 14 September, Duntersville's force set sail for its base in the Iranian port of Anzali. The next day DRA and Turkish forces entered Baku and, according to the Armenian National Council, killed 8988 Armenians.[42] The Baku Soviet was replaced by the Centro-Caspian Dictatorship, which was dominated by the anti-Bolshevik Social Revolutionaries, and backed by the Armenian nationalists. On 17 September the Azeri government under Premier Khoiskiy moved from Ganja to Baku.

In early November the Turkish military command informed the DRA that its forces would soon leave Azerbaijan. The DRA government approached General V. Thomson, the British head of the Allied Supreme Command in the region, to fill in the vacuum. They reached an agreement whereby, once the Turkish and Azeri forces had left Baku, the city and surrounding oilfields would be occupied by Allied forces, with General Thomson acting as the governor-general of the Baku region, followed by the representatives of Britain, France and America establishing relations with the *de facto* government of Azerbaijan.

Elections were held to the DRA parliament in late November 1918 on the basis of universal suffrage, including women, the first such instance in the Islamic world. Of the 120 deputies, eighty-five were Azeris, twenty-one Armenian, ten Russian and the rest Polish and Jewish. The parliament met on 7 December and elected Ali Mardan Beg Topchibashev its chairman. He called on Fatah Ali Khoiskiy to form the administration.

Khoiskiy led a Musavat-dominated coalition government where Musavat's intellectuals shared power with the feudal lords of western Azerbaijan and wealthy oil magnates of Baku. With the feudalists providing the bulk of the 50,000-strong Azeri army, they soon emerged as the most powerful element in the government. Unsurprisingly, the administration postponed implementing the agrarian reform law adopted by the parliament, ordering the return of the estates, seized earlier by landless peasants, to their owners. It also found itself unable to balance the books in the wake of the soaring costs of maintaining an inflated army and state bureaucracy, a steep decline in petroleum revenue due to sharply reduced demand from a war-ravaged Russia, and lack of fiscal backing by Russia.

On top of this the DRA found itself embroiled in a dispute with the Dashnak Republic of Armenia over the possession of the mountainous region of Karabakh. Soon after declaring its independence,

Armenia made excessive territorial claims on Turkey and also soured relations with Georgia, paving the way for a war with the latter.

The Khanate of Nagorno Karabakh, an extension of the Armenian plateau, inhabited by Armenian farmers and traders and semi-nomadic Azeri herdsmen, was captured by the Russians in 1805 – twenty-one years before the Armenian territories around Yerevan – and attached to the eastern section of Trans-Caucasia. Though ruled by Muslim potentates since the eighth century, its Christian Armenian inhabitants had resisted all attempts by their Muslim rulers to embrace Islam. In 1846 the Tsar incorporated this territory of 4400 square kilometres (1700 square miles) into the Baku Province, and then into the Ganja Province in 1868. Following the founding of the DRA in May 1918, the Armenians of Nagorno Karabakh set up their own National Council in late August 1918 – an enterprise in which they were aided by the Dashnak Republic of Armenia. The basic problem was that the Azeri nomads had for centuries taken their livestock up the Karabakh Mountains in summer and brought them down to the plains in winter. With Armenia now claiming the Karabakh Mountains and insisting on regulating the Azeri nomads' movements, the stage was set for a confrontation between Armenia and Azerbaijan. General Thomson in Baku sided with the DRA, and appointed Khosrobeg Sultanov the governor-general of Karabakh, thus confirming Azerbaijan's suzerainty over the area. This occurred against the background of deep turmoil in 1919.

Following the suppression of the Baku Soviet in August 1918, the local Bolsheviks joined the Himmat Party. Six months later one of their leaders, Anastas Mikoyan, an Armenian, was released from jail owing to poor health. He assumed the leadership of the local Bolsheviks. The increasingly assertive Bolsheviks caused a split in the Himmat between them and the non-Bolsheviks, and laid the foundation for the Communist Party of Azerbaijan (CPA).

From then on the Bolsheviks/Communists, firmly established in the industrial region of Baku and in touch with fellow-Communists in Moscow, employed a combination of means – political manipulation, threats of force and military intervention by the powerful Red Army – to overthrow the DRA, which derived its legitimacy from a popularly elected parliament. They succeeded partly because of the DRA's failure to win diplomatic recognition by the Allies.

A DRA delegation lobbied various government representatives at the peace conference at Versailles, near Paris, in the spring of 1919 to recognize the Democratic Republic of Azerbaijan as an independent, sovereign state, but failed. This happened partly because of the bitter dispute it conducted with its Armenian counterpart on the ownership of Karabakh and Nakhichevan, a province where Armenians constituted forty per cent of the population. Relations between Azerbaijan and Armenia worsened.

The disagreements over Karabakh and Nakhichevan were symptomatic of the long enmity between Armenians and Turks (an ethnic term which included Turko-Azeris) – dating back to the struggle between the Ottoman, Persian and Tsarist empires, from the sixteenth century onwards, for Trans-Caucasia. As devout Christians, the Armenians in the region preferred Russian hegemony to Ottoman or Persian. Those Armenians who came under Ottoman control suffered periodic pogroms as they tenaciously resisted the imposition of Turkic culture and religion. What compounded their sin, in the Ottoman mind, was the fact that their kinsmen in the Russian-controlled Trans-Caucasia blocked Ottoman expansion to Baku, the prized oil city – and the creation of an unbroken hinterland of Turkic Islamic communities from the Mediterranean to the Chinese border. The description of Armenia by Arsalan Demirbey, a pan-Turkic intellectual, as 'a dagger in the heart of the Islamic world'[43] aptly summed up the popular Turkish feeling. During the First World War the Armenian nationalists in the Ottoman empire sided with the enemy, the Russian troops, and, to settle past scores, participated in massacring Turks and Kurds in eastern Anatolia. This in turn led to a series of massacres of Armenians by the Ottoman Turks during and soon after the First World War.

As for the DRA, by late 1919 its standing had deteriorated considerably at home and abroad. In December a corruption scandal caused the downfall of the Khoiskiy government. The next cabinet was headed by Nasibbek Yusubbekov (Yusufbek). It split into anti-Bolshevik and pro-Bolshevik factions, with the latter, led by M. H. Hajinskiy, interior minister, arguing that Soviet Russia would leave Azerbaijan alone if its government was friendly with the Bolsheviks. Enjoying substantial support in parliament and the ruling party, Hajinskiy convinced President Muhammad Rasulzadeh of the merits of a policy of friendship with Moscow.

Responding to Russia's call to Azerbaijan on 2 January 1920 to join in the campaign against General Denikin's counter-revolutionary forces, Azerbaijan averred that it was ready to do so as an independent state, and demanded recognition of its sovereignty as a pre-condition. On 23 January Moscow described Azerbaijan's

stance as a pretext for withholding cooperation. Azerbaijan denied
this. Unaided, the Eleventh Red Army gained an upper hand over
Denikin's troops to the north of the Caucasus. By then other contingents of the Red Army had captured all of the Trans-Caspian region
to the east of the Caspian Sea.

At home the DRA faced a rising Bolshevik tide. At its First Congress in February 1920, held secretly in Baku, the Communist Party
of Azerbaijan called on the workers and peasants of Trans-Caucasia
to overthrow 'the rule of the khans, the begs, the nationalists and
the capitalists' and establish 'a workers' and peasants' Soviet regime'.

Moscow's bargaining power with Baku improved when the
Eleventh Red Army captured Daghestan to the north of Azerbaijan;
and so did Hajinskiy's position within the ruling Musavat and the
administration. At the party conference in March he won a majority
for his friendly line towards Moscow. Premier Yusubbekov
resigned. President Rasulzadeh called on Hajinskiy to form the next
government as reports poured in of the Eleventh Red Army units
massing along the Azeri frontiers. Aware of the military pressure on
the DRA, the Armenians in Nagorno Karabakh revolted on 22–23
March. The Baku government rushed most of its 50,000-strong
army to quell the rebellion. This, and the deliberate delay in the
forming of the new cabinet by Hajinskiy, heightened public tension.
On 22 April Hajinskiy informed the parliament of his inability to
constitute the next government.

Having liaised with the Eleventh Red Army Military Revolutionary Council, the Baku Communists worked out a strategy for seizing
power. On 27 April at noon the Central Committee of the CPA and
the Baku Bureau of the Caucasian Regional Committee of the All
Russian Communist Party gave an ultimatum to the chairman of the
Azeri parliament that state power be handed over to them by mid-
night. They also circulated reports that the Eleventh Red Army had
entered Azerbaijan and was advancing towards Baku. The parliament assembled and decided that power should be transferred to the
Communists immediately. On 28 April the CPA's Central Committee sent a telegram to Lenin, chairman of the Council of People's
Commissars in Moscow, offering the Russian Soviet Republic 'a
fraternal union of a common struggle against world imperialism',
and appealing to him to 'give us immediately real help by sending
here detachments of the Red Army'.[44] This marked the official
demise of the two-year-old Democratic Republic of Azerbaijan, and
the founding of the Azerbaijan Soviet Socialist Republic.

Five months later Azerbaijan SSR signed a treaty of military and economic union with Soviet Russia. Thus the Azerbaijan SSR and its incorporation into the Union evolved differently from the way the Muslim-majority regions in Central Asia had evolved as parts of the new Soviet entity. Indeed, their paths diverged further when in March 1922 Azerbaijan joined Armenia SSR (established in December 1920) and Georgia SSR (founded in February 1921) to form the Trans-Caucasian Soviet Federated Socialist Republic.

The question of Nagorno Karabakh, then ninety-four per cent Armenian, was debated by the Caucasian Bureau of the Communist Party during its meeting in early July 1921 in Tbilisi (then Tiflis), Georgia. According to one account, its majority decision on 4 July to attach Karabakh to Armenia was reversed the next day owing to the intervention of Stalin, then the Commissar of Nationalities in Moscow, on the urging of Nariman Narimanov, an Azeri leader close to him. 'In view of the need to instal national peace between Muslims and Armenians, of the economic link between the Mountainous and Lower Karabakh, of their permanent links with Azerbaijan, it is decided to leave Mountainous [i.e. Nagorno] Karabakh inside the frontiers of Azerbaijan, giving it a large measure of regional autonomy, and having at its centre the town of Shusha, forming part of the autonomous region,' the Bureau's resolution stated.[45] There was more to Stalin's decision than friendship with Narimanov. Stalin, who had spent the early years of his political life in Baku, was well aware of the crucial role that Baku had played as the island of Bolshevik strength in Trans-Caucasia during the bloody civil war. Allocating Nagorno Karabakh to Azerbaijan was his way of rewarding the Bolsheviks of Baku for their loyal support of the revolution. The fact that there were no roads to connect Nagorno Karabakh with Armenia – only mountain paths through the strip separating the two territories – also added weight to the Azeri argument.

In earlier, similar moves, Moscow had strengthened the hand of Azerbaijan. In July 1920, after the Red Army detachments stationed in Nagorno Karabakh had clashed with the forces of the Dashnak Republic of Armenia in the Zangezur region, they had occupied Zangezur and Nakhichevan. Intent on securing its borders with post-war Turkey, ruled by Mustafa Kemal, Soviet Russia signed a treaty with Turkey on 16 March 1921. It stipulated that Nakhichevan must remain part of Azerbaijan, and that its status could not be altered without the consent of Azerbaijan. This treaty was endorsed by the

Kars Treaty of 13 October 1921 between Turkey and the Trans-Caucasian republics of Azerbaijan, Armenia and Georgia. It ceded Kars and Ardahan districts to Turkey.

In February 1924 the Azeri government gave Nakhichevan, separated from the mainland by Armenia's Zangezur district, the administrative status of an Autonomous Soviet Socialist Republic. The Armenian wedge between Azerbaijan proper and Nakhichevan broke the territorial continuity of the Turkic people from the Mediterranean to the Caspian Sea, thus delivering a body-blow to the concept of pan-Turkism, a development that pleased Stalin. Even the Nakhichevan enclave of Azerbaijan lacked a common frontier with Turkey – until January 1932, when Ankara exchanged territory with Tehran in order to have a ten-kilometre- (seven-mile-) long border with Nakhichevan, thus making for a tenuous contact with Turko-Azeris.

Regarding the enclave geographically within Azerbaijan, the Armenian-dominated Nagorno Karabakh Autonomous Province, the government published a decree on the subject in July 1923, and appointed a joint commission to demarcate its frontiers. It then moved the enclave's capital from Shusha to Khankendi (literally khan's village), later renamed Stepanakert after Stepan Shahumian, a Bolshevik hero of Baku, now the fifth largest city of the USSR. The frontiers fixed in August excluded, the western corridor of Lachin and Getabek from the enclave.

By then Azerbaijan was on its way towards socialism, undergoing social, political and economic changes along the same lines as Central Asia. In 1922 it became the first Muslim republic to alter the script of its language, Azeri, from Arabic to Latin. The agrarian reform benefited the peasantry which in the pre-revolution era owned only two per cent of the arable land. The 3.49 million acres of land taken from the feudal lords, Muslim endowment trusts and Christian churches and monasteries were redistributed to landless peasants. The First Five Year Plan, launched in 1929, placed special stress on industrialization, with the government claiming an increase of 111 per cent at the end of the plan.[46]

Azeri oil was as crucial to the Soviet economy as it was to the Tsarist. Its output, down to 2.9 million tons in 1920 from the pre-revolution figure of 7.7 million tons, needed to be raised urgently. Large-scale capital investment and technological modernization, including offshore drilling, boosted oil production in 1937 to 21.4 million tons, or 430,000 barrels per day, amounting to three-fifths of the total Soviet output,[47] enabling the Communist Party to claim that Azerbaijan had become an industrialized and collectivized republic. It was right to use the term 'republic': following promulgation of the 1936 constitution the Trans-Caucasian Soviet Federated Socialist Republic had given way to three separate republics, each of them becoming part of the USSR directly. Among other things, this made Nagorno Karabakh more dependent on Baku.

As elsewhere in the USSR, the purges of 1937–8 had a devastating effect on Azeri life and society, with many intellectuals and party leaders executed or exiled to labour camps in Siberia for either being bourgeois nationalists or practitioners of Islamic rituals and customs. The young cadres, who replaced the older ones, were totally loyal to Moscow. On the eve of the Second World War, therefore, Stalin was confident of the local Azeri leaders shoring up Muslim backing for the USSR should it find itself engaged in hostilities. He was not to be disappointed. Within eighteen months of the Soviet Union joining the war in June 1941, more than half of the 79,100 CPA members had enrolled in the military.

Of the four Muslim Spiritual Directorates that Stalin allowed to be established in the USSR in 1943, the one for Trans-Caucasia was based in Baku. Since nearly three-quarters of Azeri Muslims, forming two-thirds of the republic's population,[48] were Shia, the chairman of the directorate, Shaikh-al-Islam Ali Aga Suleiman, was a Shia, and his deputy a Sunni.

By the time of Stalin's death a decade later, Azerbaijan had been re-shaped in the same social mould as the republics of Central Asia, with the script for its language now altered to Cyrillic, Muslim women released from their traditional bondage, taking up more than forty per cent of the places at higher educational institutes,[49] and interest in religion and religious rituals reduced to a bare minimum.

ONE

Turkey: From Militant Secularism to Grass-roots Islam

Modern Turkey is a successor to the Ottoman Turkish empire, the heart of the Islamic world for four centuries, from 1517 to 1918. It is populated by Osmanli, or Ottoman, Turks. They and Seljuks, or Oghuzs, have been the two Turkic groups prominent in West Asia and East Europe. Classified as Western Turks, they are distinct from Eastern/Central Asian Turks and Tatars/Turko-Tatars.

Original Turks were hunting people in the Altai Mountains of Western Mongolia at a time when the steppes were occupied by Scythians, Huns and other pastoral nomadic peoples, and the plains of Mongolia by the Kyrgyz/Kazakh people. As Turks moved westwards they adapted pastoral nomadic life and occupied the steppes, reaching the shores of the Caspian Sea in the middle of the first millennium. They were followed from the ninth to the eleventh centuries by Seljuks, who played an important role in the ethnogenesis of Turkmens. In the tenth century Mongols conquered Mongolia, displacing the Kyrgyz/Kazakh people, and causing a migration of Turks and Turko-Mongols over the next several centuries. The Kyrgyzs/Kazakhs moved south to present-day Kyrgyzstan and East Kazakhstan. Other Turks made forays into the Syr Darya region. Of the various Turkish realms that sprang up in the region, the Ottoman principality emerged as the most powerful under Osman I (1259–1326), a leader of Osmanli Turks who had by now embraced Islam, with its capital in Bursa, 100 kilometres (sixty-five miles) from Istanbul (then Constantinople). When Muhammad II (1451–81) seized Istanbul in 1453 he became heir to the Byzantine empire. Under Selim I (1512–20) the Ottoman empire acquired Islamic primacy by usurping the caliphate from the Mamluks based in Cairo, the Ottoman ruler thus becoming the Sultan-Caliph, the secular-religious ruler. The empire expanded until the late seventeenth century, stretching from the Persian Gulf to Algeria, and from Sudan in the south to southern Russia in the north-east, and just beyond Budapest (in the Balkans) to the north-west. Like its rivals, the Tsarist and Persian empires, it had Muslim, Christian and Jewish subjects.

By the early nineteenth century, owing mainly to rapid advances made by European powers in technology and administration, the military balance began to turn against the Ottoman empire. Sultan Mahmud (1808–39) tried to rectify the situation by introducing administrative and military reforms along European lines under the title of Tanzimat (literally Reorganization) in 1827. European powers favoured Tanzimat; but that did not deter them from attacking the Ottoman empire. Tsarist Russia was the most aggressive, determined to act as the militant protector of twelve million Eastern Orthodox Christians under the Ottomans. It was at the same time consolidating and expanding its territories in Central Asia, inhabited by Muslims.

Taking their cue from Russian aspirations towards the Christians of the Ottoman empire, the leaders of the Central Asian Muslims appealed to Sultan Abdul Aziz (1861–76) to establish himself as the guardian of the Muslims in Tsarist Russia. To them the Ottoman empire – containing the holy cities of Mecca, Medina and Jerusalem, as well as the leading Islamic cultural centres of Cairo, Damascus and Baghdad – was the prime embodiment of Islamic civilization and power.

But Abdul Aziz, heavily indebted to European powers, could do little. In the mid-1870s, at Russia's behest, Bulgaria, Bosnia, Serbia and Montenegro rebelled against Istanbul. This paved the way for the overthrow of Abdul Aziz by Midhat Pasha, the leader of the Young Ottomans, a powerful group formed in 1859 with the main objective of securing an elected assembly of the believers.

Midhat Pasha produced a constitution, which formalized the religious status of the Ottoman sultan, and included a bill of rights and a provision for an elected chamber. It was promulgated by Sultan Abdul Hamid II (1876–1909) in December 1876.

In April 1877 the Russian army crossed the Ottoman borders with the objective of winning freedom for Slavs, and reached Istanbul. The sultan had to sign the humiliating Treaty of San Stefano in March 1878. It was revised in July by the Treaty of Berlin. Under its terms, Cyprus was handed over to Britain, and Tunis to France, and Russia was left in control of the districts of Kars, Batum and Ardahan.

The continued loss of territory, coupled with growing interference in the internal affairs of the Ottoman empire by the Europeans, convinced Abdul Hamid II that the fifty-year-old Tanzimat pro-gramme had failed to reassure either European powers or his Christian subjects. It was therefore time to change direction.

In February 1878 he suspended the constitution and dissolved parliament. He arrested Midhat Pasha and banished the Young Otto-mans to different parts of the empire. He repudiated Islamic modern-ism and turned to traditional Islamic values and thought. He tried to regenerate cohesion in Ottoman society by activating the masses on a religious platform around the Islamic banner and harnessing their energies. In order to succeed in the venture he activated Sufi brotherhoods and used them as channels of communication to reach the masses. His strategy succeeded since there had all along been a widespread current of Islamic feeling among the humbler Muslim subjects of the Ottoman empire.

However, by the early twentieth century Abdul Hamid II's popu-list approach to Islam at home and espousal of pan-Islamism abroad had proved inadequate to revitalize the disintegrating empire. In 1908 the army officers of the empire's European territories and a group of young intellectuals, later to be called the 'Young Turks', com-pelled the sultan to reinstate the 1876 constitution. They stood not for pan-Turanism/pan-Turkism, the concept of uniting all Turks in Asia and Europe in one state; or pan-Islamism, the idea of uniting all Muslims in one state; but for pan-Ottomanism, the concept of forging a single Turkish-speaking nation out of the various peoples of the empire.

Soon after the 1908 coup, Crete announced its union with Greece, Bulgaria proclaimed its independence, and Austria annexed Bosnia and Herzegovina. In April 1909 came an unsuccessful attempt to overthrow the Young Turks. They in turn deposed Sultan Abdul Hamid II, hoping that would improve the health of the empire. It did not.

The Balkan War of 1912–13, which resulted in the Ottoman empire's loss of its remaining European territories as well as Libya, once again underlined its weakness. The latest conflict destroyed the concept of pan-Ottomanism; and by reducing the empire it made it religiously more homogeneous. This encouraged the Young Turk triumvirate of Enver Pasha, Jamal Pasha and Talat Bey – which assumed effective power in Istanbul in 1913 – to highlight pan-Islamism and pan-Turkism. It was therefore receptive to the sugges-tion by the Kaiser of Germany in 1914 to liberate fellow-Turks and fellow-Muslims from Russian bondage in Central Asia, and thus compensate the Ottomans' loss of empire in Europe and north Africa. Hence Ottoman Turkey joined Germany in the First World War in October 1914.

Encouraged by Enver Pasha, the Ottoman war minister, Sultan-Caliph Mehmet VI (1909–23) urged Muslims worldwide to mount a jihad against their imperial masters – Britain, France and Russia. This call was taken up by the Muslims of Azerbaijan, but only after the Tsarist regime in Russia had collapsed, and the triumphant Bolsheviks had pulled out of the war. The result was the founding in May 1918 of the Democratic Republic of Azerbaijan, which signed a treaty with Ottoman Turkey. Their joint forces entered Baku in mid-September 1918. Six months earlier, in March, the Bolsheviks had concluded a peace treaty with Germany at Brest-Litovsk which involved *inter alia* Russia returning to Ottoman Turkey the districts of Kars, Batum and Ardahan it had appropriated forty years before.[1]

Elsewhere, though, the Ottoman forces found themselves pounded by the Allies. The Young Turk ministers resigned, and the sultan appointed a new cabinet. It signed an armistice with the victorious Allies on 30 October 1918, twelve days before the German surrender.

For the next several years the situation in Turkey, the nucleus of the old Ottoman realm, remained turbulent as its new regime tried to break with its past as the centre of the Islamic empire and create a new nation-state after it had regained its full sovereignty from the occupying Allied forces. During this period the unprecedented problems of the nature of sovereignty and the relationship between state and mosque had to be addressed.

EMERGENCE OF THE TURKISH NATION

In a duplicitous move, the Allies permitted Greek forces to occupy the Turkish port of Izmir on 15 May 1920. As the Greeks began marching east with the stated objective of annexing Western Anatolia to create a Greater Greece, the Muslims of Anatolia took up arms under the leadership of Mustafa Kemal (1881–1938) to wage what they called the War of Independence. Because of his brilliant performance on the battlefield in the defence of the Dardenelles and Gallipoli against the British offensive during the First World War, Mustafa Kemal had emerged as a war hero.

In February 1920 the Ottoman parliament adopted a nationalist manifesto, demanding self-determination for the Arab regions of the empire, but insisting that all other Muslim-majority areas should remain an undivided whole. The Allies were displeased, and showed it. On 16 March the British troops occupying Istanbul arrested 150 nationalists, including several parliamentarians. Sultan-Caliph Mehmet VI acquiesced in this. Protesting at the arrest of its members, the parliament prorogued itself indefinitely on 18 March. The next day Mustafa Kemal ordered elections to a new emergency parliament, to be called the Grand National Assembly (GNA), to convene in Ankara, where the Turkish nationalists had established their head office. On 11 April Sultan-Caliph Mehmet VI dissolved the parliament.

The collaboration of Sultan-Caliph Mehmet VI with the occupying forces accelerated the transformation of Ottoman nationalism, the driving force of the Young Turks, into Turkish nationalism.

The Grand National Assembly met in Ankara on 23 April 1920 under the chairmanship of Mustafa Kemal. The constitution it adopted read: 'Sovereignty belongs unconditionally to the nation. The government is based on the principle of the people's direct rule over their own destiny'; and 'the Grand National Assembly is the only real representative of the people . . . the holder of both legislative and executive power'.[2] But there was no apparent contradiction in being a nation-state and being Islamic, maintaining the religious traditions of the Ottoman empire. The parliament later appointed a clergy-dominated Sharia committee to vet all legislation for conformity with Islamic law. Also, the earlier practice of having a minister for Sharia – a successor to the traditional office of the Shaikh-al-Islam, the Wise Man of Islam, the paramount religious official – continued.

The Treaty of Sèvres between the Allies in August 1920, which confirmed the dissolution of the Ottoman empire, was accepted by Sultan-Caliph Mehmet VI, but rejected by the Grand National Assembly. Later this treaty was to be overturned by the Treaty of Lausanne in July 1923.

Kemal's prestige rose sharply when he secured a decisive victory over the Greeks at the Sakarya River in August 1921. By the following year the Turks had formally won their War of Independence against the Greek army – an event that paved the way for Allied recognition of the sovereignty of Turkey under the Treaty of Lausanne.[3]

At Kemal's behest, the Grand National Assembly passed a law on

1 November 1922 that marked the formal end of Ottoman rule, depriving Sultan-Caliph Mehmet VI of all secular power in the new Turkish state, thus ending the ruling dynasty originating with Osman I in 1259. But the new law left untouched the caliphate, a religious office now on a par with the Pope in the Catholic world. To justify his action Kemal referred to the Abbasid period (750–1258) when the caliphs had lost all political authority and become symbolic figures of Islamic unity. Thus the Assembly finally abrogated the principle of 'sovereignty of an individual', which had been the foundation of Islamic empires, further underscoring its earlier commitment to the principle that sovereignty belonged to the nation. As for the caliphate, the GNA accepted the Ottoman dynasty's claim to it with the rider that it would choose as caliph 'that member of the Ottoman house who was in learning and character most worthy and fitting'. Since it did not consider the deposed Mehmet VI to be so qualified, he went into exile in 1923 after losing his office of sultan, and the mantle of caliphate fell on his cousin, Abdul Majid.

Once Turkey, a nation of a mere twelve million people, had secured its sovereignty internationally through the Treaty of Lausanne, enforced in July 1923, its Grand National Assembly amended the constitution on 29 October to describe the country's governmental form as 'a republic', with the power to choose the republic's head resting with the GNA, based in Ankara. It elected Mustafa Kemal president.

With Caliph Abdul Majid based in Istanbul, the Turkish state had to define its relationship with Islam. Its constitution declared that 'The religion of the Turkish state is Islam'; and the GNA continued to have its Sharia committee, and the cabinet its minister of Sharia.

However, having established a republic, a fledgling entity, Kemal resolved to strengthen it by eliminating the other centre of power that existed in Turkey, the caliphate, which had the potential of rallying the opposition to the new order. Riding the surge of Turkish nationalism, a powerful force, Kemal decided to strike at the caliphate while it was recovering from recent traumatic experiences. Whether by design or chance, the struggle of Kemal and his aides against the *ancien régime* came to include a campaign against religion and religious infrastructure, which were bound to be used by the caliph's camp to regain secular authority. Also Islam, transcending national frontiers, was ideologically antithetical to the concept of a Turkish national identity, which Kemalist forces were striving to engender. Anticipating resistance and counter-attack by the caliph's followers, the new regime set up 'independence tribunals' to try those accused of attempting to restore the old system, and promulgated a stringent Law for the Maintenance of Order.

Addressing a new session of the GNA on 1 March 1924, Kemal stressed the need to have 'a unified system of education' – that is, to abolish religious schools and colleges – and to 'cleanse and elevate the Islamic faith by rescuing it from the position of a political instrument to which it has been accustomed for centuries'.[4] Two days later the 290-member GNA passed Kemal's proposals, with only one voice dissenting. This led to the deposition of Caliph Abdul Majid, and the abolition of the caliphate, a 1292-year-old tradition. Equally importantly, the Turkish government exiled all members of the Ottoman family, thus aborting any chance of them becoming a rallying force against the republic. This occurred at about the same time as the supporters of Mustafa Kemal were reorganized as the Republican People's Party (RPP), a body that claimed the loyalties of all parliamentarians and most civil servants of various ranks.

The amended constitution, guaranteeing equality before the law, and freedom of thought, speech, press and association, was promulgated on 20 April 1924.

In May, in what proved to be the second phase of secularization, came a wholesale abolition of the religious infrastructure: the office of the Shaikh-al-Islam, the ministries of Sharia and *waqf* (religious endowments), the Sharia courts, religious schools, and Sufi lodges and hostels. The income from the religious trusts, now placed under the directorate-general of religious endowments, was transferred from the clergy to the public treasury. All Sharia judges were retired. The government retained control of mosques as well as the education, appointment and salaries of the preachers (khatibs) and prayer-leaders (imams) through the newly created Directorate-General of Religious Affairs (DGRA) under the prime minister. It instructed the ministry of education to train a new generation of preachers and prayer-leaders, and the DGRA to organize the teaching of Quranic courses by schools.

Along with secularization went westernization – at first in dress. 'Boots or shoes on our feet, trousers on our legs, shirt and tie, jacket and waistcoat – and of course . . . [a] "hat",' Mustafa Kemal stated in a speech in August 1925.[5] His subsequent decree prescribed hats for all men, and made wearing the traditional fez a criminal offence. Interestingly, while describing the veil for women as 'a ridiculous object', he refrained from banning it. Another crucial step towards westernization was the supplanting, in December 1925, of the Islamic calendar – beginning with the migration of Prophet Muhammad from Mecca to Medina – by the Gregorian calendar beginning with the birth of Jesus Christ.

Having curbed the orthodox Islamic infrastructure, Kemal focused on destroying the network of Sufi brotherhoods, which, he said, fostered superstition, thus retarding modernity and civilization. He disbanded them, outlawing their rituals and prayers, and confiscating their assets, including their lodges and convents.

Since this set of social reforms impinged directly on the everyday life of citizens, about eighty-seven per cent of whom were rural and conservative, it elicited more resistance than the earlier package, centred chiefly around Islamic institutions. The regime dealt with it by actively maintaining its instruments of coercion: the 'independence tribunals' and the Law for the Maintenance of Order.

In 1926 came the final instalment of reform – of the law. The current combination of the Ottoman statutes and the Sharia gave way to the Swiss Civil Code, the German Commercial Code and the Italian Penal Code. The Swiss Civil Code changed the legal position of women overnight, ending polygamy and the inequity suffered by women under the Islamic rules of inheritance, and legalized civil marriage. (However, women had to wait another eight years for the right to vote.)

Thus, between 1922 and 1926, using state authority, Kemal effected revolutionary changes at the macro- and micro-levels – from the abolition of the caliphate to the compulsory wearing of hats. Finally, in 1928, at his behest, the Grand National Assembly deleted the constitutional clause which stated that 'The religion of the Turkish state is Islam'.

During the same year, the GNA, following the lead of Azerbaijan SSR, adopted a law introducing a Latin-based alphabet to replace the Arabic script, which was banned. As in the Soviet republics of Central Asia and Azerbaijan, this had the immediate and dramatic effect of cutting off society from its literature, religious and secular. Furthermore, over the years the Roman script created an ever-widening gap between Turkey and other Muslim countries.

Secularization and westernization continued until Kemal's death in 1938. Educational reform manifested itself in making attendance at secular elementary schools compulsory in 1930 and the downgrading of Istanbul University's Faculty of Divinity to Institute of Islamic Research within the Faculty of Letters in 1933. Religious reform took the form of the call to Islamic prayer to be given in Turkish, instead of Arabic, in 1932 – an interference with the most frequent ritual of Islam, which caused widespread resentment. Further westernization came with the replacement of Friday, the weekly day of rest in public offices, with Sunday; and the introduction of surnames in the European style in 1935. Mustafa Kemal took Ataturk (literally father of Turks) as his surname, and his lieutenant, Ismet, Inonu. More importantly, in 1937 the GNA inserted secularism or 'laicism' as one of the fundamental principles of the state laid out in the constitution.

The strength of the Kemalist revolution was that it was thoroughgoing. Besides reforming or enfeebling Islamic institutions, it impinged on the daily existence of citizens: dress, family relations, children's education, alphabet, the weekly holiday, etc. Its primary weakness was that it depended too much on a single leader. The tremendous esteem and popularity that Kemal had won as a result of his triumphs during the War of Independence helped him virtually to impose his will on the largely illiterate masses, who lacked self-confidence. There was support for his ideas among military officers and liberal intellectuals, based mainly in Istanbul. He was opposed, consciously, only by religious and secular conservatives. His major problem was the sheer inertia of traditional customs and patterns of thinking deeply embedded among the mainly rural masses. His strategy of relying on state coercion to suppress resistance was effective in curbing overt opposition by a literate minority, but it lacked an instrument to educate and inform the illiterate populace. It was only in 1932, a decade after the deposition of the sultan, that he used his Republican People's Party to initiate a programme of adult education. Lacking a fully fledged ideology beyond its commitment to Turkish nationalism and secularism, the RPP was a less powerful instrument of change than the Communist Party in Soviet Central Asia and Azerbaijan. This deficiency was to become increasingly obvious as the years rolled by after Kemal's death.

AFTER KEMAL

Following the Kemalist dictum of 'Peace at home, peace abroad', the Turkish government remained neutral in the Second World War – until January 1945, when it joined the Allies. But it could not insulate itself from the economic hardships caused by the armed conflict. The peasantry and the traditional middle classes – artisans, craftsmen and petty traders – who had gained nothing, socially or economically, from the Kemalist revolution, became disenchanted, and remembered fondly the old Islamic era of the Ottomans.

Sensing popular restiveness, President Ismet Inonu, the successor to Kemal, allowed the formation of opposition parties. Of these the Democratic Party (DP), constituted mainly of former RPP members, and led by Celal (Jelal) Bayar and Adnan Menderes, proved to be the most important. While committing itself to upholding Kemalism, it diverged slightly from the ruling RPP: it called for less governmental intervention in the economy and religious affairs. Its demand that religious freedom be treated as 'a sacred human right' proved popular. When, in 1949, the government offered an optional two-hour course on Islam on Saturday afternoons in schools, parents rushed to enrol their children. Attendance at mosques rose. In defiance of the law, Arabic inscriptions began appearing in shops, cafés and taxis.

In the May 1950 election the DP won a landslide victory – 408 seats to the RPP's seventy-nine – on a popular vote of fifty-five per cent. Bayar was elected president, and Menderes prime minister. The new government's first measure was to abrogate the penalty for reciting the prayer call in Arabic. It proved popular. In the next parliamentary poll, in May 1954, the DP improved its popular vote to 58.4 per cent. It made religious education compulsory at the primary level and optional at the secondary, and recognized preacher-prayer leader (imám khatib) schools and colleges. The state-controlled radio began transmitting Quranic recitation and sermons. And new mosques were built at an annual rate of 200-plus.

Such an environment proved conducive to the publication of the 130-volume *Risale-i Nur* (Treatise of Light), consisting of commentaries on the Quran by Bediuzzman Said Nursi (1873–1960). A native of south-eastern Turkey, and a one-time partisan of Kemal in the War of Independence, Nursi turned against the war hero when he launched his secularization and westernization programme. As a result Nursi faced periodic imprisonment followed by exile to a small village in western Turkey where he wrote his Quranic commentaries in Turkish in a series of pamphlets. These proved popular. '[H]e made Islamic theology accessible to the masses without robbing it of its mystic qualities; and his approval of technology and science as "steeds that one should mount" and of progress as "a train" that one should follow made his teachings attractive to many Turks . . . especially craftsmen, artisans and (rising) businessmen,' noted Serif

(Sherif) Mardin, a Turkish academic.[6] His followers, who included many former shaikhs of the (Sufi) Naqshbandi order, came to be known as Nurculuk (singular Nurcu/Nurju). Though disallowed under the law, the Nurcu movement was tolerated. In due course, commanding the loyalty of a quarter of a million members, it edged its way into the political arena.

With a series of record harvests coming to an end in 1954, the economic situation suddenly worsened. As food prices rose, inflation jumped to fourteen per cent. This hurt urban residents more than rural. Already such influential segments of society as military officers, bureaucrats and the urban middle class had become disaffected with Menderes whom they saw favouring illiterate peasantry at the cost of urbanized, westernized citizens. Little wonder that the DP's share of the vote at the next general election fell, but not enough to deprive it of power. This made the opposition restive. To counter this challenge the Menderes government passed legislation that authorized it to retire judges and civil servants, and ban political gatherings and party coalitions. But since the root cause of its troubles – mismanagement of the economy – remained unresolved, the opposition refused to be cowed. In April 1960, at the behest of Premier Menderes, the Grand National Assembly appointed a commission of inquiry to investigate 'the opposition and a section of the press', and search and arrest suspects. This amalgamation of legislative and executive authority was a clear infringement of the principle of the separation of powers specified in the constitution.[7] There were protest meetings which the government suppressed brutally. On 27 May the military, headed by General Celal (Jelal) Gursel, seized power to safeguard what it called 'Kemalist values', arrested Menderes and banned all political parties.

In practice, restoring Kemalist values meant an end to a governmental endeavour to amalgamate legislative and executive powers, and a return to the religious reformist phase of Kemalism, abandoning its militantly secular phase, implying an attempt to refurbish the image and content of Islamic faith. 'Islam is the most sacred, the most constructive, most dynamic and powerful religion in the world,' General Gursel said. 'It demands of those who believe in this faith always to achieve progress and higher wisdom. But for centuries Islam has been explained to us negatively and incorrectly.'[8]

A National Unity Committee of thirty-eight military officers under General Gursel assumed the powers of the Grand National Assembly. In January 1961, as a freshly appointed Constituent

Assembly began drafting a new constitution and electoral law, the military junta lifted the ban on political parties.

Article 2 of the new constitution specified that secularism was 'the foundation stone' of the state. Article 19 read: 'No individual can exploit religion with the aim of changing the social, economic, political or legal structure of the state so as to promote religious principle, neither can he use religion to promote his personal or political interests.' Article 21 specified that religious education 'should proceed in accordance with the foundations of modern science and education'. Article 57 required political parties to conform to the principles of secularism. (Later Article 163 of the criminal code was used to prosecute individuals or groups 'believed to endanger the principle of secularism'.)

At the same time the constitution exempted the following laws from judicial review: unification of education, wearing of a hat, abolition of Sufi hostels and lodges, the civil code clause permitting civil marriage, and the Latin alphabet.

The constitution specified a two-chamber parliament, with one-third of the 150-member Senate resigning every two years, and the deputies of the 450-strong Grand National Assembly holding office for four years. The introduction of proportional representation made possible the rise of small parties, thus allowing the incipient leftist forces to participate in the electoral process.

In the October 1961 election, the RPP secured 36.7 per cent of the vote, and the Justice Party (the renamed Democratic Party), led by Suleiman Demirel, 34.7 per cent. At the military junta's insistence, the two leading parties formed a coalition government under Ismet Inonu. In the next general election, however, the JP emerged as the clear winner, with forty-three per cent of the vote, and the RPP a loser at twenty per cent.

The JP government extended religious education from the lower grades of secondary schools to the upper. And by setting up higher Islamic institutes in Istanbul and Konya, an important religious centre, it completed an official system to educate and train a new generation of orthodox clerics, *ulema*, thus undoing an important element of Kemalist secularism.

In the private sphere, charitable associations centred around mosque construction, and Quranic schools approved by the Directorate-General of Religious Affairs became the chief instrument of Islamic revival. Between 1951 and 1967 the number of religious charities rose nearly eleven-fold, from 237 to 2510.[9] Most of these associations sprang up in provincial towns. This was not surprising because it was in such places that the supporters of Islamic charities – local craftsmen, petty traders and middle peasants – found themselves exploited by big business, based mainly in Istanbul and tied to Western capital.

However, their backing for the Justice/Democratic Party waned when at the insistence of its leader, Prime Minister Demirel, Turkey acquired associate membership of the European Economic Community (EEC), which was committed to the lowering of tariffs between its full and associate members. Since such an arrangement was bound to damage the material well-being of the traditional middle classes – artisans, craftsmen and traders – the backbone of the JP, they felt betrayed, and accused the JP leadership of selling out to business, the chief beneficiary of the EEC link. Their desertion of the JP led to the formation of several small parties, including the National Order Party (NOP), headed by Necmettin (Nejmettin) Erbakan.

As a Justice Party parliamentarian, Erbakan repeatedly attacked Demirel for being pro-American in foreign policy and being pro-big business at the expense of small traders. Consequently, he was denied the party ticket in the 1969 parliamentary election. He contested as an independent and won a seat from Konya. Once in parliament, he gathered a few other like-minded MPs, and formed the National Order Party. A member of the Naqshbandi order, he won the backing of the widespread Nurcu movement. The first party congress opened in 1970 with the Islamic cry '*Allahu Akbar* (God is Great)', something that had not been heard at political gatherings in Turkey for almost half a century.

Not surprisingly, after the military had forced Prime Minister Demirel to resign in March 1971 owing to his failure to contain the rise of the leftist tide in urban centres, and facilitated the installation of a government 'above parties' led by Nihat Erim, a former RPP deputy, it took the NOP to the Constitutional Court, charging it with violating the constitution by using religion for political purposes. The court upheld the charge, and banned the party.

Undeterred, Erbakan formed the National Salvation Party (NSP) in October 1972 when another military-backed government led by Ferit Melen was in office. Erbakan argued against Turkey's membership of the EEC, 'a product of a new Crusader mentality', because such a step would merely perpetuate Turkey's role as an economic underling of 'Western-Christian capitalism'. Instead, he advocated independent industrial development as had been pursued by Japan.

He attacked such aspects of the state-sponsored arts as Western dancing, ballet and theatre which, he said, were alien to 'real' Turks. Above all, he bemoaned the disintegration of the traditional Turkish family under Western influences of the mixing of sexes and disrespect for elders. He stressed 'morality and spiritual values' as the nucleus around which Muslim society needed to be organized.

In the October 1973 general election the NSP emerged as the third-largest party, winning nearly twelve per cent of the vote and forty-nine seats, mainly in deprived rural areas and conservative districts of urban centres, and holding the balance between the left-of-centre RPP and the right-of-centre JP.

Erbakan became deputy premier in the two coalition governments formed between 1974 and 1977. Defying the constitution, he propagated Islamic ideas, and called for the formation of an Islamic Common Market consisting of Turkey and the Arab Middle East. Though the NSP's vote declined to 8.6 per cent in the June 1977 election, Islamization of politics and education did not. An example was the government's decision to let a graduate of the imam-khatib (preacher–prayer leader) colleges become a teacher of general subjects in primary schools, a virtual subversion of the Kemalist principle of 'unification of education'. Summing up the current situation, Turkey's interior minister said in April 1978: 'Politics had even entered the mosques and lower forms of secondary schools.'[10]

By the late seventies the NSP had emerged as the national voice of a sizeable section of the lower and middle classes. 'In so doing, the NSP invested the Islamist movement with the legitimacy of a national party platform,' noted Ronnie Margulies and Ergin Yildizoglu, co-editors of a Turkish newsletter. 'The very existence of the NSP forced all major parties to take the existence of the "Islamic" vote into account and court it more explicitly.'[11]

A revived Islam began to compete with the ideologies of secular right (fascism) and left (Marxism) as a saviour of the disillusioned urban youths sunk in nihilism. Reflecting an accelerated emigration from the villages – with urban population, up from seventeen per cent to twenty-six per cent during 1935–60, rising to forty-six per cent during the next generation[12] – the number of youths in city slums grew sharply. Given the economic recession, caused by steep oil price increases, and the country's huge foreign debt, stemming from recklessly expansionist policies, joblessness shot up. Unemployed youths became ready recruits for extremist parties of the left and right, which resorted to violence for political purposes.

Apparently, Kemalism had failed. Unlike Marxism or liberal democracy, it was not an all-encompassing ideology that explained society and history. Nor was it a socio-ethical system in the form of a conventional religion. Its ascendancy over the past half-century had left Turkish society without moral-ethical moorings which in the past had been provided by Islam. Its main achievement had been to foster Turkish nationalism. But once nationalism had taken root, Kemalism lost most of its *raison d'être*. It was in this moral-ideological vacuum that the parties of the militant left and right thrived, and with it political violence.

As strife in urban areas spilled into villages, it rekindled old racial and sectarian hatreds, between Turks and Kurds, and Shia and Sunni. The underprivileged, pro-leftist Alawis (a sub-sect within Shia Islam), forming one-sixth of the national population, became targets of attacks by ultra-nationalists – organized under the banner of the National Action Party (NAP), led by Alparslan Turkes (Turkesh) – who worked in league with such militant Sunnis as Nurcus, who regarded Alawis as 'worse than unbelievers'. Emulating the NAP and its youth wing, called the Grey Wolves,[13] the NSP formed its youth wing, Akincilar (Akinjilar), which took to attacking leftist students and teachers as well as Alawis. A three-day sectarian-political riot in the south-eastern town of Kahramanmaras (Kahramanmarash) in December 1978 left 117 people dead, most of them Alawis. Premier Bulent Ecevit (Ejevit) put twelve eastern provinces under martial law to reassure the Alawis. But, overall, political violence did not subside. Indeed, by the summer of 1980 it claimed more than 100 people a week.

On 6 September 1980 a rally in Konya by the World Assembly of Islamic Youth for the Liberation of Palestine, sponsored by the NSP, and attended by delegates from twenty Arab countries, drew large crowds. Among other things the rally called for the founding of an Islamic state in Turkey. This triggered a military coup on 12 September and the removal of the coalition government led by Prime Minister Suleiman Demirel of the Justice Party. The communiqué issued by the military leaders, headed by General Kenan Evren, the Chief of the General Staff, described their action as being against 'the followers of fascist and communist ideologies as well as religious fanatics'.[14] The junta arrested Erbakan and other NSP leaders and prosecuted them under Article 163 of the penal code for attempting to change 'the fundamental principles of the state' and organizing a demonstration against the secular laws of the country. It suspended not only all political parties, confiscating their assets, but also the leftist trade union movement, DISK (*Devrinci Isci Sendikalari Konfedasyony* – Confederation of Revolutionary Workers' Unions), which had broken away from the conservative Turk-Is.[15]

AFTER THE 1980 COUP

While the immediate aim of the military junta, formally constituted as the five-member National Security Council (NSC) and led by General Evren, was to halt the slide towards a civil war, its medium-term objective was to rid Turkish society of Marxist ideology and parties. It therefore saw merit in encouraging Islamic ideas and education as an antidote to Marxism. In 1982 it made the teaching of Islam compulsory in secondary schools, something that had been optional since 1967.[16] Repeating the view of Islam expressed earlier by another general, Gursel, who had led a military coup in 1960, Evren said: 'We interpret Westernization as setting our people on the road to becoming the most prosperous and civilized nation . . . In fact, the real nature of Islam is always open to science, civilization and development.'[17] The military regime celebrated the birthday centenary of Mustafa Kemal Ataturk in 1981 with great fanfare, portraying itself as a staunch upholder of the Kemalist legacy. A year after seizing power it dissolved all political parties.

In early 1982 the National Security Council appointed a hand-picked 160-member constituent assembly to draft a new constitution and electoral laws. With thirty-three lawyers, twenty-nine engineers, twenty-one retired military officers, nineteen academics, sixteen civil servants and nine economists as its members, the assembly was widely regarded as unrepresentative and right-wing. Little wonder that while retaining many of the articles of the earlier constitution, the latest document whittled down certain basic freedoms. For example, it effectively emasculated trade unions, curbing collective bargaining and depriving them of any 'political activity'. It authorized the president to veto legislation and appoint judges to the Constitutional Court which among other things was required to pass judgements on political and human rights specified in the constitution. It abolished the Senate.

Once the NSC had modified the draft constitution somewhat it was put to the vote in early November 1982. The referendum also included the appointment of Kenan Evren, who resigned his military post, as president for a seven-year term. Both proposals received massive support. Following this, political life was revived, but only those parties approved by the military were allowed to function. Among these was the Motherland Party established by Turgut Ozal, who had served as the economic overlord under the military junta, and who had in 1977 unsuccessfully contested a parliamentary seat as an independent supported by the National Salvation Party. By late 1982 most of the leaders of the (pan-Islamic) National Salvation Party and the (pan-Turkic) National Action Party had been released whereas the leading Marxist figures were either in prison or self-exile. The left was thus annihilated as an opposition force. In contrast, the rightist opposition was allowed to secure jobs in those sections of the civil service and educational institutions where the left had been influential before the coup. Lacking political outlet, lower and middle cadres of the now-dissolved NSP and NAP joined the Motherland, thus turning the new organization more into a coalition than a unified party.

In the November 1983 parliamentary poll, held under an electoral law that discriminated against small parties, the Motherland won a slight majority in parliament, and Ozal became the prime minister. In the local elections in March, the Motherland repeated its performance, securing forty per cent of the popular vote.

Under the presidency of Evren, son of a prayer-leader from a provincial town in Alasehir (Alashehir), and the premiership of Ozal, a pious man never without his prayer beads, Islamic revival continued. In 1985 there were 72,000 mosques in Turkey, up from 20,000 in 1945, a three-and-a-half-fold increase, whereas the population during that period had grown only two-and-a-half times, from 18.7 million to 51.4 million. In other words, in 1945 there was one mosque for every 1000 Turks; and forty years later there was one for every 700, an index of religious piety that equalled the one prevalent in the Emirate of Bukhara before the Bolshevik revolution. A study by Professor Besir (Beshir) Atalay of Kirikkale, a town of 200,000 near Ankara, revealed a high degree of urban religiosity. It showed that 65.4 per cent of the working-class men and sixty-one per cent of the merchants prayed daily.[18] Unlike rural Turks, who were religious by tradition, urban Turks had been influenced by the mass media.

The adoption of Islamic dress by a growing number of women of all classes could be partly attributed to Islamic programmes on television, especially a two-hour-long women's programme every

Thursday evening. As Emile Serdengenchti, a sales assistant in Bursa, put it: 'Women wear the veil voluntarily, out of fear of leading a sinful life. The idea of sin has come to them from the religious men who preach on the women's television programme [begun under the military regime] every Thursday evening.'[19]

Prime Minister Ozal, a teetotaller and political conservative, was widely known to be sympathetic to Islamic elements, including Sufi brotherhoods. The orders of Naqshbandi, Nurcu and Suleimanci (Suleimanji) became more visible and popular than before, with the pro-Naqshbandi monthly, *Islam*, selling over 110,000 copies. The Quranic courses, specializing in the memorization of the Quran, offered by the Naqshbandi and Suleimanci orders, brought them young pupils. And their programmes of providing free tuition and accommodation in their hostels to the students taking university entrance examinations helped them influence the educated generation of the future. The largest of these brotherhoods, the Naqshbandi, played an important role in electoral politics, offering and withdrawing its support to a leading political party.

Three of the country's twelve dailies were Islamic in outlook. The *Milli Gazete* (National Gazette) was the mouthpiece of the Welfare (Rifah, in Turkish) Party, the reincarnation of the National Salvation Party. Paralleling the rise of an Islamic press was the boom in Islamic publishing. According to Ahmet Kot, a Turkish researcher, at the height of Kemalism, in 1934, religious books accounted for only 1.7 per cent of the total published, whereas in 1985 the figure was seven per cent. In the latter year the number of Turkish pilgrims to Mecca was 280,000 – twice the figure for the Islamic Republic of Iran, which had about the same population.[20]

Buoyed by the satisfactory economic performance of Turkey under his helmsmanship, Ozal applied for full membership of the European Community (EC) in April 1987. With political life returning to normal, excepting the continued exclusion of the Marxist left, competition for voter loyalty increased. Aware of this, the Grand National Assembly tinkered with the electoral law to benefit the Motherland Party. The result was thirty-six per cent of the vote for the party in the October 1987 parliamentary election, but sixty-four per cent of the seats – a remarkable achievement under a proportional representation system.

The governing party's ploy was to fix a high threshold of ten per cent for a political group to qualify for seats in the GNA. Aware of this, Erbakan's Welfare Party coalesced with Turkes's Nationalist

Labour Party (the renamed National Action Party) and another small group to fight the election. With a total vote of 10.9 per cent, including seven per cent for the Welfare Party, the alliance scraped through the barrier. The lead in the GNA was taken by the Motherland Party, followed by the Social Democratic Populist Party (the successor to the Republican People's Party), and the right-of-centre True Path Party (the renamed Justice Party) headed by Suleiman Demirel. The governing coalition excluded the Welfare Party-dominated alliance.

Lack of power helped the Welfare Party to widen its base. Since the socio-economic conditions spawning leftist politics in the 1970s persisted, and since the left was virtually outlawed, the role of opposition fell increasingly on the Welfare Party. The success of Islamic forces in 1979 in Iran, where they toppled the powerful pro-Western monarch, Shah Muhammad Reza Pahlavi, and ten years later in Afghanistan in securing the withdrawal of the Soviet troops (stationed there since late 1979), established that Islam was capable of successfully confronting both Western capitalism-imperialism and Marxist socialism. It thus established its credentials as an indigenous third way, wedded neither to East nor West.

To widen the popular base of his party, the Motherland, Ozal continued to court the Islamic constituency. In July 1988 he went on pilgrimage to Mecca, and became the first eminent leader to do so since the founding of the republic sixty-five years previously. In a sense he was following a trend that had been set by the military regime. Breaking with the country's precedent of sending its foreign minister to a summit meeting of the Islamic Conference Organization (ICO), established in 1969, it had despatched the prime minister to such a gathering in Taif, Saudi Arabia, in January 1981. Following the Islamic summit, the military government reduced its relations with Israel to the second-secretary level. Diplomatic recognition of Israel was part of the price America had extracted from Turkey before letting it join the North Atlantic Treaty Organization (NATO) in 1952. But this had not inhibited the Turkish government from recognizing the Palestine Liberation Organization (PLO), allowing it to open a mission in Ankara, and warmly receiving the PLO leader, Yasser Arafat, in March 1986.

Soon after Ozal's pilgrimage to Mecca, his government became embroiled in a controversy on the wearing of a headscarf by women students on a university campus. When some of them did so, they were ordered by the rector to remove it or face expulsion. Aware that the gap between secularism of the state and religiosity of the people – which had been at the root of a series of political crises since the death of Kemal Ataturk – needed to be bridged, and that along that path lay more and more votes for his party (with local elections looming in March 1989), Ozal intervened. He had the Grand National Assembly pass a bill legalizing the headscarf. But President Evren vetoed it, and asked the Constitutional Court to pass judgement. In late February 1989 the Court overturned the bill on the ground that it contravened the secularist articles of the constitution.

Islamists mounted noisy countrywide demonstrations which were broken up by the police. Iran joined the protest, with its Turkish-language broadcasts attacking President Evren as a blasphemer. The tension between the two neighbours reached a point where Turkey recalled its ambassador to Tehran in protest at Iran's meddling in its internal affairs.

In the municipal elections of March 1989, the Welfare Party improved its vote from seven to ten per cent, whereas the Mother-land's vote nearly halved from the forty per cent it had gained five years before. In early 1990 the controversy on the headscarf/turban was revived, when Islamic students staged a sit-in at Ankara's Middle Eastern Technical University in protest at the wearing of a headscarf/turban. Seizing the opportunity to regain the lost electoral ground, the Ozal government issued a decree authorizing an individual university to decide whether or not to allow the (banned) headscarf/turban on the campus. Later that year women students at a university where the headscarf was prohibited took their case to the local court. It repealed the ban on the ground that it infringed personal human rights. The subject became so charged that the students and teachers involved in the controversy resorted to boycotting classes. This time President Evren refrained from intervening. He reckoned, rightly, that if he did, women students would take their case to the European Court of Human Rights, and win. In short, the secularist side found itself on the defensive as it attempted to reconcile Kemalist precepts with the right of religious freedom within a democratic context.

Breaking with the Kemalist tradition, the Ozal government per-mitted Islamic finance houses, mostly controlled by the Naqshbandi order, to operate. This allowed it to channel funds to support Islamic activists who were by now to be found in all government depart-ments, especially the secular educational system. The extent of Islamist infiltration of civil and military services became apparent when, in February 1990, the government sacked forty officials within the ministry of education for propagating Islamic fundamentalism, and dismissed fifteen air force officers for attempting to establish Islamic cells. The expansion of the Suleimanci, an important Sufi order, could be gauged by the fact that it managed 1900 Quranic schools – over one-third as numerous as the 5197 such schools, with a student body of 290,000, run under the supervision of the official Directorate-General of Religious Affairs under the prime minister.[21] Reflecting the rise in popular interest in Islam, the staff of the DGRA grew sixteen per cent annually, from 47,000 in 1985 to 84,000 five years later, including 69,000 full-time clerics operating from mosques in Turkey, and 800 preachers and prayer-leaders attached to twenty-one Turkish embassies and consulates to serve Turkish expatriates abroad.[22]

By then Turgut Ozal had been elevated to the presidency, following the end of President Evren's term in November 1989. Prime Minister Yildirim Akbulut, who succeeded Ozal, included in his cabinet Memet Kececilir (Kejejilir), the leader of the Islamic wing of the ruling Motherland Party, which included the new president's two brothers: Tokrut Ozal, a businessman with extensive Saudi connections, and an active member of the Naqshbandi order, and Yusuf Ozal.

In early 1990 the EC decided to defer, indefinitely, negotiations on Turkey's full membership. It justified its decision on economic and political grounds: the high price of integrating the Turkish economy into the EC, and Turkey's failure to bring its adherence to human rights up to European standards. But this explanation did not dispel the popular perception among Turks that their country was being excluded on religious grounds, a perception strongly expressed by the pan-Islamic and pan-Turkic press.

Already pan-Islamist and pan-Turkic elements in Turkey had begun looking east – towards Soviet Azerbaijan and Central Asia. They evinced keen interest in the dispute between Azerbaijan and Armenia over the Nagorno Karabakh enclave, which erupted in early 1988, and which they perceived as a confrontation between Muslim Azeris and Christian Armenians, an ethnic group much disliked in Turkey. When, in January 1990, Moscow despatched Soviet tanks to the Azerbaijani capital of Baku to restore order after large-scale Azeri attacks on the Armenian minority in the city,[23] the Welfare Party and the pan-Turkic Nationalist Labour Party (NLP) protested vehemently, arguing that Christian Armenians had collaborated with the atheist regime of Gorbachev to attack the innocent Muslims of

Azerbaijan. Their action helped create a nationwide clamour for a decisive governmental move to help Muslim Azeris resist the Soviet Union's iron-hand policy. This happened because, thanks to media propaganda and historic bonds, most Turks came to think of Azeris as their kith and kin. But Ozal failed to reflect this feeling. All the Turkish government did was to issue a public protest at Soviet behaviour in Azerbaijan. Later, at a meeting in Washington, Ozal reportedly remarked that since an overwhelming majority of Soviet Azeris were Shia, that republic was of more interest to Iran than Turkey.[24] Ozal highlighted the sectarian affiliation of Azeri Muslims because he knew that in a predominantly Sunni Turkey, Shias, a variant of the much-disliked Alawis (of Turkey), were unpopular. This was his way of dissipating the popular pressure that was being applied on his government. This angered Islamists who did not wish to get bogged down in sectarian differences within Islam, and who persisted in portraying the Azeri–Armenian conflict in religious terms.

On the positive side, taking advantage of the liberalization of religious freedom and foreign travel in the USSR during the latter part of perestroika (restructuring), 1989–91, hundreds of Welfare and NLP activists travelled to the Muslim-majority Soviet republics to build up contacts with anybody and everybody interested in Islam and/or pan-Turkism, and help the people there rediscover their Islamic and Turkish roots.

In Turkey itself, with the prospect of economic-political integration into Europe almost dead, and the Marxist forces at home and abroad in decline, the popular attraction of Islam as a viable social ideology increased.

Islamic sentiment reached a high point on the eve of the Gulf War between Iraq and the US-led United Nations forces in mid-January 1991, because of the economic loss due to the termination of Turkey's trade with Iraq following the UN embargo against Baghdad, and the presentation of the conflict by the Iraqi president Saddam Hussein as a struggle between believers and unbelievers.

Sensing the popular mood, the government revived the Higher Islamic Council (HIC), composed of senior clerics and theologians, which had been disbanded after the 1980 military coup. When the secular press presented the development as a precursor of the reformation of Islam, something secularists have wished since Ataturk's days, it was disabused of the notion by Hamdi Mert, deputy president of the DGRA. 'Our religion is an unchanging system,' said Mert. 'We believe it's the final revealed religion, so reform is out of the question.'[25] The repeal of Article 163 of the penal code, dealing with those who challenged secularism, in April 1991, gave a further fillip to Islamist forces.[26] When the Iranian president, Ali Akbar Hashemi Rafsanjani, visited Turkey early the following month, cheering crowds greeted him with shouts of '*Allahu Akbar* (God is Great)', an unprecedented spectacle in the history of the republic.

What had by now irretrievably undermined the Kemalist heritage, currently upheld only by an elite of military officers and senior bureaucrats, was the unprecedented extension of access to information and personal mobility – television, telephones and cars – to ordinary Turks during the decade of economic liberalization and prosperity under Ozal, with the Gross Domestic Product (GDP) growing at seven per cent annually during 1986–8. With an equally rapid expansion of higher education during the earlier decades, the religious beliefs of a ninety-eight per cent Muslim society had by now permeated the top layers of a civil administration headed by popularly elected politicians since the return of parliamentary democracy in 1983. The establishment by fifty-three Turkish intellectuals of an Islamic Human Rights Group in Istanbul in the spring of 1991 was another indication of a new trend in Turkish life. In other words, religious revival in Turkey had followed the form of Islamic perceptions quietly gaining ground in popular thought and practice within the shell of secular law, by and large avoiding a clash with the secular legal system or existing legal interpretations of a secular constitution.

That Islamic consciousness existed at the highest political level and played a major role in shaping perceptions was well encapsulated by a remark by President Ozal in late 1991. When asked by a reporter from *Der Spiegel* (The Mirror), a German magazine, why he thought Turkey was not accepted into the EC, Ozal replied: 'I think it is because you [Europeans] are Christian and we [Turks] are Muslim'.[27]

By then the October 1991 elections had again shown Islamist forces gaining ground. The Welfare Party-led alliance won seventeen per cent of the vote, and sixty-two seats, forty of these being Welfare's. The Motherland was reduced to 115 seats, and gave way to a coalition of Suleiman Demirel's True Path Party (TPP) and Erdal Inonu's Social Democratic Populist Party (SDPP). The new government headed by Demirel, and supported by 266 deputies in a house of 450, took office in late November.

The Motherland's lacklustre performance was due to poor

economic growth, down from 9.2 per cent in 1990 to 1.9 per cent in 1991 (owing partly to the Gulf War), and a lack of dynamic leadership previously provided by Ozal who, as president, was required to stay away from party politics. During the same period, reflecting seventy-four per cent annual inflation, the average exchange rate for the Turkish Lira rose from TLs 2609 to one US dollar to TLs 4172. The high inflation caused interest rates to rise above 100 per cent a year, a clear example of usury which, the Welfare Party pointed out, was forbidden by the Quran. It called for an increase in the number and size of interest-free institutions, a popular demand.

As the inheritor of an economic mess, the new coalition government knew that it had a tough task on hand, and felt depressed. But its depression was soon to be dispelled by an event outside Turkish boundaries: the break-up of the Union of Soviet Socialist Republics in mid-December 1991 into fifteen independent states, which led to the rise of Turkic nationalism in Azerbaijan and the five republics of Central Asia, and opened up vast economic, diplomatic and cultural possibilities for Turkey at official and private levels.

The assistance that the Turkish state was able to offer the former Soviet Union's Muslim-majority republics in the cultural field included religion. Like their kinsmen in Turkey, the Muslims in Central Asia belonged to the Hanafi school, one of the four leading schools of Sunni Islam. Turkey's DGRA and one of its departments, the Religious Affairs Foundation, provided voluntary aid: shipments of the Quran and other religious books, despatch of clerics, and scholarships to students from the former Soviet republics for the study of Islam in Turkey. With 50,000 students graduating annually from the religious vocational high schools, intended to provide vocational training for the clergy, there was no dearth of qualified Turkish clerics to be sent abroad.[28] Not surprisingly, Turkey became one of the first countries to send Islamic clergy to former Soviet Central Asia, starting with the despatch of 357 Turkish clergy to these and other states, including Outer Mongolia, during the holy month of Ramadan in March 1991.[29]

Yet in its public pronouncements, the Turkish government stressed its secular image, and projected itself as a rival to Iran, which was shown to be intent on exporting Islamic fundamentalism to these new Muslim-majority countries.

Such a presentation was also at odds with the change that had occurred within Turkey in the aftermath of the Soviet Union's collapse. The euphoria created by the disintegration of the barriers between Turkey and the Turkic populations of Central Asia and Azerbaijan lowered tension between secularists and Islamists in Turkey. 'Secularists have stopped accusing Islamists of being funded by Iran and of having extra-territorial loyalties,' said Fehmi Koru, the chief columnist of the *Zaman* (Time), an Islamist paper. 'In any case there is not much hostility to Islamists from the government and the political establishment. After all, there is an Islamic faction within each of the two leading parties: the True Path and the Motherland. Strong opposition [to Islam] is now confined to diehard secularist intellectuals and military leaders.'[30]

This was the background against which Ankara devised its overall policy towards former Soviet Central Asia and Azerbaijan in collaboration with Washington.

The official stance of Turkey, actively encouraged by America, was to offer itself as a role model to Central Asia and Azerbaijan: a secular regime, free-market economy and Islamic culture. As a country with a well-developed industrial base and considerable commercial dealings with Europe and America, Turkey was capable of providing the newly independent 'Turkic' (the adjective routinely used by the Turkish media) republics industrial know-how and managerial and commercial expertise – as well as practical advice on how to change over from a centralized, planned economy to a market economy.

In the cultural field, Turkey intervened in the debate about changing the alphabet for Azeri and Central Asian languages then in progress in these republics. It strongly advised a switch-over from the present Cyrillic script to the Roman: a step which in time was bound to wean the new states away from the Russian orbit towards Turkey and the West. As a gesture of practical help, Ankara shipped Turkish typewriters, dictionaries and printing presses to these states. To its delight, the Azerbaijani parliament opted for the Roman alphabet in January 1992. It is worth noting, however, that it was Azerbaijan which had pioneered the move away from the Arabic to the Latin/Roman script as early as 1922, inadvertently paving the way for Turkey to follow, which it did six years later.

The presidents of Central Asian states were quick to recognize the importance of Turkey and, within a month of their republics becoming independent in mid-December 1991, visited Ankara. President Ozal reciprocated the gesture soon after.

Given its size and strategic location, Turkey was in a position to play an active role not only in the region to its east but also to its north and west. Out of this arose the idea of a Black Sea Cooperation Council (BSCC) consisting of the countries surrounding the Black Sea – and Azerbaijan, even though it did not share a Black Sea shoreline. A preliminary meeting took place in Istanbul in early February.

Later that month, during his visit to Washington, Premier Demirel presented President George Bush with a thirteen-point programme on Central Asia, led by the proposal that all assistance to the region by America, other Western powers and Turkey be coordinated through the recently formed Central Asian Trade Bank in Turkey. Ankara's problem, he confessed, was that, given its financial problems at home, it could not unilaterally provide much fiscal aid to these new states. With the burgeoning federal deficit in the US showing no sign of abating, Bush's hands were tied too. In the political sphere, Demirel reportedly reassured Bush that by providing the Central Asia republics with a viable secular model, Turkey would act as an American conduit to these states, thus joining Washington's battle to keep Iran and its version of Islamic fundamentalism out of the region.

While projecting itself as a rival to Iran, Turkey had to cooperate with it at least in economic matters. Along with Pakistan, they were both members of the Economic Cooperation Organization (ECO), which was originally established as the Regional Development Council (RDC) in 1967, when all three countries were firmly in the Western camp. Now, at Iran's initiative, it was decided to expand ECO by including Azerbaijan and all Central Asian republics except Kazakhstan. A summit of the expanded ECO took place in Tehran on 17 February. Much to the chagrin of Turkey, the Iranian president, Rafsanjani, the host, began portraying the enlarged body as an Islamic Common Market of nearly 280 million people.

To the further embarrassment of Turkey, Rafsanjani announced that a Caspian Sea Cooperation Council composed of the countries around the Caspian Sea – Azerbaijan, Russia, Kazakhstan, Turkmenistan and Iran – had been formed at the initiative of Tehran.

But then came a boost for the Turkish side. In mid-March all Central Asian states and Azerbaijan attended a meeting of the North Atlantic Cooperation Council which included the sixteen members of NATO. Earlier they had participated in a gathering of the Helsinki-based Conference on Security and Cooperation in Europe (CSCE), which had accepted them as members. Both these events were portrayed in the Turkish media as unmistakable signs that Central Asians and Azeris were going with Europe and Turkey, and not with Iran and the Muslim world. Equally importantly, Turkey had taken under its wing countries that were untutored in the art and craft of diplomacy.

The predominantly secular Turkish media combined self-congratulatory reporting and analysis – 'The Twenty-first century will be the Turkish century', 'We are the leaders of 200 million Turkic peoples extending from the Black Sea to China', 'We have won the race against a fundamentalist, obscurantist Iran' – with jibes at Tehran for having fits of jealousy over losing out to Ankara in a competition for influence in the Muslim-majority republics of the former Soviet Union. Chauvinism in the media reached such a high pitch that even President Ozal, with a reputation for showmanship, found it excessive. 'We have historic and cultural ties with them, and they want us as a model,' he said. 'But . . . this is getting a bit exaggerated. This could induce over-optimism, and backfire against Turkey.'[31]

While the Turkish media and government were busily attacking Iran's Islamic obscurantism, the official Directorate-General of Religious Affairs, pursuing its little-noticed policy, despatched sixty-seven clerics to Central Asia during the month of Ramadan (which started on 5 March) to lead prayers in mosques and give sermons, followed by an appeal to the Turkish faithful for funds to build 100 mosques in the region. It also disclosed that it was funding 197 scholarships to students from the Muslim-majority territories of the former Soviet Union at several Quranic schools in Istanbul, and that it had shipped more than 200,000 religious books to these areas.[32]

Among many Turkish newspapers, it was only the *Zaman*, an Islamist daily, which acted immediately to take advantage of the new situation. Its management arranged to publish editions in Baku twice a week, and in Alma Ata twice a month, setting its pages in both Roman and Cyrillic scripts. Established in Ankara, in November 1986, with a circulation of 10,000, the newspaper had seen its sales rise to 120,000 by the spring of 1992, most of the gains having been made during the past three years.

On the governmental side, state-run Turkish television also showed enterprise and speed. On the eve of Premier Demirel's tour of Central Asia and Azerbaijan in late April, Turkish television's 'Avrasya (Eurasia)' channel began beaming programmes to Azerbaijan. The idea was to strengthen cultural ties by transmitting television programmes and popularizing the spoken Turkish of Turkey in Azerbaijan – and areas further east. Ankara claimed that in due course there would be a two-way television traffic between Turkey and its eastern neighbours. But that seemed unlikely in the same way that despite repeated statements by Demirel that Turkey would not act as the Big Brother, senior civil servants and leading commentators in the media continued to display a patronizing attitude. This was well reflected by Kurtulus Tashkent, deputy director-general of the Turkish foreign ministry's eastern section, when he said: 'We feel moral and political responsibility towards Azerbaijan and other Turkic republics, and want to lead them in establishing a secular democratic system and free-market-oriented economy.'[33] In any event, it was unrealistic to expect that any of the these former Soviet republics, with populations ranging between 3.6 million and twenty-one million, could feel equal to Turkey with its fifty-seven million people.

During his visits to Azerbaijan, Turkmenistan, Uzbekistan, Kyrgyzstan and Kazakhstan, Premier Demirel stressed the historical connection. 'The star of history is shining for the Turkic people,' he said. 'We do not want any pan-Turkic aspirations. But this region is the land of our forefathers.'[34] Among the many agreements he signed, provision was made for 10,000 high-school and university students from these republics to receive further education and professional training in Turkey. More importantly, Demirel promised $1,200 million in aid to these countries: $600 million in soft loans for buying Turkish wheat and sugar; and $600 million from Turkish Eximbank for funding Turkish exports, construction and investment.

While its cultural affinity and historic ties with Central Asia provided Turkey with strong cards, geography was against it. Turkey did not share frontiers with any of these states (except a ten-kilometre (seven-mile) common border with the Nakhichevan enclave of Azerbaijan, separated from the mainland by a strip of Armenia). And continued instability in the Caucasian states of Azerbaijan, Armenia and Georgia limited Turkey's overall geographical asset of being a bridge between East and West. Also, despite all the talk about getting together with long-lost Turkic cousins, private Turkish companies were more interested in such large markets as Russia and Ukraine than in sparsely populated Turkmenistan (3.6 million), Kyrgyzstan (4.5 million) or Tajikistan (5.2 million).

As the struggle between Azerbaijan and Armenia over Nagorno

Karabakh intensified in May–June 1992 after the Armenians had established a corridor between Armenia and Nagorno Karabakh, which had slipped out of Azeri control, the Turkish government came under popular pressure to side with Azerbaijan militarily. Aware of the Western military and trade embargoes that followed Turkish military intervention in Cyprus in 1974,[35] Demirel refused to yield to such pressures. More importantly, he had to take into account the warning issued on 20 May by Marshal Yevgeny Shaposhnikov, supreme commander of the military of the Commonwealth of Independent States (CIS), the virtual successor to the USSR, that foreign intervention in the Nagorno Karabakh dispute 'could lead the world into the Third World War'.[36] His statement came soon after the establishment of the Collective Defence Treaty (CDT) by six members of the CIS – Russia, Armenia, Kazakhstan, Kyrgyzstan, Tajikistan and Uzbekistan – which did not include Azerbaijan. It was based on the premise that since Turkey was a member of NATO, its attack on Armenia would trigger a response by the CDT, to which Armenia belonged, igniting a conflict between two multilateral defence pacts. It had a chastening effect on Turkey.

Premier Demirel, as well as President Ozal, now concentrated on the fate of Bosnia-Herzegovina, once part of the Ottoman empire, where the Muslim community, forming forty-four per cent of the population, was under attack by the smaller but better-armed (Christian) Serb community. Breaking with precedent, Turkey decided to use the forum of the Jiddah-based Islamic Conference Organization to shore up support for the suffering Bosnian Muslims. At its behest, foreign ministers of the forty-seven-member ICO gathered in Istanbul in mid-June 1992 and adopted a Turkish plan to lobby for United Nations military intervention in Bosnia to stop the Serbian aggression. For a country claiming to be secular, this was an extraordinary step to take. But there was little doubt that the official action was popular. Islamic feeling in Turkey was on the rise. In the elections to 342 mayoral posts in the country on 7 June, the Welfare Party won fifteen per cent – only a shade behind the 18.5 per cent won by the Motherland, the main opposition party.

The election of Abulfaz Elchibey (born 1939) as president of Azerbaijan in early June was a plus for Turkey and a minus for Iran in their competition for influence in Azerbaijan. Much to the disappointment of Azeri Muslims, the Islamic Republic of Iran had not taken their side in the conflict, but had acted as a mediator between

Muslim Azerbaijan and Christian Armenia, brokering ceasefires, which had proved short-lived. Apparently Iran had concluded that a stable, strong Azerbaijan on its doorstep would encourage irredentist tendencies among Azeri Iranians, about eight million of whom lived in the provinces of East and West Azerbaijan contiguous with the newly independent Republic of Azerbaijan. It was therefore content to see a weak Azerbaijan struggling to maintain its territorial integrity. In other words, Iran chose to put national interests above any purely ideological consideration of unequivocally helping fellow-Muslims in Azerbaijan.

Iran's policy encouraged President Elchibey to strengthen ties with Turkey. He had all along been a Turkic nationalist. He was prominent among those who greeted Turkes, head of the pan-Turkic Nationalist Labour Party in Turkey, during the latter's visit to Baku in early 1992. He was pleased to note that, despite its own severe economic problems, Turkey had granted $250-million credits to Azerbaijan – including $100 million to its Nakhichevan enclave with a population of a mere 300,000 – to buy Turkish goods and services. In contrast, Iran had provided no such economic aid. Overall, given Turkey's political and commercial links with the West, it was better equipped to help Azerbaijan than Iran. On the other side, given its abundant petroleum and gas resources, Azerbaijan was in a position to complement the economy of Turkey which, unlike Iran, lacked oil. However, the speed of economic reform and foreign investment in Azerbaijan hinged on domestic stability, which in turn depended on the resolution of the festering Nagorno Karabakh crisis, which President Elchibey promised to resolve by retaking the lost enclave of Nagorno Karabakh militarily after the collapse of the CSCE-sponsored peace talks in Rome in early August.

Azerbaijan's steady military effort from August until early January 1993 to recover Nagorno Karabakh led to its recapture of about a quarter of the enclave. But it lost most of this territory when the Armenians mounted their counter-offensive on 20 January. Indeed, their next major offensive in mid-March resulted in the establishment of a second corridor between Armenia and northern Nagorno Karabakh, thus bringing roughly ten per cent of the Azerbaijani territory under their control.

Turkey joined Azerbaijan in a diplomatic effort to isolate Armenia for its aggression against Azerbaijan. But little came of it. The only concrete way that Turkey could help its neighbour was by providing it with military assistance. But this was not on the cards despite Premier

Demirel's warning to Armenia that Ankara would 'run out of patience' if its 'oppression of the Azeri people does not end shortly'.[37]

Armenia did not take Demirel's statement seriously. It was aware that Ankara's hands were tied in more ways than one. Since Turkey had only a short common border with the Nakhichevan enclave of Azerbaijan, a Turkish military involvement would have meant invading Armenia in places that were far removed from the current theatre of fighting. Secondly, Demirel's assessment that military action by Turkey would turn the conflict into a Christian–Muslim confrontation was realistic. Armenia felt confident that if Ankara intervened militarily it would find itself isolated in NATO, where it was the only Muslim member, and that public opinion in the West would swing towards Armenia.

Turkey's ostracism by the West in the wake of its invasion of Cyprus in 1974, and the continued non-recognition by the world community of the subsequently established Republic of Northern Cyprus (except by Turkey), were the arguments most often advanced by those who urged moderation on Demirel, who publicly envisaged 'others helping Armenia' in case Turkey sided militarily with Azerbaijan.[38] These arguments were more popular among the elite in Istanbul, the centre of the newly emergent business class, than in the Anatolian hinterland. Aware that more than half of Turkish exports went to the EC, the business elite of Istanbul was deeply apprehensive of any Western trade embargo most likely to follow Ankara's military intervention.

In other words, Turkey's commercial-economic links with the West, which had been presented as assets to the Muslim-majority republics of the former USSR, now proved to be its liabilities. They narrowed Ankara's options, and foreclosed military aid to its closest Turkic neighbour to repel Armenian aggression. That this stance was bound to hurt Turkey's future prospects in Central Asia was not lost on many influential Turkish figures, including President Ozal, who happened to be in the midst of a tour of the Central Asian republics and Azerbaijan when the latest crisis erupted.

During his three-day visit to Baku in mid-April, Ozal offered Azerbaijan a defence pact – something which, strictly speaking, was not within his powers.[39] But because such a gesture was in tune with popular feeling in Turkey, his public standing at home rose sharply. This was illustrated amply by the huge crowd which turned up at his funeral following his sudden death on 17 April due to heart failure. Large sections of the funeral procession were made up of the supporters of the Welfare Party. They came carrying green flags of Islam and placards paying homage to 'Our Pious President', and shouted '*Allahu Akbar*' – religious cries which mingled strangely with the officially sanctified funereal music of Frédéric Chopin.

President Elchibey's impotence in the face of Armenian aggression undermined his position at home. This became dramatically clear when his power was seriously threatened by Geidar (Heidar) Ali Rezaoglu Aliyev (born 1923), a pre-eminent Azeri politician during the Soviet era, and Colonel Suret Husseinov, a military officer dismissed by Elchibey, in mid-June. When, fearing for his safety, Elchibey fled Baku in the middle of the night for his birth-place in Nakhichevan, Turkey continued to recognize him as president, stating that 'effective removal of Azerbaijan's elected President Abulfaz Elchibey was unacceptable to the civilized world'.[40] It had the full support of America. Therefore when Elchibey was finally removed from office by parliament which, acting within the constitution, passed on his powers to its chairman, Aliyev, Ankara suffered a humiliating diplomatic defeat.

Turkey's Islamic opposition, on the other hand, had few tears to shed for Elchibey, who had allied himself with America and Israel. At home, though, it was taken aback when Tansu Çiller (Chiller), an erstwhile minister of economy, was elected leader of the senior partner in the coalition government, the True Path Party, following the elevation of Demirel to the presidency in mid-June – thus becoming the first woman prime minister of Turkey. The event might encourage the Islamic faction within the True Path Party to leave and join the Welfare Party, which was gaining ground due to the continued failure of the Turkish government to assist Azeri Muslims and Bosnian Muslims to counter aggression respectively by Christian Armenians and Christian Serbs. A dramatic indication of rising Islamic sentiment in Turkey came in early July when in the central city of Sivas a demonstration by several thousand Muslims against Aziz Nesin, a newspaper editor and translator of Salman Rushdie's novel *The Satanic Verses*, considered blasphemous by many Muslims, escalated into arson at his hotel, resulting in thirty-six deaths.[41] The rioters also toppled the bust of Kemal Ataturk in the city centre, an unprecedented event in the chronicles of the Turkish republic. The Sivas episode was a contrast to the isolated assassinations of prominent secularists in Turkey which had been blamed on Iran. This was a violent public protest, and opened a new chapter in the recent history of Islamic forces in Turkey.

With the Motherland Party weakened by the death of its charismatic founder, Turgut Ozal, and the True Path Party redefining its identity under a new, untested leader, Tansu Çiller, the Welfare Party seemed set to gain further ground. Once its popular vote reaches the fifteen to twenty per cent band, a likely prospect, its chances of sharing power in a future coalition government would improve.

Among other things such a development would enable Azerbaijan to strengthen its ties with Turkey without alienating Iran, combining its pan-Turkic proclivities with Islamist tendencies. After all, before the formation of the Democratic Republic of Azerbaijan in 1918, Azeris had not existed as a nation, and had derived their identity primarily from Islam; and with most of them being Shia, they had been drawn willy-nilly to the overwhelmingly Shia Iran.

TWO

Azerbaijan: Limits of Pan-Turkic Nationalism

As part of the Communist Party of the Soviet Union, the Communist Party of Azerbaijan was deeply affected by the proceedings of the Twentieth Congress of the CPSU which lasted from 14 to 25 February 1956. In a long speech, Nikita Khrushchev (1894–1971), the party's First Secretary, exposed numerous misdeeds by Stalin, including trampling upon socialist legality, fostering a personality cult, and committing monstrous violations of basic Leninist principles in his nationalities policy by banishing entire nationalities to the far corners of the USSR on flimsy grounds. In the wake of Khrushchev's denunciations came a shake-up of the party, starting at the top, with the weeding out of diehard Stalinists: a development noted by A. N. Guliev, a party bureaucrat, in the *Great Soviet Encyclopedia*, thus: 'After the Twentieth Congress of the CPSU, with the aid of the Central Committee of the CPSU, the Communists of Azerbaijan strengthened and heightened the combat capacity of the Party organizations and intensified its activities.'[1]

The severity of the purges implemented in the early 1950s, and then again five years later, was such that the growth in party membership during the decade was only thirty-two per cent, from 108,800 to 143,700 – down from ninety-eight per cent during the 1940s.[2]

While Khrushchev was intent on ending the state terror that Stalin had institutionalized, his militant atheism brooked no compromise with religion and religious traditions. Encouraged by him, members of the Communist Youth League began a sustained anti-veil campaign in 1955, bringing it to a climax in 1959, that marked the official end of the veil in the USSR. It also signalled a campaign by the freshly revived Union of Atheists against places of worship as well as religious schools and monuments. During the next five years the number of working Russian Orthodox churches fell by half, to about 10,000, and synagogues by four-fifths, to ninety-five.

The closure of mosques continued long after Khrushchev had been removed from power in 1964. During the period 1958–68 the number of functioning mosques in the USSR decreased from 1500 to 500.

Renewed Communist Party pressure on religion and religious traditions created ill-will against the regime among Muslim and Christian believers. Since they were unable to express it, their feelings were channelled along inter-ethnic lines, reviving animosity between (Muslim) Azeris and (Christian) Armenians which had been dormant since the mid-1920s. The controversy over Nagorno Karabakh resurfaced. In May 1963, some 2500 Armenians in Karabakh stated in their petition to Khrushchev that the Azerbaijani authorities had neglected the economic development of the enclave, and demanded incorporation into either Armenia or the Russian Federation. They drew a blank. But their action aroused enough Azeri anger to trigger anti-Armenian riots in Baku and Sumgait, an industrial suburb of the capital.

Khrushchev's removal as the CPSU's First Secretary in October 1964 did not affect the position of his Armenian colleague, Anastas Mikoyan, on the twelve-member Politburo, the supreme organ of the party. Mikoyan was also the chairman of the Presidium of the Supreme Soviet, the country's highest law-making body. This encouraged Armenia to petition Moscow in 1966 that it be given jurisdiction over Karabakh, but in vain.

Simmering tension between Azeris and Armenians in the enclave escalated in 1968 into rioting in the capital, Stepanakert, where most Azeris lived. Mutual distrust and hostility remained high until 1973, when Boris Kevorkov, the only Armenian member of the CPA's Central Committee, was appointed First Secretary of the Nagorno Karabakh Regional Committee of the CPA. This allayed Armenian feelings somewhat.

During the 1970s USSR authorities were favourably inclined towards Azerbaijan primarily because of the unprecedented high position acquired by one of its politicians, Geidar Aliyev, in Moscow. A native of Nakhichevan, Aliyev held important posts in Azerbaijan, including the chairmanship of the republic's KGB (*Komitet Gosudarstvennoy Bezopasnosti*/Committee for State Security) from 1967 to 1969, before being promoted to First Secretary of the CPA. Elected a member of the CPSU's Central Committee in 1971, he made a deep impression on Leonid Brezhnev (1906–82) – Khrushchev's successor as First Secretary of the CPSU – and rose to become a candidate member of the Politburo in 1976. The interests of Azerbaijan were thus in powerful hands.

In contrast, the task of presenting the Armenian case fell to stray intellectual partisans. One such was Sero Khanzadian, an Armenian author. In October 1977 he petitioned Brezhnev to re-unite Karabakh with Armenia. But nothing came of it.

When Yuri Andropov, the chairman of the USSR's KGB, became the First Secretary of the CPSU after Brezhnev's death in November 1982, he initiated a campaign to improve labour discipline and productivity and eliminate corruption, which had increased dramatically during the Brezhnev era. Since Aliyev had supervised a crackdown on corruption in Azerbaijan as the local KGB chief in the late 1960s, Andropov assigned him a similar task – with its focus on Central Asia and Azerbaijan, which were widely regarded as the most corrupt regions in the USSR. Aliyev was elected a full member of the Politburo in November 1982; and a year later he became the first deputy chairman of the Council of Ministers. However, Andropov's tenure proved short. He died in February 1984 and was succeeded by Konstantin Chernenko. He expired just over a year later, and was followed by Mikhail Gorbachev. A member of the Politburo, Gorbachev had obtained the backing of Aliyev in his successful bid for First Secretary in March 1985.

Gorbachev initiated glasnost (literally, transparence) and perestroika (restructuring) at the Twenty-seventh Congress of the CPSU in February 1986. Glasnost was part of the lexicon of Lenin, who believed in exposing the Communist Party and the government to public examination. And perestroika was the term used by Stalin radically to transform the socio-economic structures of the pre-revolutionary period.

It took about a year for these processes to get going. The subsequent liberalization considerably altered the political environment in the USSR. Much to the surprise and frustration of Gorbachev and his aides, among other things this brought to the fore the nationalities problem which, in the Central Asian and Azerbaijani context, had strong religious connotations. (Gorbachev should not have been surprised. During his year as the Politburo member in charge of party ideology, he had allowed the Russian nationalist trend in literature to reassert itself, while failing to give similar latitude to non-Russians who then saw their chance to catch up under perestroika.)

As it was, 'parallel' or 'unofficial' Islam had made strides in Azerbaijan, especially after the success of the Islamic revolution in Iran in early 1979. The fact that it was not Marxism-Leninism, but Islam, a faith which the Soviet authorities dismissed as feudal and backward, which had inspired the Iranian masses to overthrow an oppressive pro-Western monarchy, made a mark on the region's Muslims. Since Azeris shared their language with those living in the border provinces of Iran, and since many of them had blood relations across the frontier, they were more interested in Iranian events than were other Soviet Muslims. Some of them had taken to listening to the Azeri radio programmes that the Iranian authorities began beaming towards the Caucasus after the Islamic revolution. Later, following the lead of Riyadh Radio, the Iranian broadcasters offered courses on Islamic theology, thus encouraging the growth of 'unofficial' mullahs in Azerbaijan and elsewhere in the USSR. Rising Armenian nationalism, with its long history of symbiosis with the Church, also provided an impetus to the underground Islamic movement in Azerbaijan, which perceived the Armenian–Azeri conflict in a religious context. Little wonder that small, radical Islamic groups sprang up. One such body, headed by Ali Reza Khalqin, was discovered by the KGB in Baku in 1984, and suppressed.

Noting that religion was still a force among sections of the Azeri population, and that there were self-appointed mullahs and holy places, Abdul Farid Dashdamiryev, a Communist intellectual, writing in *Nauka i Religia* (Knowledge and Religion) in December 1986, outlined the reasons for the phenomenon. 'Religion is trying to find its place in the sphere of national relations,' he wrote. 'In recent years the interest of our intellectuals and masses in national culture, the sources of our culture and the traditions and customs of our people has increased noticeably. The confusion between the national and the religious, the replacement of one by the other, takes place mainly on the level of mass consciousness. The idealization of religion, the over-estimation of its role in the life of the nation, generally accompany nationalistic attitudes and the glorification of the national style of life.'[3]

Earlier that year, in February 1986, the importance of Abel Aghanbegian, an Armenian, who had emerged as chief economic adviser to Gorbachev, had become obvious at the Twenty-seventh Congress of the CPSU. It was one of the many signs that the star of Aliyev was waning, and with it the advantage that Azerbaijan had enjoyed so far in Moscow.

In the Caucasus, political liberalization led to the revival, in early 1987, of the Armenian United National Party (AUNP) – a nationalist group that had been suppressed by the KGB in 1971 – and changes in the Communist Party of Armenia. The new grouping began protesting openly against the alleged discrimination that Armenians were suffering in Nagorno Karabakh, and called for the enclave's retrocession to Armenia. Many members of the Armenian Academy of Sciences addressed a letter to Gorbachev in which they called Azerbaijan 'a Turkish Fifth Column in the USSR', and warned that Azerbaijan was planning to expel not only Armenians but also Russians. In order to widen the AUNP's base, Armenian nationalists living in Baku and Sumagit started contacting fellow-Armenians in Nagorno Karabakh, pointing out that the province had been denied the prosperity that high prices of exported Azeri oil had brought to Azerbaijan from the mid-1970s onwards, and arguing that keeping the enclave underdeveloped was a ploy to encourage the Armenians, then forming three-quarters of the total population of 185,000,[4] to emigrate to Armenia. The Azeri authorities disputed the facts and analysis presented by the Armenian nationalists. They argued that with the central planners investing large amounts in developing petroleum reserves in Siberia from the early 1960s onwards, the oil output of Azerbaijan had declined from the peak of 450,000 b/d (barrels per day) to the current level of 250,000 b/d. They were upset to hear Aghanbegian declare publicly in November 1987 that he had made a proposal to Gorbachev recommending that Nagorno Karabakh be returned to Armenia. Since Aliyev had fallen out with Gorbachev two months earlier, disputing the way he was handling the nationalities problem, and had lost his place in the Politburo, the Azeri leadership in Baku had all the more reason to dread the influence Aghanbegian had come to wield in Moscow.

On the other side, encouraged by Aghanbegian's rising star, delegations of Armenians from Karabakh journeyed to Moscow three times between mid-November 1987 and mid-February 1988 to lobby the USSR Supreme Soviet's Presidium and the CPSU's Central Committee. They mistook the sympathetic hearing they received from some officials as a promise to review the status of the enclave. In late January, a group of Armenian nationalists in Karabakh attacked Azeri neighbourhoods in Stepanakert and clashed with militiamen. This led to calls from the Azeris in Baku and Sumagit for retribution against Armenians. There were fist-fights between the two communities in Sumagit. The authorities turned a blind eye, partly because the party hierarchy, dominated by hardliners – including Kamran Bakerov, First Secretary since 1983 – wished to lay the blame for the worsening situation at the door of Gorbachev for his policies of glasnost and perestroika. A delegation of senior Azeri officials visiting Karabakh on 12 February ruled out any territorial change. But its statement was ignored by the local Armenian community, especially when it clashed with the estimation of the latest Armenian delegation to Moscow which, on its return to the enclave on 18 February, described its mission as 'successful'. Taking their cue, the local soviets began voting immediately for reunification with Armenia. The climax came two days later. One hundred and ten Armenian members of the 186-strong Soviet of Nagorno Karabakh supported a resolution calling on Azerbaijan and Armenia to reach a 'positive decision' regarding the transfer of Karabakh from Azerbaijan to Armenia.

Moscow tried to black out the latest news while the CPSU's Politburo coupled the immediate rejection of the Armenian demand with an order to the Communist parties of the two republics to 'normalize the situation'. Its opposition to any territorial change owed as much to ideology (the Leninist view of nationalism as a bourgeois phenomenon) as to practical considerations. Any alterations to the boundaries of Azerbaijan and Armenia would open a flood-gate of demands and counter-demands all over the USSR, and overwhelm the party and the government. Secondly, among the seven million people living in the republic there were some 420,000 Armenians in Azerbaijan outside Karabakh, and about 200,000 Azeris in Armenia with a population of nearly 3.5 million.[5] The central leadership feared that any change in the status quo was bound to affect adversely the fate of the Armenian and Azeri minorities.

Despite Moscow's effort to suppress the news of the Karabakh vote, it reached Yerevan, the Armenian capital, almost instantly. And it led to large demonstrations in favour of the Karabakh resolution, with the participants urging the government to support it. The size of the demonstrations increased daily, reaching 100,000 on 23 February 1988, and culminating in 750,000 on 26 February when the capital was paralysed by sympathy strikes. Gorbachev responded by making a television appeal for calm, and privately complaining to an Armenian delegation that by their actions the Armenians were stabbing perestroika in the back. His appeal had come too late for the inhabitants of the enclave: by then communal violence had claimed two Azeri lives.

The news of the Azeri deaths in Karabakh spread fast, with Baku Radio broadcasting the killings. This triggered a massacre of

Armenians in Sumagit, an ethnically mixed dormitory suburb with a majority of industrial workers, many of them male and single, in the habit of getting drunk over the weekend. On the evening of Saturday, 27 February, young Azeris went on a rampage, setting alight Armenian residences and businesses. When the Armenians formed defence groups, local Azeri youths called on reinforcements from their allies in Baku. By the time violence died down two days later, official figures claimed twenty-six Armenians and six Azeris dead – as against the Armenian claims of 300 – and hundreds more were injured. Troops patrolled the streets to maintain order; but they could not stem the outflow of frightened Armenians from Azerbaijan to Armenia, and the counter-flow of Azeris from Armenia.

The Sumagit incident led to a chain of events which over the next few years were to alter radically the political landscape of the Caucasus, raising nationalist passions in Azerbaijan and Armenia to the point where it was hard to believe that the two republics were part of the same Union, and leading *inter alia* to a rapid rise of the anti-Communist, nationalist Popular Front (PF) in Azerbaijan at the expense of the Communist Party.

Given the degree of violence in Sumagit, and the march of 300,000 demonstrators in Yerevan on 8 March in protest against the Sumagit massacre, Moscow had to act decisively. It did. On 9 March, Gorbachev called the top officials of the two republics to the Kremlin and told them that a special commission would be appointed to examine the Karabakh problem. This seemed to be a conciliatory gesture holding an implicit promise of change. But two weeks later the Presidium of the USSR Supreme Soviet condemned 'self-styled formations' pressuring the authorities to alter frontiers, and reiterated its constitutional obligation to safeguard the sovereignty and territorial integrity of the Union republics, thus rejecting at the outset Karabakh's transfer to Armenia. On 24 March, the CPSU's Politburo unveiled a plan to raise living standards in Karabakh. The same day Soviet troops were deployed in Yerevan to prevent any demonstrations. It was thus that Moscow won a brief respite.

Two months later the CPSU's Politburo dismissed the First Secretaries of the Communist parties of Azerbaijan and Armenia, and replaced them respectively with Abdul Rahman Vazirov and Suren Harutiunian. They in turn purged the party and administration of nationalist elements, resulting in the expulsion of 600 party members and the dismissal of 200 senior government officials in Azerbaijan.[6]

Similar purges were carried out in Armenia, but failed to douse the nationalist fervour. On 28 May, the seventieth anniversary of the founding of the Dashnak Republic of Armenia, its red-blue-orange flag (instead of the Armenia SSR's red-blue-red flag) was displayed. Two weeks later the Armenian Supreme Soviet unanimously demanded the restoration of Nagorno Karabakh. Azerbaijan responded by cutting off its railway link with Armenia. Ignoring Gorbachev's statement to a party meeting on 28 June in Moscow that there was no prospect of republican borders being altered anywhere in the USSR, a fortnight later the Nagorno Karabakh Soviet adopted a specific resolution to secede from Azerbaijan. This was rejected by the Presidium of the USSR Supreme Soviet. In return, the Armenians paralysed the enclave with periodic strikes; and their supporters in Armenia began forming branches of the Karabakh Committee which, over the ensuing months, emerged as an alternative to the Communist Party of Armenia.

The escalating conflict with Armenians, in whose demonstrations priests played a leading role, revived Islamic feeling among Azeris. Also significant was the fact that the Soviet regime had allowed the Russian Orthodox Church in 1988 to celebrate a millennium of Russian Christianity on a grand scale, thus lessening inhibitions about Islam and Islamic rituals among Soviet citizens with a Muslim background. Since most Soviet Azeris were Shia, they were keen to undertake the ceremonials of the first ten days of Muharram, the first month of the (lunar) Islamic year, beginning on 20 August 1988, culminating in public mourning for the murder of their revered Imam Hussein ibn Ali on the tenth, Ashura (in Arabic).[7] For the first time since the fall of the Democratic Republic of Azerbaijan in 1920, tens of thousands of Shias staged Ashura processions in the streets of major Azerbaijani cities. The mourners carried the green flags of Islam and the portraits of such eminent Shia religious figures as Ayatollah Ruhollah Khomeini (1903–89), the supreme leader of Iran, Ayatollah Muhammad Kazem Shariatmadari, an ethnic Azeri of Iran, and Ayatollah Abol Qassim Khoei, based in the holy Shia city of Najaf, Iraq. This led to clashes between the marchers and security forces, and injuries to several hundreds of people. The incident created ill-will against the central authorities among Azeris. Even the cautious Shaikh-al-Islam Allah Shukur Pashazadeh, the Shia chairman of the Muslim Spiritual Directorate of Trans-Caucasia, was moved to attack the 'enemies of Islam' and urge mobilization and vigilance among the believers.

Later, Hassan Saidov, the chairman of the Azeri Council of

Ministers, who had refused to ban the Ashura processions, and who had also failed to curb a spurt of violence in Karabakh in September, was to be made a scapegoat, and was replaced by Ayaz Mutalibov, who promised to prohibit such religious rituals. But that did not stop some of those participating in the demonstrations against the Armenian position on the Nagorno Karabakh controversy from displaying the green flag of Islam and portraits of Khomeini and Khoei, a development that drew the attention of foreign observers in Baku.[8]

With the Kremlin becoming unpopular in both Armenia and Azerbaijan, Gorbachev – elected chairman of the Presidium of the USSR Supreme Soviet in October – resorted increasingly to blaming 'the enemies of perestroika' for the violence in the two republics on the ground that the 'vested interests' there were threatened by political and economic reform, and were therefore stoking up feelings about the ethnic issue of Karabakh in order to maintain their popular support.[9]

Inter-ethnic strife showed no sign of abating, claiming 100 to 400 mainly Armenian lives in 1988. At different times leading Azeri and Armenian cities were placed under martial law, accompanied by large-scale arrests and confiscation of illegal arms and printing presses. On 7 December a severe earthquake in Armenia destroyed Leninkan and Spital, killing 50,000 people and displacing over 200,000. But so strained were Armenian–Azerbaijani relations that Azerbaijan refused to lift its railway blockade of Armenia, thus holding up badly needed fuel and building materials.

Following a report by its commission on Karabakh, the Presidium of the USSR Supreme Soviet conferred a special administrative status on the enclave on 12 January 1989: direct administration by Moscow through a special commission headed by Arkadi Volsky. The local Armenian-dominated soviet expressed its disapproval by staging periodic protest strikes. The new arrangement was also to prove unpopular with the Azeri public, which saw no reason why its republic should be deprived of its right to govern a territory within its boundaries.

Throughout 1989 the exodus of Armenians from Azerbaijan and Azeris from Armenia continued unabated. The (officially) unrecognized Karabakh Committee in Armenia, whose eleven leaders had been arrested following Gorbachev's visit to the republic in the wake of the earthquake, was absorbed into the Armenian United National Party, which enjoyed official recognition.

Paralleling the AUNP in Armenia was the Popular Front in Azerbaijan, an organization formed in mid-1988 by a few score Azeri intellectuals who were inspired by similar bodies in the Baltic republics. Nationalist and anti-Communist in its general orientation, the PF's social, political, economic and cultural demands were similar to the ones made by the Popular Fronts in the Baltic Republics of Estonia, Latvia and Lithuania. Additionally, it called for the release of political prisoners; the declaration of Azeri as the only official language – thus implying elimination of Russian, then the sole language of the Soviet military, foreign services (including international trade) and the KGB; and the retrieval of Nagorno Karabakh from central control. One of its leaders, Abulfaz Elchibey, had been a long-term opponent of the regime, having been imprisoned in 1974 for 'anti-state activities', and later consigned to a job as an Arabic calligrapher. Since the PF was not officially recognized, it could not contest the multi-candidate elections to the 2250-strong Congress of People's Deputies of the USSR – the super-parliament from which a smaller Supreme Soviet was to be drawn – that were held in March 1989. But lack of recognition did not inhibit the PF from organizing demonstrations and strikes for the return of Karabakh to Azerbaijan. These reached a peak with a 500,000-strong rally in Baku on 19 August 1989. Yet the government still refused to recognize the PF.

It was not until 11 September, when a week-long PF-led strike had paralysed the capital, that the administration reversed its stance. It registered the PF, and convened a special session of the republic's Supreme Soviet to take stock of the current situation in Azerbaijan and its enclave of Karabakh. The Supreme Soviet endorsed the PF's demand that it should regain control of Karabakh. More importantly, reflecting the nationalist fervour the PF had engendered, the Supreme Soviet published a new constitution for Azerbaijan in October. It specified greater sovereignty for the republic within the USSR, and reiterated its right to secede from the Union if this were decided by a referendum. Oddly, by stealing the political clothes of its rival, the PF, the Communist Party ended up highlighting the growing importance of the PF.

Realizing that its policy of depriving Azerbaijan of jurisdiction over Nagorno Karabakh was increasing the popularity of the PF, the Kremlin dissolved the special Karabakh commission on 28 November 1989, thus virtually returning the enclave to Azerbaijan – but without reducing the size of the Soviet military contingent in the territory, believed to be 6000. By so doing, Moscow angered the Armenian government, which retaliated by forcibly expelling its remaining Azeri citizens, much reduced from the pre-crisis total of 200,000 – an action which further aggravated the situation.

The arrival of tens of thousands of homeless Azeri refugees from Armenia fuelled anti-Armenian feeling in Azerbaijan, especially in Baku, which housed most of the republic's Armenians who had numbered over 400,000 before 1988. Moreover, with Armenia now totally free of Azeris within its boundaries, the Azeris lost the restraint they had felt in expressing their hostility towards the Armenians in their midst so long as tens of thousands of their kinsmen were settled in Armenia.

On 13–14 January 1990 mobs of mainly homeless Azeri refugees carried out a pogrom of the Armenians in Baku, killing fifty and injuring hundreds, ignoring not only calls by the government to stop the violence but also appeals by the Popular Front. The event had repercussions beyond the capital. It undermined the credibility of the Communist authorities, with the Popular Front local committees taking over several provincial towns. PF committees also helped to restore order in Baku, a task facilitated by the fact that virtually all Armenians had fled the city.

Thus strengthened, PF leaders challenged the Communist regime. On 18 January, addressing a large rally of their supporters, they urged the government to resign immediately, thus bringing seventy years of Communist rule to an end, and called on their supporters to stage a general strike to hasten the downfall of the regime.

The Kremlin concluded that it was beyond the powers of the republic's administration to meet this challenge. Therefore it decided to step in directly, and act. Warning that 'all necessary steps would be taken to stop today's tragedy turning into tomorrow's national catastrophe', it declared a state of emergency on 20 January and despatched 20,000 armoured troops to Baku. They crushed the opposition, killing 131 people and wounding 744.[10] The purpose of the military intervention was expressed by the Soviet defence minister, Dmitri Yazov, thus: 'Our task is . . . to destroy the structure of power that has formed at all enterprises and offices'.[11] By 'the structure of power' he apparently meant the Popular Front. Denouncing 'extremists, vandals and criminals in Baku', Gorbachev justified using arms against 'the instigators of disorder'.

Once order was restored, Abdul Rahman Vazirov, the CPA's First Secretary, was dismissed for incompetence and inaction, and replaced by Ayaz Mutalibov, then chairman of the Council of Ministers. But the party he headed had been considerably reduced in size. Following the Soviet military action in Baku, thousands of party members returned their party cards or destroyed them, thus causing a large drop in the party membership of 326,000.[12]

The trauma that seized Azerbaijan in the aftermath of the Soviet military action encouraged Armenia to harden its stance. On 20 February it abrogated its decision to accept the 5 July 1921 resolution of the Caucasian Bureau of the Communist Party, and formally backed Nagorno Karabakh's demand for reunification with Armenia.

In Azerbaijan, Mutalibov tried to follow in the footsteps of Gorbachev, his political godfather. In March, after Gorbachev succeeded in getting the 1977 USSR constitution modified to create the job of an executive president, he had the Supreme Soviet elect him to that post: it carried wide powers, including mobilizing the armed forces and declaring a state of emergency. Mutalibov followed suit, and became the executive president of Azerbaijan.

However, the rise of Gorbachev's rival, Boris Yeltsin, also began to affect the fortunes of Mutalibov. On 1 June 1990, Yeltsin was elected chairman of the newly formed 1041-member Supreme Soviet of the Russian Soviet Federated Socialist Republic by a margin of four votes. Under his guidance the RSFSR parliament declared its sovereignty on 12 June 1990. That is, from then on, Russian laws held primacy over Soviet laws – a step which in retrospect was to prove to be the beginning of the end of the USSR. The Russian lead was soon followed by Georgia, Moldova and Ukraine. At the Twenty-eighth Congress of the CPSU in early July, Yeltsin announced his resignation from the party, and called for the repeal of Article 6 of the 1977 USSR constitution, which described the Communist Party as the leading organ of the state and society, thus making it the *de jure* power. This demand gained a great deal of popular support in the form of demonstrations. During the summer, Russia under Yeltsin began signing bilateral agreements with the Baltic republics as between independent countries. Since Estonia, Latvia and Lithuania had been incorporated into the USSR in 1940, at a time when their populations had a strong sense of national identity, these republics had now emerged as bastions of ethnic nationalism.

Encouraged by these trends within the USSR, and responding positively to Popular Front pressures, the Azeri government under Mutalibov initiated negotiations with Iran on oil and gas exploration in the Caspian and the establishment of joint ventures. It also began signing agreements with Tehran for the training of Azeri Shias at various Iranian theological colleges.

In the general election to the 360-member Supreme Soviet held in September 1990, the Communist Party of Azerbaijan won 329 seats, the remainder going to those sympathetic to the PF, which boycotted the poll, partly because it was held under a state of emergency.

Finding that the rise of nationalism in the Baltic republics was posing a threat to the unity of the USSR, President Gorbachev decided to act. In January 1991 he despatched to the Baltic republics contingents of the recently formed Special Purpose Militia Units, Omon (*Otryady militsiy osobovo naznachenia*), to curb nationalist extremism there and to bring them into line with the centre. As a result fourteen Lithuanians were killed by the troops in Vilnius on 13 January. Among those who condemned this action was the Azerbaijani Popular Front. It perceived the state violence in Vilnius as a re-run of the Soviet forces' actions in Baku a year before. It therefore felt pessimistic about the future of Azerbaijan within the USSR.

Gorbachev's intent was to curb extreme nationalism with a view to forging a looser union between the fifteen republics of the USSR. On 17 March a referendum was held on the subject throughout the Union. The question was: 'Do you consider it necessary to preserve the USSR as a renewed federation of equal sovereign republics, in which human rights and freedom for all nationalities will be fully guaranteed?' The poll was boycotted by the Baltic states as well as Georgia, Armenia and Moldova. Of those citizens who participated, two out of three answered 'Yes', thus providing a basis for a new Union Treaty: a result that pleased Gorbachev.

The reason for the boycott by several republics was more economic than political. It had to do with the sharing of public property between the Union and republican governments. According to the 1977 constitution, the major part of the USSR's wealth – land, natural resources, military and machine-tool industries, power plants, transport and communications systems, banks, etc. – belonged to all Soviet citizens and was managed by the central administration in Moscow. This left housing, educational institutions, other social infrastructure, cooperatives and local transport and trade networks in the hands of the republican governments. The 500-day radical plan proposed by economists Stanislav Shatalin and Grigory Yavlinksy in the autumn of 1990, and endorsed by Gorbachev and Yeltsin, envisaged the first stage of privatization thus: the central government would relinquish its ownership of major industries, and allow them to be transformed into 'trans-republican share companies', with each republic receiving shares commensurate with its population. This egalitarian plan was opposed by those republics with small populations but a proportionately large number of industrial enterprises, such as Armenia (population 3.5 million), Estonia (1.7 million), Georgia (5.6 million), Latvia (2.8 million), Lithuania (3.8 million) and Moldova (4.5 million). They wanted the centrally owned enterprises in each republic to be transferred outright to the republican government. The plan was backed by the most populous Russian Federation, accounting for a little over half of the 286 million Soviet citizens, and the comparatively poor Central Asian republics.

Following the referendum on a new Union Treaty, Gorbachev tried to conciliate the opposing views. He settled for a compromise that vested the land and natural resources of a republic in the hands of its regime, with all industrial and power plants, transport and communications systems to be retained by the central government – the latter to be privatized according to a modified version of the Shatalin–Yavlinsky proposal. In early July, Gorbachev took this plan to London, where the chief executives of the seven most industrialized nations, known as the Group of Seven, had gathered for their annual summit. It did not go down well with the Western leaders. So, in response to his plea for economic assistance for the USSR, all he received was a promise of associate membership of the International Monetary Fund (IMF), which ruled out credits. His futile cap-in-hand exercise before the Western and Japanese leaders damaged his standing at home where his rival, Yeltsin, was beginning to outshine him.

In the election for presidency of the RSFSR on 12 June 1991, a year after the RSFSR's parliament had declared its 'sovereignty', Yeltsin won. The voter turn-out was seventy-five per cent, and fifty-seven per cent voted for him, three times the figure for his nearest rival, Nikolai Ryzhkov, a former premier under Gorbachev.[13] Thus Yeltsin acquired the sort of legitimacy President Gorbachev lacked.

After his return to Moscow from London, Gorbachev resumed his consultations with the republican presidents and others on the terms of the new Union Treaty. His final compromise on sharing public property between the Union and the republican governments met criticism from both conservative centralists, who reproached him for giving away too much, and republican decentralists, who accused him of conceding too little. Despite this, Gorbachev announced on 2 August that the new Union Treaty would be ready for signing by eight republics on 20 August. This was not to be.

On Monday, 19 August, when Gorbachev was on holiday at his official dacha in the Crimea, a State Committee for the State of Emergency, consisting of five of the eight members of the high-powered Security Council of the USSR, assumed power. They were Vice-President Gennady Yanayev, Prime Minister Valentin Pavlov, Defence Minister Dmitri Yazov, Interior Minister Boris Pugo, and KGB Chairman Vladimir Kryuchkov. Tanks rolled into the streets of Moscow. The Russian Supreme Soviet and President Yeltsin opposed the coup, and tried to muster popular support. The coup leaders, who had not foreseen any resistance, were unable to decide how to cope with the unexpected situation. Their indecision, coupled with Gorbachev's outrage at their action, destroyed the chances of the coup holding. By the afternoon of Wednesday, 21 August, as the tanks began to withdraw, it became apparent that the plotters' bid for power had failed. Gorbachev was back in Moscow on Thursday morning.

During the coup, Ayaz Mutalibov was on a state visit to Tehran. There his off-the-cuff remark was taken to mean that he backed the coup leaders. Later he was to dispute this interpretation.

On 23 August, during a session of the Russian Federation's Supreme Soviet, President Yeltsin, in the presence of Gorbachev, signed a decree suspending the Communist Party. Yeltsin's order could apply only to the 'Russian Federation' Communist Party. But since there was no separate Communist Party for the Russian Federation, the decree in effect applied to the Communist Party of the Soviet Union within the boundaries of the Russian Federation, resulting in the immediate sealing of its offices, dismissal of its employees, and freezing of its assets.[14] That left the fate of the republican branches of the CPSU outside the Russian Federation in the hands of the respective republic-level Supreme Soviets.

On 30 August the Azerbaijani Supreme Soviet declared its republic independent, and called a presidential election. It was boycotted by the Popular Front. That left Ayaz Mutalibov as the only candidate. The authorities claimed a turn-out of seventy per cent, with ninety-eight per cent voting for Mutalibov. As the popularly elected head of state, Mutalibov resigned from the Communist Party, and recommended that the party dissolve itself. It dutifully did so on 8 September.

A fortnight later, following mediation by Yeltsin and President Nursultan Nazarbayev of Kazakhstan, Mutalibov and his Armenian counterpart, Levon Tet Petrossian, signed a document calling for a ceasefire in Nagorno Karabakh until 1 January 1992 and withdrawal of all armed forces, except the Soviet troops, from the territory.

But that did not inhibit Mutalibov from creating a national defence force in the republic separate from the Soviet troops to safeguard Karabakh, and co-opting Itibar Mahmedov, a pro-PF chief of the already established voluntary militia, known as the National Defence Army. However, this Azeri force proved inadequate to fight the better-organized and motivated Armenian contingents in the enclave. As the Armenian units began capturing Azeri villages in October/November, the PF called for firmer action. In early December, Mutalibov announced the establishment of a regular Azeri army, consisting chiefly of PF volunteers whom he could scarcely afford to trust politically. But before the new force could emerge as a serious factor in the complex equation – involving the Azerbaijani and Armenian governments, AUNP and Dashnak Party militants in Armenia, the Armenians in Karabakh, the Azeri PF, and the Soviet troops – events of much greater import gripped the attention of Mutalibov and other Azeri politicians.

On 8 December the leaders of Russia, Ukraine and Belarus (then Belorussia) – the three Slav republics that had formed the core of the Union after the Bolshevik revolution around which the USSR was later created – meeting in Minsk, Belarus, announced the formation of the Commonwealth of Independent States (CIS). Five days later, the Central Asian republics decided to join the CIS. This prepared the ground for a summit meeting in Alma Ata on 21 December of the presidents of all the republics that wished to join the new commonwealth, expected to be led as before by Russia. Ignoring the strong anti-Moscow feelings among Azeris because of the brutality of the Soviet troops in Baku nearly two years before, Mutalibov took his republic into the CIS. On 25 December Gorbachev resigned as president of the Soviet Union, and the USSR ceased to exist on 31 December 1991, with its seat as a permanent member of the United Nations Security Council going to the Russian Federation.

AFTER THE SOVIET BREAK-UP

With the collapse of the Soviet Union, both Azerbaijan and Armenia became truly independent sovereign states. Among other things they lost any inhibitions they had had as members of a centralized union, the USSR, in pursuing their interests in Nagorno Karabakh. This led to an increased resort to violence in their dispute over the territory – the cause of over 1000 deaths so far – especially after the previously agreed ceasefire expired on 1 January. The issue was now pushed to the centre stage of Azeri and Armenian politics.

Facing accusations of bias from both sides, the high command of the CIS (former Soviet) armed forces decided to withdraw the 366th Motorized Infantry Regiment from the enclave. As CIS units began leaving, the Azeri military resorted to bombarding the enclave's capital, Stepanakert. But that did not alter the situation on the ground where the better-organized and better-led Armenian fighters, many of them belonging to the ultra-nationalist Dashnak Party of Armenia, kept on seizing Azeri villages. Upset by these setbacks, the Popular Front increased pressure on the Baku government to intensify its war effort. Mutalibov acted to unify the nation by co-opting the PF. In mid-February he dissolved the Supreme Soviet, and replaced it with a fifty-member National Council, split evenly between pro-PF democrats and former Communists. The newly appointed government also included ministers associated with the PF.

Once almost all CIS troops had pulled out of Karabakh by late February, violence escalated sharply as Armenia became directly involved in the fighting, with the well-armed men of the Karabakh Committee, freshly revived in the newly independent Armenia, participating in combat. The Azeris in Karabakh alleged that on 27 February, during their attack on Hojali (Khodzhali), a strategic settlement of 6000 near Stepanakert, Armenian gunmen slaughtered 1000 Azeris fleeing from the village. They produced convincing evidence of Azeri civilians, including women and children, murdered on the frozen hills outside Hojali. Azerbaijan declared three days of mourning on 29 February. The fighting in Karabakh continued, with the Armenians making further gains.

Following an acrimonious debate in the National Council, popularly known as the Supreme Soviet, on 4 and 5 March, against the background of outraged demonstrations about the Hojali massacre outside the parliament and elsewhere, President Mutalibov resigned on 6 March. The chairman of the Supreme Soviet, Yakub Mahmedov, a former Communist, succeeded him as caretaker president.

The president's resignation, the first of its kind in the Muslim-majority former Soviet republics, created diplomatic ripples – affecting not only Turkey and Iran but also the US and the Conference on Security and Cooperation in Europe, to which Azerbaijan and

Armenia had been admitted in February. America, which had withheld its recognition of Azerbaijan owing to its poor human rights record, reversed its policy, realizing that its non-recognition was seen as encouraging Armenia to pursue a hard line on the Karabakh issue. It opened its embassy in Baku on 15 March.

This step was welcomed by Turkey. Its prime minister, Suleiman Demirel, was under pressure from the opposition – consisting not merely of Islamists and pan-Turkists but also left-of-centre politicians – to aid Azerbaijan militarily in view of the Armenian government's involvement in the offensive in Karabakh. He resisted, arguing that Ankara's use or threat of force against Armenia would turn the West against Turkey, and that it was best for his administration to stay neutral. Thanks to his diplomatic efforts, the CSCE as well as NATO issued calls for a ceasefire. But nothing came of them. With more Azeri villages in Karabakh falling into the hands of the Armenians, who started attacking the Azeri town of Agdam (a base for the Azeri artillery guns) outside the enclave, the Turkish broadcasting media focused on the worsening situation in Karabakh. However, by the time the Turkish National Security Council, headed by President Turgut Ozal, met in mid-March to consider the issue, the combatants had agreed to a ceasefire brokered by Iran. Later that month the CSCE appointed a mission to help resolve the dispute.

Azerbaijan found itself at a disadvantage owing to the absence of a properly elected president. The incumbent, Yakub Mahmedov, was a caretaker holding office for a maximum of three months within which a presidential poll had to be conducted. As a leader without charisma or a strong constituency, Mahmedov was susceptible to deposition through conspiracy. And that was what happened. By activating the support he had among the ex-Communist half of the National Council, and working in conjunction with Rafiq Sadiqov, the former deputy chief of the republic's KGB, Mutalibov got himself restored to the presidency on 14 May. He immediately declared his intention to take Azerbaijan into the CIS Collective Defence Treaty (CDT) that had been drafted for signature at the CIS summit scheduled for 15 May in Tashkent. But before he could consolidate his position, the Popular Front mobilized its supporters on a large scale in Baku. They marched up the hill to the Supreme Soviet building. Following heated but virtually bloodless confrontation with the armed police, they had Mutalibov on the run early on 15 May. He took a flight to Moscow from the CIS base near Baku. The timing of Mutalibov's move gave rise to a theory that the Russian government, unhappy at the PF's repeated declarations of intent to withdraw from the CIS, had plotted to put Mutalibov back in power. Those who discounted this theory argued that when the chips were down neither the CIS forces stationed in Azerbaijan nor the Azeri security and military units had backed Mutalibov. It was most probable that the Russian government was involved; but like the anti-Gorbachev hardline plotters in Moscow in August, it had not foreseen a popular resistance to its move, and when that materialized it and its henchman, Mutalibov, beat a hasty retreat. The subsequent refusal of Azerbaijan to join the CIS Collective Defence Treaty, which was concluded in Tashkent on 15 May, coupled with Armenia's decision to join, played a major role in shaping the subsequent history of the Karabakh dispute.

The PF consolidated its political power by installing Isa Gambarov, the chairman of the Supreme Soviet, as the republic's acting president. But there was little the PF could do about the economic power that rested with those (former) Communist managers who ran industry and public services. Since, in the absence of experienced managers, it could not replace them, it had to reach a *modus vivendi* with them.

With Azerbaijan mired in a debilitating political turmoil, the Armenians considered the time opportune to strike out. Breaking the ceasefire, they went beyond the territory of Karabakh: they seized the strategic town of Lachin situated halfway along the eleven-kilometre (seven-mile) corridor connecting the enclave with Armenia. The seizure of the corridor was justified on the ground that without supplies from Armenia the enclave could not survive. To keep the Azeris on the defensive, the Armenian gunners then severely shelled Sadarak, a settlement on the border of Nakhichevan. The latest bout of violence raised the total death toll in the crisis to 2000.

Yerevan claimed that Karabakh had been taken over by a militant Armenian militia over which the regime had no control. Besides being unconvincing, this Armenian explanation wounded Azeri pride. Azeris could not accept the idea that their republic, three times the size of Armenia and twice as populous, rich in oil and gas, had been defeated not by a regular army but by a militia. They sought solace in attributing their setbacks to conspiracies hatched by a variety of forces: pro-Armenian Russian officers in the CIS army and powerful politicians in Moscow; the well-heeled and influential

Armenian diaspora in league with the Dashnak extremists; the fanatic Iranian mullahs in Tehran; and the treacherous Azeri 'mafia',[15] who allegedly sold Azeri arms to the Armenians for huge profits.

Pressure built up on Ankara to side militarily with Azerbaijan. Turkey's premier, Demirel, was reluctant to do so; and he found himself provided with a powerful argument by the CIS supreme commander, Marshal Yevgeny Shaposhnikov. He warned on 20 May, five days after the promulgation of the Collective Defence Treaty signed among others by Armenia, that foreign military intervention in the Karabakh dispute could lead the world into 'the Third World War'.[16] If nothing else, Shaposhnikov's statement underscored the point that by staying out of the CDT, Azerbaijan had put itself at a major disadvantage vis-à-vis Armenia.

With the military option ruled out, Turkey intensified its diplomatic effort to isolate Armenia, and succeeded. At the fifty-two-member CSCE, America moved a motion calling for Armenian withdrawal to international frontiers. It received the backing of all except Armenia, which vetoed it. (Since the CSCE worked on the consensus principle, its resolutions had to be passed unanimously.) During his visit to Moscow on 26 May, Demirel succeeded in getting President Yeltsin to endorse a statement condemning Armenia. This was ironic, to say the least, in view of Moscow's covert military involvement in the latest offensive by Armenia, with which it had signed a bilateral defence agreement as early as February.[17] Russia had been upset by the repeated insistence of the PF leader, Elchibey, tipped to win the forthcoming presidential election, on pulling Azerbaijan out of the CIS. Afraid that Azerbaijan's withdrawal could start a chain reaction and result in the demise of the CIS, Russia decided to keep Azerbaijan weak and on the defensive. With CIS troops stationed in both Azerbaijan and Armenia, Moscow had a powerful card to play. And it played it by discreetly diverting weapons and military expertise to the Armenians through the Russian-dominated CIS forces, thus enabling them to score military victories.

As part of the continuing Turkish effort to forge closer ties with Azerbaijan, on 28 May Demirel opened a bridge over the Aras River to link Turkey with the Azerbaijani enclave of Nakhichevan ruled by Geidar Aliyev as chairman of the local Supreme Soviet, thus establishing a physical link between Turkey and a Turkic republic of the former Soviet Union, the only such bond. This and earlier Turkish diplomatic moves enabled Demirel to resist successfully the opposition demand that the government should at least secure parliamentary consent for the deployment of troops, a preliminary step towards actual use of force. 'Direct intervention would plunge Turkey into such trouble that we would be unable to disentangle ourselves in 20 years, and it would turn the matter into a Muslim–Christian conflict,' explained an official Turkish spokesman.[18]

On 28 May 1992 the Azeri government made a point of celebrating with great fanfare the seventy-fourth anniversary of the founding of the Democratic Republic of Azerbaijan – whose tricolour flag and national anthem it had adopted as its own – thus linking itself firmly with the political entity that existed for two years between the collapse of the Tsarist empire and the rise of the Union of Soviet Republics, and popularizing the DRA president, Muhammad Rasulzadeh, as the father of the Azeri nation. This enabled the nationalist authorities to give the present Republic of Azerbaijan an identity that the Central Asian republics lacked.

Attention then turned to the presidential poll in Azerbaijan. The front-runner, Elchibey of the PF, promised democracy, human rights, respect for law, and fresh parliamentary and local elections. He favoured close ties with Turkey, America and Israel, and sought defence alliances with Turkey and the United States. He accused Iran of meddling in Azerbaijan's internal affairs, and promised to keep state and religion apart. A fervent nationalist, he vowed to pull Azerbaijan out of the 'semi-slavery' of the CIS, arguing that Mutalibov's decision to join had not been endorsed by the Supreme Soviet (as had happened in all those states which had come together).

None the less, Elchibey found himself outflanked on the nationalist front by Nizami Suleimanov, a maverick scientist. He gained support late in the campaign by playing on the Azeris' recent exaggerated sense of self-importance. He proposed to market Azerbaijan's oil and gas so extensively that within two years the republic would become a Kuwait-by-the-Caspian. He promised a military-industrial complex a hundred times more powerful than Armenia's, and a solution to the Karabakh problem within three weeks.[19]

The one candidate who would have probably beaten them both was absent from the contest. He was Geidar Aliyev, the current head of Nakhichevan's Supreme Soviet. Aware of his charisma, Mutalibov had been instrumental in the Supreme Soviet's insertion of a clause in the constitution in November 1991 barring the republic's presidency to anyone over sixty-five, a step clearly aimed at disqualifying sixty-eight-year-old Aliyev from supreme office.

As expected, Elchibey won the presidential election on 7 June, but gained only fifty-nine per cent of the vote, with Suleimanov securing thirty per cent. Elchibey became the second nationalist intellectual to achieve supreme power in Trans-Caucasia, the first being Zviad Gamsakhurdia of Georgia. Among those who supported Elchibey was the Islamic Progress Party (IPP), one of the two Islamist groups established in September 1991. The prime reason for this was the anti-Communist credentials of Elchibey. The IPP operated from the office of Haji Sabir, the Sunni deputy to Shaikh-al-Islam Allah Shukr Pashazade, chairman of the Muslim Spiritual Directorate of Trans-Caucasia, in the compound of the Taza Pir mosque in Baku, one of the two mosques allowed to function since 1943. The IPP wanted compulsory Islamic education in schools 'just as in Turkey', and longer and more frequent religious programmes on the state-run television than the current one-hour weekly programme of Quranic recitation and commentary.[20] As it was, the Azerbaijani state recognized Islam as an important part of the national life, the green band in its tricolour flag signifying Islam.

Once elected, Elchibey lost no time in launching an offensive against the Armenians on 12 June to recover Nagorno Karabakh. The success the Azeri forces enjoyed in retaking seven villages around the strategic town of Mardakert in the north-east and a further eighteen villages in the south helped to restore, partly, damaged Azeri pride. And the timing was right – the eve of the CSCE-sponsored meeting of eleven countries in Rome on 15 June. Elchibey feared that if he did not act in advance of that meeting, the follow-up peace conference in Minsk would recognize the status quo, thus legitimizing Armenian control of the enclave. When, at the Rome meeting, Armenia insisted that the assembled participants condemn the Azeri offensive, it drew a blank. After all, the Armenians had taken Nagorno Karabakh and a corridor through Azerbaijan by force. Armenia's appeal to Russia to intervene under the Collective Defence Treaty also fell on deaf ears, partly because the CDT's four Central Asian members, being Muslim, would not have agreed, and partly because of Azerbaijan's strong links with Turkey, a member of NATO.

Armenia responded by announcing general mobilization in the republic on 16 June; and the Armenian authorities in Karabakh drafted 40,000 men, and declared a state of emergency. 'For the Armenian militias, the "defence forces", the right-wing Armenian nationalists and the Dashnak guerrillas . . . the conflict is one of titanic proportions: Christianity struggling in the face of an Islamic onslaught,' reported Robert Fisk from Yerevan. 'Azeris, Russians, Turks, Uzbeks, Iranians, Libyans – there is no end to the real and imagined enemies who are threatening their [Karabakh] enclave.'[21] But for different reasons the three Muslim countries involved directly or indirectly in the dispute refrained from portraying the conflict in religious terms. Demirel was reluctant to do so on the ground that this would make Turkey's position in NATO shaky and sink any prospect of its being accepted as a full member by the EC. Elchibey knew that religious interpretation of the fighting would lead his country into the arms of the Islamic regime of Iran, which he disliked. Reciprocating Elchibey's sentiment, the Iranian leadership had decided to keep Azerbaijan weak – all the more so since a strong Azerbaijan was likely to become a magnet for its Azeri minority living in areas adjacent to Azerbaijan. It was therefore content to see the simmering conflict between Azerbaijan and Armenia continue.

As it was, renewed fighting cast a shadow over the CSCE-sponsored conference in Rome which adjourned on 7 July. Peace talks finally collapsed a month later. On 9 August Azeri troops captured the tiny Armenian enclave of Artsvashen situated within Azerbaijan – a poor consolation for their loss of the Karabakh enclave to the Armenians. From then on, however, there was a steady improvement in the performance of the Azeri army. Gradually it regained about a quarter of Karabakh by December. But the cost was heavy: the military came to consume more than a third of the national budget. Feeling that the steadily improving situation on the battlefield had strengthened his hand, Elchibey entered into secret talks with the Armenians through the Russians. But he found the terms offered unacceptable, and the negotiations broke down. This upset Moscow, which had been displeased by the decision in early October of the Azeri National Council, acting as parliament, to withdraw from the CIS; and as before, with the tacit backing of the Russians, the Armenians hit back.

In a major counter-offensive, which lasted from 20 January to mid-February 1993, the Armenians retook most of the Karabakh territory they had lost. The Azeri débâcle badly damaged the credibility of the Baku government. Seeking a scapegoat, President Elchibey sacked the military administrator of Karabakh, Colonel Suret Husseinov, aged thirty-four. He protested, saying it was unfair to single him out for the setback. A former textile-factory manager who had taken to wool trading in Yevlakhi, west Azerbaijan, and made a lot of money, he had switched from the Communist Party to the Popular Front in the winter of 1991–2. Impatient at the Mutalibov government's inaction in the face of the Armenian onslaught, he spent his own funds to buy weapons and hire recruits from the disintegrating Soviet units, and built up a fighting force. When his party leader, Elchibey, won the presidential poll in June, he handed over part of his arsenal to the official army, but maintained a brigade of his own. As the commander of the Azeri forces that gained victories in Karabakh during the summer and autumn, he became a protégé of the defence minister, Rahim Gaziyev, who promoted him to colonel. During late 1992, when Baku was full of rumours of an impending military coup against the president, who had by now proved inept, both politically and administratively, Elchibey dismissed his conspiring defence minister. The defeat of Azeri forces in Karabakh gave Elchibey the opportunity he was seeking to remove Husseinov, a charismatic field officer whose authority and popularity had increased much too swiftly for his liking. But when Husseinov, still commanding a large force personally loyal to him, set up a base in Ganja, the republic's second city, Elchibey thought it wise not to confront him.

As before, the in-fighting in the Azeri leadership encouraged the Armenian camp to strike out, coordinating the moves of the forces within Karabakh with those of the units inside Armenia. The next round started on 17 March and reached a climax a fortnight later, when the Armenians from Armenia, using mechanized units and airborne troops, captured the strategic Azeri town of Kelbajar as their counterparts from Karabakh approached the town from the opposite side. They thus established another corridor between Karabakh and Armenia. Together they now controlled a swathe of 4000 square kilometres (1545 square miles) of Azeri land, almost as large as the Karabakh enclave itself, the two jointly taking up all of southwestern Azerbaijan, about one-tenth of the republic. The latest bout of violence pushed the total death toll to over 3000.

While eye-witnesses testified to assaults on Kelbajar from the side of the Armenian republic, Yerevan claimed that it was the soldiers of the 'Republic of Nagorno-Karabakh' who were involved in the fight, that they had been 'reacting' to an Azeri offensive from Kelbajar, and that they opened a second corridor to Armenia 'by coincidence'.[22]

On 6 April the United Nations Security Council passed Resolution 882 on the subject. While condemning Armenia's latest action and demanding that Armenian troops be withdrawn from the Azeri territory, it failed to specify action against the Armenians if they failed to comply with its resolution. This was because three of the five permanent members of the Security Council – Russia, America and France – were reluctant to penalize Armenia. Russia had been supporting Armenia covertly; and there were powerful Armenian lobbies in the US and France.

Little wonder that, ignoring the Security Council resolution, the Armenians began shelling Fizuli, situated twenty-nine kilometres (eighteen miles) from the Iranian border. It was only after Elchibey had despatched his prime minister, Panah Husseinov, to Tehran urgently to seek Iranian assistance, and President Rafsanjani had described the fighting in Fizuli as threatening Iranian security,[23] that the Armenians took heed, and discontinued their offensives on 15 April.

Elchibey insisted that he would not resume negotiations with the Armenians until they had vacated Azeri territory. The Armenian aggression had rallied domestic support for him and dissipated the threat to his office from military officers. Thus strengthened, he imposed a state of emergency, banning marches and rallies. A week later, yielding to Turkish pressure, he softened his stance towards Armenia: he had a meeting with the Armenian president, Levon Ter Petrossian, in Ankara, where both had arrived to attend Ozal's funeral. Elchibey agreed to 'informal talks' under the CSCE – a blunder that cost him and the Turkish government dear. 'Every time Turkey, at the behest of the West, forces Azerbaijan to the negotiating table, the Azeris lose something militarily or politically,' noted Alexis Rowell in the *Observer*. 'Add to that the opening of Turkey's border with Armenia to foreign aid, again under huge pressure from the West, and it is easy to understand why Turkey has no credibility in Turkic-speaking Azerbaijan right now.'[24] When the Azeri–Armenian talks in Moscow in mid-May under a tripartite sponsorship that included Turkey failed, there was not much surprise or disappointment in the region.

At home the prestige of Elchibey fell steeply while that of Husseinov rose as thousands of civilians and government soldiers, expelled from the freshly lost Azeri territory, took refuge in Ganja, where Husseinov and his fighters were based. Misreading the public mood, Elchibey thought the time right to crush the renegade force of Husseinov. On 4 June he ordered his loyal troops to attack Husseinov's men. But the rebels, who got wind of Elchibey's move, beat off the loyalist attack. The battle, which left sixty-eight dead, established Husseinov's fighters as superior. Commanding a force of several thousand experienced troops equipped with tanks, surface-to-surface missiles and helicopters, Husseinov captured Ganja and Yevlakhin. He held Elchibey and his prime minister, Panah Husseinov, responsible for the bloodshed, and demanded their resignations. These were not forthcoming.

The renegade soldiers began marching on Baku, and encountered no resistance. It seemed that within a year popular support for Elchibey and the Popular Front had evaporated. By the weekend of 12–13 June the rebels were within 100 kilometres (sixty-two miles) of Baku. Minor skirmishes between the two sides were reported at Haji Kabul forty kilometres (twenty-five miles) from the capital. The severe crisis brought to the centre stage the most skilled politician Azerbaijan had: Geidar Aliyev. Invited to Baku from his home base of Nakhichevan, he was asked to mediate. He held a meeting with Husseinov, who combined his backing for Aliyev's return to power with the dismissal of the entire Elchibey government. To smooth Aliyev's path to office and partly meet Husseinov's demands, the chairman of the National Council, the acting parliament, Isa Gambarov, resigned on 13 June; and so too did Prime Minister Panah Husseinov.

Aliyev wanted the fifty-member parliament to dismiss Elchibey but, yielding to pressure from Washington and Ankara to respect the democratic process, he temporized. On 15 June, by thirty-four votes to three, the parliament elected him its chairman, his supporters including all twenty-five former Communists plus nine disgruntled PF members. But Husseinov wanted nothing less than Elchibey's resignation: his men continued their march towards the capital. On the night of 17 June, army commanders told Elchibey that they would not resist the rebel soldiers if they entered Baku. In the early hours of 18 June Elchibey flew to his home town of Ordubat in Nakhichevan. That morning Aliyev declared on television that as parliamentary chairman he was taking over the powers of the president who had left Baku. It was clear to most deputies that both Husseinov and Aliyev were popular, and that Elchibey had had his day. But they wanted to operate within the constitution (even though they themselves had not been elected). They backed Husseinov, and called on Elchibey to present himself to the parliament by 24 June. When he failed to do so, the house invoked Article 133 of the constitution by thirty-three votes to three, and handed over presidential powers to Aliyev for three months. On 27 June, Aliyev and

Husseinov signed an agreement whereby rebel troops near Baku would withdraw, be incorporated into the Azerbaijani army, and help fight the Armenians in Karabakh. Three days later parliament ratified Aliyev's proposal to appoint Husseinov prime minister with direct control of defence, interior and security ministries. Forgetting how Elchibey had dug his political grave by promising to liberate Karabakh within six months, Husseinov, a novice in politics, declared: 'If the diplomatic efforts fail [in Karabakh] everything will be done by military means, and the war will end only in the victory of Azerbaijan.'[25]

Husseinov's statement came three days after the Azeris had lost their only urban possession in Karabakh, Mardakert, to the Armenians, who were seriously threatening to capture the Azeri town of Agdam. The Armenian moves ensued despite the fact that the Karabakh parliament had, under severe pressure from President Ter Petrossian, narrowly passed the CSCE peace plan which visualized Armenian withdrawal from Kelbajar and a (renewable) sixty-day ceasefire in exchange for an end to Azeri 'hostile acts', meaning the lifting of the rail blockade which had crippled Armenian industry and left Armenians without heat during the winter. But instead of implementing the plan from 20 June as proposed, Karabakh requested one month's postponement to allow local authorities to reassert control over some defiant military units. The interval would also give time to the new government in Baku to consolidate its position.

In the end, just as in the case of Mutalibov, the military setbacks in Karabakh paved the way for Elchibey's downfall. Additionally, he showed a lack of administrative, political and diplomatic skills. He failed to overcome the limitations of his academic background. He also failed to grasp the geopolitics of his country, trapped as it was between powerful neighbours to the north (Russia) and south (Iran), and a long-time foe to the west (Armenia). He alienated Russia by pulling out of the CIS, thus breaking the commonwealth's geographical continuity.[26] He did not moderate his invective against Iran after winning power. He lacked the natural aura of authority that Aliyev had, and the combat experience that Husseinov quickly acquired.

Finally, the overthrow of Elchibey, who was strongly backed by Turkey and America, was a severe setback for Ankara. Turkey's failure to provide military aid to Azerbaijan to beat off Armenian aggression was deeply disappointing to pro-Turkic nationalists.

They realized with bitterness that Turkey was so tightly integrated into NATO, and its economy so dependent on concessions from the European Community, that it dared not upset Western, Christian Armenia, which had powerful lobbies in Washington and Paris. In another sense the experience of independent Azerbaijan illustrated the limitations of pan-Turkic nationalism just as the brief existence of the Democratic Republic of Azerbaijan in 1918–20 had shown the limitations of a secular democracy in the midst of Bolshevik revolution.

On the other hand one diplomatic setback for Turkey did not mean it had lost out in the Great Game for influence in the vast Turkic region. After all, it had done nothing so far to damage its standing in Central Asia, where the giant-size Kazakhstan, with boundless grasslands, loomed larger than any other republic.

THREE

Kazakhstan: Between Russian Bear and Turkic Grey Wolf

In late 1953 Nikita Khrushchev decided to make the USSR self-sufficient in food grains and meat within three decades by transforming the vast, underused land in the Urals, the Volga region, north Caucasus, southern Siberia and Kazakhstan into fertile agricultural fields, with the last two areas contributing the most.

To implement this Virgin Land plan, the plenum of the Central Committee of the Communist Party of Kazakhstan (CPK), meeting in February 1954, supplanted Jumabai Shaiahmedov (Dzhumabai Shaiakhmetov), the First Secretary, and I.I. Afanov, the Second Secretary, respectively with P.K. Ponomarenko and Leonid I. Brezhnev, a Moscow-based protégé of Khrushchev. Their target was to transform 3.5 million hectares of grazing land into 300 new state farms within a year, as the first step towards bringing under plough a total of sixteen million hectares of pasture land. The success of this programme depended on attracting volunteers from outside Kazakhstan, a proposition unpopular with native Kazakhs, who had seen their proportion in the republic's population decline by nearly half from fifty-seven per cent in 1926 (a census year) while the proportion of European settlers – Russians, Ukrainians and Germans – had risen by about half from thirty-four per cent.[1] The failure of Ponomarenko to overcome Kazakh resistance to the Virgin Land plan led to his replacement by Brezhnev in July 1955.

Brezhnev adroitly used the stick and carrot to dissipate Kazakh opposition to the plan, an achievement that accelerated his rise in the CPSU hierarchy. He was quick to promote those who were energetic and enthusiastic, thus gaining their loyalty and swiftly expanding a network of cadres, both Slav and Kazakh, who were personally faithful to him. He initiated a programme of transforming collective farms into state-run enterprises, thus putting Kazakh farmers, unfamiliar with modern agricultural and livestock breeding practices, under the supervision of highly trained Slav cadres, and improving output as well as economic integration of the new agricultural lands into the USSR economy.

In March 1956 Brezhnev moved to Moscow to take up a better party job, but assiduously maintained his contacts with his loyalists in Kazakhstan. I. D. Iakovlev, who became the next First Secretary, lasted until December 1957 when, following poor crops, he was replaced by N. I. Beliayev. In January 1960 he gave way to a Kazakh protégé of Brezhnev, Dinmuhammad Ahmedovich Kunayev (1912 –93), who became the fifth leader to hold the job in six years. A graduate of the Moscow Institute of Non-Ferrous Metals and Gold, Kunayev started his working life as a machinist at a copper-smelting plant and moved up to become the director of administration in a mine. He joined the Communist Party in 1939 and within three years became the vice-chairman of the Council of Ministers, with the special task of overseeing the republic's industry during the Great Patriotic War against the Germans. After ten years in that post he became president of the Academy of Sciences of Kazakhstan, and in 1955 the chairman of the Council of Ministers. Now, as the republican party's First Secretary, he concentrated on improving the productivity of land under cereals which had shot up from seven million hectares in 1953 to twenty-three million hectares.[2]

To cope successfully with such a dramatic rise in agricultural land was a task that proved beyond Kunayev's considerable leadership skills. And like his predecessors he found himself replaced swiftly. He returned to his old post of chairman of the Council of Ministers in December 1962, with the job of First Secretary going to I. Yusupov (Yusuf). However, Kunayev's comparative eclipse proved short-lived.

The rise of Brezhnev as supreme leader, following the downfall of Khrushchev in October 1964, prepared the ground for the re-emergence of Kunayev as the party chief in Kazakhstan. The CPK's Central Committee elected him to this post in December. He now ruled over a republic of about eleven million, which had during the past decade absorbed a predominantly Slav workforce of about a million. This time around he stressed scientific management of agriculture, and steered the state farm sector, consisting of 1500 units, away from acquiring gigantic fields. His strategy proved successful in raising productivity – with 2059 state farms providing two-thirds of the republic's agricultural output by 1970.[3] The commanding role played by the agrarian sector, run directly by the state, made the republic's economy more diverse than it had been a generation ago.

Little wonder that Kunayev, who had been elected a candidate member of the CPSU's Politburo in 1966, was elevated to full membership in 1971 – an unparalleled honour for a Central Asian leader.

The arrival of hundreds of thousands of young, politically conscious Russian and Ukrainian volunteers to participate in the Grow More Food campaign during the decade of 1954–63 led to a substantial increase in the membership of the CPK,[4] and strengthened the Slav hold over the party, a development which troubled most Kazakhs. Aware of this, Kunayev tried to redress the balance by reactivating traditional Kazakh-dominated networks, thus encouraging Kazakhs to join the party and play an active role. Having a Kazakh as the party chief made the native population feel that the hijacking of their republic by Slavs had virtually ended. While steadfast in his loyalty to Brezhnev, Kunayev set out to consolidate his power base by generously rewarding those he believed to be serving the party and state well, making no distinction between Kazakh and Slav. By so doing, Kunayev (married to a Russian) healed the breach that had developed between these leading ethnic groups before he became First Secretary – in the process creating an ethnically mixed team of senior cadres committed to developing Kazakhstan along socialist lines.

Little wonder that by the late 1970s the republic managed to meet its targets for food grain production, as measured by four-year running averages, with its contribution to the central food pool varying between five million tons (in 1975) and twenty million tons (in 1976).[5] With three-quarters of the workforce engaged in agriculture, this achievement was a matter of national pride. Much progress was made in industrialization as well. By the early 1980s Kazakhstan, with six per cent of the USSR population, produced ten per cent of Soviet coal and five per cent of Soviet oil, with its economy more fully integrated into the central system than before. It had also acquired a massive space complex at Baikonur; and alone among the Central Asian republics it provided testing sites for nuclear arms in its Semipalatinsk region, and had nuclear weapons stationed on its soil.[6]

Mirroring the modernization of agriculture and industry, the social mores of Kazakhs underwent a sea-change. Gone were the feudal ways dominated by *bais*, village notables, and *aksakals*, clan or tribal elders. Instead, socio-economic prestige came to rest chiefly with the party leaders, or sometimes with the directors of collective farms if they had a *bai* or *aksakal* background.

The influence of mullahs and Islam – brought to the nomadic Kazakhs by peripatetic Tatar clerics from outside the region, and having tenuous hold over Kazakhs – had also ostensibly withered. The anti-religious drives conducted during the 1930s and again during the Khrushchev era had led to large-scale closures of the places of worship and religious schools, reducing the number of mosques in the capital, Alma Ata, from sixty-three during the pre-revolution days to one. The total number in the republic now was a mere thirty, based mainly in the south, where Kazakhs outnumbered Slavs, and where the mausoleum of the much-revered Hoja Ahmed Sultan was situated.

Before the Bolshevik revolution, Kazakh intellectuals were engaged in a debate about the relationship between Islam and Kazakh culture, and between the Sharia, Islamic law, and the *Adat*, customary law, which had evolved over the centuries among the predominantly nomadic Kazakhs. Many intellectuals argued that Islamic practices should follow the cultural needs of Kazakhs, rather than precede them. They thus manifested superficiality in their conversion to Islam, which was typical of the community at large which, after formal conversion to Islam, had maintained strong pagan beliefs and practices and, being nomadic, had failed to get into the habit of praying regularly at mosques, which were few and far between in pasturelands. The peripatetic majority among Kazakhs had embraced Islam in the early nineteenth century under the dual pressure of wandering Tatar clerics, often of the Sufi ilk, and colonizing Russians, who perceived Islam (already prevalent among settled Kazakhs) as a cementing force for the disparate nomadic tribes, thus making them easy to control. Those Kazakh intellectuals who maintained that Islamic practices should reflect Kazakh culture also preferred the use of the *Adat* to the Sharia in Kazakh courts. They included Ali Khan Bukeikhanov, the head of Alash Orda,[7] the leading Kazakh nationalist party. 'Kazakhs are non-Muslims or at very most half-Muslims,' he said. 'The preservation of customs and traditions is useful to Kazakhs. The Sharia is harmful to Kazakhs.'[8]

It was accepted by both Kazakh and non-Kazakh intellectuals that language was an essential part of Kazakh identity. This was as true of the pre-Bolshevik era as of the revolutionary period. But as Russian influence increased in all facets of Kazakh life, especially after the compulsory collectivization and rapid settlement of nomads during the 1930s, there was a reaction to Russification by Kazakhs, who became universally literate by the late 1960s. In order to preserve and strengthen a separate cultural identity, a minority among Kazakh intellectuals began stressing the significance of Islam in Kazakh history and culture, aware that Islam was alien to Russians. This view was articulated by N. Ashirov, a Kazakh academic, in his book *Islam i Natsiya* (Islam and Nation), published in 1975. Stating that 'some intellectuals and party elite of Central Asia have tacitly accepted Islam as an important component of their national history and cultural heritage', he argued that 'Islam is therefore worth preserving or at least [worth] special treatment by the regime.'[9]

That Islamic customs remained a significant factor in Kazakh culture was confirmed by the findings of a survey by T. Saidbayev, a Kazakh researcher, which were published in 1978. The survey showed that fifty per cent of the respondents observed Muslim rituals whereas only ten per cent had any grasp of the Islamic doctrine. It also revealed that most Kazakhs feasted on major Muslim religious days, gave at least 'ceremonial importance' to religion to commemorate birth, marriage and death, and that circumcision of male children was virtually universal.[10] The persistence of Islamic traditions pertaining to personal existence, especially among the old, who enjoyed the respect of their juniors, was a known phenomenon. What the 1978 survey disclosed was that a growing number of young Kazakhs were turning to Islam because they felt a need to fill the moral-ethical vacuum left by the erosion of morality among the party cadres, characteristic of the latter years of Brezhnev's rule. Increasingly, the party hierarchy, arrogating greater powers to itself than ever before, was losing touch with the people. Many farm and factory workers were losing motivation; and attitudes towards public property were deteriorating, with widespread pilfering, bribery and nepotism giving impetus to a parallel economy. The fact that during his final years Brezhnev was too ill to know what was really happening, and was therefore open to manipulation by his close aides, was another negative factor. Saidbayev's findings captured symptoms of rising public unease at the way the country was run. But the party leadership failed to examine the cause of the deepening malaise with a view to remedying it, concentrating instead on decrying the effect.

The subject of religion came up at the Sixteenth Congress of the CPK in early 1981. In his address, the First Secretary, Kunayev, noted that far from declining in its influence, Islam was gaining acceptance even among party members, some of whom were encouraging others to observe Islamic customs and rituals. He urged a reversal of this trend. The party militants and the Communist Youth League (CYL) took up his call, and resorted to highlighting the failure of the party cadres in this sphere. But there was an extraneous element working against them: foreign broadcasts. From the late 1970s onwards, Islamic campaigns on radio beamed at the southern republics of the USSR were launched independently by Iran, the anti-Communist resistance in Afghanistan, the Persian Gulf monarchies, especially Saudi Arabia, and the Washington-funded Radio Liberty and Radio Free Europe. Despite the jamming ordered by the central authorities in Moscow, some of these transmissions were received and recorded. Many of the broadcasters tried to combine religion with nationalism, a potent mixture. This encouraged unofficial mullahs in Kazakhstan to try to get through to non-believers by encouraging them to understand Kazakh cultural practices in the light of Islamic teachings.

By the mid-1980s, on the eve of perestroika, Kazakh mullahs and secular intellectuals, both demanding greater cultural autonomy, seemed to have found a common denominator: a recognition that Islam was an important part of Kazakh identity. Beyond that the two groups diverged. Clerics saw no role for Marxism-Leninism in society. In contrast, secular intellectuals wished to adapt this doctrine, seen as dynamic, to Kazakh cultural values which, they concurred, were formed partly by the moral-ethical values of Islam. The situation had parallels with what prevailed, politically, in the early 1920s when a special body of Muslim Communists was established in Soviet Russia. The difference this time around was that the new intelligentsia was well versed in Russian, the common language of most Soviet citizens, and was therefore able to address a large body of Muslims and others. Now, as then, the party elite at the centre was unprepared to abandon its claim to be the sole authority to regulate doctrinal purity, be it in economic management, nationality relations or culture.

These developments occurred against the background of the diminishing power of Kunayev. The first sign came during the rule of Andropov. He wanted to diverge from the Brezhnevite line whereas Kunayev was for continuing the old policies. The brief tenure of Kunayev's close friend, Chernenko, as the First Secretary of the CPSU failed to reverse the trend. With Gorbachev in power, the downward slide of Kunayev, aged seventy-three, accelerated.

Kunayev managed to get re-elected as the First Secretary of the

CPK in February 1986, but failed to prevent the removal of his half-brother, Askar, from his jobs as the chairman of the Kazakh Academy of Sciences and the Gosplan (State Plan). Later that month, at the Twenty-seventh Congress of the CPSU, he retained his seat on the Politburo. But he was so much at odds with the policies being implemented by Gorbachev that a dénouement was inevitable, especially when loosening party discipline emboldened Nursultan Nazarbayev (born 1940), the chairman of the Kazakh Council of Ministers, to air criticism of Kunayev and his record. It came on 17 December 1986.

That day it was announced in the state-run media that the fifth plenum of the CPK's Central Committee had chosen Gennadi Kolbin, a native of Ulyanovsk, Russia, to replace Kunayev, who had resigned as First Secretary because of 'poor health and old age'. A former Second Secretary of the Georgian Communist Party, Kolbin was then serving as the First Secretary of the Communist Party of Ulyanovsk. His elevation to the highest party job in the second-largest republic in the USSR at a time when Kazakhs had reached demographic parity with Russians sent shock waves throughout the republic. The appointment of Zakash Kamalidenov (Kamaluddin), a Kazakh, as Second Secretary failed to pacify the popular mood since it reversed the order of giving primacy to Kazakhs that had prevailed for the past twenty-two years. In sum, replacing Kunayev with Kolbin sharpened the contradiction that had existed between the centre (Moscow) and the periphery (Alma Ata), strengthening Kazakh nationalism even within the Kazakh ranks of the CPK.

The next day there was a demonstration by some 10,000 people, mainly students, including Communist Youth League members of both leading ethnic groups, Kazakh and Russian, in Alma Ata. They carried placards saying, 'We are for Kazakhstan', and 'Where is Kunayev?', with some of them shouting 'Kazakhstan for Kazakhs!'. They were ordered to go home by the armed guards. They refused. The Communist Party leadership organized a counter-demonstration by workers, who came armed with metal bars and cables. They attacked the student demonstrators. In the subsequent mêlée, which involved the police opening fire, between two and twenty people lost their lives, and between 763 and 1137 received injuries. Between 2212 and 2336 demonstrators were arrested.[11] Attempts were made in twelve of the republic's twenty provinces to mount pro-Kunayev demonstrations, and thousands of protesting pamphlets were distributed. The situation was so serious that the violent outbreak was reported in the Soviet media. The Kremlin rushed a team of CPSU bureaucrats under M. S. Solomentsev to calm the situation.

On arrival in Alma Ata, now being patrolled by soldiers wearing bullet-proof vests, Solomentsev deplored the fact that 'extremism' had become popular. The authorities put it about that Kunayev had been behind these disturbances. The facts were to the contrary. Kunayev wanted to pacify the rioters but Kolbin, the new party chief, did not allow him to.[12] It was not until mid-1988, when Kunayev had been out of the CPSU Politburo for a year, and when glasnost had progressed further in the USSR, that the Moscow-based *Izvestia* (News), the organ of the Soviet government, conceded that the removal of Kunayev was seen 'by certain young people' as 'a blow against national esteem and pride, as a personal tragedy, as the eclipse of their hopes'.[13] It also emerged later that the demonstration was not a purely Kazakh affair: there were many Russian participants.

The event was a watershed in the history of Kazakhstan, giving birth to a party called Jeltoksan (literally December), the Decembrists. It was later to be portrayed as the first spontaneous 'democratic uprising', involving both Kazakhs and Russians. Indeed, one of the three leaders – Andrei Statetin, M. Akuyev and D. Kunayev – arrested and convicted for the rioting was a Russian. He received the most severe punishment, eight years' hard labour for 'stealing public property', and was expelled from the party. Despite this, the violent disturbances came through as basically anti-Russian, or at least a rebellion by young Soviet-educated Kazakhs against the Russian 'elder brother'. The presence of many people from the countryside led Yegor Beliayev, a Soviet expert on Islam and the Muslim world, to see the hand of Sufi brotherhoods.[14]

Kolbin, the new party leader, reacted sharply, singling out the CYL for a severe purge, saying repeatedly that his move was not aimed solely at the Kazakh members – a statement received with scepticism by the native population. He also stepped up action against those who were found participating in religious ceremonies or rituals. Said Aqa Ziayev, the head of the party in Jambul Province, was sacked for a 'public show of respect for religious rites'. Later another party official was accused of diverting public finances for the construction of an unauthorized mosque.[15] Both these cases were highly publicized, thus further inflaming Kazakh susceptibilities.

For about a year Kolbin pursued a hard line. Then he changed direction under orders from the Kremlin, which realized both the highly explosive nature of the nationalities problem throughout the USSR and the inadequacy of means to tackle it. The year 1988 therefore started with a multi-candidate election for the leadership of CYL organizations in Alma Ata, followed by a government decision to widen the use of Kazakh in the social-cultural life of Kazakhstan. Action against Islam was limited to rooting out underground Islamic organizations, with one such group headed by Kalim Kurbanov in Jambul being discovered and disbanded in March 1988.

With Moscow lifting central trade monopolies in May 1988, Kazakhstan and other republics set up their own trade organizations, with Kazakhstan and Kyrgyzstan establishing trading links with China. While this and other economic liberalization measures gave greater powers to the republics and large, individual enterprises, these changes in the highly centralized economic system caused a drop in output, inducing recession and enlarging the pool of the unemployed. In the spring of 1989 word went around in the cities of western Kazakhstan that the refugees from Armenia, which had suffered a devastating earthquake in December, were being offered scarce housing. This triggered riots which were quickly suppressed. The event, which was symptomatic of rising frustration, especially among the young unemployed, provided Gorbachev with a rationale to return the top republican party job to a Kazakh.

This happened in June 1989 when Prime Minister Nursultan Nazarbayev was elected First Secretary of the CPK's Central Committee; a step which cooled Kazakh passions, but did not guarantee peace.[16] Born into a peasant family in Chemolgan, a village in Alma Ata Province, Nursultan Abishevich Nazarbayev studied metallurgy at a technical college in Karaganda. He started his working life as a steel worker, simultaneously taking a correspondence course in economics. A party member at twenty-two, he became a party official seven years later. He caught the attention of Kunayev, and under his patronage rose steadily from being secretary of the CPK's Central Committee to chairman of the Council of Ministers in 1984. Finding a rapport with Gorbachev, who assumed supreme power in Moscow the following year, Nazarbayev began drifting away from his mentor, Kunayev. His relations with Kunayev worsened after the latter lost his job as First Secretary of the CPK, and remained tense until after Nazarbayev's elevation to the highest party post in mid-1989. Subsequently they patched up their differences, with Nazarbayev recognizing Kunayev as an elder statesman.

Unable to do much on the economic front, Nazarbayev found

ways of asserting Kazakh autonomy in order to palliate rising grass-roots pressure. He protested to Moscow at the continued use of Kazakh territory for nuclear testing and for having created environmental pollution. At the same time he allowed social and political liberalization to proceed.

Sensing the rising mood in favour of devolution, Haji Radbek Nisanbayev, the chairman of the republican branch of the Muslim Spiritual Directorate of Central Asia and Kazakhstan, mounted a coup against the head of the regional body, based in Tashkent, in December 1989, by getting himself elected mufti of Kazakhstan at the republican Muslim Congress in December 1989, and establishing an independent Muslim Spiritual Directorate of Kazakhstan. It soon made plans to open new mosques with voluntary donations, and an Institute of Islamic Studies in Alma Ata and Jambul in the autumn, with an intake of sixty students for a two-year course for a prayer-leader and preacher.[17]

Among the numerous political groups that sprang up was one that aimed to rehabilitate those who had demonstrated in Alma Ata in December 1986. Out of this emerged the Kazakh National Democratic Party, popularly known as Jeltoksan, the Decembrists. In early 1990 its supporters, mainly Kazakhs with a sprinkling of Russians, condemned Kolbin, Kamalidenov and Solomentsev, and upheld 'December Events/Glasnost/Rehabilitation'.

Feeling freer, the 360-strong Supreme Soviet, elected in March 1990 with 338 Communist deputies, appointed a committee to inquire into the events of December 1986. Its report, published on 24 September 1990, was something of a political bombshell. 'The demonstration was not nationalistic but part of perestroika,' it stated. 'It was not against law and order. It was protest by youth, and it had occurred because the Communist Party and its leaders had neglected the consciousness of the people. It was a spontaneous demonstration by the working and university youth. The assessment by the Central Committee of the Communist Party [that it was an extremist outrage] was an insult to the nation. Since the leaders of this demonstration challenged the legitimacy of the forces of the republic's new party leader [Kolbin], they freed themselves from accepting the decisions of the local governors as well as other high and low executive organs. A narrow circle of leaders decided to send troops [from their regions] to Alma Ata to suppress the demonstration.'[18] The report's findings were accepted by the Supreme Soviet which ordered an appropriate tablet to be placed at a corner of the Square of the Republic, formerly Brezhnev Square.[19]

The report summed up the sea-change which the republic's governing organs had undergone since the bloody episode of December 1986, from being a mouthpiece of Moscow's will to mirroring the genuine feelings of the people they were expected to serve, thus shifting the balance decidedly in favour of ethnic Kazakhs, away from the Russian bear and towards the Turkic grey wolf, the animal which, according to legend, led the migrating Turkic tribes in different directions.

It was applauded outside the chamber, especially by the Jeltoksan, by Alash Orda, the old Kazakh nationalist party which had been crushed by the Red Army during the civil war, and by the Azat (i.e. Free) Movement, which combined Kazakh nationalism with pan-Turkism. Alash, led by Aron Atabek Nutushyev, came to life in late 1989. It became active in 1990, and offered a three-plank platform of pan-Turkism, Islam and democracy. Its vehement criticism of the government and Russian citizens and its call for a revolt against 'Russian colonial policy' made it a target of official harassment. Its meetings were broken up by security forces. Nutushyev was charged with insulting the president, a crime, because his party had coined the slogan: 'Nazarbayev, Stop Double-dealing'. The case against him failed. But, unable to bear further persecution, Nutushyev fled to Moscow in February 1991 and went underground. Here he managed to publish the party journal *Haq* (Truth).[20] By contrast, the Azat Movement was less strident, although equally committed to pan-Turkism, which it tried to popularize through such Turkic symbols as a grey wolf and the crescent and star. It had grown sufficiently by early October 1990 to start its own fortnightly journal, *Azat*, in Alma Ata. By then conflict in leading urban areas during the summer over rising demand for schooling in Kazakh and the continued housing shortage had shown that there was much that the opposition could highlight.

To meet the rising demand for autonomy, the Kazakh Supreme Soviet followed the lead of its Russian counterpart, and on 28 September 1990 declared the primacy of Kazakh legislation over Soviet laws, a milestone in Kazakhstan's history.

This provided the framework within which parliament could translate Kazakh nationalism into specific legislation, especially when fifty-three per cent of the deputies were Kazakh and only thirty per cent Russian. It passed a law making Kazakh the official language,

In the office of the caretaker of a Muslim shrine near Baku, Azerbaijan. Despite seventy-
four years of Communism, reverence for Islamic symbols continues.

Haji Sabir, deputy chairman of the Muslim Spiritual Directorate of Trans-Caucasia, is also the leader of the Islamic Progress Party, a registered political grouping in Azerbaijan.

Entrance to the Taza Pir mosque, one of only two mosques in Baku, Azerbaijan, which were kept open during Soviet rule.

Part of the oil industry of Azerbaijan, once the life-blood of the Soviet economy, now in decline due to persistent under-investment since the 1960s.

A mural of the Communist Youth League, or Komsomol, in Baku, Azerbaijan, in spring 1992: a continuing presence of the symbols of the Soviet era.

The main administrative building of Baku. The statue of Vladimir Lenin was removed from the pedestal in the foreground during the Popular Front-led nationalist demonstrations in September 1991.

Graves of the Azeris in Baku killed by Soviet troops despatched by the Kremlin to quash an incipient Popular Front-led nationalist uprising against the Communist regime in January 1990.

Abulfaz Elchibey, the first popularly elected president of independent Azerbaijan in June 1992, fled when faced with armed rebellion a year later. *Associated Press*

Geidar Aliyev, former First Secretary of the Communist Party of Azerbaijan and a member of the Politburo of the Communist Party of the Soviet Union, succeeded Elchibey in June 1993 as acting president; he was duly elected four months later. *Associated Press*

Dinmuhammad Kunayev, aged 80, the most powerful Communist in Central Asia for many years until his forced resignation in December 1986, and the mentor of President Nursultan Nazarbayev of Kazakhstan.

Under the guidance of Haji Radbek Nisanbayev, the mufti of the Muslim Spiritual Directorate, Kazakhstan, since December 1989, the number of mosques in the republic rose by almost four a month, reaching a total of 140 in September 1992.

President Nursultan Nazarbayev (third from left in front row) advances the market economy by inaugurating the first fast-food restaurant in Alma Ata, Kazakhstan.
Jeremy Nicholl/Katz

Above: The old administrative buildings, in the vicinity of the new Soviet-style administrative-political centre, are still in use in Bishkek, Kyrgyzstan.

Left: Even though Communist rule is over, a statue of Lenin dominates the administrative-political centre of Bishkek.

Above: 'Leninism is our banner': a symbol of the Communist past in Bishkek, November 1992. *Nina Bektemisova*

Right: Kyrgyzstan's membership of the Commonwealth of Independent States is underlined by its president, Askar Akayev (left), chairing a CIS summit in Bishkek in October 1992.

limiting certain civil service posts to Kazakh speakers, and specifying 1993 as the date for its full implementation with Slav-majority areas getting a two-year extension. The measure proved popular with Kazakhs; and this manifested itself with more new members, mainly Kazakh, enrolling in the CPK than the year before, bringing the total to nearly 800,000 in mid-1991.[21] On the other side, many Russian citizens disapproved of the new linguistic law. Some among them advocated the establishment of a Russian autonomous region in the north. Luckily for Nazarbayev, this disaffection did not graduate into sustained political action by Russians.

As the leader of the second-largest republic, rich in resources, which had as many Russians as Kazakhs, Nazarbayev occupied a special place in the USSR hierarchy. Aware that nearly two-thirds of the eleven million Russians settled in Central Asia were based in Kazakhstan, Gorbachev had particular reason to pay attention to Nazarbayev's ideas on the new association of sovereign states under discussion before and after the referendum on the subject in March 1991. This paid off, as Nazarbayev seemed to have played a pivotal role in reconciling Presidents Gorbachev and Yeltsin, thus making possible the signing of an interim agreement between nine Soviet republics and the centre on the shape of a new Union in April. Nazarbayev's political autobiography, *Bez Pravykh i Levykh* (Without Rights or Lefts), published in late spring, gave flesh to his ideas on political and economic reform, and showed him to be a balanced thinker. In the political field, like his Central Asian colleagues, he was for political autonomy rather than outright independence, a stance that obviated Gorbachev's fear of presiding over the disintegration of the USSR. Nazarbayev advocated an inter-republican concord that would maintain economic union of an integrated Soviet system of long standing. At the same time he lobbied hard for republican control of their resources, foreign trade and hard currencies. Apparently the hardline centralists in the Kremlin felt that too much power was being conceded to the republics by the new Union Treaty to be signed on 20 August; and that spurred them to mount a coup against Gorbachev. Unlike most Central Asian and Azerbaijani leaders, Nazarbayev, who was on good terms with Yeltsin, came out against the coup. As a result, its failure was as enthusiastically received in Alma Ata (with a majority Russian population) as it was in Moscow.

On 26 August 1991 Nazarbayev resigned as First Secretary of the Communist Party of Kazakhstan, saying the party had 'discredited itself in the eyes of the people'. Later he advised the leadership of the party to dissolve it. The CPK's Central Committee, meeting in October, did so by 586 votes to four. Efforts were then made, successfully, to re-constitute the old organization as the Socialist Party of Kazakhstan.

After the Law on Public Associations – based largely on a 1932 Decree of the CPSU on establishing 'voluntary societies and public organizations' – came into effect on 1 September, the Jeltoksan and Alash Orda refused to register, even though they were confident of comfortably meeting the minimum membership requirement of 3000. They protested at the provisions of the law which required the party leadership to submit a list of party members with addresses, phone numbers and signatures to the Ministry of Justice, suspicious that the information would be used by the intelligence and security departments to harass the membership.

In Russia, spurred by the upsurge in his popularity in the aftermath of the failure of the coup, President Yeltsin declared that he was 'prepared' to 'question' the borders between Russia and its large neighbours – Ukraine and Kazakhstan – arguing that these had been delineated in disregard of the ethnic complexities during a period when a single-party Soviet state seemed destined to last indefinitely.

In the case of Kazakhstan it would have meant moving the Russian frontier southwards since seven northern provinces had Slavic majorities, and since the settlements of the Ural and Siberian Cossacks, mostly of Russian blood, had been excluded from the Russian Federation. Historically, Cossacks, four million strong at the turn of the century and constituting a separate community of military pioneers who had defended Christendom from the invading Mongols and Tatars, were settled in eleven military colonies, extending from the Don River across Siberia to the Ussuri River bordering China, each colony signalling the extension of the Tsarist empire. Since they opposed the Bolshevik revolution militarily, Lenin ordered dispersement of their armies. Later Stalin's compulsory collectivization took its toll of Cossacks. In the late 1980s, besides the seven million Cossacks in the Russian Federation, there were two million outside the Federation, mostly in the Ural and Siberian parts of Kazakhstan.

Now in Russia most people saw Yeltsin's threat of incorporating Russian-majority parts of Kazakhstan into Russia as a clever move to knock some sense into the Kazakh leadership, whose decision to make Kazakh the official language was strongly disapproved of in the Russian Federation. But Yeltsin's ethnic argument was dangerous, set to produce more problems than it would solve. It unnerved Nazarbayev, and fuelled Kazakh nationalism, represented by the Azat Movement and Alash Orda, which reacted sharply to the meetings of Cossacks in north Kazakhstan in support of Yeltsin's statement. They claimed that the historical border of Kazakhstan was further north, following the line of Orenburg, Orsk, Kurgan and Omsk.

Nazarbayev protested vehemently, warning against 'a drive for a tsarist empire' and a 'new chauvinism'. Yeltsin backed down, insisting that Russia would be 'an equal among equals', and sending a peacemaking delegation to Alma Ata, which soothed ruffled feathers somewhat.[22] His public protestations against Yeltsin notwithstanding, Nazarbayev understood the facts on the ground. Were his government to yield further to strident Kazakh nationalist demands, it would trigger irredentist movement among Slav citizens who, settled primarily on cooperative or state-owned farms and cattle-breeding centres, formed sixty per cent of the population of seven northern provinces, five of them contiguous with the Russian Federation: they would opt for a merger of their territory with Russia. This scenario came to act as a damper on the Nazarbayev regime in its drive for Kazakhization. Overall, it was in his republic's interests, economic and otherwise, to work for a renegotiated union of the twelve republics of the USSR.

Nazarbayev participated actively in the discussions to finalize a Union Treaty, advocating a strong centre in order to maintain control over the military and economic infrastructure of the USSR – also the aim of the Russian democrats now led by Yeltsin – and institute uniform economic reform. Intent on constructing a new social order without dissipating the achievements of the existing one, they wanted to preserve the present Union, albeit in a modified form. Nazarbayev presided over a conference of the leaders of twelve republics in Alma Ata on 2 October to discuss a strong economic union. The participants initialled an agreement that laid the ground for a Union-wide economic structure. On 18 October eight republican leaders signed the document in Moscow, with the presidents of Azerbaijan, Georgia, Moldova and Ukraine abstaining. (Following the failure of the August coup the three Baltic republics had seceded from the USSR and won international recognition as sovereign independent states.) The new agreement was meant to provide a guideline for a similar set-up in the political arena, the two together producing the Union of Sovereign States to replace the Union of Soviet Socialist Republics.

In order to implement more effectively the forthcoming reform in Kazakhstan, Nazarbayev decided to hold a popular ballot for the presidency. Feeling that winning by a wide margin was not enough, he resolved to go for an absolute victory. He rationalized his decision thus: 'Now, when transitions to unpopular measures are beginning, only a politician backed by all the people can be sure of himself.'[23] At his behest the Supreme Soviet had passed an electoral law that required a prospective candidate for presidency to produce signatures of 100,000 supporters over a period of eight weeks. In practice, the electoral commission gave only nine days' notice to the candidates to show proof of 100,000 backers. Despite this, Hasan Kojahmedov, the leader of the Jeltoksan, capitalizing on falling living standards due to a twenty-two per cent economic downturn during the year, made sufficient progress to unnerve Nazarbayev. Two days before the deadline, Kojahmedov was attacked in the street by government militiamen, who snatched the list of signatures from him. So on polling day, 1 December, there was only one candidate: Nazarbayev. Of the nearly ten million electors, ninety-two per cent reportedly turned out. And ninety-eight per cent voted for Nazarbayev.

On the same day, ninety per cent of the voters in Ukraine opted for independence, thus upsetting Gorbachev's plan, which had perceived the Slav heartland of Russia and Ukraine acting as the axis around which a multinational union of sovereign states was to be formed.

When the presidents of the three Slav republics of Russia, Ukraine and Belarus announced the creation of a Commonwealth of Independent States on 8 December in Minsk, they aborted Soviet President Gorbachev's attempt to form a new confederal union on the territory of the USSR. But Gorbachev was not the only one to be upset by this development. President Nazarbayev was too when he noticed the Minsk declaration stating: 'The state-members of the Commonwealth intend to . . . guarantee unified control of nuclear weapons and their non-proliferation'.[24] His republic had nuclear arms on its soil, and unified control over the nuclear arsenal of the 'state-members of the Commonwealth' could not be complete without Kazakhstan's inclusion in the new political entity. On the other hand the Minsk declaration stated that the new agreement was open to all members of the USSR who shared 'the goals and principles of its founders'. This provided an opening for Nazarbayev to intervene actively in the process of rearranging the inter-republican relationship.

After holding discussions with Yeltsin, Nazarbayev took the initiative of assembling the leaders of the Central Asian republics. They met in Ashqabat, Turkmenistan, on 12 December, and decided to join the CIS, but only on equal terms, necessitating some rewriting of the Minsk declaration. The Slav countries agreed on 13 December. By aborting the prospect of the USSR splitting into Slav-centric and Turko-centric parts, the latest decision brought especial relief to Alma Ata and Moscow. It reassured the Slavs of Kazakhstan, forming forty-three per cent of the population, that they would not be left out of a Slav-centric grouping of former Soviet republics. At the same time, aware of the susceptibilities of the eighteen per cent mainly Asian and Muslim minorities in the Russian Federation, most Russian citizens were somewhat relieved not to belong to an exclusively European union.

On 16 December the Kazakh Supreme Soviet became the last body of its kind in the region to declare its republic an independent sovereign state. Once the treaty encompassing all the constituents of the USSR, except Georgia, was signed in Tashkent on 21 December 1991 to form the Commonwealth of Independent States, the stage was set for a formal dissolution of the Soviet Union.

AFTER THE SOVIET DISINTEGRATION

From early on, aware of Kazakhstan's forty-eight per cent European (i.e. Slav and German) population, the highest proportion in the Muslim-majority republics, Nazarbayev visualized Kazakhstan as a bridge between Russia and Central Asia. He realized that if any of the constituent republics of Central Asia were to come under the sway of Islamic militancy it would make Kazakhstan's bridge-building task extremely difficult. During his first visit to a European country, Austria, in early February, he declared that Kazakhstan had 'a special responsibility', along with Russia, to steer other Central Asian states away from Islamic fundamentalism and Iranian influence.[25]

The other unusual feature of the republic, its possession of nuclear arms, also engaged the attention of the Kazakh leadership as well as the Western powers, especially America, which wanted to see proper controls maintained over the nuclear arsenals outside Russia.[26] In late

February, Nazarbayev promised to transfer Kazakhstan's 650 tactical nuclear weapons to Russia, but insisted on keeping the strategic nuclear arms and destroying them only if the US, China, Russia, Ukraine and Belarus did the same. The fear in Western capitals was that the Muslim states of Pakistan and Iran, intent on advancing their nuclear ambitions, would prevail upon Kazakhstan, a fellow-Muslim state, to sell them nuclear arms and/or technology for hard currency. The reports in the Western media, based on information provided by an Iranian resistance organization in March (later proved to be baseless), that Alma Ata had sold three tactical nuclear weapons to Tehran added to Western apprehension. Washington increased its pressure on Kazakhstan to give up all its nuclear arms. In early May Nazarbayev explained that he could not do so because some politicians in Russia were claiming Kazakh territory, and textbooks in China continued to show parts of Kazakhstan as Chinese territory. The other factors that worried him were the uncertain futures of the CIS and the current Russian leadership.

As it was, there was sufficient protest at home to divert Nazarbayev's attention away from foreign affairs. Kazakhstan had begun its life as an independent state unpropitiously, with the workers in ten coal mines of Karaganda going on strike, demanding fulfilment of promises made by the government during the past two years. The shut-down continued for a month. Then, in late February, there was a mutiny against poor working conditions by the troops of the construction battalion at a base near the Baikonur Space Centre. It led to the deaths of three soldiers. After dismissing many officers, the authorities promised to improve conditions.[27]

Political opposition, especially pro-Turkic, also became active. A Jeltoksan delegation, led by Hasan Kojahmedov, participated in the Congress of the Supporters of Turkestan in Tashkent in early March. The assembly decided to work for the unification of the Central Asian republics into a supra-state to be called Turkestan, an unpalatable prospect for the Slav settlers in Kazakhstan. Following a resolution by the Congress to send military help to the Azeris in Karabakh, Kojahmedov proposed that a Muslim battalion be despatched from Kazakhstan to Karabakh.[28]

Not to be outflanked by the Jeltoksan on the pan-Turkic front, the Alash Orda leadership had combined pan-Turkism with Islam in its programme, thus producing a powerful mixture of Islamic pan-Turkism. It believed in Islamic revival since, it argued, Islam upheld the ethics it wished to see revived. It was also committed to reviving the old Turkestan as a first step towards creating Turanistan, stretching from Turkey to the Chinese border, a dream of the early proponents of pan-Turkism. But these aims were not to be achieved at the expense of democracy, which was perceived as essential for maintaining harmony in a multi-ethnic republic like Kazakhstan.[29]

But the deeds of Alash members were not always in line with their words. On 13 December 1991 five young Alash activists assaulted Haji Nisanbayev and injured him. Accusing him of not being sufficiently nationalist either in his public utterances or in his dealings with the Nazarbayev government 'run by former Communists', they forced him to sign a letter of resignation. In his defence Nisanbayev could have argued that thanks to the pressure from him the authorities had introduced an hour-long television programme on Islam every Friday, including a sermon by him, not to mention two to five religious programmes on radio every week. That aside, the progress of Islam had been quite impressive. During his two-year tenure as the mufti of Kazakhstan, each week had seen the opening of a new mosque or the re-opening of an old one, bringing the total of working mosques to 140. At his central mosque, which contained his office, the average size of the congregation for Friday prayers had risen from about 500 mainly elderly people before perestroika to 3000–4000 believers of all ages. The number of Muslims going on the hajj pilgrimage to Mecca had grown from a handful to forty-eight. On his relationship with the regime he could rightly say: 'The government respects us, and we respect it. At the same time we are separate from the state.'[30]

Those who attacked Nisanbayev were arrested. They and other Alash militants were tried in the spring of 1992 for insulting the president, organizing unauthorized rallies, and attacking Haji Nisanbayev, found guilty, and given prison sentences of varying lengths. These trials did little to subdue the registered opposition groups which began gaining support as the economy shrank, despite the best efforts by the administration to reverse the trend.

It was only in external affairs that Nazarbayev could notch up dramatic successes. At the CIS summit in Tashkent on 15 May, he was able to announce that Kazakhstan had reached an agreement with Russia on the joint use of Baikonur and Plesetsk space facilities. At the same meeting a Collective Defence Treaty, encompassing six states, including Russia and Kazakhstan, was concluded, enabling Nazarbayev to describe Russia as 'a political and military ally'.

Referring to the CDT as 'the guarantee Kazakhstan had sought for its security', he announced on the eve of his visit to America on 18 May that Kazakhstan would sign the Nuclear Non-Proliferation Treaty which Washington had been pressing it to do. Following his return home, the US, Russia, Ukraine, Belarus and Kazakhstan reached an agreement on 23 May on the destruction of all strategic nuclear weapons by former Soviet republics, except Russia, and the despatching of all tactical nuclear arms by Kazakhstan, Ukraine and Belarus to Russia.[31] Two days later Nazarbayev flew to Moscow to sign a bilateral treaty of friendship, cooperation and mutual aid between Kazakhstan and Russia. This committed the two sides to establishing joint military areas with common use of military installations and a 'common economic area' – and more importantly, recognizing the inviolability of each other's borders, thus setting to rest ethnic Kazakhs' fears about future Russian claims on Kazakhstan's territory.

As for the ethnic Slavs of Kazakhstan, they found much to worry about when the Supreme Soviet, now called the Supreme Kenges, published the proposed 148-article draft constitution on 2 June for public discussion. The draft described Kazakhstan as 'the national state of Kazakhs'. (In reality, Kazakhstan was a bi-national state, with six Russians to every seven Kazakhs.) The constitution retained Kazakh as the state language but guaranteed free development for all others, making Russian in practice the language of inter-ethnic communication. The 'Fundamentals of the Constitutional Order' included one that guaranteed 'political parties and public organizations . . . equal opportunities', and added that 'the ideology of political parties and other public organizations, including religious organizations, may not be established as state ideology'. This foreclosed the possibility of pan-Turkism or Islam being adopted as the state ideology if either the Alash Orda or Jeltoksan won power singly or jointly through constitutional means. Other provisions put restrictions on 'registered public associations'. They were required to open their membership to all Kazakh citizens irrespective of race, nationality (i.e ethnic origin), sex, language, social origin, domicile or attitude towards religion. That is, to win official registration, the Alash Orda would have to open its membership to ethnic Russians, Ukrainians or Germans. Equally, Slavic- or other European-dominated political parties would have to be open to all citizens to secure official registration.[32]

The registered pan-Turkic parties – the Azat Movement, the

Republican Party and Jeltoksan – joined the debate on the draft constitution. They rejected its articles on the language and political associations, demanding that Kazakh should be made the sole language of the republic, and the registration requirements for a political group should be far less stringent. This, and their general dissatisfaction with the Nazarbayev government, led them to call a protest demonstration on 17 June. (The unregistered Alash Orda backed the move surreptitiously.) Appealing to 'all those who consider themselves Kazakh', the sponsoring parties said: 'Until now yesterday's Communists have been ruling us. The Communists do not take into account the opinion of the nation. The government lurched into the market economy without any preparation. Speculation is rife.' They demanded a coalition government involving all the registered parties, including the governing Socialist Party. The new administration, they continued, should divide the assets of the former Communist Party among the registered parties, and dismiss the officials responsible for selling land to the Russians in the past as well as those responsible for selling public property cheaply to bogus foreign companies during the recent privatization programme. They called on the Supreme Soviet to appoint commissions on (a) repatriation (of European settlers), (b) the language issue, (c) the freedom of the press, (d) rescinding of the treaty with the US on nuclear weapons, and (e) abrogation of Kazakhstan's recent defence and security agreement with Russia since it legitimized the stationing of the 40th Russian Army in Kazakhstan in the guise of CIS forces.[33] They were clearly taking a strongly Kazakh nationalist position with a view to establishing clear Kazakh hegemony in the republic.

The opposition's call was taken up by some 5000 supporters. They demanded a meeting with President Nazarbayev, who refused to see them, accusing them of 'generating instability'. So they mounted pickets outside the Supreme Kenges. These went on for two weeks. Finally the protesters were removed forcibly by the security forces in the middle of the night.

With Kazakh nationalists flexing their muscles at the expense of Slavs, the Cossacks in Northern Kazakhstan, noted for their fighting prowess, and their kinsmen across the border in Southern Siberia became restive. A meeting of the 'Large Cossack Circle of Siberia and the former Steppe Krai [i.e. Northern Kazakhstan]' in Omsk, Russia, just north of the Kazakh border, protested against the violation of the rights of Russians in Kazakhstan on 1 July. Strongly condemning the renaming of Russian settlements and the destruction of Russian monuments in Kazakhstan, it called on the Supreme Soviets and presidents of Kazakhstan and Russia to protect the rights of Russians in Kazakhstan, and allow them dual citizenship. It reiterated its right to defend 'its [Russian] brothers [in Kazakhstan] by all available means'. Taking their cue from their kinsmen across the border, the Russian settlers in Northern Kazakhstan sent a delegation to Alma Ata. In its meeting with Nazarbayev it urged amending the draft constitution to prohibit discrimination against non-Kazakh speakers and postpone the switch-over to Kazakh for official business.[34] Given the large size of the Russian population in his republic, and a virtually unguarded land frontier of 4000 kilometres (2500 miles) between Kazakhstan and Russia, Nazarbayev could hardly afford to ignore the demands being made by the ethnic Slavs.

To withstand the mounting pressure from the militant Kazakh and Slav lobbies, the Nazarbayev administration needed to activate the political organization that had the backing of nearly eighty per cent of the parliamentarians – the Socialist Party – in order to demonstrate its popular standing. Although, intent on being president of all citizens, Nazarbayev had decided not to join any grouping, his premier, Sergei Tereshchenko, had enrolled in the Socialist Party. But the organization was a shadow of the former CPK. Whereas the CPK had 866,262 full and candidate members, the Socialist Party had only 60,000 full members.[35] Inevitably, therefore, political life came to revolve around the policies and actions of Nazarbayev.

Nazarbayev was advised that one way to contain the tide of Kazakh nationalism was to direct it into non-threatening cultural channels. He therefore sponsored a World Congress of Kazakhs in Alma Ata – with a Russian to Kazakh ratio of 2.3:1 – in early October. Attended by 750 delegates from abroad, including Turkey, Russia, Uzbekistan, Afghanistan, Egypt and Germany, its proceedings were televised to popular acclaim among Kazakhs. Nazarbayev combined his appeal to the Kazakhs living abroad to return to the motherland with an offer of instant citizenship, a step intended to increase the Kazakh proportion in the republic's population.

However impressive, such assemblies failed to mask the economic fact that living standards were falling owing to a steep drop in the GDP, stemming from the closure of many factories because of a lack of raw or semi-finished materials and a shortage of hard currencies, and that unemployment was rising. High inflation was making a mockery of properly assessing the value of industrial assets as part of privatization plans, which were more advanced in Kazakhstan than in many other former Soviet republics. This was so partly because Nazarbayev had a good grasp of economics, and partly because he had taken on board Grigory Yavlinsky, one of Gorbachev's radical economists who had left the Soviet leader in late 1990. Also, given Kazakhstan's vast resources not only in copper, zinc, lead, titanium, gold and silver but also in oil, natural gas and coal, Western companies showed considerable interest in investing, making Kazakhstan the third most favoured republic, after Russia and Ukraine. However, prosperity ensuing from such investments lay in the future.

Nazarbayev felt that the republic's economic ills would be cured if there were better economic integration of the CIS through supra-governmental structures. But his proposal on these lines was rejected by his fellow-presidents at the CIS summit in Bishkek, Kyrgyzstan, on 9 October. Then he took to criticizing his own administration for blindly following the Russian reform programme which, in his view, was going nowhere. He asked parliament for additional powers so that he could administer a strong anti-crisis medicine. Despite this his popular standing fell ten points in a month, reaching fifty-nine per cent in late October.[36] The following month Prime Minister Tereshchenko halted further privatization in view of the persistently high inflation. Any hopes that the forthcoming CIS summit in Minsk would produce a general economic strategy that would ease the crisis in Kazakhstan were dashed when the meeting was postponed.

As if this were not enough, some 15,000 Russian protesters gathered in Ust-Kamenogorsk, the capital of East Kazakhstan Province, on 7 December calling for an equal status for Russian along with Kazakh as a state language, and a law allowing dual nationality. They demanded that their province be given 'self-determination' in language, culture and natural resources. Since this large demonstration was the first of its kind inside Kazakhstan, Nazarbayev realized apprehensively that, far from subsiding, ethnic tensions in the republic were rising, and that this could lead to irredentist agitation by ethnic Russians and a revival of Moscow's claims over parts of Kazakhstan.

It was against this troubled background that Nazarbayev flew to Tashkent to attend a summit of Central Asian leaders on 3–4 January 1993 to coordinate regional economic and financial policies. While the host, President Islam Karimov of Uzbekistan, stated that the existence of the CIS and the rouble zone did not preclude the creation of a Central Asian Common Market with unified customs, pricing and export policies, Nazarbayev went one step further. Expressing his doubt that the CIS would 'ever meet again', he urged the union of Central Asian people along the lines of the Association of South-Eastern Asian Nations (ASEAN). He went on to suggest that the five regional states should adopt a plane tree with a single root and five branches as a common symbol. This, and his agreement to replace the Soviet designation of 'Republics of Middle Asia and Kazakhstan' with 'Republics of Central Asia',[37] signalled that Nazarbayev had finally opted for integrating Kazakhstan into Central Asia at the expense of its links with Russia if need be. Evidently he reckoned that he had an area of manoeuvre only so long as Russia was divided and weak as it was then, with its president and parliament locked into a power struggle; and that it was time to get closer to fellow-Turkic peoples. 'Nazarbayev is scared that when Russia strengthens again, it will come after those [Russian] people [in Kazakhstan], especially since their area [of settlement] is full of oil and gas resources,' said an ambassador in Tashkent. 'He feels that he would be stronger . . . with the 50 million people of Central Asia behind him.'[38]

Later Nazarbayev distanced himself further from Russia. Addressing the Kazakh parliament during the last week of January, he blamed the failure of the first phase of economic reform on 'the ground rules dictated by Russia', and promised as part of his anti-crisis package a greater interventionist role on the part of the government, a policy out of favour in Moscow.

Prudence demanded that such policy shifts be balanced somewhat, if only to ensure the continued loyalty of ethnic Russians and to see that they did not feel alienated from the state. This view was shared not only by the president but also by an overwhelming majority of parliamentarians then engaged in finalizing the constitution after a seven-month debate inside and outside the chamber. The final document adopted by 309 deputies on 28 January demonstrated this. While according Kazakh the status of official language, it recognized Russian as the *lingua franca*, and required merely that the country's president should 'speak Kazakh fluently', thus making it possible, theoretically, for a Kazakh-speaking Slav to be elected to the highest office.[39]

In other words, caught between the Russian bear and the Turkic grey wolf, Nazarbayev had, by design or chance, devised a policy of two steps towards the wolf, then one step back.

It was a policy most suited to another republic with a large proportion of Russian settlers: Kyrgyzstan.

FOUR

Kyrgyzstan: A Democratic Niche, an Islamist Void

The ethnic make-up of Kyrgyzstan in the 1950s was similar to that in Kazakhstan. That is, at forty per cent of the population, native Kyrgyzs were only as numerous as European settlers – Russians, Ukrainians and Germans.[1] Later this was to change, primarily owing to the high birth-rate among Kyrgyzs. But it was not until the late 1980s that Kyrgyzs were to become a bare majority in a republic named after them.

With three-quarters of its territory covered with mountains, Kyrgyzstan has proved to be richly endowed with minerals. It emerged as the leading source of mercury and antimony in the USSR, and one of the main producers of Soviet coal and uranium. In the early 1950s it also had a potential for developing further its agriculture and animal husbandry. The Kremlin was aware of this, and included it in its Virgin Land project. The Seventh Congress of the Communist Party of Kyrgyzstan (CPKz), meeting in February 1954 in Bishkek (then Frunze, named after the eminent Red Army general), duly pledged itself to advance the scheme.

Equally obediently, the republican Communist Party promised to restore 'the Leninist norms of party life and strengthen socialist legality' which, according to the speech delivered by Nikita Khrushchev to the Twentieth Congress of the CPSU in February 1956, had been violated by Joseph Stalin. But it was not until four years later that the party leadership in Moscow used the unsatisfactory progress made by Kyrgyzstan in the Virgin Land programme to instal a comparatively young party member, Turdahun Usubaliyev (Yusuf Ali), as First Secretary of the Communist Party of Kyrgyzstan. He had graduated from the Senior Party School of the CPSU's Central Committee, and then became an instructor in Communist ideology at the institute. This enabled him to forge contacts with the rising stars in the party's central bureaucracy.

Little wonder that the replacement of Khrushchev by Leonid

Brezhnev in mid-October 1964 did not affect the fortunes of Usubaliyev. He rapidly insinuated himself into the good graces of Leonid Brezhnev, during whose rule the party became even more powerful, and more distant from the people, than before. 'We were a highly centralized party, which did not ask the people what they wanted,' said Kybanychbek Idinov (Uddin), chairman of the Kyrgyzstan Supreme Soviet Commission on Inter-parliamentarian Relations, who joined the Communist Party in 1972. 'We considered ourselves the embodiment of the nation, and that was it.'[2]

An unrelenting obsession with meeting economic targets, despite mounting problems of bureaucratic red tape, unethical behaviour among managers and low morale among workers, engendered corruption and nepotism in the economy and government administration. As the quality of leadership at the centre deteriorated, republican party bosses like Usubaliyev found greater chances to strengthen their grip over local networks. Drunk with power, and running a distant republic at the back of beyond, Usubaliyev fostered a personality cult which was in full bloom when Brezhnev died in 1982. With the advent of Yuri Andropov, who pledged to weed out corruption and restore worker discipline, Usubaliyev's future looked shaky. Luckily for him, Andropov's rule proved transient. And Konstantin Chernenko, who succeeded Andropov, was a long-standing friend of Usubaliyev: they had been room-mates in their university days in Moscow during the Great Patriotic War.

It was not until Mikhail Gorbachev became First Secretary of the CPSU in March 1985 that the future of Usubaliyev, now sixty-six, was really threatened. The axe finally fell on him on 4 November when, after more than a quarter of a century in power, he was replaced by Absamat Musaliyev (Musa Ali), the erstwhile mayor of Bishkek. A mining graduate of Moscow University, Musaliyev had worked in mines in Kyrgyzstan and had then gone over to the party organization and become active in party politics. The following year another Kyrgyz with an engineering/science background followed a similar path, moving from a technological/scientific job to a position in the party bureaucracy at the CPKz's Central Committee secretariat. He was Askar Akayev. Born in 1944 in Kyzyl Bairak in Northern Kyrgyzstan, he had graduated from St Petersburg (then Leningrad) Institute of Exact Sciences and Optics as a nuclear physicist.

Musaliyev set out to reform the party and the social system, which had become atrophied under Usubaliyev; but he proved unequal to the task of remedying the distortions and drawbacks of the system

which had persisted for decades. He was therefore shunted sideways
to take over the job of chairman of the Presidium of the Supreme
Soviet, with Jumgalbek Amanbayev (Amanbai) becoming First
Secretary of the republican Communist Party. Rivalling him was
the up-and-coming Akayev. Elected a deputy in the March 1989
elections to the USSR Congress of People's Deputies (CPD), he
became vice-chairman of the Commission on Foreign Affairs of the
Supreme Soviet, the super-parliament, whose 460 members were
drawn from the larger CPD. At the Twenty-eighth Congress of the
CPSU in July 1990, at the behest of Gorbachev, Akayev was elected
to the Central Committee.

As elsewhere in the USSR, perestroika and glasnost brought to the
fore inter-ethnic tensions which were all the stronger in Kyrgyzstan
owing to the insecurity felt by the largest group, Kyrgyzs, which
until recently had not constituted a clear majority. It was only in
1989 that the census showed Kyrgyzs to be 52.4 per cent of the total
population – with Russians down to 21.5 per cent, and Uzbeks steady
at thirteen per cent.[3] Most Uzbeks lived in the southern province of
Osh, containing part of the fertile Fergana Valley, and accounting
for more than a third of Kyrgyzstan's area and over two-fifths of its
population of 4.26 million.

Responding to the rising tide of ethnic nationalism, the Supreme
Soviet declared Kyrgyz the official language in November 1989, and
specified an eight-year period for a complete changeover from the
current practice of treating Kyrgyz and Russian on a par. This proved
popular with the Kyrgyz majority and helped the Communist Party
to gain over eighty-five per cent of the 350 seats in the Supreme
Soviet in the multi-candidate election held in March 1990, with the
rest of the seats going to independents who propounded Kyrgyz
nationalism and/or democracy.

Prominent among the ethnic minorities that disapproved of the
republic's new linguistic policy were Russians and Uzbeks. Relations
between Uzbeks and Kyrgyzs, especially in the Kyrgyzstan–
Uzbekistan border region in the Fergana Valley, had been dis-
harmonious over a long period. Ethnic differences had been
compounded by the dearth of arable land in the predominantly
mountainous Kyrgyzstan, resulting in frequent disputes between the
two communities over land and supplies of irrigation water originating from the large Fergana Canal. The authorities in Bishkek maintained that the Uzbek population of Osh Province was being
encouraged by the clandestine Birlik (i.e. Unity) Popular Front (of

Uzbekistan) to agitate for autonomy with a view to getting a future Autonomous Region of Osh to join Uzbekistan. To make matters worse, in many urban settlements of the province, especially Osh, minority Uzbeks monopolized commerce and trade, and this made them unpopular with the majority community. With unemployment among Kyrgyzs, especially young men, growing sharply, tension between the two ethnic groups rose.

It was against this backdrop that Kyrgyz–Uzbek rioting erupted in the province of Osh in early June 1990, with Uzbeks getting the worst of it. The trigger was the forcible takeover of a large piece of land belonging to an Uzbek-dominated collective farm by local Kyrgyzs in the Kyrgyzstan–Uzbekistan border area on 4 June, accompanied by much violence and arson in which Uzbeks were the victims. The evicted Uzbeks sought and received assistance from fellow-Uzbeks across the border. The subsequent fighting ceased only after a large-scale intervention by Kyrgyzstan's security forces. The initial figure of 116 dead and 500 injured during three days of violent disorder, which spread to Osh city, was later revised upward to 300 killed, most of them Uzbeks. But these figures were considered low by many observers.[4] The blame for instigating the bloodshed was attributed to Birlik supporters among Uzbeks by one side, and to the leaders of a newly established group known simply as 'Kyrgyzstan', backed by those local CPKz figures who wanted to underscore their nationalist credentials, by the other. Whatever the truth, the severity of the violence shook public confidence in the governmental and party leadership. What made matters worse for the authorities was the open demand for autonomy by Uzbeks once they had recovered from the shock, which in turn increased ethnocentric sentiment among Kyrgyzs who complained bitterly of housing shortages and joblessness.

Matters came to a head in early November when about 1000 Kyrgyz protesters, led by the Unit of Builders, a grass-roots organization focusing on unemployment and homelessness among Kyrgyzs, undertook a hunger strike in the administrative centre of the capital. They had been inspired by the spontaneous demonstration by several thousand people in June demanding 'objective news' about the events in the province of Osh. To divert the rising public protest, and to follow the lead of the USSR Supreme Soviet, Musaliyev, chairman of the Presidium of Kyrgyzstan's Supreme Soviet, persuaded the chamber to create the new post of executive president. Going by the precedent set by Moscow, this job should have gone to the chairman of the Supreme Soviet's Presidium, Musa-liyev. But with street protest in full swing in Bishkek, President Gorbachev thought it prudent to give a genuinely free choice to Supreme Soviet deputies scheduled to settle the matter on 22 November. He deputed Vladimir Kryuchkov, the KGB chief and a Politburo member, to oversee the election.

Eleven aspirants, including Musaliyev, offered themselves for the job. None of them managed to obtain the absolute majority needed. A stalemate ensued. It was broken only when, prodded by Gorba-chev and Kryuchkov, Akayev flew in from Moscow and offered himself as a candidate. He won. Encouraged by Akayev's victory, the anti-Musaliyev elements in parliament and outside decided to form the Democratic Kyrgyzstan Movement (DKM), an over-whelmingly Kyrgyz party, along the lines of the CPKz, including dues-paying members. To placate Musaliyev, the CPSU leadership offered him the job of First Secretary of the CPKz.

Even though the parliamentary poll had given the Russian min-ority a share of seats commensurate with their proportion in the population, about twenty per cent, they were increasingly apprehen-sive of their future in Kyrgyzstan. This was due to the rising tide of Kyrgyz nationalism: it grew at the expense of the Russian language and hegemony that had been an integral part of the Bolshevik revol-ution in the region. Little wonder that of the 920,000 Russians in the republic, more than 74,000 left during the first six months of 1991,[5] most of them possessing high technical, scientific or mana-gerial skills which they were confident of selling elsewhere in the former USSR. This was a serious problem for the Kyrgyz authorities who were determined not to alienate ethnic Russians. As for the Russian minority, most of its members preferred to stay on since food and housing in Kyrgyzstan were better than in the Russian Federation, and there were ample supplies of vegetables and fruit as well, an important consideration. On the negative side, they were aware of the rising tension between them and Kyrgyzs, especially the young among them.

An important positive factor from the Russian viewpoint was the weakness of the Islamic fundamentalist forces. Kyrgyzs came under the influence of Islam late – largely as subjects of the Khanate of Kokand in the 1830s. However, as a nomadic people, they did not develop the tradition of going to the mosque on Fridays, and Kyrgyz women continued to work unveiled alongside their men. As pagans of long standing they found it hard to adjust to the strait-jacket of monotheism. 'Given our style of life and our cattle-breeding economy, we still have a pantheistic outlook,' said Ulan Orozaliyev, a former Communist editor-turned-businessman. 'We were children of nature, our God. We worshipped the wind, sun, fire and sky before embracing Islam.'[6] Under Soviet rule religion was suppressed to the extent that in all of Kyrgyzstan only twenty-five mosques were allowed to function, most of them in the province of Osh in the Fergana Valley, where Uzbeks and Tajiks with long histories of settlement were more drawn to the mosque than were Kyrgyzs. In this region Islamic customs regarding birth, male circumcision, marriage and death persisted during the Soviet era. Almost all Muslim funerals were conducted according to the Islamic tradition. Between 1984 and 1987 an estimated 5000 'exclusively religious marriages' were solemnized.[7] With the general relaxation that came in the wake of glasnost and perestroika from 1986 onwards, more and more people began attending the mosque or church. Also, by then the quality of clerics, graduating from the officially run theological colleges, had improved considerably. Commenting on this change, Moldo Kasimov (Kasim), a Kyrgyz researcher, wrote in the *Leninchil Zhash* (Leninist Youth) of 6 August 1987: 'In the past they lectured on atheism but now they wear turbans and have become mullahs.'[8]

Following the secession of the Kazakh branch from its parent body, the Muslim Spiritual Directorate of Central Asia, in late 1989, the Kyrgyzstan branch under Kazi Kismanbai Abdurahmanov (Abdul Rahman) began to act independently.

There was a growth in secular organizations too, since perestroika allowed voluntary social and cultural groups, such as the Unit of Builders, claiming a membership of 20,000 in the late 1980s. This gave a general impetus to the democratic movement in the republic. A majority of the economic enterprises were controlled by Moscow and the directors appointed by it. Most of them employed Kyrgyzs chiefly in manual and semi-skilled jobs. Increasingly Kyrgyz youth felt alienated. During the latter half of the 1980s, with the progress of glasnost and perestroika, this problem acquired political dimensions. In 1988–9 socially conscious Kyrgyzs started forming Youth Democratic Forums. Finally, encouraged by the success they had in frustrating Musaliyev's ambition to become the republican president in late 1989, these elements, consisting largely of Kyrgyz writers, journalists and university teachers and students, formed the Democratic Kyrgyzstan Movement in Bishkek in May 1990 – a perfectly

legal move since a republican law now allowed the formation of
political parties so long as they were not based on religion, race or
ethnicity. Though the DKM was open to all citizens of Kyrgyzstan,
there was little support for it among Russians. By and large they did
not encounter unemployment and homelessness like their Kyrgyz
fellow-citizens; and the well-off among them, engaged mainly in
technical, scientific or managerial work, and earning good salaries,
had scant grounds for complaint or for joining newly formed opposition groups. Overall, therefore, the democratic stream in Kyrgyz
politics came to be virtually monopolized by Kyrgyz nationalists.

Unlike in the Soviet Union, where Gorbachev, the CPSU's First
Secretary, also became the USSR's executive president, in Kyrgyzstan the two positions came to be occupied by different leaders:
Musaliyev and Akayev. Since Musaliyev had contested the republic's
presidency and failed to win, he did not take kindly to President
Akayev. It therefore seemed logical that Akayev should reciprocate
by cold-shouldering the power base of Musaliyev, the Communist
Party, and turning a benign eye on the emergent democratic opposition. With other Central Asian republics following the centre's lead
in having the top party leader also assume executive presidency of
the republic, Kyrgyzstan emerged as an exception, a democratic
niche. And it began attracting democrats from elsewhere in Central
Asia.

Indeed, democrats from the region assembled in Bishkek in late
May 1991. They formed the Democratic Congress of Central Asia
and Kazakhstan as a discussion forum and a coordinating body with
its headquarters in Bishkek. Its first conference concentrated on ethnic issues, and concluded that 'any reconsideration of [current inter-
republican] borders could cause inter-ethnic conflict that could
become international.'[9] Among other things the establishment of
this organization boosted the morale of the democratic forces in
Kyrgyzstan, and thus of President Akayev.

This manifested itself during the dramatic days of the hardliners'
coup in Moscow in August 1991. Unlike most other Central Asian
presidents, Akayev publicly and strongly opposed it, thus arousing
the ire *inter alia* of the local military and KGB bosses (since their
superiors in Moscow were among the coup leaders). Following the
lead of Vladimir Kryuchkov, the Soviet KGB chief and one of the
main plotters, his deputy in Bishkek arrived at the presidential palace
to arrest Akayev. The move boomeranged. He found himself
arrested by the security men guarding the president, who despatched

loyal troops to surround the headquarters of the Communist Party, a rival centre of power. He ordered television and radio stations to broadcast the Russian President Yeltsin's appeal for resistance to the coup. Following the collapse of the coup, Akayev resigned from the Communist Party, and emulated Yeltsin's moves against the organization: suspension coupled with confiscation of its properties. The party in Kyrgyzstan, with 154,650 full and candidate members on its rolls,[10] had reportedly acquired substantial funds through the underhand economic activity of its apparatchiks. As the founders and managers of many cooperatives, chiefly in small enterprises, from 1986 onwards, several of them had become involved in shady dealings, including the laundering of black money, which had started to grow during the latter part of the Brezhnev era in an environment of economic stagnation.[11] Now, with the Communist Party extinct, most of its top bureaucrats fled Kyrgyzstan, heading mainly for Moscow. As for the parliamentarians who had been elected on the party ticket, they ceased to belong to any recognized organization, and became independent. They unanimously supported the Supreme Soviet motion on 30 August declaring Kyrgyzstan an independent, sovereign state.

The government came to rely increasingly on the personal popularity of Akayev, who refused to join any party. Aware of the important task of establishing democracy in Kyrgyzstan, Akayev turned down Gorbachev's offer of vice-presidency of the USSR.[12] He set the tone for democratic tolerance by making it part of his weekly agenda to consult the leaders of all political hues inside and outside parliament on important matters.

Yet when it came to contesting the presidency of independent Kyrgyzstan in a popular poll on 12 October, Akayev temporized. Expecting to be opposed by Jumgalbek Amanbayev, a former First Secretary of the CPKz, Akayev spiked his guns by getting parliament to pass a law that required a presidential candidate to secure 25,000 signatures within two weeks,[13] a near-impossible task for any opposition leader to accomplish in the absence of an established party network. The voter turn-out was eighty-three per cent, and 98.5 per cent voted for Akayev, the sole candidate.

During the consultations among Central Asian leaders that followed after the three Slav republics had announced the formation of the Commonwealth of Independent States on 8 December 1991, Akayev advocated a looser link between Soviet republics along the lines of the British Commonwealth, but his proposal did not prevail.

This was just as well: Akayev had failed to work out the economic consequences of a looser association on his republic.

The collapse of the USSR, which resulted in the immediate loss of the central subsidies amounting to seventy-five per cent of Kyrgyzstan's budget, played havoc with the republic's economy. Kyrgyzstan managed to survive economically because of the subsidies that President Yeltsin offered it from the treasury of the Russian Federation. Little wonder that Kyrgyzstan was quick to follow Russia's example in early January 1992 when it came to raising prices on basic and other goods.

Sharing common borders with China and Tajikistan, Kyrgyzstan needed to have CIS/Russian troops on its soil; but it lacked funds to maintain them even partially. Once again Russia came to its rescue by volunteering to pay the full costs. In turn Kyrgyzstan confirmed that it would honour its commitment to provide recruits to CIS forces, its annual supply of conscripts being 21,000. It also joined the Collective Defence Treaty that was forged by six CIS members in Tashkent in mid-May.

While Kyrgyzstan's links with China had strengthened, especially in the economic field, following the establishment of republic-level trading organizations after spring 1988, its relations with Tajikistan had deteriorated in the same period because its demand for readjustment of borders had been rejected by the Tajik government. The root of the problem was that the fertile Fergana Valley, a multi-ethnic settlement, had been split three ways in the 1920s – between Uzbekistan, Tajikistan and Kyrgyzstan – in a manner that had failed to satisfy all the republics. But Moscow was against re-opening the border issue in this instance on the same ground as in the case of Karabakh: any such move would prove to be a Pandora's box, creating more problems than it solved. As it was, the Kyrgyz province involved in the border controversy with Tajikistan, Osh, had not returned to normal two years after the Kyrgyz–Uzbek riots. Indeed, following large-scale Islamic demonstrations in the Tajik capital of Dushanbe in the spring of 1992, partly encouraged by the victory of the Islamic Mujahedin in Afghanistan in April 1992, the political situation in Tajikistan had become unstable,[14] and this had a knock-on effect on Osh. An increasingly nervous Akayev dismissed the provincial governor for failing to ameliorate the tense situation in Osh.

Among other things the turmoil in Tajikistan, caused mainly by Islamist forces, made Akayev realize that he had taken the right decision by formalizing the division between state and religion in his republic, and banning parties based on religion. Later, in October, he prevailed upon the parliamentary commission on the constitution to drop the statement in the preamble of the draft constitution that the country was 'in the process of a spiritual rebirth oriented toward Islamic values'.[15] Since this reference to Islam in a spiritual-cultural context pertained to a society with three-quarters of its members having a Muslim background, it was quite valid and, strictly speaking, not at odds with the republic's commitment to keeping state and religion apart. On the other hand it was crucial for Akayev to distance his administration firmly from anything even vaguely smacking of Islamism in order to reassure the Russian minority, possessing much needed skills, as well as Moscow, which continued to shore up the fragile Kyrgyz economy with subsidies – not to mention the International Monetary Fund, dominated by the US, poised to provide financial assistance to Bishkek.

Akayev was anxious to see an end to Islamic turmoil in Tajikistan, a source of his troubles at home. As the host of the CIS summit on 8–9 October in Bishkek, he sought and won the backing of his colleagues to pursue a peace-making mission under the leadership of his vice-president, Felix Kulov. But when it was announced that Kyrgyzstan would send a contingent of 450 troops to Tajikistan for peace-keeping, the proposal was received coolly by parliamentarians and the public. The mothers of the Kyrgyz soldiers likely to be despatched to Tajikistan mounted a picket outside the defence ministry in protest. This had an impact on many parliamentary deputies, who argued that if a CIS peace-keeping force had to be sent to Tajikistan, it must be composed of all the remaining five members of the Collective Defence Treaty, and not only Kyrgyzstan. On 19 October the Supreme Soviet rejected the government proposal for a peace-keeping mission in Tajikistan – a triumph for grass-roots politics which made Kyrgyzstan stand out in the region.

But a single such victory did not mean that democracy had struck firm roots in Kyrgyzstan. Lacking a political democratic tradition, Kyrgyzstan was then in the midst of a declining economy and tense inter-ethnic relations, with its president publicly admitting that law-enforcement agencies had failed to apprehend 'armed bands' who were smuggling weapons and narcotics from Tajikistan and Afghanistan, with many Tajik refugees in Kyrgyzstan acting as conduits. To remedy the situation he resorted to appointing local governors directly and abolishing local soviets that had the authority to elect such officials. This alarmed the opposition groups. Eleven of them, including the Democratic Kyrgyzstan Movement, the Democratic Party of Erkin (Free) Kyrgyzstan, and the Party of National Unity, banded together in January 1993 to issue a warning against the return of dictatorship.

Though Bishkek continued to be the freest capital in the region, providing once again the venue for the Second Conference of the Democratic Congress of Central Asia and Kazakhstan in December, all local opposition groups were kept under vigilance. Phone-tapping was the most common technique used. 'I use a scrambling device in my telephone,' said an opposition leader in Bishkek. 'But I don't use it all the time because that way the [local] KGB would get suspicious.'[16] The opposition claimed that Akayev found it easier to get along with technocrats than with democrats, and that his circle of close advisers was bereft of members of the democratic parties.

Since most of the Kyrgyz political groups were sympathetic to pan-Turkism, and looked up to the democratic order in Turkey, they had good relations with the Turkish embassy. Within months of Kyrgyz independence, Turkey had emerged as an important foreign player in Bishkek. During his visit to the Kyrgyz capital in May 1992, Premier Demirel had offered $75 million in credits to Kyrgyzstan, as well as training for its university students in Turkey. Earlier, Ankara had reiterated Turkic fraternity with Kyrgyzstan, stressing common linguistic and cultural origins, to such an extent that rhetoric had overwhelmed reality. As a member of the Central Turkic group, Kyrgyz is not as close to the Turkish of Turkey as Azeri is. This became obvious when, during their tour of Central Asia and Azerbaijan in April–May 1992, Demirel and his party had to engage interpreters everywhere except in Azerbaijan. Later, television programmes in Turkish beamed at Kyrgyzstan failed to gain much of an audience: Kyrgyzs had a problem understanding the Turkish of Turkey.

None the less, efforts to bind Turkey closely with the Central Asian republics and Azerbaijan continued unabated. In late October 1992, Ankara played host to a meeting of the heads of these states (except Tajikistan, then in the throes of a civil war) with the specific aim of developing transportation and communication links.

Unlike in Azerbaijan, where Turkey faced competition from Iran, the cards were stacked heavily in Turkey's favour here. The areas of commercial or cultural cooperation between Iran and Kyrgyzstan were limited. Even in religion there was not much room for exchange: Kyrgyzs and Uzbeks were Sunni whereas Iranians were

Shia. Neither Iran nor Afghanistan, a Sunni-majority state, shared borders with Kyrgyzstan.

With the civil war in Tajikistan ending in December 1992 with the defeat of the Islamist-led alliance, the Akayev administration could heave a sigh of relief, confident that its commitment to separating the state and mosque and banning religious parties, now written into the new draft constitution, was unlikely to be tested.

The final draft of the new constitution, a result of much deliberation and rewriting by the constitutional commission, was debated by the Supreme Soviet in April. Much to the disappointment of Russian and Uzbek citizens, it rejected the clause describing Russian as the language of inter-ethnic communication. It also turned down the provision for dual citizenship, which had been demanded by the Russian and Uzbek minorities. But it approved the change in its own name – to Zhogorku Kenesh – and that of the country, to Kyrgyz Republic. It thus broke the regional pattern of using the suffix of 'istan' (meaning 'land') after the leading ethnic group: Uzbek-istan, Tajik-istan, etc. The draft constitution was unanimously adopted by the Supreme Soviet on 5 May, and promulgated on the same day.[17] Kyrgyzstan thus became the last of the four Central Asian states to adopt a new constitution, with Tajikistan continuing to function by amending its 1978 constitution.

It was not accidental that Kyrgyzstan, the most democratic of former Soviet Central Asian republics, was the last to promulgate a new constitution while Turkmenistan, the most authoritarian, was the first.

FIVE

Turkmenistan: Secular
Autocracy Intact

With Khrushchev as the leader of the CPSU from 1954 onwards, there was much stress in the Kremlin on raising the output of agricultural produce, including cotton. This, and the general principle of division of labour applied to the constituents of the USSR, resulted in increased effort to turn Turkmenistan into a cotton-producing republic. As elsewhere in Central Asia, the achievement of this goal involved giving preference to qualified ethnic Russians, either born locally or brought in from Russia, for top jobs – a policy with which Suhan Babayev, First Secretary of the Communist Party of Turkmenistan (CPTu), disagreed. He felt that the Russians, forming only one-sixth of the republic's population, had a disproportionate share of senior positions. His protest led to the CPSU leadership replacing him with Balish Ovezov in 1959. Since nearly eighty per cent of Turkmenistan is desert, and since cotton production depends heavily on a reliable source of water, something highly innovative needed to be done. Out of this arose the idea of constructing, in stages, a tributary of the Oxus River (known locally as Amu Darya) flowing into the Caspian Sea, to be named after Lenin and Karakum (Black Sand).

Work on the Lenin Karakum Canal commenced in 1960 from the Oxus River end. By 1967 the 850 kilometre- (530 mile-) long canal had reached the capital, Ashqabat (then spelt Ashkhabad), providing irrigation to an area extending fifteen to twenty kilometres (nine to thirteen miles) from each of its banks. This caused a sixty-two per cent growth in the sown acreage of the republic, most of it used for cotton cultivation. The ten per cent annual increase in cotton production during 1960–65 was maintained during the following decade, partly through growth in acreage and partly through a rise in productivity. Actual output, which was 211,000 tons in 1940, shot up to 920,000 tons thirty years later.[1]

The impressive increase in the cotton-growing acreage began

about the same time as the commercial extraction of natural gas – in the early 1960s. By 1971, with proven total gas reserves at 6000 billion cubic metres, the annual production had risen to seventeen billion cubic metres, with some of the exports being pumped to Western Europe. Oil output was up too, running at 310,000 barrels per day, the third highest in the USSR, after Russia and Azerbaijan. The year 1971 saw the election of Muhammad Nazar Gapusov (Hafiz) as First Secretary of the CPTu, whose membership had increased from 40,000 to about 66,000 during the past decade.[2]

Like his fellow-leaders in Central Asia, Gapusov tried to ingratiate himself with Leonid Brezhnev, the CPSU's First Secretary, by exceeding the economic targets set for his republic, especially in cotton. Little wonder that by the early 1980s cotton output reached 1.4 million tons, making Turkmenistan the second-largest producer of the commodity in the USSR after Uzbekistan. As in Uzbekistan, there was some padding of production figures, involving corrupt practices, but not to the same extent. However, this issue was highlighted by Mikhail Gorbachev in 1985 at the time of the replacement of Gapusov with Saparmurad Niyazov (born 1940) – the First Secretary of the Communist Party of Ashqabat, his home town, since 1980 – if only to impress on the republic's populace that a new corruption-free era had begun. Indeed, following Gapusov's removal from the top party office, an inquiry was instituted into corrupt practices. Its report concluded that during Gapusov's leadership of the CPTu, party cadres were often promoted to important posts on the basis of 'personal loyalty, family ties or birth-place'.[3]

In the important agricultural sector of cotton, there were other malpractices besides the doctoring of crop figures. Since cotton-harvesting is labour-intensive, and the supply of mechanical harvesters was always limited, during Gapusov's rule the directors of collective and state farms had increasingly resorted to using child labour. The practice had become so entrenched that the removal of Gapusov made little difference. A study in 1988 showed that rural children spent fifty-six to sixty-eight schooldays a year working in the cotton fields.[4]

Such social malpractices aside, overall socio-economic progress under Gapusov was impressive, largely because of the sharp rise in gas extraction, which reached seventy-two billion cubic metres in 1985, and which boosted the contribution of industry to the annual GDP to forty-seven per cent, more than twice that of agriculture. The universal literacy achieved in 1970 (from a base of 2.3 per cent in 1926) had gone hand in hand with the continued emancipation of women, who now provided forty-two per cent of the workforce and forty-five per cent of the membership of local soviets. Of the fourteen members of the Presidium of the Supreme Soviet, which exercised legislative powers between parliamentary sessions, five were women.[5] Three decades of Marxism-Leninism had muted the impact of tribalism, which had been the root cause of continual warfare between the leading tribes – Tekke, Yomut, Salory, Ersary and Sariki[6] – until the Bolshevik revolution.

The hold of Islam in Turkmenistan had been almost completely eliminated. Whereas in 1911 there were 481 mosques, continued anti-religious propaganda and action reduced the number to five by 1941. The single mosque in Ashqabat was destroyed in the earthquake of 6 October 1948, and never rebuilt.

Following the 1979 Iranian revolution, Radio Gorgan, operating 240 kilometres (150 miles) from Ashqabat, began beaming Islamic programmes in Turkmen, and gradually built up the size of its audience in a republic of 2.75 million, eighty-five per cent of whom had a Muslim background. But it was not until several years later that the signs of rising interest in Islam could be discerned. In 1986 it was due to the efforts of a young (registered) cleric, Annamuhammad Annaberdi, that the Taltahana Baba mosque was renovated. There was also clandestine Islamic activity afoot. This came to light during the winter of 1987 when the authorities uncovered two underground Islamic cells operating in Charju and Ashqabat, now a city of some 450,000, three-quarters of them with a Muslim background, but still lacking a mosque. It was only in 1988 that a new mosque was opened in the capital.

By then, Niyazov, a graduate of St Petersburg (then Leningrad) Polytechnical Institute, who in the mid-1970s had undergone political-ideological education at the Senior Party School of the CPSU's Central Committee in Moscow, had consolidated his power base. The fact that he belonged to the largest tribe, Tekke, estimated to claim the loyalties of more than a third of Turkmens, helped him, though not overtly. Yet Niyazov was unable to reverse the economic downturn. The basic problem was that in the centralized economy of the USSR, Turkmenistan's natural gas was being sold to other Soviet republics at five kopeks, or three US cents, a cubic metre, a paltry sum, especially by comparison to the price in the international market. There was therefore no improvement in the living standards of Turkmen citizens, with fifty per cent of peasant families and forty per cent of industrial worker households below the official poverty line. The annual subsidy of nearly R2 billion (or US $1.2 billion at the official rate) that Moscow gave to Turkmenistan would have been unnecessary had the republic been paid a realistic price, if not the international one, for its gas. In agriculture, cotton output had fallen by twelve per cent during 1980–85 mainly owing to the overuse of soil and chemical fertilizers. More seriously, the modest growth in the economy was unable to keep pace with the annual 3.5 per cent growth in the birth-rate. The disaffection caused by high unemployment among young people escalated into urban rioting in the first half of May 1989. But, unlike in other Central Asian republics, the opposition forces were unable to take advantage of the situation to establish themselves as political groups. The republic's KGB was much too powerful, and Niyazov far too authoritarian to brook any opposition, however muted.

After the elections to the 330-member Supreme Soviet in March 1990, heavily dominated by the Communist Party, Niyazov became chairman of the Supreme Soviet's Presidium. On 22 August, following the example of the Russian Supreme Soviet, the Turkmen parliament declared its sovereignty, thus placing its own laws above those of the USSR. Later it took a lead in creating the new post of directly elected executive president of the republic. The election was held on 26 October with Niyazov as the only candidate. He won, securing 98.3 per cent of the votes cast.

Turkmenistan's example was emulated by the Russian parliament, and the result was the election of Boris Yeltsin as president in June 1991, although in his case it was a multi-candidate contest. His position as the first popularly elected president of Russia played an important role in frustrating the plot of the Communist hardliners to overthrow President Gorbachev two months later. During the August coup, Niyazov stayed neutral. A few days after the failure of the coup, at his behest, the Supreme Soviet in Ashqabat declared Turkmenistan an independent sovereign state. This was ratified in a referendum on 26 October.

Within a week of the decision of the five Central Asian republics to join the newly formed Commonwealth of Independent States on 13 December 1991, the Communist Party of Turkmenistan met to dissolve itself, and re-emerged as the Democrat Party, with Saparmurad Niyazov as its chairman. But there were differences between the old and new organizations. Whereas the Communist Party was an integral part of the state, formed on the basis of the dictatorship of the proletariat, the Democrat Party was neither the sole party allowed to function nor was the state now expected to be based on the dictatorship of any class or nationality. When the Communist Party was dissolved, its members were free to abstain from politics altogether or join the Democrat Party or some other political group. More than half felt they had had enough of politics, so that the Democrat Party could attract only 50,000 of the former Communist Party's 119,000 members.[7]

Following the formal break-up of the USSR on 31 December, the Turkmen government decided to concentrate on developing bilateral relations with former Soviet republics and ensuring that the loose association implied in the CIS did not graduate into an active, multilateral relationship.

To underscore its newly won independence – and disregarding Washington's public warnings to the Muslim-majority former Soviet republics not to fall under the influence of Iran – Turkmenistan soon declared that it was willing to sell gas, oil and electricity to Iran, with which it shared a 1500-kilometre (940-mile) border, and proposed a direct telephone link with it. This was followed by a meeting between senior officials of the two countries in April when they decided to cooperate on oil exploration. The next month Turkmenistan joined the Caspian Sea Cooperation Council, an economic organization, proposed by Iran.

President Niyazov considered it prudent to balance these moves with cultivating Saudi Arabia, a powerful Islamic state and the custodian of Islam's two holiest shrines in Mecca and Medina, the respective birth- and burial-places of Prophet Muhammad. In April, accompanied by eighteen secular and religious aides, including Kazi Nasrullah ibn Abdullah, the head of the Directorate of Religious Affairs, formed after Turkmen independence in October 1991, Niyazov flew to Saudi Arabia. Together they undertook an *umra*, a short pilgrimage to Mecca. During the visit Niyazov paved the way for Turkmenistan's membership of the Jiddah-based Islamic Conference Organization (ICO). It joined the ICO at the foreign ministers' meeting convened in mid-June to consider ways of assisting the Muslims of Bosnia.

In May, Niyazov welcomed the Turkish premier Demirel's visit to Ashqabat, especially when it was accompanied by the latter's offer of US $120 million in credits to Turkmenistan, and the provision of higher education for up to 2000 Turkmen students in Turkish institutions. There were strong cultural and linguistic ties between the two countries: Seljuks (Oghuzs), who set up an empire in Turkey before the Osmanli Turks, came from Turkmenistan. And Turkmen, being part of the South Turkic group of languages, is nearer to the Turkish of Turkey than, say, Kyrgyz, belonging to the Central Turkic group.

At home Niyazov was cautious in introducing economic reform, warning that speedy liberalization of prices and complete privatization would result in impoverishment of many people. He argued that indifference by the regime towards a sizeable section of society for the sake of prosperity in the future smacked too much of Bolshevik thinking, and proposed introducing a market economy gradually, starting with the privatization of small- and medium-sized enterprises.[8]

Niyazov's hands were strengthened after the draft constitution – which stated 'Power is held by the president who is elected by the people' – was ratified by a referendum on 18 May 1992. Turkmenistan thus became the first Central Asian state to adopt a new constitution. It named the *Halk Maslahaty* (People's Council) – the supreme council of the representatives of the executive, legislative and judicial branches – as the second-highest organ of authority, with the popularly elected *Majlis* (Assembly) acting as parliament. It guaranteed citizens' rights to private property as well as other rights such as freedom of expression, except 'on revealing state secrets', and freedom of religion with the proviso that 'religion should not have influence on the government'. Article 28 gave citizens the right to form political parties except 'those (a) which aim to change the constitutional system through force, (b) which oppose constitutional rights, (c) which propagate hatred against race, nationality or religious tolerance, or (d) which aim to set up military rule'.[9]

The constitution tackled the ticklish problem of the language by specifying Turkmen as the official language and adding that 'all citizens are guaranteed to use their own language', a statement intended to reassure Russian settlers. And unlike elsewhere in the region, it allowed dual citizenship – a provision much valued by the small (less than ten per cent) but highly skilled Russian minority. By providing them with a device guaranteeing their return to the motherland as full citizens, it reassured them as individuals while ensuring that Turkmenistan continued to use their much-needed services during its hazardous transition to a market economy. The attitude shown towards ethnic Russians stemmed as much from pragmatism as from the fact that Niyazov was married to a Russian and had several Russians as senior advisers.

However, a pro-Russian bias did not prevail when it came to the question of the script for Turkmen: it was decided to change the present Cyrillic script after some deliberation. The debate on the choice of the Arabic or Latin alphabet was summed up by Murad Annapesov, vice-president of the Academy of Sciences, thus: 'If we switch over from the Cyrillic to the Arabic script, then we would be integrated only with Iran and the Arab world. But if we adopt a Latin alphabet then we would get closer to Turkey and Europe.'[10] Not surprisingly, following the adoption of the new constitution which specified Turkmen as the official language, the *Majlis* opted for a Latin script to be used from 1 January 1995.

In line with its policy of steering clear of multi-national treaties, Turkmenistan did not join the Collective Defence Treaty that was established at the CIS summit in mid-May in Tashkent. It was the only Central Asian state to stay out. Equally, in line with its policy of developing bilateral relations, it signed a three-year military cooperation agreement with Russia on 8 June. The signatories agreed that while Turkmenistan would form its own military on the basis of former USSR army units in the republic, then 120,000-strong, it would submit such forces to the joint control of Moscow and Ashqabat. As for the air force and air defence units, these were to remain under Russian command. The cost of maintaining the troops was to be shared by the two states.[11] Russia was keen to have 'special' relations with Turkmenistan because of its common border with Iran, which it visualized as a source of destabilization in the region. The signing of this pact during the run-up to the presidential election on 21 June under the new constitution raised further the already high prestige of Niyazov: it showed that Turkmenistan was dealing with Russia, the erstwhile Big Brother, on an equal basis.

In the presidential election more than eighty-five per cent of the 1.86 million eligible electors participated, with 99.5 per cent voting for the sole candidate, Niyazov. With this, he became the only Central Asian leader to continue to govern since achieving supreme power during the early days of the Gorbachev era. Indeed now, under the new constitution, President Niyazov's authority was all-pervasive since the legislative and judicial bodies were subordinated to him as well. His executive powers entitled him to appoint not only the members of the People's Council and the cabinet but also the governors of five provinces and the administrative heads of forty counties.

However, once the political system had been changed to popular elections for an executive president, Niyazov altered his leadership style. He opted for meritocracy and consensus, and gave a stake in the system to all major tribes without saying so. Indeed, he resorted to stressing the 'Turan' nation rather than any particular tribe. That is, instead of attacking tribalism, as Marxist-Leninists had done earlier, he tried to subsume tribalism into Turan/Turkic nationalism. On major issues he consulted as many groups and individuals as possible, but once the decision was taken he implemented it strictly. He revived the traditional Council of Elders (which each tribe used to have), and set up a forum to consult university students. And he ensured that his consultations received maximum publicity in the state-run media.[12] Overall, he tried to project himself as the Chief of Turkmens – Turkmenbas – in the footsteps of Mustafa Kemal Ataturk, the Father of Turks. But perhaps as someone who lost his father in his infancy, and the rest of his family in an earthquake at the age of eight, the need for Niyazov to be the Father of the Nation had deeper psychological implications. He quickly transformed the popularity he acquired among his fellow-countrymen as a strong leader who had maintained stability in the republic into a personality cult. Following the awarding of the Order of the Hero of the Turkmen People to him by the Turkmen parliament,[13] in early October 1992, local papers devoted most of their space to panegyric letters from their readers congratulating their president on his achievement. Soon an important thoroughfare in Ashqabat bearing Lenin's name was renamed after Niyazov; and so too was a collective farm near the capital, as well as the Lenin Karakum Canal, the lifeline of the cotton-growing area. 'Some people make comparisons with Stalin, with his dictatorship and cult of personality,' Niyazov told a press conference. 'But Stalin achieved his personality cult through repressive measures whereas I achieved my popularity without conflicts.'[14]

While the censorship section of the republic's KGB was formally abolished when Turkmenistan became independent, it reappeared in the form of the Department of Protection of State Secrets in the Media. This, and the Press Centre established at the headquarters of the Presidential Council, kept the media on the 'right' path. 'We have to keep well clear of about 200 points of censorship,' said a senior journalist in Ashqabat. 'It is just not possible to publish straight criticism, and even indirect criticism is risky.'[15]

Whereas there were no known political prisoners in Turkmenistan, opposition was systematically harassed through 'wire tapping, provocations, dismissals from jobs, all kinds of intrigues, telephone threats'.[16] When US Secretary of State James Baker visited Ashqabat in February 1992, the government put twenty opposition leaders under house arrest. Of those opposed to the present administration, Agiz Birlik (Unity Party), led by Burburdi Nurmuhammadov, and the Democratic Party (not to be confused with the ruling Democrat Party), headed by Durdimurad Khojamuhammad, were the best known. The law on political associations required a party to have a minimum of 1000 members dispersed throughout the republic, and not to be based on religion or have foreign links. Khojamuhammad claimed that his party, established on 22 December 1991, had 1500 members, yet it was denied registration with the argument that it did not exist, a Kafkaesque situation. When its activists despatched part of the print-run of the first issue of their journal, *Daianch* (Day), published in Moscow, to Turkmenistan, it was tracked down by the Turkmen authorities and confiscated.[17] The Agiz Birlik leader, Nurmuhammadov, who was tried three times for insulting the president, a criminal offence, spent some time in jail. He and other dissidents were prevented from attending a human rights conference convened by the Democratic Congress of Central Asia in Bishkek in early December 1992.

The reasons for the suppression of the opposition were summarized by government officials and others thus: since the current stage in our political development required consolidation of our independence, and concentration on nation-building, now was not the time for opposition politics. 'At this time there is no need for a multi-party system,' wrote Tagan Jumakov, a senior journalist, in *Ashqabat Vecherni* (Ashqabat Evening). 'Many problems have to be solved, social problems, and we must raise living standards. When our living standards are high, and we are economically independent, then we can have a multi-party system. But if this happens now then there will be anarchy.'[18] Addressing a meeting of the *Halk Maslahaty* in December 1992, President Niyazov mentioned a period of ten years for Turkmenistan to achieve 'economic prosperity'.

Meanwhile, to meet the rising criticism in Russia and the West, Niyazov, like his counterpart in Uzbekistan, President Islam Karimov, came up with the idea of fostering 'loyal' opposition in the form of the Young League of Turkmenistan and the Peasants Party.

Unlike in Uzbekistan and Tajikistan, there were no obvious signs of opposition from Islamic quarters, despite the fact that the size of the congregations and the number of mosques were growing dramatically. During 1987–92 the number of mosques in the republic shot up from four to 114, and that of the Ashqabat-based pilgrims to Mecca from ten to 141. As during the Communist rule, there was 'official' Islam in the form of the Directorate of Religious Affairs. To meet the growing demand for clerics, the Directorate sent 116 religious students to Turkey for a four-year course in Islam, specifically the Hanafi school of the Sunni sect prevalent in Turkmenistan.[19] Thus it was Turkey, and not Iran, a Shia country, that was at the centre of Islamization in Turkmenistan.

As during Soviet rule, opposition to official Islam came to be expressed intermittently. It came from Hazratkuli Khanov, the cleric in charge of the capital's largest mosque. Describing the current secular regime as an administration 'run by the same old Communist functionaries whom the people did not trust', and criticizing the official Islamic leadership, headed by Kazi Nasrullah ibn Abdullah, as 'weak and obedient', he predicted 'some sort of Islamic regime in all Central Asian republics'.[20] But this was more a statement based on wish-fulfilment than a serious assessment of the situation, present or future.

The threat to the determinedly secular, authoritarian regime of President Niyazov from the opposition, secular or religious, was negligible. The reasons were cultural – absence of political democratic tradition – and, more importantly, economic. The natural resources of the republic, with a population of a mere 3.7 million in the early 1990s, were stupendous. At the current global prices, its annual gas output of eighty-five billion cubic metres, the third-highest in the world, was worth US $6 billion. Of this, seventy-five billion cubic metres were available for export. Once its plan to lay a new pipeline to carry thirty billion cubic metres of gas to Iran, Turkey and Europe had been accomplished, a project expected to take about three years to complete, it would have acquired a solid foundation for its prosperity. Even now, under fairly unsettled economic conditions, Turkmenistan had met the precondition for launching its own currency – foreign reserves of US $300 million in hard currencies – within a year instead of the expected three. It therefore did not sign the rouble-zone agreement reached at the CIS summit in Bishkek in October 1992. Under the circumstances, Niyazov could easily afford to raise the salaries of public employees threefold in a year, provide free gas, electricity and water to citizens, and continue hefty subsidies on food and other items as before.

Confident of its economic future, Turkmenistan was drifting away from the CIS just as Azerbaijan had done. It had visualized the CIS as a political club, a consultative body, lacking any central coordinating mechanisms. When the summit at Bishkek in October 1992 included in its agenda the signing of a CIS charter, Niyazov developed a 'diplomatic illness', and stayed away. In the event the document failed to materialize. Finally, when the CIS charter was presented for signature at the next CIS summit in Minsk on 22–23 January 1993, Niyazov abstained. The presidents of Ukraine and Moldova did the same. But they as well as the remaining seven leaders of CIS member-states signed a more generally worded document. This enabled Turkmenistan to stay in the CIS while it considered its long-term position.

Besides the unrivalled economic wealth of Turkmenistan, and (at seventy-five per cent) the predominance of Turkmens in the republican population, there was another crucial factor that reinforced Niyazov's confidence in the durability of his regime. This was the solidity of the ruling Democrat Party: it was a virtual reincarnation of the Communist Party, maintaining the same structure and occupying the same premises, but swiftly creating and consolidating its indigenous power base, and fostering the idea of Turkmen nationalism within a vaguely defined concept of Turanism.

This was also by and large the case in the neighbouring Uzbekistan, the most populous and complex republic of the region.

SIX

Uzbekistan: The Complex Hub of Central Asia

Following Stalin's death in March 1953 there was much jostling for power at the highest levels of the CPSU, involving *inter alia* Nikita Khrushchev, Vice-Premier Vyacheslav Molotov, and the head of the NKVD (forerunner of the KGB), Lavrenti Beria. It was not until the autumn of 1954 that Khrushchev emerged as the unbeatable front-runner, and began to initiate deStalinization. It affected all republics, including Uzbekistan. As a result, Usman Yusupov (Yusuf), the chairman of the Uzbek Council of Ministers, a die-hard Stalinist, lost his job in November 1954. It went to Nuritdin Mukhitdinov (Nuruddin Muhyiuddin). A year later, during his visit to Tashkent, Khrushchev supervised the promotion of Mukhitdinov as First Secretary of the Communist Party of Uzbekistan (CPU), replacing Amin Niyazov, another Stalinist.

This was a few months before Khrushchev's revelation to the Twentieth Congress of the CPSU that Stalin had grossly violated basic Leninist tenets about nationalities – a step which created a milieu that allowed some freedom to non-Russians to speak about their culture and identity without the risk of being denounced as 'bourgeois nationalists'.

In October 1956 the CPU leadership convened a Congress of the Intelligentsia of Uzbekistan. It attracted 1200 delegates. Mukhitdinov set the tone of the gathering. Calling Central Asia 'one of the most ancient centres of the development of human culture', he urged the delegates to take the lead in developing the nation's culture. Among other things the conference decided that the government should give greater prominence to Uzbek in administrative and social-cultural spheres. As a result, some modifications were later made to the Cyrillic script (used to write Uzbek) to enable it to be more faithful to the spoken language.

Following the promotion of Mukhitdinov to a central party job at the CPSU secretariat in Moscow in December 1957, the chairman of the Council of Ministers, Sabir Kamalov, became First Secretary of the CPU. But he did not last long. At the Fourteenth Extraordinary Congress of the CPU in January 1959, he gave way to Sharaf Rashidov, a journalist and a wounded war veteran. Under Rashidov deStalinization continued. Indeed, following the Twenty-second Congress of the CPSU in October 1961, the process was accelerated, with more of Stalin's depredations made public. The first authorized history of the CPU, published in 1962, provided a long official list of the Uzbek leaders executed during the 1937–8 purges.

At the Twenty-second CPSU congress in October 1961 Khrushchev announced that the USSR had entered 'mature socialism', and that during this period the dialectics of national relations would follow the line of 'blooming, rapprochement and amalgamation': the twin processes of blooming (fullest national self-realization of each Soviet nation) and rapprochement (coming together of nations, through mutual cross-fertilization, sharing a common socialist economy and social formations) resulting in rapid progress towards ultimate amalgamation. Later this assessment was to prove too optimistic, and had to be modified.

Khrushchev's fall in October 1964 slowed the deStalinization process but did not stop it. Rashidov proved adroit enough to use the downfalls of Kamalov (in Tashkent) and later Khrushchev (in Moscow) to strengthen his power base in Uzbekistan, the most populous republic in the region, and the leading producer of cotton in the USSR.

The earthquake of 26 April 1966, which destroyed much of Tashkent, changed the political landscape as much as it did the physical. The national disaster brought the erstwhile adversaries together. This manifested itself in the way the government and party showered praise on Usman Yusupov, a staunch Stalinist, on his death in May, naming the Fergana Canal after him. Such behaviour had more to do with the excessive reverence a feudal society offers its elders, 'white beards', than with any ideological assessment or reassessment. This was borne out by the fact that honouring an old Stalinist had not resulted in any reversal of the trend towards Uzbek nationalism which thrived, at least in part, on resentment of Russian domination. Indeed, following a further growth in the Russian population of Tashkent due to Moscow's decision to give twenty per cent of new apartments to the mainly Russian workers who had volunteered to rebuild the city after the earthquake,[1] there was a spurt in anti-Russian feelings.

These came to the fore in early May 1969 during what was later labelled as the 'Pakhtakor Incident', Pakhtakor being the name of the leading sports stadium in Tashkent. Following a football match, there was fighting between Uzbek and Russian youths. Thousands of young Uzbeks went on a rampage, shouting 'Russians, get out of Uzbekistan'. Rioting subsided only after Soviet troops were deployed in the streets. There were also unconfirmed reports of ethnic demonstrations in other Uzbek cities. Moscow instituted an inquiry, which reportedly concluded that Rahmankul Kurbanov, the chairman of the Uzbek Council of Ministers, had been misusing his official position. He was tried, found guilty and sentenced to ten years' imprisonment. Another important politician, Yadegar Nasruddinova, the chairwoman of the Uzbek Presidium of the Supreme Soviet, was transferred to Moscow, and given a minor job there. These events allowed Rashidov to place his nominees in their posts and further consolidate his position.

Another sign of rising national consciousness came in early November 1969 when, on the eve of the celebration of the anniversary of the Bolshevik revolution on 7 November, leading Russian-language newspapers in all Central Asian republics printed a joint issue, commemorating the fiftieth anniversary of Lenin's letter to the special Commission for Turkestan Affairs, calling for the 'elimination of Great Russian chauvinism' in Soviet Turkestan.[2]

By the mid-1960s, a new generation of Uzbeks and other Central Asians had grown up, reared on Soviet education, possessing the kind of confidence that had eluded its parents. Many young Uzbek intellectuals tried to rediscover their national and cultural roots; and because these were intertwined with Islamic heritage, their quest led them to Islam. The resulting rise in interest in Islam could not be properly satisfied by the Official Islamic Administration, which was tightly controlled by the government. Consequently, there was growth in 'unofficial' or 'parallel' Islam. By 1966 the situation had reached a point where L. Klimovich, a party official active in anti-religious campaigns, acknowledged that the clergy of the 'out of the mosque' (unofficial) trend in the USSR were stronger than those of the 'mosque' trend.[3] Since Tashkent was the headquarters of the Muslim Spiritual Directorate of Central Asia and Kazakhstan, which supervised 230 mosques, nearly half of the USSR total, the city came to reflect emergent nationalist and religious consciousness among Uzbeks.

As the CPSU's First Secretary, Leonid Brezhnev reassessed the national question and concluded that his predecessor's scenario of the merger of all Soviet nations was too idealistic and would have to await the global triumph of socialism over capitalism. At the Twenty-third CPSU congress in March 1966, therefore, he took a realistic stand, declaring that the party would continue to show 'solicitude' for the interests and characteristics of each of the peoples who constituted the USSR.

There was a similar compromise by Brezhnev in his treatment of the Central Asian republics. He ended the excesses of anti-religious propaganda initiated by Khrushchev, and attempted to palliate the Official Islamic Administration by authorizing a programme of restoration of religious monuments. The rebuilding of all the mosques destroyed by the 1966 earthquake in Tashkent, capped with a plan to construct more places of worship, reflected Brezhnev's continued commitment to the new policy. The following year the Presidium of the USSR Supreme Soviet cleared the Crimean Tatars, Khemshins (Armenian Muslims), Kurds and Meskhetian Turks of the treason charges levelled against them by Stalin during the Great Patriotic War. In 1968 the Muslim Spiritual Directorate in Tashkent was authorized to publish a magazine entitled *The Muslims of the Soviet Union* in Uzbek, Arabic, Persian, English and French. Its international department continued to maintain contacts with Muslims abroad and make arrangements for the Muslims in the region to make the pilgrimage to Mecca. Fifty scholarships were offered to those Soviet Muslims who wished to study Islamic theology and law in Cairo and Damascus, the Arab capitals then allied with Moscow. Encouraged by the state, Shaikh Ziauddin Babakhan, the mufti of the Muslim Spiritual Directorate of Central Asia, assisted by the Council of Ulemas (religious-legal scholars),[4] organized an international Islamic conference in Tashkent in 1970, the first such event in Russian or Soviet history: it signalled a concordat between state and mosque that had last been seen, briefly, during the Great Patriotic War. Islamic clerics often rationalized their cooperation with the Soviet state on the ground that its ideology, Marxism-Leninism, was primarily focused on running the economy and government, whereas Islam was concerned first and foremost with matters of human spirit and ethical behaviour. This perception helped to keep the relationship between official and parallel Islam almost trouble-free,[5] since the latter also dealt with moral-ethical issues.

During the 1970s the state and party did not have to worry overmuch about the rise of Islam, a phenomenon that had then affected only a section of the intelligentsia, leaving the vast majority of Soviet Muslims untouched. According to an official Soviet survey published in 1979, only thirty per cent of 'formerly Muslim peoples' described themselves as 'believers' – the majority of them rural, old and semi-literate – with twenty per cent as 'hesitant', and the remaining fifty per cent as unbelievers.[6]

But with an Islamic regime emerging in Iran in early 1979, and the Communist government in Afghanistan – originating in a military coup in April 1978 – falling asunder owing to internal rivalries, and inducing Soviet military intervention on 27 December 1979, the situation began to change.

Regarding Afghanistan, the Kremlin claimed that it had been invited by the Kabul government to help foil conspiracies against it by the US Central Intelligence Agency (CIA) and pro-American Pakistan, actively encouraging insurgency along Afghanistan's eastern and southern borders – as well as by Islamic Iran, backing subversion along Afghanistan's western frontier. The Soviet intervention led to the killing of the radical Afghan leader President Hafizullah Amin, and the installation of Babrak Karmal, a moderate, as president. He immediately restored the country's original green–black–red flag, which had been replaced in August 1978 by an all-red flag. He also restored the customary invocation to Allah which is used by pious Muslims as a preamble to all public statements. But these gestures had no impact on Afghanistan's Muslim neighbours, Pakistan and Iran. Karmal's letter to Ayatollah Ruhollah Khomeini, the supreme leader of Iran, in early 1980 proposing 'consolidation of fraternal and friendly Islamic relations between Afghanistan and Iranian peoples' with the objective of delivering 'an ultimate rebuke to the world-craving imperialism and Zionism' went unanswered.[7]

Addressing the Twenty-sixth Congress of the CPSU on 23 February 1981, Brezhnev described the Iranian revolution as a major international event, and stated that Islamic slogans could be used for reactionary as well as progressive ends. On balance, despite attempts to the contrary, the Iranian revolution had emerged essentially as 'an anti-imperialist revolution', he concluded.[8] He explained that the Soviet Union's military intervention had stemmed from 'a direct threat to the security of . . . [its] southern border'. With the Soviet military presence in Afghanistan increasing steadily from the initial 50,000 troops to 115,000 in the mid-1980s, the importance of the Central Asian republics in providing men, materials and logistical

back-up grew. Soviet citizens were told that troops were being sent
to Afghanistan to meet the USSR's obligation under Article 4 of the
Treaty of Friendship and Cooperation concluded between the two
countries in December 1978, which required the signatories to 'take,
by agreement, appropriate measures to ensure the security, independence and territorial integrity of the two countries', which were
being threatened by imperialist aggression. Once the CPSU Politburo had taken the decision to act militarily, the leaders of the Central
Asian republics backed it. Intent on making the Soviet military presence appear racially as unobtrusive as possible, the USSR armed
forces high command decided to include a high proportion of Uzbek,
Tajik and Turkmen troops in the units that were despatched to
Afghanistan, a country whose citizens also belonged to these ethnic
groups.

Following the Kremlin's action in Afghanistan, the American
administration of President James Carter intensified the Cold War
against the Soviet bloc. Carter's pledge to defend the 'Persian Gulf
region' was interpreted by his national security adviser, Zbigniew
Brzezinski, as including Baluchistan, the Pakistani province that lies
between Afghanistan and the Arabian Sea. In its intensified anti-
Soviet campaign, orchestrated by Brzezinski, America relied heavily
on Islam and Islamic forces, combining its material and military aid
to the Islamic groups of Afghans with radio propaganda, broadcast
by the US-funded Radio Liberty and Radio Free Europe, against
the Soviet system, directed specifically at the Muslim population in
Central Asia and Azerbaijan. Washington's lead was immediately
followed by Saudi Arabia, which combined propaganda broadcasts
with courses on the Quran and Islamic law; and later by Egypt, a
close American ally since 1972, Kuwait and Qatar.[9]

Writing in the October 1981 issue of the *Kommunist*, the party's
ideological journal, S. Tsvigun, the first deputy head of the KGB,
noted that 'reactionary Islamic organizations abroad' had intensified
their anti-Soviet propaganda, 'trying to capitalize on events in Iran
and around Afghanistan'.[10] The Communist leaders of Muslim
origin in Central Asia and elsewhere tried to combat the Islamic
onslaught against the USSR. They combined an ideological campaign with an intensified effort to root out underground Islamic
organizations. In 1982, in a series of raids, the Uzbek KGB discovered four such groups, run either as study circles or Quranic
schools, in Tashkent, and had their leaders, including Sayyid Karim
Khojayev, author of *The Truth about Islam*, imprisoned. As the chair-

man of the Presidium of the Governing Councils of the Preservation of Monuments in Uzbekistan, Nuritdin Mukhitdinov, a former CPU First Secretary, made repeated attacks on the reactionary role of Muslim clerics. Another Uzbek leader, Nasruddinova, then chairwoman of the USSR Soviet of Nationalities, the second chamber of the USSR Supreme Soviet – with thirty-two members from each of the fifteen constituent republics – kept up her criticism of Islam for being discriminatory against women. On the political-diplomatic front, however, the Kremlin failed to win the backing of any of the heads of the four Muslim Spiritual Directorates (in Baku, Makhachkala, Tashkent and Ufa) on the Afghanistan issue.

In the mid-1980s the domestic issue of corruption engaged much public attention in Central Asia, especially Uzbekistan. Following the demise of Brezhnev in late 1982, his successor, Yuri Andropov, mounted a campaign to improve labour efficiency, which had declined during the Brezhnev era, and curtail corruption throughout the USSR. With malpractice being more common in Central Asia than elsewhere, the anti-corruption drive had more impact on this region than others. It was overseen by Geidar Aliyev, a member of the CPSU's Politburo and the first deputy chairman of the USSR Council of Ministers. Since, as the head of Azerbaijan's KGB during the period 1967–69, Aliyev had supervised an anti-corruption campaign there, he was well qualified for the new task. Yet he failed to make much headway in Uzbekistan, principally because the party's First Secretary there, Sharaf Rashidov, who had become extremely influential during the Brezhnev era, was far from cooperative. It was only after Rashidov's death – either self-inflicted or due to heart failure caused by unbearable KGB pressures – in October 1983 that the KGB was able to investigate thoroughly the allegations made against Rashidov and his aides. The charges included not only widespread bribery and nepotism but also large-scale embezzlement of funds, stemming from fraudulent cotton output statistics inflated by up to a quarter, and general economic mismanagement. Since Uzbekistan accounted for two-thirds of the USSR's cotton production which reached nearly eight million tons in the mid-1970s, this was a serious matter.

Inamjan Usmankhojayev (Usman Hoja), who succeeded Rashidov as the CPU's First Secretary, pursued the anti-corruption drive vigorously while replacing Rashidov's appointees, mostly from his native Jizk region, with his own, often from the Fergana Valley, his home base, or Tashkent;[11] and missing no chance to highlight other failures of the Rashidov era. In an interview with the Moscow-based *Izvestia* in early November 1984 he revealed, for instance, that Islam and other 'outdated and backward views' were still a problem in Uzbekistan, with many highly educated party members participating in Muslim religious rituals.

At the CPU Congress in January 1986, held within a year of Mikhail Gorbachev assuming supreme party office in the USSR, Usmankhojayev extended his criticism of Rashidov beyond bribery and falsifying cotton output by listing the latter's other failings: 'major miscalculations' in the selection, placement and education of ideological cadres, neglect of anti-religious propaganda, and failure to combat vigorously 'unofficial Islam', thus allowing class enemies to resuscitate outdated concepts like pan-Islamism and inflame 'nationalist passions'.[12] Working in association with Rafiq Nishanov, the new chairman of the Uzbek Supreme Soviet, and top CPSU leaders in Moscow, Usmankhojayev finally ended the political legacy of his towering predecessor, Rashidov. Of the twelve members of the CPU Politburo, ten lost their positions, the two exceptions including Usmankhojayev. Their replacements deprived Uzbeks, then forming two-thirds of the republic's population, of their long-standing majority in the Politburo – a development that hurt Uzbek pride and inflamed nationalist feeling. Of the Central Committee's 177 members, all but thirty-four lost their jobs. Those who replaced them were often young, educated cadres more interested in building their careers by monitoring developments at the CPSU secretariat in Moscow than at the republican level in Tashkent. They were therefore more suitable for the inter-republican exchange of cadres announced the following month at the Twenty-seventh Congress of the CPSU by the secretary for personnel, Yegor Ligachev, who had taken over the supervision of the anti-corruption drive in Central Asia from Aliyev. Many of those who lost their party positions attributed their downfall to their national origins, thus fanning the embers of Uzbek nationalism.

Among those who lost their Central Committee membership was Vahabjan Usmanov, minister of cotton-ginning. He was later arrested for falsifying the figures of cotton production by twenty-five to thirty per cent, something he had achieved by bribing officials all the way up to Yuri Churbanov, son-in-law of Brezhnev, and getting the producers paid by the central government. As for the kickbacks he received for his services, these were so abundant that he had thrown one envelope containing R40,000 into a corner of his office where police found it two years later. He was sentenced to death in late August 1986.[13]

The results of the full investigation into corrupt practices published in 1987 showed that during his twenty-four-year tenure as party boss, Rashidov was instrumental in milking the public treasury of the equivalent of $2 billion by getting payments for inflated cotton production figures. More than 2600 officials in Moscow and Uzbekistan were arrested for their participation in the long-running fraud.[14] The purges in the party, government and economic organizations before, during and after the major investigation were extensive, and weakened the party and administration. Contrary to official expectations, instead of restoring popular faith in the system which had flushed out corrupt elements, the scandal and purges left the populace, especially the Uzbek majority, confused and cynical, and less trusting of the system than before. The leading role played by the Moscow-based media, and the speed with which officials and newspapers in the Soviet capital resorted to using the terms 'the Uzbek Affair' and 'corruption' interchangeably – despite the fact that the bulk of the kickbacks had landed in the Soviet capital – reinforced the affront that most Uzbeks felt as a result of the uncovering of the scandal. The initial hurt was then transformed into a communal consensus to resist Moscow; and this prepared the ground for the emergence of nationalist or religious opposition to the Soviet system. 'The crackdown they [Usmankhojayev and Nishanov] presided over – and the abrupt break with established ways under the guise of cleaning up local corruption – contributed to mounting local disorder and dissent,' noted Donald S. Carlisle, an American specialist on Uzbekistan. 'It stimulated resistance to Moscow, created grievances to be exploited by opposition forces within the Uzbek intelligentsia, and reawakened restive religious feelings.'[15]

Containing two-thirds of the 230 functioning mosques in Muslim Central Asia in the mid-1980s, Uzbekistan was the single most important Soviet republic in terms of Islam. Developments in this field were therefore of great interest not only to the republic-level leadership but also to the central regime. At the Plenum of the CPU's Central Committee in October 1986, many speakers referred to the 'complicated religious situation' in the republic, providing the CPSU organ, *Pravda*, with a chance to criticize the CPU for its failure to conduct atheistic propaganda effectively enough to combat rising Islamic influence. The following month, during a brief stopover in Tashkent on his way to Delhi, India, Gorbachev urged 'an uncompromising struggle against religious manifestations and the strength-ening of political work among the masses and of atheistic work'. He criticized those party members who paid 'lip service to our [party] morals and ideals', warning that 'even the slightest discrepancy between words and deeds in this matter' was 'impermissible'.[16] Such admonitions came in the wake of the news, published by *Literatur-naya Gazeta* (Literary Gazette), that Sayid Taherov, a leading Com-munist and director of the telecommunications centre in Tashkent, and Sabir Tarsuenov, leader of the local Communist Youth League, had been caught conducting semi-clandestine Quranic studies at the centre.[17]

Following Gorbachev's speech, the CPU leadership tightened up its requirement of atheism for party members; and this gave added impetus to expulsions from the party of those found to be morally or ideologically deficient. In the first six months of 1987, CPU leaders expelled fifty-three members from the party for organizing and parti-cipating in religious rituals – often those concerned with birth (cir-cumcision for male children), marriage and funerals.[18] It was also revealed that in the province of Jizak, once one of Rashidov's strong-holds, party members had spent R500,000 to restore a mosque. And A. Karimov, the veteran First Secretary of the party in Bukhara, was charged with sponsoring construction of mosques and tombs, and building approach roads to them with state money.

However, as the year progressed, Gorbachev's warning lost much of its force, partly because, during the run-up to the millennium celebrations in 1988, the Russian Orthodox Church was accorded an honoured place in the Russian Federation. The Soviet media waxed eloquent on the inextricable bond between the Russian Church and culture, and the significance of religion in the history of Russia, applauding the glorification of the nine new saints of the Orthodox Church in the summer of 1988 in Zagorsk near Moscow. Noting that while continuing to call Islam backward and reactionary the Soviet press had taken to stressing the 'progressive significance' of the adoption of Christianity in Russia, Amin Usmanov, an Uzbek writer, asked in June 1988: 'Why have we not tired of looking in a one-sided manner at the dark aspects in Islam in our past culture? . . . Has not the time come to speak fairly of both the positive and negative aspects of religion?'[19] With the pace of political liberalization accelerating in the late 1980s, during the latter part of perestroika, this sort of questioning of official policies became increasingly routine.

In the political–diplomatic field, Gorbachev's agreement in early

February 1988 with the Afghan Communist leader, Muhammad Najibullah, to start withdrawing 115,000 Soviet troops from Afghanistan from mid-May onwards, signified a political-ideological setback for the Soviet Union in the face of the continuing armed struggle by Islamic guerrillas against the Kabul regime. This seems to have tempered Gorbachev's views on Islam. During his visit to Tashkent in April 1988, Gorbachev's remarks on Islam were described as 'affable', a contrast to what he had said eighteen months earlier.[20]

By then the CPU had experienced one more change at the top, with Rafiq Nishanov replacing Usmankhojayev as First Secretary in January 1988. A veteran Communist, Nishanov had been sidelined during the ascendancy of Rashidov with a job as Soviet ambassador in the Middle East, to be recalled to Uzbekistan after Rashidov's death. Following his removal from the highest party post and then from the party itself, Usmankhojayev found himself arrested on corruption charges, and found guilty – an ironic development since he had made a career of condemning his predecessor, Rashidov, as a corrupt leader.

The continual purges, which had reduced party membership by 58,000, the relentless publicity in the media about the misdeeds of erstwhile respected figures, and the convictions of many party and government officials on criminal charges, resulting not only in long prison sentences but also in executions, had a devastating impact on the party faithful and – with one out of six households contributing a member to the party – society at large. It created an environment conducive to the rise of opposition groups, nationalist and Islamist, both formally and informally.

Some of those turned off by the stench of the scandals took to religion. In the streets of Uzbek cities there was an increasing presence of men with beards and women with headscarves: visual signs of the rising influence of Islam. In 1987 the findings of a survey of undergraduates with a Muslim background at Tashkent University – with sixty per cent describing themselves as 'Muslim', thirty-three per cent being 'hesitant', and only seven per cent calling themselves 'atheist'[21] – jolted the Communist leadership. In the past, such surveys had shown religion to be strong only among older, rural people. Now many of the undergraduates declaring themselves to be Muslim were at the same time members of the Communist Youth League. The fact that there was a religious revival in that region of the USSR, which had registered fifty per cent population growth between 1959 and 1979, rising from 16.4 million to 32.77 million, was all the more worrisome to the party and government.

The authorities had begun responding to the Islamic revival by activating the houses of atheism and the scientific atheism departments in the philosophy faculties of universities. Following the old strategy of combating religiosity, these institutions sponsored lecture series and special days of atheism. They were not as effective as they should have been because those undertaking the task were deficient in numbers and qualifications. In the absence of a full grasp of Islam, a complex ideology, the atheist propagandists had failed to forge an appropriate tool to counter it. Also, unlike in the past, the general level of education of the new believers was high, and some of them were sophisticated thinkers.

Addressing a seminar on the problems of Islam and inter-ethnic relations in the spring of 1988, M. Khalmuhamedov (Hal Muhammad), the secretary to the CPU's Central Committee, pointed out that the observance of Islamic rituals and traditions had risen among young citizens and even among party members. The challenge, he observed, was how to bring about 'the emancipation of their consciousness from the narcotic of religion which is partly forced [upon the people] by the clergy under the cover of national [tradition]'. He advised the participants to make a comprehensive study of the anti-religious campaigns in the mid-1920s and mid-1930s, and devise appropriate solutions.[22] Since this meant essentially more of the same, using blunt weapons in frontal offensives against religion, positive results were unlikely to ensue in changed circumstances.

It was left to an erudite atheistic ideologue – I. A. Makatov, deputy director of the Institute of Scientific Atheism of the CPSU Central Committee's Academy of Social Sciences – to tackle the problem with some sophistication in a long article in the June 1988 issue of the *Kommunist Uzbekistana*. Having examined the results of the surveys on religion, which had depressed the authorities, he questioned their basic premise of defining religiosity on the basis of the observance of religious rituals rather than belief in the supernatural. He then offered a breakdown of the elements of religiosity and atheism, and provided different grades of each. He also categorized Muslim clerics, describing them as registered, unregistered/self-employed, and those belonging to the Sufi movement. He singled out self-employed clerics as the main threat: they combined the performance of Islamic rituals for the faithful with spreading Islam among the unbelievers and the 'hesitant'. The solution, he stated, lay in registering the self-employed clerics, thus enabling the authorities to monitor their activities.[23] As for the already-registered religious bodies, it was important to differentiate between their political stance towards the party and government and the religious ideology they propagated within the places of worship, so that atheistic effort could be focused on countering religious ideas promoted by the clergy. He emphasized that the atheistic campaigns must not infringe the constitutional right of freedom of conscience, and advised a subtle approach in Muslim regions, with an emphasis on education and the reclaiming of those who had newly embraced Islam, meticulously avoiding hurting religious sensibilities.[24]

Besides the young in general, a particular social group that had come under rising Islamic influence was the old trading class of the traditional bazaar. Having been dormant for many decades in the aftermath of the Bolshevik revolution, several merchant clans among Uzbeks showed signs of revival as traders as the state opened up opportunities for the cooperative sector – a euphemism for the private sector – in the economy. They had earlier carved out a niche in the 'black' economy that had arisen during the latter part of Brezhnev's rule. Given the historical link between the bazaar and the mosque, it was not long before religious charities, supported by traders, sprang up – following the passing of an all-Union law that permitted social and cultural organizations, including those engaged in repairing or constructing places of worship.

Such traders were in the vanguard when it came to staging a demonstration in late January 1989 against the mufti of the Central Asian Muslim Spiritual Directorate in Tashkent, Shamsuddin Babakhan, son of the previous mufti, Ziauddin Babakhan, and a relic of the Brezhnev era. The protesters accused him of drinking alcohol and mixing with women who were not closely related to him, and therefore being unfit for the high religious office of mufti. In another context, ignoring the recent Islamic revival, his directorate had not cared to bring out a new edition of the Quran, the last one having been published in 1984. Yielding to popular pressure, he resigned – an event that signalled a success for grass-roots politics, applied in this case to a religious matter. In March the delegates to the Fourth Congress of the Muslim Spiritual Directorate elected Shaikh Muhammad Sadiq Muhammad Yusuf as mufti. Later that month he was elected to the USSR Congress of People's Deputies, one of seven religious deputies in a house of 2250.

By now, as a result of political liberalization, popular demonstrations for specific demands were coming into vogue. On 3 December 1988 a meeting called to honour Uzbek at Tashkent University turned into a spontaneous forum for Uzbek nationalism. When students were allowed to express their views on the subject from the platform, their spokesmen urged CPU leaders to declare Uzbek as the official language of the republic, while their colleagues in the hall displayed placards reading, 'Don't Let Our Language and Cultural Heritage Be Turned into a Graveyard!' Much to the unease of the local officials present, some students unfurled the green flag of Islam and recited the first verse of the Quran. Such a display of a bond between religion and a secular demand concerning the Uzbek language was an unorthodox development, which puzzled and worried the government, already aware of the disaffection among young people due to high unemployment, then affecting more than a million people in a country of some 4.2 million households.

The growing joblessness, especially among young men, twenty-seven per cent of whom were unemployed, and the rising awareness of severe economic problems facing the republic, brought to the fore friction between majority Uzbeks and ethnic minorities, including Tatars – also known as Meskhetian Turks – who, forming about four per cent of the total population, were concentrated in the Fergana Valley. Inhabitants of Georgia, who had adopted Islam and the Turkish language, Meskhetian Turks were punished collectively in 1944 by Stalin for being pro-German, and deported to Central Asia.

During the first half of June 1989 Uzbeks in the Fergana Valley attacked their Meskhetian Turk neighbours, burning their settlements and killing and maiming them. The result was nearly 200 killed, and over 1000 injured, mostly Turks. More than 160,000 Turks were rendered homeless, and had nowhere to go as Georgia refused to take them back. The news of these bloody riots reached Tashkent where a plenum of the CPU's Central Committee was in session. The First Secretary, Rafiq Nishanov, leading a delegation of party luminaries, and accompanied by Mufti Muhammad Yusuf, immediately flew to the disturbed area to calm the situation.

The unprecedented violence shook the people of Uzbekistan, especially the minorities, including Russians, forming eleven per cent of the republic's population, and diminished further the power and prestige of the leadership of the party which, having experienced purges and large-scale arrests of its members for corruption and fraud over the past five years, was itself confused and demoralized. The situation was made worse by the arrival from Moscow of nearly

300 officials of different ranks to fill the posts of those locals who had been purged from the party, government or economic organizations. Unfamiliar with the language or national character of Uzbeks, or with the republic's cotton-oriented economy, the new arrivals found it expedient to blame the alliance of Uzbek nationalists and local mafiosi for their failures.

Spurred by the bloody Fergana Valley episode, Gorbachev decided to act swiftly. He eased Nishanov out of the top party position in Tashkent by offering him promotion to a job at the CPSU secretariat in Moscow. Going by the past pattern, Nishanov's position should have gone to M. Ibrahimov, chairman of the Uzbek Supreme Soviet. But it did not. The fact that Ibrahimov had been part of the leadership during whose tenure severe rioting had taken place in the Fergana Valley went against him. The winner was a comparative outsider, Islam Abduganiyevich Karimov (born 1938), First Secretary of the party in the Kashka Darya Province. Born in Samarkand, Islam Karimov graduated from the local Polytechnical Institute in 1960. Starting his working life as a semi-skilled engineer in Tashkent, he simultaneously pursued the study of economics. He joined the ministry of finance in 1966 and moved up the civil service scale to become minister of finance seventeen years later. A long-time member of the CPU, he was elected a member of its Central Committee in January 1986, the year in which he was appointed chairman of Uzbekistan's Gosplan, the state planning department. During the incumbency of Nishanov as the CPU's First Secretary he was demoted, and despatched to a province bordering Turkmenistan as party chief. His brief career as a party functionary was enough to satisfy Gorbachev, who was looking for a youngish leader untarnished by past scandals. Gorbachev was painfully aware that the opposition movement, Birlik Halk Harakiti (Birlik Popular Front), founded in May, was rapidly gaining political ground lost by the CPU in the wake of continued economic and other scandals combined with unprecedented violence against Meskhetian Turks.

Karimov acted with firmness, and imposed an immediate ban on public meetings to cool tempers. 'There could have been another six or seven Ferganas without firm action by the government,' he explained later. 'In Leningrad [St Petersburg], Russia and the Baltic republics, you could have meetings which could go on for hours peacefully, but here people get easily excited. Once roused it would be easy enough for people to shout "Kill the Koreans" or "Kill the Russians".'[25] In other words, the democratic process had to be slowed down to avert further outbreaks of inter-ethnic violence.

However, by now the main opposition force, Birlik, had developed sufficiently to become an important actor on the political stage. An informally established public movement headed by intellectuals, Birlik grew rapidly in 1988 on a programme of democracy, nationalism and economic liberalization, inspired by nationalist Sajudis in Lithuania, also the model for the Popular Front in Azerbaijan. Its two prominent leaders were Abdurahim Pulatov (Abdul Rahim Pulat) and Muhammad Salih, the former a scientist, and the latter a poet and a leading member of the Writers Union. Birlik quickly appropriated the student demand to make Uzbek the official language, and set up an office at the Writers Union in Tashkent.

The other issue that Birlik appropriated was the welfare of Uzbek draftees in the Soviet military. Following the bloody events in the Fergana Valley, in which Uzbeks had acted aggressively, it was alleged that conscripts from the region faced attacks, sometimes fatal, from their non-Uzbek comrades. Birlik staged protest demonstrations in Tashkent on 1 and 15 October 1989. These were preceded and followed by demonstrations demanding the adoption of Uzbek as the state language. Both these were popular, emotional issues; and their vociferous espousal by Birlik helped the fledgling organization, which had already held a national congress as a recognized 'public movement', but not as a political party,[26] to widen its appeal quickly, especially among intellectuals and students. As an umbrella organization, which had by now appropriated such causes as a confederation of all Central Asian republics, propagation of Islam, and a wider use of the Arabic alphabet for Uzbek, it had attracted not only Uzbek nationalists and pan-Turkists but also Islamists.

With nationalist feelings rising sharply, Karimov considered it expedient to echo them. He was better equipped to do so than any of his predecessors. Being a comparatively new figure in the party hierarchy, he had escaped any categorization – 'conservative', 'radical', 'pro-Moscow', 'pro-nationalist', etc. – before being made the head of the CPU. He now began to highlight the plight of the republic's citizens, implicitly blaming the Kremlin for it. At the CPU Central Committee's plenum on the 'national question', he underlined the fact that the average per capita income of forty-five per cent of the republic's population was below the official subsistence level of R78 a month, and that there were more than one million jobless in the republic.[27]

To rebuild a popular base for the CPU and its leader, Karimov courted Mufti Muhammad Yusuf, aged thirty-seven, who responded positively, willing to forge a concordat on the basis of their common distrust of what the mufti called 'the elusive dimension of Islam' – meaning the Sufi brotherhoods and Wahhabis, a Saudi Arabia-based puritanical sect within the Hanbali school of Sunni Islam – which both of them held responsible for endangering inter-faith and inter-ethnic harmony. At the Fourth Congress of the Muslim Spiritual Directorate of Central Asia in March 1989, the delegates had referred to the presence of extremist Muslim groups insisting on the segre-gation of sexes in educational institutions, the use of headscarves by women, and discontinuation of European dress by Muslim men and women. The mufti was opposed to such groups as well as Sufis on theological grounds, and the government on political grounds. But there were also certain positive elements which the two sides shared. These were spelled out by a Communist writer, N. Usmanov, in the June 1989 issue of the party journal, *Kommunist Uzbekistana*. Alluding to Islamic commandments which 'correspond to communist morality', he proposed joint action against 'alcohol-ism, drug addiction, prostitution, bribery, fraud, embezzlement and other disgusting ills of our society which would be condemned by any religion'.[28]

There were other signs of rapprochement between state and mosque. The media campaign initiated in Central Asia in early 1989 to repair some of the damage done by the biased presentations of Islam in the past gathered momentum as the year progressed. The literary journal *Zvezda Vostoka* (Star of the East) printed a Russian translation of the Quran in instalments. In its January, May and June 1989 issues, the prestigious *Nauka i Religia* (Science and Religion) published a series of articles on the life of Prophet Muhammad and the importance of the pilgrimage to Mecca. Later issues offered a Russian translation of numerous chapters of the Quran.

The CPU's manifesto for the Uzbek Supreme Soviet elections scheduled for March 1990 summed up the governing party's stance on religion thus: 'The republican Party organization is actively in favour of *freedom of religion and the legal rights of believers*, and for cooperation with religious organizations . . . Believers are entitled to all opportunities for participation in the public, political and cul-tural life of the Republic.'[29]

Since Birlik's status as a public movement had not been changed to that of a political body and recognized by the government as such, it could not contest these elections. Consequently the CPU, often offering more than one candidate for a seat, emerged with a near-monopoly in the chamber. It won 450 out of 500 seats, with the remainder going to well-known members of the opposition and independents. Among those who lost was Anvar Usmanov, a pro-Birlik journalist, contesting a seat in the capital as an independent. He found the list of candidates containing two A. Usmanovs: himself and an obscure academic called Alisher Usmanov. The resulting confusion led to a split in the votes for Anvar Usmanov, who lost by twelve votes.

Within Anvar Usmanov's favoured party, Birlik, differences between the minority and majority factions, led respectively by Salih and Pulatov, reached a breaking point. For Salih, working for Uzbekistani independence was the foremost priority, leaving democracy for later. In contrast, Pulatov stressed democracy – meaning the toppling of the Communist regime of Karimov – leaving independence for later.

In April 1990, barely a year after the founding of Birlik, Salih and two other leaders left to establish the Democratic Party of Erk (Freedom), which claimed the loyalty of thirteen deputies. They adopted the flag of the Kokand Autonomous Government, which had existed from November 1917 to February 1918, as their party banner, thus stressing national independence.

The split in the opposition was good news for Karimov, who had worked behind the scenes to bring it about, and who was now preparing to address the CPU's Twentieth Congress in early June. In a wide-ranging review he outlined the awesome problems facing the party and government, some of which had been created or accentuated by the posting of party cadres sent from, and controlled by, 'outside', meaning Moscow, who lacked a proper grasp of local conditions. (A prime example, unmentioned by Karimov, was B. F. Satin, a Slav, who had been transferred in 1983 from the CPSU secretariat in Moscow to Tashkent to become First Secretary of the city party, a post he occupied until mid-1990.) The way to tackle the problem, Karimov said, was to have Uzbekistan act as a sovereign republic, and seek local answers. As a step towards that objective, the delegates resolved that Uzbek be adopted as the official language of Uzbekistan. More importantly, to establish firmly that a new era was about to unfold, Karimov persuaded congress to replace all the members of the Politburo except himself, and three-quarters of the Central Committee membership of 261.

Karimov also touched on the question of corruption and its almost exclusive association with Uzbekistan in the Soviet psyche, which had hurt Uzbek pride. Here again the role of the Moscow-based press, especially the *Komsomolaskaya Pravda* (Truth of the Komsomol) and *Moscow News*, was a sore point. Taking advantage of glasnost, followed by the relaxation of press censorship that came in 1987, it had played a leading part in investigating and exposing corruption in Central Asia, particularly Uzbekistan. Its reporting had created a negative image of Uzbekistan and Uzbeks among Soviet citizens of European origin, who increasingly associated them with corruption and inefficiency. Now, feeling free to speak out, Uzbek spokesmen and journalists argued that fabrication of the figures of cotton output stemmed from the pressure to meet ever-rising, unrealistic targets set by the central bureaucracy, which had raised the Uzbek proportion of the total cotton area in the USSR from forty-five per cent in 1940 to sixty per cent in 1980: a period during which the land under cotton in the Soviet Union had grown merely by half, from two million to three million hectares, but the yield fourfold – from 2.24 million to 9.1 million tons – with Uzbekistan contributing fifty-nine per cent of the total. However, continued over-use of soil for decades had led finally to depleted yields, so that at 4.9 million tons in 1987, Uzbekistan was 1.8 million tons behind the target of the latest Five Year Plan.[30] Secondly, so the Uzbek argument ran, the corruption could only have been sustained with the cooperation of high officials in Moscow, mostly Russian, who received the lion's share of embezzled money. They were more responsible for the sorry state of affairs than Uzbeks. The arrest and conviction in 1987 of Yuri Churbanov, a former son-in-law of Brezhnev, on corruption charges, provided convincing evidence. Above all that, there was much to be said against the cotton monoculture that had been imposed on Uzbekistan by the central bureaucracy, which had failed to expand the republic's textile industry, which processed only fifteen per cent of the locally produced cotton. It was cotton that was at the centre of the corruption scandals that had afflicted the republic and its leaders. Karimov was aware of this and, to put the whole saga in perspective, he focused on the deeds of Rashidov, a legendary Uzbek leader, who was now routinely portrayed in the Soviet press as the progenitor of corruption. Karimov counselled a balanced assessment of the departed leader, weighing both his flaws and his achievements. He thus indicated that he was going to end the pattern of continuous purges that had bedevilled the party since 1984, and turn a new leaf in the organization's history.[31]

With politics becoming more Uzbek-oriented, the secular opposition party, Birlik, strengthened by its second national congress in May 1990, was able to set the agenda. The status of Uzbek and the treatment of Uzbek draftees were the two issues it pushed to the fore with meetings, demonstrations and newspaper articles. As a strong rebuff to the Soviet military commanders, who kept up their denials of any wrongdoing to Uzbek conscripts, an opposition journal published two illustrated articles in early March 1990, detailing particulars of fatal incidents involving Uzbek servicemen, and the general mistreatment of Uzbek draftees, who were often assigned to the notorious construction battalions commanded mainly by officers suffering from alcoholism or some other psychological malady. Such substantiated reports of the Uzbek conscripts' deaths at the hands of their sadistic Russian officers gripped the imagination of local intellectuals, created revulsion against the authority of Moscow, and spurred the Birlik movement to demand the founding of a truly sovereign Uzbekistan.

Aware of the potency of the issue, and determined not to let Birlik gain further popular ground, the government issued a decree stating that there would be a cut in the number of conscripts assigned to the construction battalions, which would be posted only within the Turkestan (i.e. Central Asian) Military District,[32] with a corresponding rise in the number of draftees assigned to regular units.

Following the CPU lead in June, the Supreme Soviet declared Uzbek as the state language, and appointed a commission to recommend the pace of implementation – from street names and public announcements to the broadcasting media and communications with official organizations.

As an integral part of the CPSU, the Communist Party of Uzbekistan was sensitive to political events in Moscow. Its leader, Karimov, noticed that in March 1990 the CPSU's First Secretary, Gorbachev, had got himself elected as executive president of the USSR, and that three months later, under the chairmanship of Yeltsin, still a member of the CPSU, the Russian parliament had placed its legislation above that of the USSR.

Taking his cue, Karimov had the Uzbek Supreme Soviet take similar steps: declaring its sovereignty in October 1990, thus giving primacy to Uzbek laws over Soviet laws, and electing him executive president of the republic.

With this, Karimov felt freer to give vent to nationalist views. In a speech in late November he blamed the current economic plight of the republic on two major factors: a long period of economic planning by the centre which had turned Uzbekistan into 'a raw materials base', and the 'unjustly low prices' that Moscow paid for Uzbek cotton.[33]

Karimov had continued his policy of co-opting official Islam as personified by Mufti Muhammad Yusuf, who had taken to projecting a high public profile, giving interviews to the media on current problems, interpreting and analysing them from an Islamic angle. With each week marking the opening of new mosques or the recommissioning of old ones, the influence of Islam was rising; and with it the power and prestige of the mufti. Both he and Karimov had a common aim of marginalizing the militant Islamic tendency, be it in the form of Sufi brotherhoods, Wahhabis, or the Islamic Renaissance Party (IRP). The IRP, with its headquarters in Moscow, held its founding convention in June 1990 in Astrakhan, a port on the Volga Delta on the Caspian Sea in the Russian Federation. An all-Union organization, it aimed primarily at obtaining concessions and religious freedoms equal to those granted to the Russian Orthodox Church under President Gorbachev, thus enabling Muslims to 'live according to the Quran'. It organized a demonstration in Moscow demanding a higher number of permits for the hajj pilgrimage, the figure in the previous year being only 1300 for fifty-three million Soviet citizens with Muslim names; and this led the KGB to inspire reports that the IRP was a fundamentalist body funded by Saudi Arabia. The IRP's Uzbek branch became active under the leadership of Abdullah Yusuf at about the same time. It declared itself ready to undertake political activity in order to 'establish Islam as the Muslims' way of life in this republic'. Both Karimov and Mufti Muhammad Yusuf wanted to channel rising popular disaffection through such officially recognized forums as the mosque and the refurbished CPU. The state-controlled broadcasting media followed this policy, as did Muslim clerics who, for instance, tried actively to cool popular tempers in the wake of the anti-Meskhetian Turk riots.[34] But there were instances when these efforts proved inadequate in preventing violence between different ethnic groups.

Much to the embarrassment of the authorities, violence had erupted between Uzbeks and Tajiks in Samarkand. The official figures of about 100,000 Tajiks and 140,000 Uzbeks in the city, according to the 1989 census, were generally believed to be off the mark, since many Tajiks, conscious of their domicile in Uzbekistan, voluntarily registered themselves as Uzbeks to avoid any discrimination. With political liberalization, this attitude changed. Aware of their historic dominance of Samarkand, a leading centre of Tajik culture and Islamic learning, Tajiks in the city began to assert themselves. And so too did Tajiks in Bukhara, another such settlement. In mid-1988, inspired by the Armenian actions in Karabakh, Tajiks in Samarkand and Bukhara demonstrated, demanding attachment of these cities to Tajikistan. Any such change was out of the question, and for the same reasons as applied to the Karabakh issue: re-opening the issue of transfer of territory between republics would trigger too many claims and counter-claims. But that did not subdue Tajik aspirations. The result was the emergence of the Tajik Liberation Front in Samarkand, and the worsening of relations between Tajiks and Uzbeks. In July 1991 the Tajik police in the city roughed up Uzbek revellers so badly that thirty of them had to be hospitalized.[35] Unlike the earlier conflict between Uzbeks and Meskhetian Turks, alien to Central Asia, Tajiks were natives of the region, formed large minorities in Samarkand and Bukhara, and also had their own republic, Tajikistan. Any violence between them and Uzbeks in Uzbekistan had the potential of spreading to Tajikistan, with the Tajiks there persecuting the Uzbek minority in their midst.

One way to dampen inter-ethnic tensions was to direct popular disaffection at Moscow for its exploitative policies of the past, ignoring the fact that central aid to Uzbekistan amounted to about a third of its annual budget. Yet anti-Moscow feelings in Uzbekistan were not as sharp as in the Baltic states, Georgia or Moldova – the republics which boycotted the referendum on a new Union Treaty in mid-March 1991. But after the popular vote had decided overwhelmingly in favour of a renegotiated Union Treaty, Karimov as well as other Central Asian leaders pushed hard for republican control over local economic resources, foreign trade and hard-currency earnings. Their apparent success in this matter was one of the main factors that induced a hardline coup in Moscow on 19 August 1991.

Karimov favoured the coup partly because he had found Gorbachev deficient in providing firm leadership during a tumultuous time. 'Sometimes I cannot be sure that Gorbachev is president,' he told a press conference in Tashkent in mid-September.[36] However, once the coup had collapsed, he swiftly fell in line with the constitutionalists.

At the same time, as a member of the CPSU Politburo since the party congress in July 1990, Karimov challenged the right of Gorbachev, First Secretary of the CPSU, to suspend the constituents of the CPSU outside the Russian Federation, following the suspension of the 'Russian' Communist Party by Yeltsin, arguing that only the Supreme Court had the right to decide whether the CPSU had acted illegally.[37] He then announced that the Communist Party of Uzbekistan was breaking away from the CPSU because of the latter's 'unprincipled and cowardly position during the coup'.

Following the lead given by the three Baltic republics, which declared themselves independent and were so recognized immediately by the West, the Uzbekistan Supreme Soviet passed the Act of Independence on 31 August 1991. It set out the constitutional law and basic principles of sovereignty, including the fundamental concepts of domestic and foreign policies centred around a multi-party system and the building of a market economy, and served as an interim constitution.

On 2 September, Gorbachev and the presidents of the twelve constituent republics agreed to transform the Soviet Union into a confederation with a strong centre. All Central Asian leaders, with the exception of President Askar Akayev of Kyrgyzstan, backed Gorbachev's idea of a strong centre.

Having seceded from the suspended CPSU, the Communist Party of Uzbekistan met in Tashkent on 14 September, dissolved itself, and re-emerged as the People's Democratic Party (PDP). As chairman of the newly named party, Karimov announced that Uzbekistan would take immediate control of recruitment for the Soviet military and ensure joint control of Soviet military activities on Uzbek soil, thus ending a practice whereby Soviet generals had in the past acted unilaterally and done what they wished – such as bombing targets in Afghanistan from Uzbek airfields without first securing the approval of the government in Tashkent. He gave the slogan 'Discipline and Order' to the nation. It was well received, especially by the intellectuals, an influential section of society. 'The local intelligentsia are frightened that in Uzbekistan democracy will lead either to extreme nationalism or Islamic fundamentalism,' said Albert Musin, a Birlik supporter.[38]

Overall, the PDP government had actually benefited from ethnic divisions so far, projecting itself as the only authority that could prevent inter-ethnic violence. The secret hand of the republican KGB in instigating the inter-ethnic conflict in the Fergana Valley in June

1989 was widely alleged. Having gained from such violence, the Karimov administration, which came to office on the heels of the Fergana riots, was determined to control it lest it should get out of hand and lead to its downfall.

Intense negotiations continued in Moscow to settle the shape of the confederation to be forged out of the old USSR, but showed little sign of success. Impatient with the slow progress, President Yeltsin unfolded a radical economic and political programme to the Russian Congress of People's Deputies on 28 October. Two weeks later he appointed three reformers as deputy prime ministers to accelerate the process of political-economic liberalization, thus setting the pace for the proposed new confederation which showed scant signs of emerging.

On 8 December the presidents of two other Slav republics, Ukraine and Belarus, joined Yeltsin in a common decision to form a Commonwealth of Independent States.

Feeling left out, the leaders of the Central Asian republics met in Ashqabat four days later, and resolved to join the CIS if they were listed as founder-members. Once this was agreed, the remaining republics, except Georgia, also resolved to affiliate with the new body, thus setting the scene for the dissolution of the USSR, which happened formally on the last day of 1991.

THE POST-SOVIET ERA

Once Turkey had recognized the Central Asian republics as independent countries 'on an equal footing and on mutual respect for existing borders' on 16 December, Karimov became the first regional leader to visit Ankara. 'My country will go forward by the Turkish route,' he declared on 20 December. 'We have chosen this road and will not turn back.'[39] A fortnight earlier he had told the Ankara-based *Cumhuriyet* (Jumhuriyet: Republic): 'We want to implement a free market . . . I don't think fundamentalist Islam has much chance [in Uzbekistan]. Turkey's secularism is also a model for us.'

His trip to Turkey had as much to do with domestic affairs as foreign. A presidential poll and a referendum on the constitutional law were scheduled for 29 December. And Karimov, the candidate of the ruling PDP, wanted to underline his pro-Turkic credentials in order to erode the backing for his electoral rival, Muhammad Salih, whose Erk party was pan-Turkic.

Using subterfuge, Karimov's administration had succeeded in blocking the candidature of Abdurahman Pulatov, the Birlik chief and a political heavyweight, for the presidency.[40] Salih, a comparative lightweight, was allowed to run as a member of the (recognized) Writers Union, and not as the leader of the opposition Erk. The election campaign was far from fair. Large sums were spent on Karimov's campaign by the provincial governors, city mayors and others belonging to the ruling PDP. State-run television featured Karimov daily in its news bulletins broadcast nationally. All Salih got was a slot of fifteen minutes on local television a week before polling day, after three minutes of his speech had been censored.[41]

On 29 December, eighty-nine per cent of the eleven million eligible electors turned up to vote, with eighty-six per cent opting for Karimov, and thirteen per cent for Salih. With the strong line taken by Erk (and Birlik) on Uzbek nationalism, rooted in pan-Turkism, non-Uzbek voters, forming thirty per cent of the total, felt alienated from Salih. They therefore voted for Karimov. The other area in which he was strong was the countryside, containing sixty per cent of the electorate, mainly because of his 1989 decree giving land for private homes and cattle-grazing to the members of cooperative farms – which in 1991 had benefited 2.5 million families to the tune of 550,000 hectares – and the publicity surrounding this measure.[42] But the opposition refused to accept the result, claiming that Salih had gained forty-six per cent of the vote. This vitiated the atmosphere, and Karimov found himself facing protest in the streets.

The price decontrol in Uzbekistan, and elsewhere in the CIS, on 1 January 1992 led to dramatic rises, and caused much suffering to those on fixed incomes or grants. University students began demonstrating against the price explosion on 16 January, and continued for the next four days, citing human rights violations, and demanding Karimov's resignation. Clashes between the demonstrators and security forces led to the deaths of two students.

To calm the situation, Karimov instituted an inquiry into the shootings, and restored old prices for students. While accusing the opposition of manipulating the demonstrators for political purposes, he replaced the force responsible for the deaths with a Special Militia Battalion. Karimov treated the student protesters with some restraint, partly because he badly needed to have the US open a diplomatic mission in Tashkent, without which Uzbekistan could not gain access to such financial world bodies as the International Monetary Fund and the World Bank.

Following the formation of the CIS, Washington had publicly listed five conditions for establishing diplomatic links with its constituent members: acceptance of all US–USSR agreements, respect for human rights, a free market, democratic elections, and a functioning multi-party political system. Later, America modified its stance, saying that it was enough to show that progress was being made towards these objectives to win US recognition.

During his visit to Tashkent in mid-February 1992, the US Secretary of State, James Baker, told President Karimov that Uzbekistan needed to demonstrate that it was advancing along the path of democracy and a free market. To make his point that America was committed to staying in touch with the local opposition as an important ingredient of its foreign-policy doctrine, Baker visited Salih and Pulatov in their offices.

Karimov had therefore to curb his authoritarian tendencies, and liberalize the administration – at least until Uzbekistan had been admitted to the United Nations and its allied organizations, the Conference on Security and Cooperation in Europe, the IMF, and the World Bank.

This allowed the opposition greater freedom than before. Taking advantage of this, the pan-Turkic Erk and Birlik sponsored the Congress of the Supporters of Turkestan in Tashkent on 7 March. The assembly was attended by pan-Turkic elements from other Central Asian republics. While in general sympathy with the concept of pan-Turkism, especially in its cultural sense, the Karimov government did not like the event: sponsored by Uzbek opposition leaders, it had managed to make the Uzbek government appear lukewarm towards the idea of resurrecting Turkestan.

The religious opposition – now consisting of the IRP and the newly established Adalat (Justice), a socio-religious association – also became more active, especially in the Fergana Valley, the traditional stronghold of Islam, where a quarter of the republic's population lived.

These groups were encouraged by the rift that had opened up in the Official Islamic Administration. It came to the surface at the Fifth Congress of the Muslim Spiritual Directorate in Tashkent in late February 1992, with some delegates openly accusing Mufti Muhammad Yusuf of cooperating with the KGB. Though he managed to get re-elected, the allegation tarnished his public image.

Of the two religious organizations, Adalat, with its headquarters in Namangan, a bastion of Islam, began to impinge on the everyday life of Muslims in the Fergana Valley. Even under Communist rule many local Muslims, including Communist Party members, in Namangan used to have Islamic ceremonies for marriage (*nikah*) and birthdays (*sumat*) – but in secret. Since the advent of perestroika in the mid-1980s, and especially after Uzbekistan's independence in December 1991, there was a rapid revival of Islam in the Fergana Valley and elsewhere. The number of mosques in Namangan, a city of 360,000, rose from two to twenty-six. The province of Namangan (population 1.5 million) accounted for 130 mosques, more than half the total in all of Central Asia before perestroika – with another 470 in the rest of Uzbekistan. Until 1989 only four Muslims from the Namangan province were allowed to undertake hajj, the pilgrimage to Mecca. Three years later the figure was 1500, accounting for nearly two-fifths of the republic's total of 4000.[43] Unsurprisingly, it was in Namangan that Adalat formed vigilante groups to impose the veil on women and a ban on the sale of alcohol, and made citizen's arrests of suspected criminals. The accused were tried by Islamic judges, who often restricted themselves to sentencing the guilty to forced labour on the construction or repairs of local mosques. The more serious cases were transferred to the police.

This state of affairs was insupportable to the government. Once it had achieved its objectives of admissions to various international bodies, and the opening of the American embassy by early March 1992, it moved to curb the opposition.

Aware of the hostility Washington felt towards Islamic fundamentalism, it targeted the IRP and Adalat first. On the eve of Karimov's visit to Namangan in mid-March it arrested seventy leading members of the IRP and Adalat in its first strike against these organizations, and shut down an Islamic centre that had been established in the premises of the former Communist Party.[44]

It then extended its pressure on the secular opposition, concentrating on Birlik since, unlike Erk, it had real potential to become a mass party and a serious challenge to the PDP. Birlik's handicap was that it had been denied registration as a political party. (The law on political parties did not allow political activity by individuals, only registered parties.) As for Erk – a registered political group whose membership of 40,000 far exceeded the legal minimum, entitled to publish its own journal, *Erk* – the government pressured it through its censorship bureau. In April/May the party could scarcely get one-fifth of its editorial material passed by the censors.[45] Some of the censored material pertained to the activities of the opposition in

Tajikistan and the success it had had in sharing power with the former Communists led by Rahman Nabiyev. Suffering official persecution, and realizing that with the establishment of a genuinely independent Uzbekistan the old argument between Birlik and Erk about different priorities for independence and democracy had vanished, Pulatov and Salih began to cooperate with each other informally on a shared programme of striving for a democratic state and society.

Aware that the Supreme Soviet was to meet on 2 July (but only for three days), they decided to sponsor a public rally in Tashkent to demand fresh elections under a new electoral law. They secured the necessary permission from the public prosecutor. But later he changed his mind (reportedly at the behest of the president's office) and pressured Pulatov on 29 June to cancel the rally. Pulatov refused. When he left the prosecutor's office he was attacked by four unknown assailants who broke his skull. Three weeks later he was discharged from a local hospital, even though he had not recovered fully. He then went to Moscow for treatment, and from there to Istanbul to recuperate. When parliament convened on 2 July, Salih tried to raise this issue, but was barred from doing so. He resigned in protest. While he continued to lead the only recognized opposition party, there was no slackening in the tapping of his phones or the surveillance under which he was kept – a fate he shared with the leaders of Birlik and other opposition groups, and even Mufti Muhammad Yusuf.[46]

While weakening an already feeble opposition, Karimov tried to sponsor 'loyal' opposition which stayed away from Uzbek nationalism and Islamic fundamentalism, and concentrated instead on fostering private property and enterprise. An example was the National Progress Party, which was led by Muhammad Azimov, who was close to the president, and which won official recognition. It tried to attract members possessing private property.

Externally, Karimov had by then consolidated the position of Uzbekistan, especially in the region. At the CIS summit in Tashkent in mid-May, his proposal for a mutual defence agreement was accepted. Six out of eleven members, including four Central Asian countries, joined the Collective Defence Treaty. Thus Karimov succeeded in linking Russia with a Central Asian defence system as an integral member and in giving the new treaty impressive military muscle. But his proposal that the CIS set up a mobile peace-keeping force to be posted in the areas of conflict – such as Tajikistan, Moldova and Nagorno Karabakh – was found to be too impractical by a meeting of CIS foreign and defence ministers in Tashkent in early July.

By then, however, Uzbekistan had signed a bilateral treaty with Russia on political, economic, cultural and scientific relations, followed by a similar treaty on security. The latter allowed the 100,000 CIS troops stationed in Uzbekistan to be transformed into Uzbek military under the control of the Uzbek government. As before, Tashkent continued to be an important military command-control-communications centre, with facilities for officer training. Moscow wanted the Uzbek administration to be stable and strong in order to stave off any chance of anti-Russian pogroms either in Uzbekistan or anywhere else in Central Asia. (By stretching the programme of making Uzbek the official language over several years, to 1997, the Uzbek authorities had eased the stress ethnic Russians felt on this score.) And Uzbekistan's neighbours wanted its government to remain powerful, fully capable of preventing inter-ethnic tensions within its boundaries escalating into violence and causing knock-on effects in the adjoining states.

In August, Karimov published a seventy-two-page pamphlet in Uzbek and Russian, *Uzbekistan: Its Own Road to Renewal and Progress*, which summed up his assessment of the current situation in the republic politically, economically and diplomatically, and set out guidelines for the future. It was used by the state-controlled media as an important educational tool, with television readings of the text which were reprinted in the press.

'Because of the perestroika experiment and decisions which were wrong, all former republics of the USSR fell into long and deep economic crisis,' Karimov wrote. 'Due to inflation and the growing cost of living, social, economic and monetary systems are in a bad state.' Pointing out that forty-four per cent of the national income was produced by agriculture, he addressed the question of land ownership. 'If land is placed into private ownership, then there will be price speculation and farmers will lose confidence,' he said. 'The main thing is to create such a mechanism which gives potential to each farmer to be the owner of his labour's result.'[47] In other words, the PDP government was committed to maintaining the present cooperative and state farming, and not to denationalizing land, a policy opposed among others by Birlik and Erk.

Karimov justified remaining in the CIS and the rouble zone. 'Until recently CIS members were one state geopolitically and administratively,' he observed. 'If all connections are broken, it would damage and destabilize the region and the international arena. The economy of the republics, their complete transport and energy systems had been formed and developed within the borders of the old Union, and their accounting was done in the rouble zone. Breaking of these relations can bring, and has already brought, a fall in production and made the economic situation worse and intensified social problems.'[48] Inflation had been so severe in Uzbekistan and other member-states of the CIS that the value of the rouble had fallen from US 60 cents before the Soviet break-up to one-third of a US cent by the summer of 1992. Price decontrol had resulted in a manyfold increase in the price of basic necessities, with the rise in wages representing only a fraction of this. Therefore, while reiterating his commitment to a 'socially oriented market economy', and describing the market as a mechanism that makes 'the producer responsive to the consumer' and provides motivation to 'move the economy in the right direction', he highlighted the problems of transition from the present system to a market economy. 'Due to the low living standard of the people in Uzbekistan, the tactic of shock therapy will not work,' he argued. 'We should move to a market economy step by step, finding the right pace which is not too slow or too fast, to prepare the people for a market economy . . . Before establishing a market mechanism we should conduct strong measures of social defence of the people.'[49] He stated that the domestic economic strategy should be 'free from the influence of any political ideology'.

Karimov was opposed to the state adopting any ideology, secular or religious. But that did not inhibit him from stressing the importance of Islam in domestic and external spheres. 'Consideration for religion and Islam plays an important part within our internal and international politics and conduct,' he stated. 'It manifests itself in the way of life of the people, their psychology and in the building of spiritual and moral values, and in enabling us to feel rapport with those who practise the same religion.'[50] He reaffirmed the policy of closer ties with other Muslim countries, especially Pakistan, Iran and Saudi Arabia – a country he had visited in May when among other things he had performed an *umra*, a short pilgrimage to Mecca. Following this he had begun prefacing his public speeches with '*Bismallah al Rahman al Rahim* (In the name of God, the Merciful and the Compassionate)'. He had then allowed a weekly programme on Islam to be transmitted on television, supervised by Mufti Muhammad Yusuf. Earlier he had taken the oath of his presidential office on the Quran. In other words, Karimov and the PDP were prepared to treat Islam as a crucial part of Uzbek culture, but were determined to maintain the secular basis of the state by maintaining a strict division between religion and government. Significantly, referring to the 'special relationship' between Uzbekistan and Turkey in his pamphlet, Karimov mentioned Turkish help in 'our efforts to achieve good relations between the state and religion, which have been conducted in the same ethnic-cultural conditions [as in Turkey]'.[51]

But political conditions in Uzbekistan and Turkey were far from alike. After a decades-long battle, Islamic forces in Turkey had finally established themselves as a legitimate political grouping, the Welfare Party. In contrast, political or even socio-political groups based on religion, such as the Islamic Renaissance Party and Adalat, were banned in Uzbekistan. However, these groupings were not prepared to take government repression lying down. Following Karimov's visit to Namangan in March 1992, Islamists in the area responded to the arrests of their activists with protest demonstrations, thus challenging the administration either to escalate its repressive policy or discontinue it. The government decided to back down. Thus the basic question of relations between the state and Islam remained in public view. It was indeed pushed to the political centre-stage because of developments in neighbouring Tajikistan. In early September 1992, after months of armed agitation led mainly by Tajik Islamist forces, freshly inspired by the success of the Islamic Mujahedin in overthrowing the pro-Communist regime of Muhammad Najibullah in Afghanistan in April, President Rahman Nabiyev of Tajikistan, a Communist, was forced to resign by Islamic militants. This prepared the way for the Islamist-led alliance to assume a dominant position in the republic's administration. The fighting before and after this dramatic event had created tens of thousands of refugees, with some 40,000 seeking haven in Uzbekistan.

Worried about the civil conflict in Tajikistan spreading to Uzbekistan, the most populous and strategically important state in the region, the Uzbek government sealed its borders with Tajikistan, and introduced internal visas for foreign visitors in late August, effectively putting the Fergana Valley, sharing borders with Tajikistan, off limits to non-citizens, especially religious Saudi nationals, many of whom had become untraceable after their overstay in the republic. The government was disturbed too by the increased activities of Wahhabis, local and foreign, in the Fergana Valley – a sharp contrast to their earlier clandestine ways. For instance, their young leader in

Namangan, Abdul Ahad, had become a Wahhabi by joining a secret group in the late 1970s, and studying Islam surreptitiously. By 1989, however, local Wahhabis felt strong enough to mount a demonstration demanding a prime venue for a mosque. Their agitation succeeded in May 1991 when the city mayor conceded their demand. Soon, work began on a mosque and a religious school while makeshift facilities were made available immediately to the faithful. The same tactic won the group, funded generously by the Saudi Arabia-based Ahle Sunna movement, important sites in such Fergana Valley urban centres as Andijan, Kokand and Margilan: part of their plan to establish a chain of religious schools to teach a total of 15,000 students. Alongside this ambitious project went funding of new mosques in the countryside – as well as teaching the believers prayers and the performance of Islamic rites and instructing them in Sharia rules, interspersed with lectures on establishing an Islamic republic after overthrowing 'the Communist government in Tashkent'. While officials claimed that militants were training a 'secret army', Wahhabi preachers maintained silence on the subject of 'military training' for their students.[52] By striking roots in the densely populated Fergana Valley of Uzbekistan – 348 persons per square kilometre (900 per square mile) – Wahhabis were placing themselves in a position to spread quickly to those parts of the valley that were incorporated into Tajikistan and Kyrgyzstan.

The options open to the Uzbek government were repressing Wahhabis and/or boosting the Official Islamic Administration in order to reduce their importance. Official Islam was as concerned about this austere sect as the government: it was sectarian, rabidly anti-Sufi and anti-Shia, and it was being financed from Saudi Arabia. But official Islam lacked the funds and imagination to compete successfully with the fast-rising Wahhabi movement and siphon off at least a section of the thousands of young unemployed Uzbeks who were flocking to Wahhabi congregations. Repression had its limitations. 'If we crack down on the [Islamic] extremists they will whip up support by accusing the government of crushing Islam,' said an official in Namangan in the autumn of 1992. 'I don't think they know in Tashkent how bad the situation is in Fergana.'[53] Even official Islam had its differences with the Karimov regime's insistence on a division between the state and Islam. 'Religion cannot be separate from life, and government is part of the citizen's life,' said Haji Bilal Khan Rustamov, the young prayer-leader of the central mosque of Namangan. 'It is therefore not possible to have the mosque and the government totally apart.' Besides the militant Wahhabis and the dissenting local official mosque, Namangan had spawned a large voluntary religious organization: the 30,000-strong Sawad Azam (Big Group). Based at Mullah Kyrgyz *madressa* (religious school), its main purpose was to collect funds for the construction and repairs of local mosques.[54] This was innocuous enough, yet the authorities felt that once such associations were formed – albeit for social or religious purposes – they could easily be transformed into militant bodies.

What compounded the problem for Tashkent was the rising power of Islamists in Tajikistan, though not in the republic's Fergana Valley region. Karimov tried to address the unstable situation in Tajikistan. Invoking Uzbekistan's membership of the Collective Defence Treaty, which included Russia, Karimov said in early October: 'Russia should take into consideration the powerful influence of pan-Islamic forces on the southern border [of the CIS]. Fundamentalism will not be limited to Tajikistan or even Central Asia. Russia, as a great powerful nation, should feel obliged to control to the fullest its interests in Central Asia as it has been doing for the past 100 years.' Describing Russia as 'the guarantor of stability in Central Asia', he called for the continued presence of the Russian troops (under the label of CIS forces) in Tajikistan.[55] He combined this public statement with covert backing for Nabiyev's forces in their efforts to retake the Tajik capital, Dushanbe.

In a surprise attack on the night of 23–24 October, pro-Nabiyev partisans captured the most important government buildings in central Dushanbe, but were unable to hold them in the face of a counter-attack by the Islamist-led forces. After this setback the Karimov regime decided to intervene directly in the Tajik civil conflict. It began training a brigade of pro-Nabiyev loyalists. And when they launched an attack on Dushanbe on 10 December, they were equipped with military hardware, including helicopter gunships, supplied by the Uzbek military. They succeeded in their mission, and expelled Islamists and their democratic allies from the capital, and later from the rest of the republic, except its Badakhshan region.[56] Thus, by the end of December, Karimov could rightly claim that he had at last resolved a problem that had been threatening the stability of Uzbekistan since the spring.

Interestingly, when the Uzbek government argued in the Supreme Soviet for a ban on Birlik under the new constitution adopted on 8 December 1992 – which confirmed a centralized presidential system, and which under Article 54 banned political parties based on 'nation-alistic or religious principles' – it presented the opposition movement as a stalking-horse for the members of the clandestine Islamic Renaissance Party whose sister organization in Tajikistan had been in the forefront of the struggle against Communists. Once the Supreme Soviet had passed the banning motion by 383 votes to seven, Birlik ceased to exist as a registered public movement. When Birlik challenged the government's decision in the Supreme Court, the justice ministry argued that during 1991–92 as many as 168 Birlik members had been charged with breaking the law. As an interim measure the Supreme Court banned the activities of Birlik until 14 April 1993.[57]

Part of the reason why the Uzbek government had highlighted the prospect of Birlik being infiltrated by Islamists was to win the approval of both Washington[58] and Moscow, both of which were antagonistic towards Islamic fundamentalism and both of which knew that instability in Uzbekistan would destabilize all of Central Asia. In any case, it was in Karimov's interests to exaggerate the threat of fundamentalism in his republic in order to encourage American diplomats to conclude that the only alternative to his government was Islamist.

So far as his party, the PDP, was concerned, President Karimov had a firm grip over it. While it did not dominate all facets of public life and economy like its predecessor, the Communist Party, it was the single most important political force in the republic, and reached out to its farthest corner. Within a year of its existence, the PDP had acquired some 550,000 members, more than four-fifths of the 664,520 that the CPU had at the time of its congress in June 1990.[59] Since it had taken over the assets of the CPU, including its multi-storey offices in city centres, it had the same physical presence as its predecessor. Yet it was plagued with a dilemma. Having lost its Marxist-Leninist moorings, the party was floundering, looking desperately for an ideology. Of the two choices available, Islam and Uzbek nationalism, it had turned its face decidedly against Islam as a socio-political philosophy. On Uzbek nationalism, as the party in power, it had to tread carefully so as not to alienate or frighten non-Uzbeks who, forming a third of the population and being mainly urban dwellers, were crucial to its economy. This meant that the opposition Birlik or Erk could easily outflank it on that front. Faced with an insoluble predicament, the PDP could do little to arrest the erosion of its power base, and became increasingly a vehicle for unprincipled opportunists.

Despite the enforcement of a constitution that specified a parliament, known as Olio Majlis, elected on a 'multi-party basis', as well as 'free mass media and no censorship', the harassment of opposition, and censorship, continued. Indeed, on the day the new constitution was adopted, 8 December 1992, the Uzbek KGB kidnapped Abdumanab Pulatov (Abdul Manab Pulat), chairman of the Uzbekistan Human Rights Association, and brother of Abdurahim Pulatov, the Birlik leader, after he had addressed a regional human rights conference in Bishkek, Kyrgyzstan, whisked him to Tashkent, and charged him on 20 January with insulting the president, a crime punishable with a maximum of a six-year jail term. The incident aroused such an international outcry that on 28 January the court ordered his release, even though it had found him guilty. Earlier, the government had banned the Moscow-based pro-democracy newspaper, *Izvestia*, after censoring it regularly, and closed down the only local independent publication, *Biznesmyen* (Businessman), after it had hinted that independent Uzbekistan was not unlike the old Soviet Union. Its editor was summoned by the president's office, and told: 'In the old days you would have been shot, so you're getting off lightly with the closing down of the publication.' The government was aware of mounting criticism in the West. 'Diplomats try to teach us lessons, but our traditions are different,' said a senior Uzbek official in January 1993. 'Uzbek people are very kind, but it is dangerous to give [them] things like democracy. We have to practise how to be a democratic state [first].'[60] Unlike in adjoining Turkmenistan, where the government wanted a virtual embargo on opposition activities until the people had become prosperous, the stress in Uzbekistan was on nation-building. 'We are telling the opposition, please wait some years,' said Jamal Kamal, the chairman of the Writers Union. 'We have no proper army, no strong borders. We must strengthen national independence and secure our national borders first. Then we will go step by step towards democracy and human rights, which will take about 10 years.'[61]

The task of building a strong nation-state was linked with the health of the economy, which was deteriorating owing to factory closures caused by lack of spare parts, raw materials and fuel, as well as the flight of many Russian technicians and managers. Since this problem afflicted all Central Asian republics, it was at the top of the agenda at the summit in Tashkent in early January 1993. The idea of a Central Asian Common Market was launched here.

On the political side, what dominated the Central Asian summit

was the state of affairs in Tajikistan, where the regime of Communists had just been restored, thanks largely to Uzbekistan's active
participation in the mission.

SEVEN

Tajikistan: The Rise and Decline of Islamists

Since the Marxist-Leninist ambience of the Soviet Union did not allow historical animosities between different nationalities to be expressed in ethnic or racial terms, such feelings were sometimes transformed into competition in achieving economic goals. This was the case with Tajik–Uzbek relations, vitiated by many centuries of authority that Uzbeks, known for their fighting prowess, had exercised over Tajiks, a predominantly sedentary community of Persian ancestry. Now, with cotton, a highly prized crop, being common to both Tajikistan and Uzbekistan, yields of the commodity became a yardstick by which the two republics measured their comparative worth. After an indeterminate race which persisted for several years following the Great Patriotic War, Tajiks, achieving an average yield of 2810 kilogrammes of cotton per hectare in 1953, clearly established their lead over Uzbeks, and indeed set an all-Soviet record.

Moscow's policy of devoting a greater proportion of sown area to cotton was given further impetus when Nikita Khrushchev launched his policy of increasing the production of food grains as well as tea, tobacco and cotton. By 1956 cotton crops in Tajikistan accounted for a third of the cultivated areas in collective farms, up from one-fifth in 1940, with the average size of a collective growing seven-fold during the same period.[1] Part of this increase had been achieved in this predominantly mountainous republic – with only seven per cent of its land being arable – by encouraging mountain Tajiks, particularly those from the Karategin region, to take up cotton cultivation in warm valleys.

By the mid-1950s, mainly due to Moscow's commitment to developing Tajik historiography, Tajiks had acquired a cultural consciousness quite apart from that of Uzbeks. This consciousness was by and large espoused by the young, Soviet-educated intelligentsia, and not the old elite. At the same time the introduction of compulsory Russian in 1938, followed by a switch-over to the Cyrillic alphabet for Tajik, and great strides made in literacy, Russian had emerged as the inter-ethnic language in Tajikistan.

As for Russian settlers in the republic, their political power outstripped their numerical strength. Though only thirteen per cent of the total population (versus Tajik's fifty-three per cent) in the 1950s, they provided forty per cent of the membership of the Communist Party of Tajikistan (CPT). Between them and Uzbeks, constituting a quarter of the population, they formed a clear majority in the CPT. Yet the policy of having a non-Slav as First Secretary of the CPT, with the Second Secretary being a Russian, which had been introduced in 1946 with Babajan Gafurov (Ghafur), continued.

When Gafurov was replaced in 1956 in the aftermath of Khrushchev's anti-Stalinist speech, his job went to Tursunbai Ulaajabayev (Ula Ajabai), erstwhile chairman of the Council of Ministers. Equally dramatically, the Tajik capital, which had been renamed Stalinabad in 1932, was given back its original name: Dushanbe.

Khrushchev's policy of economic and administrative decentralization led to devolution of power to the constituent republics, culminating in the creation of economic regions and regional bureaus within the Central Committee of the CPSU in early 1963. The result was the revival of the Middle/Central Asian Bureau within the CPSU's Central Committee, and the establishment of the Middle/Central Asian Economic Region, which excluded Kazakhstan. Laudable though this development towards regional autonomy was, the constituents of Middle/Central Asia did not benefit uniformly. Being the most populous, Uzbekistan gained most, with Uzbeks dominating the new body. This revived the old rivalry between Tajiks and Uzbeks, with each group considering itself superior to the other. The matter reached a point where the First Secretary of the Communist Party of Uzbekistan, Sharif Rashidov, addressed it at a plenum of the Central Committee in May 1963. He blamed the 'survival of nationalism' for hindering economic and cultural integration of Central Asia. '[V]estiges of [nationalism] are still tenacious among a certain segment of politically immature people,' he said. '[They manifest themselves] . . . either in a desire to idealise the past . . . or in attempts to preserve archaic and obsolete forms of national culture under the flag of national originality, or in denying that a national culture is enriched precisely through the mutual influence of the cultures of fraternal peoples.'[2]

However, the problems emanating from regional autonomy disappeared when regional organizations were disbanded within two months of Khrushchev's fall from power in October 1964. A side-effect of this was that Tajiks no longer felt dominated by Uzbeks. As a result of this, the Communist Party of Tajikistan, led since its Fourteenth Congress in September 1961 by Jabar Rasulov, a Tajik, could afford to be more self-critical than before, especially of the party's performance among Tajik masses. The Sixteenth Congress of the CPT in March 1966 singled out the party's poor agitational work, particularly in the mountainous areas, and its failure to eradicate medieval practices and traditions, feudal attitudes towards women, and clan loyalties amongst rural Tajiks, forming eighty per cent of the republic's ethnic Tajik population. Whereas village Tajiks had fully adopted the socialist mode and tools of production and were achieving their economic targets, they still clung to feudal values and practices in socio-political behaviour, perpetuated through family and informal social circles, and resisted Marxist-Leninist education imparted by the mass media and the CPT's agitational agencies.

A different situation prevailed among the urban-based Tajik intelligentsia, who had developed a commitment to the socialist system and had imbibed its socio-political values. They were concentrated in the capital, Dushanbe, and the province of Hojand (then Leninabad) which, while accounting for one-third of the republic's population, produced nearly two-thirds of its industrial output. Dushanbe was a predominantly Tajik city, having absorbed large numbers of Tajik émigrés from Bukhara and Samarkand after it became the republican capital in 1929, whereas both Hojand city and province had a substantial proportion of Uzbeks, which led to a high incidence of bilingualism and a certain amount of inter-marriage. These social developments were anathema to Samarkand and Bukhara Tajiks now settled in Dushanbe, who considered their Persian origins to be superior to the Uzbeks' Turkic ancestry. While the expression and propagation of such views was not allowed within the party, tightly controlled by the CPSU in Moscow, such perceptions undoubtedly existed.

As it was, cleavages based on geographical and clan loyalties had developed within the CPT itself, and consolidated themselves by the mid-1960s. The major factions were the Hojandis in the north, the Badakhshanis/Pamiris from the Pamir Mountains to the east, the Kulyabis to the south-east, and the Kurgan Tyubis to the south-west. The river valleys of Kulyab and Garm have been rivals for centuries. Since the Kulyab Valley was developed under Soviet rule as a cotton-growing area with many collective farms, its population rose sharply, and it became a stronghold of the CPT. In comparison, Kurgan Tyube, another of Kulyab's historical rivals, fell behind economically, and thus failed to secure its proportionate share of political power. Also, it lost its clan homogeneity with the influx of government-encouraged immigration from outside – especially from the small, narrow Garm Valley, a historic exporter of manpower; and this further weakened its political clout. Generally, party and government cadres from Moscow as well as Russian settlers in the republic got along well with urbanized Tajiks and Uzbeks in the Hojand region. Unsurprisingly, therefore, Hojand and Kulyab provinces, accounting for no more than sixty per cent of the republic's population of 2.5 million, came to monopolize political and economic power. This sowed the seeds of alienation towards Hojand and Kulyab in the rest of the republic. The feeling against Hojand was all the stronger because the region was isolated from the rest of the republic by formidable mountains; and it was to spring into an armed struggle a quarter of a century later.

Among the politicians from Hojand, the centre of a tightly knit political machine, who achieved prominence in the early 1970s was Rahman Nabiyev (1930–93), a native of the village of Shaiburhan. A graduate of the Tashkent Institute of Irrigation and Agricultural Mechanization, he joined the Communist Party of Tajikistan in 1960. A few years later he started working at the secretariat of the CPT's Central Committee, and rose up the bureaucratic ladder to become, first, minister of agriculture in 1971, and then chairman of the Council of Ministers two years later. As agriculture minister he had led a drive to expand the area under cotton cultivation, thus winning the attention and approval of Leonid Brezhnev, First Secretary of the CPSU. In his new position, Nabiyev was well placed to expand his power base through patronage with a view to securing the highest position in the republic: that of First Secretary of the CPT.

Because of the clan and blood ties between Tajiks in Tajikistan and those who had migrated to Afghanistan during the 1918–26 civil war, and because of the affinity of Tajik with Persian, the events in Afghanistan (where Persian was the official language) and Iran were more likely to have an impact on Tajikistan than on any other Central Asian republic.

In the mid-1970s Tajikistan began to feel, modestly, the impact of the rise of Islamic forces taking place in Afghanistan. Following the overthrow of King Muhammad Zahir Shah by his cousin

Muhammad Daoud Khan in July 1973, and the declaration of a republic, the new ruler tried to curb Islamist oppositionists. His repression led in mid-1974 to the flight to Pakistan of two Islamic leaders, Gulbuddin Hikmatyar and Borhanuddin Rabbani, the latter an ethnic Tajik, belonging to the Ikhwan (i.e. Brethren) movement. There they respectively set up the Hizb-e Islami (Islamic Party) and Jamaat-e Islami (Islamic Society) in 1976.

During that year their followers in Tajikistan established the Islamic Renaissance Party clandestinely. Most of the new group's backing came from Kurgan Tyube province, bordering Afghanistan, which had suffered economic neglect at the hands of a regime controlled by Hojandis in the north. Among its young activists was Muhammad Sharif Himmatzade, a mechanic, who fifteen years later was to emerge as its official leader.

The situation in Afghanistan grew increasingly unstable, with President Daoud Khan intent on becoming an authoritarian ruler, and persecuting not only Islamists but also leftists organized under the banner of the People's Democratic Party of Afghanistan (PDPA). Matters came to a head in mid-April 1978 with the assassination of a leftist trade union leader. This triggered a series of events which culminated in a coup on 27 April 1978 by military officers who belonged to the PDPA. Daoud Khan was killed, and his official positions of president and prime minister went to the PDPA chief, Nur Muhammad Taraki. As a result of this, the USSR became involved in Afghan politics.

At first the Kremlin tried to help the Marxist regime in Kabul by loaning it several hundred Central Asian – chiefly Uzbek and Tajik – administrative and technical personnel. Since ethnic Tajiks and Uzbeks in Afghanistan were part of a society politically dominated by Pushtuns, forming about forty per cent of the national population, they had always been aware of their ethnicity; and this led them to feel immediate rapport with their counterparts from Soviet Central Asia.

The victory of Islamists in Iran in February 1979 gave a boost to religious forces in the region. The broadcasts in Tajik beamed at Tajikistan by Iran's new regime began to gain a wider audience as the months went by, and helped to foster clandestine Islamic groups. And events in Afghanistan brought about increased exposure to the people and politics of that country.

As internecine fighting within the ruling PDPA grew more bloody during 1979, resulting in debilitating purges and increased resistance by Islamic partisans, Moscow started posting its troops in Afghanistan. From late October onwards Soviet Central Asian contingents began taking over guard duties from Afghan troops to relieve the latter to fight the rebels. This continued for the next two months. By the time the Kremlin decided to move into Afghanistan in force on 27 December, there were 8000 Soviet troops and 4000 military advisers in Afghanistan.

The Soviet military high command thought it expedient to bring their divisions to full strength by taking in the reserves living in Central Asia, before despatching them to Afghanistan to overthrow the government of Hafizullah Amin, an uncompromising Communist hardliner whose policies had alienated large sections of Afghan society, and instal a moderate PDPA leader, Babrak Karmal. They also airlifted many military construction units, made up almost entirely of Central Asian conscripts, to Afghanistan to construct military camps and repair air bases. All told, some 50,000 regular and 15,000 construction troops were involved. Among regular servicemen there were probably 15,000–20,000 Central Asians, mainly Tajik and Uzbek.[3] Such an ethnic mix, and the frequent parading of Central Asian troops in Kabul, indicated that the political purpose behind the exercise was to present the Soviet intervention in Afghanistan as a good neighbourly act in more ways than one.

With the Kremlin massing freshly mobilized troops along Afghan borders with Tajikistan, Uzbekistan and Turkmenistan, popular awareness of the USSR involvement in Afghanistan increased. The Soviet media explained that the friendly country of Afghanistan was being menaced by imperialist forces, and it was the duty of the USSR, according to the Friendship and Cooperation Treaty it had concluded with Kabul in December 1978, to assist the beleaguered country in its hour of need.

Sharing a 1200-kilometre- (750-mile-) long frontier with Afghanistan, Tajikistan was more exposed to developments in Afghanistan than was Uzbekistan or Turkmenistan. The authorities seemed aware of this. That is why in September 1979 Dushanbe was chosen as the venue for an international symposium on 'The Contributions of the Muslims of Central Asia, the Volga and the Caucasus to the Development of Islamic Thought, and the Cause of Peace and Social Progress', organized by the mufti of the Muslim Spiritual Directorate of Central Asia and Kazakhstan, Ziauddin Babakhan, assisted by his representative in Tajikistan, Haji Abdullajan Kalonov. It was the first time such an important gathering, attended by delegates from thirty Muslim countries, had been organized outside Tashkent, the headquarters of the Muslim Spiritual Directorate of Central Asia.

Following the Kremlin's military intervention in Afghanistan, the Soviet media rehashed the history of the Basmachi movement of the 1920s on television and in learned articles, and drew parallels with the current situation in Afghanistan, adding that this time around the neo-Basmachis were being actively assisted by foreign imperialist powers and regressive mullahs and Sufi brotherhoods. But drawing succour from the past, the authors of these educational aids assured their viewers or readers that the Soviet state would eliminate the new danger. At the same time the output of the USSR's foreign radio services beamed at Muslim countries increased sharply. The number of Soviet radio broadcasts on Islam – often delivered by muftis and kazis (religious judges) – in Arabic, Persian, Pushtu, Turkish and Urdu rose. These commentaries, offered within an Islamic context, exhorted the faithful abroad to struggle against imperialism, Zionism and racial apartheid, stressed the political concord that existed between Islam and the government in the USSR, and condemned various enemies of Islam and socialism, singling out Muslim fanatics in Afghanistan who, through their cruel, senseless acts of sabotage and attacks on civilian targets, were disgracing the peaceful message of Islam.[4]

The authorities in Tajikistan became more vigilant, with the KGB concentrating on smoking out clandestine Islamic groups, which gained ground as Soviet troops in Afghanistan failed to win a quick, decisive victory against Islamist resistance now being directed by the leaders of six Islamic parties based in Peshawar, Pakistan. The armed cadres of these parties numbered 73,000 (versus the Afghan army's strength of about 80,000), with three fundamentalist parties accounting for two-thirds of the total.[5] Prominent among those the KGB arrested in 1980 was Abdullah Saidov, a young charismatic cleric in Kurgan Tyube, inspired mainly by his father, Nuruddin Saidov, who had turned to Islam after retiring as a state farm director and become a self-appointed mullah. Two years later the KGB arrested Imaduddin Ahmedov, a young engineer, as the leader of an Islamic group based in Dushanbe. He was given a nine-year jail sentence.[6] But the most important of this generation of Islamic leaders, Himmatzade of the IRP, eluded the authorities. He slipped over into Afghanistan where he trained with the Islamic Mujahedin (i.e. holy warriors) as their struggle with the Soviet-backed regime in Kabul intensified.

In early 1982, Nabiyev became First Secretary of the CPT. He was the last of Brezhnev's protégés in Central Asia to achieve the highest party post in his republic: the Soviet leader died in November 1982. Nabiyev survived the brief tenures of Andropov and Chernenko, the Soviet leaders who initiated a drive against corruption, which particularly hit Central Asian party hierarchies and often revolved around doctoring the output of cotton, a commodity in which Tajikistan's share in the USSR total had risen to eleven per cent. However, this had failed to lift Tajikistan from its position as the poorest republic in the Soviet Union. As Nabiyev had not been directly involved with cotton production since 1973, there was only a marginal chance of his being mired in corruption.

Nabiyev continued in office for several months after Gorbachev became the CPSU's First Secretary in March 1985. When Nabiyev's downfall came towards the end of the year, it had as much to do with an important sub-faction within the Hojandi party machine turning against him as Gorbachev's desire to remove top party leaders in Central Asia as part of his clean-up drive. Kakhar Mahkamov succeeded Nabiyev, and presided over the CPT during its most turbulent period.

In foreign policy Gorbachev began to show flexibility on the Afghan issue, describing the conflict in Afghanistan as 'a bleeding wound' and expressing his wish to scale down Moscow's commitment to Kabul. In the spring of 1986 the Kremlin announced that it would withdraw 6000 Soviet troops from Afghanistan, a move that buoyed the spirits of Islamists in Afghanistan and Tajikistan.

The discovery and disbandment of clandestine Islamic groups in Tajikistan, and the increased attention paid by the authorities to Islam, indicated that the influence of religion was rising among Tajiks. Cemeteries, situated far away from normal venues for socio-political activities, had emerged as centres for Muslim festivals and celebrations, offering an environment that was freer than that prevalent in the officially managed mosques. The other salient feature of the Islamic revival was that it was making headway among the young. A profile of unregistered mullahs indicated that they were much younger and better educated than their predecessors. The predominance of youth among Islamists was apparent from the fact that most of those arrested in 1986 – including Asghar Shah Jabarov and Nematullah Inayatov of Kulyab, Abdul Rahim Karimov of Hojand, and Rajab Ali Shahyev of Dushanbe – had been born in the 1950s, a matter of concern to the government.

Addressing the party's ideological cadres in August 1986, Mahkamov, the First Secretary, revealed that some graduates of the Faculty of Oriental Languages in Dushanbe University had become (self-appointed) clerics, and urged intensification of atheist propaganda. Party discipline remained intact, with any member found practising Islamic rituals punished with expulsion, a fate that deprived the individual of the privileges that went with party membership.

Later that month Abdullah Saidov was arrested in Kurgan Tyube, and this triggered mass demonstrations for his release. These turned violent. Six months earlier, Saidov had created something of a sensation with a much-publicized petition to the CPSU congress in Moscow to establish an Islamic state in Tajikistan.[7]

A survey published in the *Leninchil Zhash* in August 1987 showed that forty-five per cent of the respondents in Tajikistan declared themselves 'believers', the highest figure ever recorded in post-war USSR. Yet these figures did not seem to surprise Mahkamov. Three months earlier he had told visiting foreign journalists: 'Islam is still a great power [here], and the number of believers has even increased.'[8] This meant that a substantial proportion of professionals and party members were observing Islamic rituals. By now it had become evident to the authorities that during the month of Ramadan, when believers are required to fast between sunrise and sunset, sales in cafeterias and restaurants fell perceptibly.

Other signs of growing religiosity, to which Mahkamov alluded in the spring of 1988, were the wearing of Islamic symbols and amulets by individuals, and the decoration of car interiors with Quranic verses. Noting that a growing number of parents were giving their babies names with Islamic connotations, he proposed that a panel of philologists and historians should produce a list of 'patriotic non-religious names'.[9] Lesser officials were more vigorous in their responses to Islamic resurgence, with Tajikistan's (nominal) foreign minister, Munavar Usmanov, describing the revivalist movement as a tool of imperialism and colonialism, and Issa Kalandarov, head of the Tajik broadcasting service, dubbing 'reactionary Islam' as 'the most determined enemy of the people'.[10]

Such statements were also reflective of the concern that Tajik authorities felt at the waning fortunes of both Soviet troops in Afghanistan and the pro-Moscow regime of President Muhammad Najibullah, who had been diluting the Marxist-Leninist content of the ruling PDPA's programme. Addressing the party conference on 27 April 1988, the tenth anniversary of the Saur (April) revolution, he urged the delegates not to underestimate the role of Islam and the prestige of clerics.[11] A joint communiqué by Najibullah and Gorbachev in early February 1988 stated that Soviet troops would start pulling out of Afghanistan in May and complete the exercise in ten months. The withdrawal signified something of a failure on the part of the USSR.

Long before this, Russian citizens of Tajikistan had sensed danger in the continuing bloody conflict between Marxists and Islamists in Afghanistan, and had begun translating their fear into action – by emigrating. Between 1979 (a census year) and 1988, some 120,000 Russians left the republic. Owing to this, and a high birth-rate among Tajiks, the percentage of Russians in the population declined from 10.4 in 1979 to 7.6 in 1989.[12]

As elsewhere in Central Asia, decline in the power and prestige of the republic's Communist Party led to the emergence of nationalist and Islamist opposition, the process gathering momentum during the latter period of perestroika starting in 1989. In the face of this challenge, CPT leaders stopped disciplining those members it found publicly practising religious rituals. And, responding to the rising nationalist fervour, the republican government tried to persuade Moscow to return Samarkand and Bukhara to Tajikistan. Whatever the strength of Tajikistan's claim to these renowned historical cities, the Kremlin realized that any transfer of territory from one republic to another in this or any other case – such as that of Nagorno Kara-bakh – would unleash an unmanageable list of disputes. It therefore turned down Dushanbe's request. This provided a palpable motive for Tajik nationalists to rally around the newly formed Rastakhiz (i.e. Resurgence) People's Organization. The Islamic Renaissance Party, which had existed clandestinely since the mid-1970s, began to show its colours gingerly. However, the IRP was just one, albeit the most politicized, element in the Islamist spectrum, the others being the traditional, rural (unregistered) Muslim clerics, and the branch of the Muslim Spiritual Directorate of Central Asia in Dushanbe, headed by Haji Akbar Turajanzade, a young kazi trained in Tashkent and Amman, Jordan. Among the publications that emerged to inform and educate Islamists, only to be suppressed by the authorities, the *Islamskaya Pravda* (Islamic Truth), founded clan-destinely in 1986, was the most notable. Ecclesiastical in its policy, it published the writings and speeches of Islamic thinkers as varied as Jamaluddin Afghani (1838–97), an Islamic thinker and philos-opher, and Ayatollah Ruhollah Khomeini, a Shia theologian who later became the supreme leader of Iran, and Sayid Abu Ala Maududi (1903–79), the Sunni head of the Jamaat-e Islami in Pakistan. The government's crackdown on unofficial Islam had resulted in fifty Muslim militants being incarcerated by the end of 1989.

At the Twenty-second Congress of the CPT in January 1990, now enjoying the support of 126,881 members,[13] leading party figures aired concern about the growth of mosques and Islamic publications, and the increasing participation of mullahs in the political process. To counter this trend, they urged the cadres to explain the party programme of economic development and social progress in a secular environment to religious leaders, and to emphasize that the republic's 1978 constitution, modelled along the 1977 USSR constitution, gave citizens freedom of conscience.

But socio-economic development, in the wake of glasnost and perestroika, was following uncharted territory, creating unprecedented problems for the authorities. Given the freedom to express their grievances, against the background of a deteriorating economic situation, ethnic Tajiks, forming sixty per cent of the population of Tajikistan, with the lowest per capita income in the USSR, became restive.

Just as in the Fergana Valley in Uzbekistan, where majority Uzbeks had turned violently against minority Meskhetian Turks, majority Tajiks – believing the rumours that Armenian refugees caused by the January 1990 anti-Armenian riots in Baku were to be given apartments while locals were being denied them – took to the streets on 12–14 February. Some of the demonstrators began attacking Armenians, and then Russians and other Slavs. The protest deteriorated into rioting. Among the more popular slogans aired was: 'Long live the Islamic Republic of Tajikistan!' This signified the blending of Tajik nationalism with Islam, something that had occurred earlier in neighbouring Afghanistan. The riots were so serious that the media in Moscow described them as 'round the clock clashes'. The Kremlin despatched its Special Purpose Militia Units, known by their Russian acronym Omon, to restore order. By the time they had done so, eighteen people were dead and another 110 wounded.

The February 1990 riots helped nationalists and Islamists to gain ground at the expense of the CPT. As a secular nationalist organization, Rastakhiz, led by Tahir Abdujabarov (Abdul Jabar), was intent on preserving Tajik identity and culture, which it saw as being threatened by two trends: mixed-nationality marriages which, having grown from 16.7 per cent to 22.3 per cent in the urban areas during

1959–70,[14] had continued to rise; and bilingualism, which was particularly prevalent in the northern Hojand Province, where a majority of the republic's 1.4 million Uzbeks lived.

In mid-1990, following the removal of state and party control over the press, it became easier for the opposition to propagate its ideas and programmes. Rastakhiz monitored rising nationalism in the three Baltic republics with great interest. Encouraged by the fast-changing political climate, IRP supporters called a meeting in late 1990 in Dushanbe to establish a branch of the party. The Supreme Soviet tried to prevent it. When it failed, it passed a law banning the party, and then adopted another which outlawed any 'religious political party'.[15] Among other things this measure alienated the head of official Islam, Haji Turajanzade. He began distancing himself from the authorities, and acting as a mediator between traditional rural mullahs, the clandestine IRP, and the underground Sufi brotherhoods; and that raised his popular standing.

When in January 1991 Moscow tried to repress nationalist forces in the Baltics by despatching Omon to these republics to quell demonstrations, Rastakhiz leaders protested.

Even an erstwhile member of the CPSU's Central Committee and a member of the USSR Supreme Soviet from Tajikistan, Davlat Khudanazarov, signed a petition as the head of the All Soviet Cinematographers' Union, protesting at the violence used by Omon militia in Vilnius, Lithuania. His disenchantment with Gorbachev's iron-fist policy towards ethnic nationalism led him to join the Democratic Reform movement – an alliance dominated by moderate Communists like Eduard Shevardnadze, the Soviet foreign minister, but also including non-Communist reformers – which was formed in Moscow in July 1991.

During the anti-Gorbachev coup from 19 to 21 August, Khudanazarov was in Moscow, and took a strong line against the plotters. On 27 August he claimed to have received documents which showed that Mahkamov, the CPT's First Secretary, and Kadriddin Aslonov, chairman of the Presidium of the Tajik Supreme Soviet, had been supporters of the failed coup.[16] Two days later Khudanazarov revealed his documents on the floor of the USSR Supreme Soviet. His charge was denied by Mahkamov and Aslonov. Their denials carried much weight in Tajikistan because they came in the aftermath of a declaration of Tajik independence by the Supreme Soviet on 24 August, made at their behest.

The revulsion felt in Moscow against the CPSU in the wake of the coup found its echo in Dushanbe, and became encapsulated in a growing demand for the removal of a towering statue of Lenin in the city's administrative-political centre. Sensing the direction in which the popular mood was moving, Aslonov urged the Supreme Soviet to ban the CPT. With ninety-three per cent of the 310 deputies, elected in March 1990, affiliated to the CPT, the Supreme Soviet refused. When Aslonov persisted, the parliamentarians voted him out of office in early September, and put Rahman Nabiyev, then in retirement, in his place.

Nabiyev allowed the IRP to register as a political party provided it agreed to keep within the law. It did so by stating that it would employ 'exclusively democratic means in pursuit of its ultimate objective: a state based on the Sharia, Islamic law', and was registered on 9 September. Nabiyev made this move partly because he reckoned that the IRP, headed by forty-year-old Muhammad Sharif Himmatzade, would grow at the expense of the following for Haji Turajanzade, aged thirty-eight, who was fast emerging as the leading star in the growing opposition camp. Already Turajanzade had established a working alliance between his directorate, now functioning independently of Tashkent and called the Kaziat (literally Pertaining to the Kazi), the IRP and Sufi brotherhoods, a considerable achievement.

Among those who had joined the opposition was Maksud Ikramov, the mayor of Dushanbe. He allowed the main statue of Lenin to be removed on 21 September, and immediately created a crisis. Denouncing the move, many Communist deputies threatened to imprison opposition leaders as well as Turajanzade. The Supreme Soviet declared a state of emergency in Dushanbe on 22 September. Nabiyev capped this with martial law, and posted interior ministry troops to guard all the remaining statues of Lenin.

Having seen the Supreme Soviet proceedings on television, many rural citizens began marching to Dushanbe in protest. The Communist deputies' action brought together leaders of all opposition groups based in the capital. They focused on getting the CPT banned and having a special commission investigate links between top party leaders and the failed coup in Moscow. With rural protesters arriving daily in Dushanbe by the hundreds, the spirits of oppositionists rose. It was their first taste of grass-roots politics, and they felt heady with confidence. They saw the first sign of success when Mamadayaz Navjavanov (Muhammad Ayaz Navjavan), the interior minister who hailed from the much-neglected Badakhshan mountainous region, refused to break up an opposition demonstration when ordered to do so by the party hierarchy. The Soviet army and Omon units declared their neutrality in domestic politics. The open split in the republic's administration, coupled with a public withdrawal of the centre's backing for it, signalled that the days of a monolithic party exercising total power under the direction of Moscow were finally over.

Realizing this, and finding martial law being openly flouted since 23 September by a round-the-clock sit-in by thousands of protesters gathered in tents in Azadi (i.e. Freedom) Square outside the Supreme Soviet, President Nabiyev lifted martial law on 6 October. Yielding to popular pressure, the Supreme Soviet endorsed the earlier order by Aslonov banning the CPT. It amended the constitution to create the office of a directly elected executive president, and fixed 27 October as the polling date. Opposition leaders felt satisfied – except for the election day, which was much too soon. Under their pressure the Supreme Soviet moved the date back to 24 November. This gave both sides enough time to devise a winning strategy.

Taking its lead from the Communist Party of Uzbekistan, a hurriedly called congress of the CPT, led by Mahkamov, dissolved the organization, and re-emerged as the Socialist Party of Tajikistan, but with the hapless Mahkamov replaced by Shudi Shahabdulov (Shah Abdul) as its head, and with only a fraction of the membership of its predecessor at 130,000. It adopted Nabiyev as its presidential candidate, who then resigned his chairmanship of the Supreme Soviet, which went to Akbarsho Iskanderov (Akbarshah Iskander).

The formal disappearance of the CPT, which had dominated state and society for seventy years, created a favourable environment for opposition groups – which since September had included the Democratic Party, a secular organization popular with younger, urban Tajik intellectuals, led by Khudanazarov – to pose a serious challenge to Nabiyev. They did. In Khudanazarov, a magnetic personality, the main opposition parties found a viable alternative to Nabiyev. There were six other hopefuls, all of them holding government jobs.

Under popular pressure, the authorities allowed debates and round-table discussions on radio and television, thus raising the political consciousness of the electorate. Inevitably, as an eminent political figure of long standing, Nabiyev received most exposure on television. Unable to gain access to Tajik television as a sole speaker, Khudanazarov, a well-established national film director, tried to tap the central television network directed from Moscow. He succeeded in getting three-minute slots which were balanced by an equal time allotted to Nabiyev. In the heat of the election campaign, five independent newspapers were launched, thus providing an unprecedented variety of political opinion and comment. Campaigning for Khudanazarov, Turajanzade expressed his preference for a parliamentary secular state with a free-market economy. 'Religion must be separated from the state so no one will ascribe the sins of society to Islam as happened with communism,' he said.[17]

On 24 November, eighty-six per cent of the 2.5 million electors voted. Of these, Nabiyev won fifty-seven per cent and Khudanazarov thirty-four per cent, with the remaining six candidates getting the rest. Khudanazarov immediately challenged the result, alleging voting irregularities. Following this, the election commission cancelled three per cent of the vote. But that did not alter the final result.

Regionally, Nabiyev did well in the traditional strongholds of the CPT, the comparatively well-off Hojand and Kulyab, which accounted for over three-fifths of the electorate. The deprived areas of thinly populated Badakhshan and the pro-Islamic Garm Valley and Kurgan Tyube supported Khudanazarov. In ethnic terms, Nabiyev vastly outperformed Khudanazarov among Uzbeks (23.5 per cent), Slavs and Germans (nine per cent), and other non-Tajik minorities. Perceiving Khudanazarov as a Tajik nationalist backed by Islamists, non-Tajik voters overwhelmingly backed Nabiyev. It was safe to assume that most of the forty per cent of non-Tajik voters opted for Nabiyev, whereas the remaining ethnic Tajik voters split almost evenly between the two leading candidates – with almost all Badakhshan electors, forming four per cent of the total, being Ismaili,[18] voting for Khudanazarov, a fellow-Ismaili. In purely personal terms, what favoured Nabiyev, aged sixty-one, were his many years of administrative experience and his authoritative style of leadership, which many of his supporters considered essential to steer Tajikistan through the painful transition to a market economy.

Nabiyev's victory was received rapturously by Communist/ Socialist stalwarts. With their leader in possession of a popular mandate, they felt they would be able to hang on to their power and privilege for another five years. In this they were not to be disappointed. The government selected by Nabiyev was dominated, as in the past, by the old nomenklatura from Hojand and Kulyab. This, and the reaffirmation of his commitment to the current five-year economic plan, showed that Nabiyev was too set in the old ways. He summed up his programme thus: 'My aim is to create a multi-party system. But before I do that I have to put food into the shops.'[19] In other words, economic aims had to be achieved first before there was meaningful progress towards political liberalization. This was the line later to be echoed by President Niyazov of Turkmenistan.

When Nabiyev attended the summit of Central Asian leaders in Ashqabat on 12–13 December 1991, he could rightly claim that alone among them he had won executive presidency in a multi-candidate contest. As the head of the poorest republic, heavily dependent on subsidies from Moscow, Nabiyev favoured a continuing association of the current constituents of the USSR. Indeed, feeling pressures on Tajikistan from Afghanistan – still in the throes of a civil war nearly three years after the departure of Soviet troops, with ninety per cent of the Tajik–Afghan border in the hands of the Afghan resistance, and containing at least as many ethnic Tajiks as Tajikistan (over 3.5 million each) – he was enthusiastic about joining a loose federation of independent republics called the Commonwealth of Independent States.

AFTER THE SOVIET BREAK-UP

Alone among former Soviet republican capitals, Dushanbe presented the establishment of the Commonwealth of Independent States as a 'revival of the Soviet Union', a term frequently used at the congress of the Socialist Party of Tajikistan on 4–6 January 1992 under the leadership of Shudi Shahabdulov. To give substance to this interpretation, the delegates decided to revert to the name of the Communist Party of Tajikistan, with their leaders arguing that since the organization had a different constitution from the old Communist Party, and was not an integral part of a supra-republican entity like the Communist Party of the Soviet Union, it was quite distinct from its old namesake. When the freshly rechristened Communist parliamentarians attended the next session of the Supreme Soviet, they enthusiastically passed laws that curtailed press freedom and the right to hold marches and rallies.

This set the scene for the government to settle scores with those who had organized grass-roots demonstrations and sit-ins in September, thus behaving in a feudal fashion more reminiscent of a tribal or clan society than a socialist or post-socialist one. On 6 March it arrested Maksud Ikramov, mayor of Dushanbe and a deputy of the Supreme Soviet, inside the parliament building, and charged him with corruption in his dealings with Iran. The opposition reckoned that Ikramov was being punished for having allowed the main statue of Lenin to be removed the previous September. If it had any doubts, these were dispelled when a week later live television transmission of the proceedings of the Supreme Soviet's presidium showed its members levelling charges of corruption at Mamadayaz Navjavanov – the interior minister who had refused to break up opposition demonstrations in September – and dismissing him.

These events acted as catalysts to bring together the main opposition groupings: the Democratic Party, Rastakhiz, IRP and Kaziat. By 21 March they set in train protest rallies and sit-ins around the administrative centre of Dushanbe. The protesters demanded the reinstatement of Ikramov and Navjavanov and, more importantly, a new constitution, dissolution of the Supreme Soviet and fresh elections. The opposition leadership, encouraged by rallies that sometimes attracted 50,000 people, threatened to establish an alternative centre of power by convening a National Council of Tajikistan.

Nabiyev's supporters argued that nobody had the legal power to disband the Supreme Soviet before its term expired in 1994, and only courts had the authority to settle the question of Ikramov's guilt. As for President Nabiyev himself, he thought it prudent not to appear inflexible. So he agreed to reinstate Navjavanov. But this was not enough to satisfy his adversaries. They kept up the pressure. They held a meeting with him in mid-April, but nothing came of it. Just then came the news of pro-Communist Najibullah's downfall in Afghanistan, followed by the arrival of the victorious Islamic Mujahedin in Kabul. This raised the spirits of the Tajik opposition, especially its religious constituents. Conversely, the morale of the Communist government in Dushanbe fell. On 17 April the Supreme Soviet agreed to concede the opposition demands for a new constitution and fresh elections in return for a three-week moratorium on demonstrations. Rejecting the offer, the anti-Communist camp set a deadline for the resignation of the hardline chairman of the Supreme Soviet, Safarali Kenjayev.

Already cracks had appeared in the governmental side. A large section of the Tajik interior ministry troops, most of them being Badakhshani and supporters of the Democratic Party or Lal-e Badakhshan, a nationalist group, had defected to the opposite camp. They had done so in the aftermath of the Supreme Soviet of Gorno Badakhshan Autonomous Region, forming forty-five per cent of Tajikistan's area, declaring the territory as Pamir-Badakhshan

Autonomous Republic on 11 April, and endorsing the opposition's demands, especially for closer links with Afghanistan and Iran.[20] With these armed men on their side, the protesters took several parliamentary deputies hostage on 21 April. The next day Kenjayev resigned, and the hostages were freed. The Supreme Soviet reciprocated by abolishing censorship, and fixing a date for the promulgation of a new constitution. President Nabiyev ordered amnesty for all those who had participated in demonstrations. Just as opposition leaders were discussing their next move, thousands of pro-government supporters from the Kulyab region, headed by Sangak Safarov and Faizali Saidov of the Popular Front, loyal to Kenjayev, a fellow-Kulyabi, arrived in Dushanbe on 26 April. Safarov, trained as a cook, had served twenty-three years in Soviet jails for committing a murder. Since his release in 1990 he had found his way into the local mafia, a network of men possessing administrative-economic influence, and had turned into an active supporter of the Communist regime. The introduction of the pro-Nabiyev demonstrators, some of them armed, radicalized the opposition which until then had been peaceful and good-natured. With the anti- and pro-government protesters occupying two squares only 250 metres (273 yards) apart, tension rose. To tackle the deteriorating situation, Nabiyev declared presidential rule. This raised the temperature further. The size of the pro- and anti-government rallies grew to some 100,000 participants each. Nabiyev ordered the formation of a National Guard answerable directly to him. This was a ploy that allowed him to arm the pro-government militias from the Kulyab and Hissar (Gissar in Russian) Valleys with automatic weapons, chiefly Kalashnikov assault rifles – a step that fuelled a civil conflict which was to rock Tajikistan, and threaten the stability of Central Asia, for many months. The size of the National Guard was put at 2000–4000. Nabiyev's action encouraged the opposition to form its own armed militia, called the People's Volunteer Corps (PVC), and arm them with weapons stolen, or bought, from the CIS forces stationed in the republic. Emboldened by the emergence of the National Guard, the Supreme Soviet reinstated Kenjayev as its chairman on 3 May, the day opposition leaders were scheduled to meet the president.

On Monday, 4 May, the simmering tension boiled over. Clashes broke out between the armed men of rival camps. The next day the opposition's PVC went on an offensive and captured the television station, which started transmitting opposition statements. President Nabiyev declared a state of emergency and curfew. Both sides ignored them. To their earlier theme of condemnation of the nomen-klatura, the opposition speakers now added their declarations of solidarity with the victorious Afghan Mujahedin who, they claimed, had sent messages promising help. Shodmon Yusuf of the Democratic Party declared that the opposition parties had the 'right' to ask for help 'from the neighbouring states', implying Afghanistan.[21] The ambience at the opposition camp at Azadi Square had become predominantly Islamic, with the place embellished with Islamic placards and slogans, many of these being copies of those in vogue in Iran. Bearded young men and veiled women declared their readiness to be martyred for Islam.[22] The opposition now raised the ante, and demanded the president's resignation and fresh elections, alleging that the result of the earlier poll had been rigged. This resulted in the two sides discussing the formation of a national reconciliation government. On 6 May the PVC seized most of Dushanbe, including the presidential palace, leaving only the Supreme Soviet building, the KGB (now renamed *Komitet Natsionalnoy Bezopasnosti*, KNB – Committee for National Security) headquarters and the radio station in the hands of the pro-Nabiyev forces. The death toll in the fighting reached sixty.

The next day the president withdrew his decrees concerning a state of emergency and the establishment of the National Guard, thus preparing the way for a compromise with his opponents. But his hand was weakened when his forces lost the radio station to the opposition, which announced the formation of a Revolutionary Council to rule Tajikistan. Some KNB employees informed the anti-Nabiyev camp that the president was inside the KNB headquarters. When PVC men approached the building, guarded by riot police in armoured personnel carriers, there was a shoot-out in which eight people died. With the disappearance of the president, the government side split between the hardliners led by Vice-President Nazrullah Dostov and Supreme Soviet chairman Kenjayev, and the moderates headed by Akbar Mirzayev. But an impasse developed between the negotiators on 9 May when the opposition refused to disarm its militia, the PVC, while the government proved unable to disarm either its supporters from Kulyab and Hissar, or the now-dissolved National Guard.

However, to stop the bloodshed the opposition re-opened talks with the moderate faction within the administration with a view to cobbling together a coalition government. These negotiations revealed a split among oppositionists, with the IRP leadership insisting on Nabiyev's resignation and the others ready to let him stay. Turajanzade argued that if Nabiyev were forced out of power it would start a war between the clans of the northern Hojand region, Nabiyev's home base, and the southern region. The example of President Zviad Gamsakhurdia in Georgia who, after being removed from power by the Supreme Soviet, had resorted to a military campaign against the regime from outside the republic, acted as a warning to those who wanted to depose Nabiyev. Khudanazarov took a constitutional line. 'It is up to the Supreme Soviet and a national referendum to decide if the republic needs a new president, and if they do, which one,' he said. 'But these matters must not be decided by clans and street rallies.'[23] While these talks continued, officials in Hojand and Kulyab provinces let it be known that they had nothing to do with the deliberations in Dushanbe, and the authorities in Hojand announced that they were considering rejoining Uzbekistan from which the province had been detached in 1929,[24] a statement that had a sobering effect on the anti-Communist camp. The commander of the CIS troops repeated that his troops had kept out of the local conflict.

On 11 May, fifty-one days after the protest had been mounted and some 150 people had been killed, it was announced that the opposition had agreed to let Nabiyev continue as president, and that it would be given a third of the seats in a twenty-four-member cabinet (corresponding to Khudanazarov's percentage of the popular vote) headed by Prime Minister Akbar Mirzayev. These included the vice-premiership as well as the defence and interior ministries. Dostov, the hardline vice-president, resigned in protest, but the Supreme Soviet chairman, Kenjayev, refused to step down. Once it was decided that the heads of the opposition parties would stay out of the government, cabinet posts went to their deputies, with Usman Davlat of the IRP becoming vice-premier, overseeing security forces. Refusing to disarm, the pro-Nabiyev militias from Kulyab and Hissar had left the capital on 9 May. And, fearing for his life, Kenjayev had reportedly escaped inside a tank of the CIS 201st motorized division.[25]

On 13 May the new government announced a plan for disarming both sides in the conflict. But the chances of its implementation were slim. The pro-Nabiyev militias, which had been drafted instantly into the National Guard and armed, had returned home; and the Popular Volunteer Corps of the opposition parties, now collectively called the National Salvation Front (NSF), refused to surrender its weapons, with many of its members returning to their strongholds in the Garm Valley and the south.

The installation of a new cabinet, bearing the comforting title of the 'national reconciliation government', did not in reality resolve the conflict, based as it was on deeply rooted clan and regional loyalties. When Nabiyev agreed to take in opposition ministers, he lost the respect of many of the Communist Party faithful who, considering him a weak-kneed leader who had betrayed the secular, socialist cause, switched their loyalty to such hardliners as Kenjayev. The failure of the coalition government to win a vote of confidence by the Supreme Soviet, heavily dominated by Communists, strengthened the hand of orthodox party members, and also made the deal between the opposition and President Nabiyev legally non-binding.

Unsurprisingly, the governor of Hojand declared on 15 May that he would obey only those orders of the president he considered 'legal', and his lead was quickly followed by the governor of Kulyab. Later, the delegates to a Sunni Muslim conference in Kulyab decided to break away from the republic's Kaziat under Turajanzade, and form alternative organs under the leadership of a Kulyabi, Kazi Heidar Sharifzade, then based in Hissar. More worryingly for the government in Dushanbe, Communist militants in Hojand and Kulyab had taken to assassinating their opponents.

On the positive side, the new government published a draft constitution to be discussed by the Supreme Soviet. It named the president as the head of state and the National Assembly (*Milli Majlis* in Tajik) as the highest law-making body. It confirmed the 1991 law on Tajik, which specified a switch-over from the Cyrillic script to Arabic/Persian over a period of five years, and limited the use of Russian. It ruled out dual citizenship, thus dimming the future prospects of Russian settlers, who often possessed much-needed skills.[26] As it was, they had already started leaving in droves.

Faced with continued defiance from officials in Hojand and Kulyab – which in turn had encouraged officials in the pro-Islamic Kurgan Tyube to do likewise – Nabiyev appointed personal representatives to explain the coalition government's decisions to the population of these provinces. But it proved to be a sterile exercise. The militia of Safarov's Popular Front had by now taken over the city of Kulyab, and was intent on settling scores with the inhabitants of the province of Kurgan Tyube, whom it regarded as its historic adversaries. Indeed, fighting between pro- and anti-Communist forces in these adjoining provinces reached a level in late June that left forty-two dead. The warring militias had resorted to equipping themselves with weapons being smuggled in from Afghanistan or bought from CIS officers and troops with US dollars, which were much in demand.

Within the ruling coalition the opposition NSF proposed that the government should claim jurisdiction over the CIS troops in the republic, and use them to end the civil conflict which was intensifying. The proposal was not adopted because it posed insoluble problems for the administration. Taking charge of the CIS force meant having to bear the cost of maintaining it, something the government could not afford, especially as the authorities in Hojand, accounting for three-fifths of the republic's industrial production, had stopped paying their budget contributions. Secondly, the officers of the mixed Russian–Tajik 201st motorized division, being almost invariably Russian, were unlikely to stay on to serve under the government of Tajikistan.

By early July 1992 civil war had begun in the south, with Kurgan Tyube and Kulyab bearing its brunt, and the number of refugees rising sharply. There was a ceasefire on 7 July which lasted only a few weeks. When the fighting resumed, it aroused strong criticism of President Nabiyev for his failure to secure peace. Owing to political instability, the republic's economy had suffered, with cotton output down by half from the peak of 900,000 tons in 1987. Because of the demonstrations in Dushanbe in April/May, the Turkish premier, Demirel, had eliminated the city from his tour of Central Asia, and had thus failed to offer Tajikistan much-needed aid and trade. A budget deficit amounting to forty per cent of the Gross Domestic Product fuelled inflation and depressed already low living standards.

Partly to get away from domestic pressures, and partly to placate the Islamists within his coalition government, President Nabiyev flew to Tehran, where he signed a treaty of friendship and cooperation with Iran, covering culture, trade, banking and science. Pleased with Tajikistan's decision to adopt the Persian alphabet for Tajik, Tehran helped Tajik linguistic experts modify the alphabet they had prepared for their language. Some weeks later, Iran offered Tajikistan 300,000 tons of free oil, worth about $40 million, to alleviate its energy crisis, which had brought public transport in Dushanbe to a virtual halt.[27]

But Nabiyev's domestic problems were far from over. During the Supreme Soviet session, which began on 12 August, the erstwhile moderate Haji Turajanzade demanded Nabiyev's resignation owing to his failure to stop political and economic disintegration of the republic. Shodmon Yusuf, the Democratic Party leader, proposed that the presidency be supplanted by a temporary State Council composed of representatives from all regions. The president's supporters rejected these demands, arguing that Nabiyev had been elected in a freely contested poll, and possessed a popular mandate to rule for five years.

Tension rose further when the KNB deputy chief, Colonel Juranbek Aminov, accused Hikmatyar, an Afghan Islamic leader, of training Tajik Islamists to overthrow the Nabiyev regime, and the chief prosecutor was murdered in Dushanbe. Nabiyev decided to act. He signed an agreement with the CIS secretariat in Moscow in late August authorizing the arrival of CIS military units in Tajikistan for peace-keeping. Since he acted without consulting the opposition cabinet ministers, they criticized him strongly. Unhappy at this, Prime Minister Akbar Mirzayev resigned on 30 August, citing severe limitations on the 'political freedoms' of President Nabiyev since the formation of the coalition government.

The open rift within the cabinet encouraged militant anti-Nabiyev elements to act. On 31 August between fifty and 100 armed opposition demonstrators (not belonging to any of the NSF parties) occupied the ground floor of the presidential palace and took thirty-five hostages, including ministers. Following talks between them and members of the government and Supreme Soviet presidium, the latter issued a statement on 2 September. It read: 'We consider that President Nabiyev has been removed from power because of his failure to end the crisis threatening the future of the country, and from now on it is not possible for him to perform his duties'. The chairman of the Supreme Soviet presidium, Akbarsho Iskanderov, called a session of the parliament on 4 September to consider the latest situation, including the fate of Nabiyev, who had taken refuge in the CIS headquarters in Dushanbe.

These dramatic events led the presidents of Uzbekistan, Kazakhstan, Kyrgyzstan and Russia to issue a communiqué on 3 September warning the government and political organizations in Tajikistan of the severe consequences of continued conflict, describing the civil war as a 'danger to the CIS', and adding that their countries intended to intervene to stop the bloodshed. Alluding to the large-scale smuggling of arms and narcotics from Tajikistan's 'southern neighbours', which raised the prospect of Tajikistan being removed from the CIS or losing its sovereignty, they announced the despatch of additional border troops to the Tajik–Afghan frontier.[28]

On 4 September the scheduled Supreme Soviet session in Dushanbe could not be held because only eighty deputies, about half of the quorum of 156, turned up. The following day there were reports of bitter fighting between pro- and anti-Nabiyev camps in Kurgan Tyube, in which between thirty and several hundred people were killed. Nabiyev, still ensconced in the CIS headquarters, declared a state of emergency in the province.

Two days later, on 7 September, Nabiyev was reported to be intending to fly secretly to Hojand to confer with the Communist Party hierarchy there. But opposition leaders were tipped off. They confronted him at Dushanbe airport's VIP lounge. After several hours of talks with them he resigned, and handed over his powers to Iskanderov, the chairman of the Supreme Soviet.[29] Nabiyev then flew to Hojand where he claimed that he had not resigned and that the signature on his resignation letter was a forgery.

Iskanderov, a Badakhshan-born politician who had earlier served as deputy premier under Nabiyev, became acting president. Attempts to convene the Supreme Soviet to consider Nabiyev's resignation and confirm Iskanderov in his new job failed due to the lack of a quorum. The new administration under Iskanderov blew up a major bridge connecting Dushanbe with the north to 'prevent military movement' – that is, to prevent armed forces from Hojand travelling south to overthrow the government in Dushanbe or aid pro-Nabiyev fighters further south. But the destruction of the crucial bridge between the industrial north and the rest of the country curtailed transport facilities, making fuel scarce. Lack of public funds and the breakdown of communications and road systems badly affected the economy and public morale.

Civil conflict escalated throughout the republic, with total fatalities exceeding 2000 by the end of September. In the anti-Nabiyev camp the major burden of fighting was borne by the militias loyal to the IRP, with a membership of 30,000 extending to village level, and the charismatic Haji Turajanzade. What aided them was the vastly increased number of mosques, many times the pre-perestroika figure of seventeen,[30] a fast-expanding network. Together these Islamist elements had marginalized secular, nationalist forces within the opposition. Outside of Kurgan Tyube, Islamic fighters came mainly from the Garm Valley, a long-standing rival of the Kulyab Valley, and were armed with weapons from Afghanistan supplied either by

Hikmatyar or Ahmed Shah Masoud. Unlike Masoud, Hikmatyar was not a Tajik, but a Pushtun. A political rival of Masoud, he retained a presence in Tajikistan's imbroglio in order to maintain influence among Tajik Islamists. Outside the Hojand region, the pro-Nabiyev forces, originating principally from Kulyab and the Hissar Valley, were armed mainly with weapons bought or stolen from the CIS depots, or supplied by such sources as the Uzbekistan government. Other, minor sources of arms supplies were the Caucasus, with shipments sent across the Caspian Sea, and Iranian air-drops.

The posting of an extra 1000 border troops from Russia, Uzbekistan, Kazakhstan and Kyrgyzstan along the Tajik–Afghan border elicited a protest from Iran. In practice, though, it made little difference, since the largely mountainous frontier was difficult to seal, and fighters on both sides of the international line had become adept in moving men and materials across the border.

During the second half of September, internal security within Tajikistan deteriorated considerably, affecting the capital, which had so far been comparatively peaceful. On 19 September a crowd of 1000 men hijacked buses in Dushanbe, and set off for Kurgan Tyube to join the fighting there. Acting President Iskanderov asked the CIS troops to assist the local interior ministry troops in guarding important public installations. The residents of Dushanbe demonstrated, calling for arms to defend themselves against attacks by pro-Nabiyev partisans. Iskanderov responded by appealing for volunteers to expand the interior ministry forces. Trying to maintain a semblance of neutrality between the opposing forces, he appointed Abdumalik Abdullajanov (Abdul Malik Abdullah Jan), an ex-Communist economist-turned-businessman, acting prime minister on 21 September, thus meeting one of the demands of the pro-Nabiyev partisans from Kulyab, others being the dismissals of the IRP leader, Usman Davlat, as vice-premier, and Turajanzade as the republic's highest ranking mullah. In the south, violence intensified as armed gangs in the countryside began settling old clan and tribal rivalries. Iskanderov set 24 September as the deadline for an end to the hostilities in Kurgan Tyube and Kulyab, and called on the CIS units to stop the fighting in Kurgan Tyube, which had produced 50,000 refugees. These were futile gestures. Nobody paid any attention to the truce deadline and the CIS high command had no intention of getting involved in local conflicts.

But, more disappointingly for Iskanderov, Russia turned down his request for the purchase of heavy weapons – for pragmatic and principled reasons. Moscow regarded the current government as 'illegitimate' since it had failed to win a vote of confidence from the Supreme Soviet, though it refrained from saying so publicly. Also, Russia was unwilling to sell weapons for anything but hard currency, which the Iskanderov administration lacked.[31] Beyond that, while loudly claiming its neutrality in the Tajik civil war and refusing to allow the Russian-dominated CIS units to be used in any capacity other than assisting the local interior ministry troops in guarding important installations, Moscow pursued its undeclared policy of helping the pro-Nabiyev forces through illicit sales of locally stored weapons and ammunition. Russia was against Tajik Islamists for practical, ideological and strategic reasons. Victory for Islamic forces would have resulted in a large-scale exodus of the remaining 300,000 Russians to a Russia where there was an acute shortage of housing and jobs, thus inflaming opinion in parliament and on the streets. This would have added to the headaches of President Yeltsin, already burdened with other, almost intractable, problems. It would have exposed him to a damaging charge from the conservative-nationalists that he was unable to protect the Russians living abroad. Moreover, a successful expulsion of ethnic Russians from Tajikistan was bound to whet the appetite of pan-Turkic nationalists in the rest of Central Asia, thus compounding Moscow's problem and creating a backlash among Russians at home, urging it to reciprocate in kind and expel the Central Asians living in Russia. Thirdly, as the leading secular democracy in the CIS, Russia was loath to see a religious state either within the CIS or bordering it. Finally, the emergence of an Islamic regime in Tajikistan would destabilize the neighbouring republics, especially Uzbekistan, the most strategically important Central Asian state. Indeed, President Karimov of Uzbekistan had taken secretly to aiding pro-Nabiyev partisans in Kulyab, using the Uzbek border town of Termez to channel arms and equipment to them.[32]

Freshly equipped with four tanks and six armoured personnel carriers, secured from the CIS 201st motorized division during the third week of September, the pro-Nabiyev Kulyabi forces mounted devastating raids on villages and towns in Kurgan Tyube, the stronghold of the IRP, killing hundreds and displacing tens of thousands. The mayor of Kurgan Tyube publicly accused the CIS troops stationed in the region of assisting the pro-Nabiyev partisans from Kulyab before his city fell into the hands of the invaders. When Acting President Iskanderov protested to Moscow about the use of Russian tanks by the pro-Nabiyev forces against unarmed civilians, the CIS command replied that an armed militia had 'stolen' these tanks after 'besieging' a CIS unit near Kurgan Tyube.[33]

Moscow's announcement on 29 September that 'a limited military contingent' of 1500 troops had arrived in Tajikistan to protect Russian troops already there, as well as their families and facilities, highlighted the worsening security situation. This statement came amid signs of growing disarray in the capital. Rumours were rife that pro-Nabiyev forces from Kulyab were on their way to Dushanbe: this encouraged the anti-Nabiyev partisans to strengthen their self-defence units in Kofarnihan (Orjonikijeabad) on the Dushanbe–Kulyab road. With thousands of refugees from Kurgan Tyube pouring into the capital, and many people demonstrating daily before the Russian embassy demanding an end to Moscow's military aid to the pro-Nabiyev camp, Iskanderov appealed to the CIS and the United Nations to help stop the armed conflict which his government was unable to do. CIS troops took to guarding the airport in Dushanbe and running the aircraft repair workshops.

In early October Western reporters visiting Kurgan Tyube and other places in the region provided evidence which confirmed the anti-Nabiyev camp's charges that CIS units in the area were assisting the pro-Nabiyev fighters. This led Usman Davlat of the IRP to compare the Russian troops currently in Tajikistan to the Soviet troops sent into Afghanistan in 1979,[34] a comparison detested by Moscow. Responding to growing public calls for the removal of Russian troops from the disturbed region, Iskanderov said that their status would be determined when military agreements were signed between Tajikistan and the Russian Federation. As for CIS troops, their chief of staff, Sviatoslav Nabzdorov, declared that following an accord with various Tajik factions on 4 October, all CIS troops were to be confined to their garrisons from the next day, except those guarding the Nurek dam and hydro-electric station near the capital.

On the eve of the CIS summit in Bishkek on 8–9 October, leaving aside the thinly populated autonomous Badakhshan region, Tajikistan was politically divided into four parts: the pro-Nabiyev Hojand[35] region in the north; Dushanbe and its environs, dominated by the anti-Nabiyev Democrat–Islamic alliance; the pro-Nabiyev Kulyab region in the south-east; and the pro-Islamic Kurgan Tyube in the south-west.

As the CIS summit grappled with the pressing problem of the civil war in Tajikistan, Nabiyev announced from Hojand that he was recalling his resignation because it had been signed under physical and psychological pressure.[36] CIS leaders agreed that since the situation in Tajikistan might threaten the security of all member-states, they would not stand idly by in the face of threats to the 'external borders' of the CIS; that they would send a CIS peace-keeping force as soon as 'the legitimate authority' in Tajikistan requested it; and that the CIS troops should not be withdrawn from Tajikistan until the situation had improved. At the same time the final communiqué stated that (Russian-controlled) CIS troops would not be involved in 'inter-ethnic conflicts', and that each member-state had to settle such problems by using its own forces, and that CIS units would defend only the 'strategically important installations' in the CIS.[37] Following the summit, the host, President Akayev, said that the CIS was ready to help Tajikistan, and that peace efforts would continue under the chairmanship of Felix Kulov, his vice-president. Kulov came up with two proposals: to lead a delegation of CIS representatives to Dushanbe to settle the conflict, and to despatch a contingent of 450 Kyrgyz troops to Tajikistan as a peace-keeping force. The latter proposal was rejected by the Kyrgyz Supreme Soviet whose chairman told a press conference on 13 October that the legislators had decided not to interfere in the internal affairs of a neighbouring state.[38]

It seemed that in Bishkek Presidents Karimov and Yeltsin reached an understanding that each of them would continue to work to expel the anti-Nabiyev forces from the seats of power they had manoeuvred to acquire. This meant that Uzbekistan would maintain its policy of arming and training the pro-Nabiyev fighters. And, as in the case of the Armenian–Azerbaijani dispute over Nagorno Karabakh, under its often-professed neutrality Moscow would see that the Russian-controlled CIS troops in Tajikistan surreptitiously continued to assist one side – in this case the pro-Nabiyev camp – by providing weapons and intelligence to it while simultaneously refusing to sell heavy weapons to the other, the Iskanderov government in Dushanbe.

Indeed, during October fighting died down considerably because both sides ran out of ammunition. This prepared the way for a ceasefire on 15 October. But it did not hold. A desperate Iskanderov established a National Security Council made up of leading members of the Supreme Soviet and the cabinet, and appointed Khudanazarov as his chief advisor. On 20 October, during a meeting with the Russian foreign minister, Andrei Kozyrev, in Moscow, Khudanazarov sought Russian assistance to end the civil conflict, but failed. Kozyrev said that Russia could not interfere in the internal affairs of Tajikistan. Obviously, Moscow did not want to help Iskanderov, dependent for his political survival on Islamists, to consolidate his power. On their part, Muslim leaders, especially Haji Turajanzade, had taken to reiterating that the aim of establishing an Islamic state could only be realized through law, and that such an outcome would require the support of a substantial majority of Muslims, and that on present trends no change could be envisaged during the lifetime of the present generation of voters. In any case, he kept saying, an Islamic republic in 'this ethnically mixed, Soviet-educated population of 5 million people in Tajikistan' was unlikely to be in 'the rigid Iranian mould', with women wearing a veil. He also made a distinction between Tajiks, who are predominantly Sunni, and Iranians, who are Shia. 'The Sunni tradition never had a place for a single authoritarian religious figure like Khomeini,' he explained. 'Besides, over the past 70 years [under Communism] we have simply acquired a different view of the world.'[39] As for secular leaders within the opposition NSF, Khudanazarov reckoned that Islamists had the backing of no more than ten per cent of the Tajik population,[40] which was only sixty per cent of the country's total of 5.4 million, an assessment disputed by his religious colleagues. But they were both agreed that Russia and Uzbekistan were actively helping pro-Nabiyev partisans.

Reiterating his charge that Moscow was assisting the pro-Nabiyev camp, Haji Turajanzade said that Russia could stop the civil war 'in two days' if it wanted to. But that would have required open, large-scale military intervention, which would have to be approved by the Russian Supreme Soviet. That was unlikely. With the distant, Muslim-dominated, mountainous Tajikistan appearing in the Russian psyche so much like Afghanistan, any military commitment in that republic would have been so reminiscent of the Soviet armed intervention in Afghanistan in 1979 that it would have undermined the authority of any Russian government contemplating such action.

However, the Uzbek military's clandestine activity aimed at toppling the present administration in Dushanbe was in full steam, facilitated by the fact that the Tajik government had lost effective control over its frontier with Uzbekistan. It bore fruit on the night of 23–24 October. Safarali Kenjayev, former KGB deputy chief and chairman of the Tajik Supreme Soviet, who had escaped from Dushanbe to Hojand and then to Uzbekistan in May, led a column of forty buses and trucks which had assembled in Tursunzade (Regar), a town forty kilometres (twenty-five miles) west of Dushanbe, near the Uzbek border. His men, including several groups of Uzbeks, were equipped with weapons supplied by the Uzbek command based in the border town of Termez.[41] Mounting a surprise attack at night, the invaders encountered little resistance in capturing the presidential palace, the Supreme Soviet building and the radio station. In his broadcast, Kenjayev accused the anti-Nabiyev coalition of establishing an Islamic fundamentalist state.

Having recovered from the shock of an unexpected assault, the anti-Nabiyev forces – consisting of the militias of the IRP, Haji Turajanzade and Juma Khan (head of the Tajikistan Youth) – mounted a spirited offensive to dislodge the rebels from their key buildings. Two days of heavy fighting, which resulted in death or injury to three of the attackers' commanders, demonstrated that the invaders' position was untenable. The besieged forces used the CIS command as an intermediary to negotiate a ceasefire and evacuation. Escorted by CIS units, they left, claiming that their action had put the question of the legitimacy of the government on the national agenda. The fighting left between sixty and 150 people dead. However, compared to the carnage in the south, which had, according to Tajikistan Radio, claimed 18,500 lives so far, the loss of life in Dushanbe was insignificant.[42]

This was an embarrassing, though not a fatal, setback for the pro-Nabiyev camp. Either its Hissar Valley-based section had moved without proper coordination with its Kulyab counterpart, or the expected reinforcements from the south had failed to materialize owing to unexpected last-minute hitches. The main reason why the pro-Nabiyev side had decided to strike was that its leadership feared that the longer its adversaries remained in power in Dushanbe the more influential they would become. It also reckoned that once its fighters had captured the administrative-political heart of Dushanbe, the capital's residents would rise up against the Iskanderov government. Finally, it felt that when push came to shove CIS troops in Dushanbe would side with it. But they did not. They remained neutral. So pro-Nabiyev partisans had no choice but to leave when faced with a much bigger force than their own.

Having survived the pro-Nabiyev attack, the Iskanderov regime tried to project a picture of active cooperation between Dushanbe and Moscow, and benign neutrality on the part of Tashkent. Contrary to popular perception in the Tajik capital, Acting Prime Minister Abdullajanov denied that there was any 'direct evidence' of Uzbekistan arming the factions opposed to his administration. He added that once Moscow had realized that the authorities in Dushanbe were not in favour of Islamic fundamentalism, it had lent its support to the government, with General Muhriddin Ashurov, the Tajik commander of the CIS 201st motorized division, announcing that his troops were maintaining curfew, guarding key buildings, manning roadblocks, and were under orders to 'use force against any group attempting to enter the capital'.[43]

But any political advantage that the Iskanderov regime managed to extract from the latest episode was likely to prove transient since its inherent position was comparatively weak. The external forces backing the pro-Nabiyev side – Uzbekistan actively and Russia tacitly – were far more powerful than the combination of a fractured Afghanistan and distant Iran, lacking a common frontier with Tajikistan, which the anti-Nabiyev camp could hope to muster. In any case, both sides knew that although the latest battle was over, the war was not. Indeed, they began preparing for the next round, with Haji Turajanzade claiming he had 8000 fighters outside Dushanbe, though many of them unarmed, and the commander of the Democratic Party planning a militia of 4000.[44]

Meanwhile, Iskanderov accelerated his efforts to find a peaceful solution to the conflict. Despite his differences with the IRP and other Islamic leaders on the subject, he asked Yegor Gaidar, the Acting Premier of Russia, during a meeting in Moscow on 2 November, to consider using the CIS 201st division as a peace-keeping force in Tajikistan. Gaidar was reluctant.

Two days later, on 4 November, the Russian foreign minister, Andrei Kozyrev, attended a meeting of the leaders of the Central Asian member-states of the Collective Defence Treaty, except Tajikistan, in Alma Ata. It more or less decided the future of the troubled republic. A joint communiqué stated that (a) the (nominally CIS) Russian 201st division should continue its 'peace-keeping' role until a proper CIS peace-keeping force had been constituted to replace it; (b) a State Council, consisting of all factions in Tajikistan, should be formed; (c) a committee of representatives of the presidents of Uzbekistan, Kyrgyzstan, Kazakhstan and Russia (henceforth the Alma Ata Committee) had been appointed to bring about peace in Tajikistan; and (d) deputy foreign ministers of these republics would supervise distribution of humanitarian aid to Tajikistan. Releasing the joint statement to the press, the host, President Nazarbayev made a placatory gesture to the anti-Nabiyev forces. He said that Rahman Nabiyev should not attempt to reclaim Tajikistan's presidency because 'not enough Tajik citizens would back him now'.[45]

In contrast to the débâcle of the Hissar-based fighters of the pro-Nabiyev camp in Dushanbe in October, the pro-Nabiyev force under Safarov of the Popular Front chalked up a string of triumphs in areas south of the capital in early November, after it had replenished its ammunition. It was particularly successful in the Shartuz and Kabodien districts of Kurgan Tyube, and was well on its way to controlling the whole province after largely depopulating it and creating hundreds of thousands of refugees. It had also succeeded in blockading the Garm Valley, an Islamist stronghold. Overall the civil conflict had so far created 430,000 refugees, with 55,000 seeking shelter in Dushanbe.

The Alma Ata Committee was now in Tajikistan actively pursuing peace. On 8 November it met civilian delegates from the pro-Communist Kulyab. They tried to convince the Committee that the administration in Dushanbe was allied with the Islamic fundamentalists in Afghanistan. They claimed that Kulyabi officials holding Kadriddin Aslonov – former chairman of the Supreme Soviet now appointed governor of Kurgan Tyube, who had been kidnapped earlier by a group of Uzbeks in south Tajikistan – had found documents showing his contacts with Hikmatyar's Hizb-e Islami in Afghanistan, and demanded Aslonov's immediate trial. Two days later, another delegation from Kulyab, that of the Popular Front militia, led by Safarov, failed to turn up for a meeting with Acting President Iskanderov and Acting Premier Abdullajanov arranged by General Ashurov of the 201st division. Freshly aware of his armed superiority, Safarov had no intention of entering into talks with his adversaries in Dushanbe. He knew that negotiations would lead to compromise, which could only diminish the impact of his military successes. Confident of his growing strength, he demanded fresh parliamentary elections and a ban on the political parties forming the anti-Nabiyev alliance. His hard line position – which signalled the demise of the proposal made at the Alma Ata summit to form a State Council composed of all Tajik factions – had a depressing effect on officials in Dushanbe negotiating with the Alma Ata Committee.

On 10 November, members of the presidium of the Tajik Supreme Soviet and the cabinet submitted their resignations to Iskanderov to enable the special session of the Supreme Soviet summoned in Hojand on 16 November to make a fresh start. The reason for selecting Hojand as the venue for a parliamentary session was that repeated attempts to hold one in Dushanbe had failed, primarily because deputies were afraid that, as in the past, they would be pressured by well-orchestrated crowds in the capital to vote in a certain way. At the Alma Ata Committee's behest, all sides agreed beforehand to abide by the decisions of the Supreme Soviet which was expected *inter alia* to discuss the legality of Nabiyev's resignation. Since the Supreme Soviet was dominated by Communists, the end result was bound to go against the anti-Nabiyev camp, albeit not starkly.

These developments occurred against the background of the worsening economic situation in Dushanbe, which had been deprived of crucial supplies from Hojand since the railway line, its only surviving link with the north, had been blown up at several places, stranding about 500 wagons of badly needed food and fuel.

On Monday, 16 November, the Supreme Soviet met in Hojand under the chairmanship of Iskanderov, with nearly 200 deputies, well above the quorum of 154 and virtually all of them Communist, attending. Three days later it accepted by 140 to fifty-four votes the resignation of Iskanderov as chairman of the Supreme Soviet and acting president of the republic. Then, by 186 to eleven votes, the deputies elected Imamali Rahmanov – the erstwhile Communist governor of Kulyab, his home base, and a former director of a collective farm – chairman of the Supreme Soviet, thus making him the effective head of state. He publicly acknowledged his debt to Safarov for the result, thus underlining his importance as the leading power-broker. By naming a former Communist economist and acting premier, Abdumalik Abdullajanov, as the new prime minister, Rahmanov satisfied Communist deputies while maintaining a link with the immediate past. The following day the Supreme Soviet decided that Nabiyev's resignation was invalid because it had been offered under duress. Having thus retrieved his honour, Nabiyev resigned voluntarily; and this was accepted by a majority vote. This ended the most fractious political episode in the brief history of independent Tajikistan. His exit satisfied those Communist deputies who considered him a weak leader. It also mollified the opposition which, having objected to the fairness of the presidential poll, had never reconciled itself with his presidency.[46] The thorny questions of who should follow Nabiyev as the republic's president and how were resolved on 27 November when the Supreme Soviet amended the 1978 constitution to 'abolish presidential rule' and declare Tajikistan a 'parliamentary republic'. It thus reverted to the old Soviet practice of conferring the title of the head of state on its chairman, Imamali Rahmanov.

Having dealt with the political aspect of the civil conflict, the Supreme Soviet addressed its military aspect. It resolved unanimously to create a CIS peace-keeping force by supplementing the already present Russian 201st motorized division with battalions from Kazakhstan and Kyrgyzstan and a mobile regiment from Uzbekistan. The anti-Communist leaders based in Dushanbe saw this as a ploy to sanctify the involvement of the neighbouring republics – especially Uzbekistan – in Tajikistan's internal conflict, which had all along been aimed at shoring up their opponents. Little wonder that Tajikistan Radio, controlled by a leader of Rastakhiz, a member of the anti-Communist alliance, demanded an immediate halt to the Supreme Soviet session, but to no avail.[47]

What the Alma Ata Committee needed now to crown its success so far was a formal ceasefire between the warring parties. It worked hard to overcome resistance from a hawkish Safarov who, determined to decimate his political enemies, especially of the Islamic variety, kept blaming the Supreme Soviet leadership for having conferred official recognition on the IRP. Conscious of their comparative weakness, the anti-Communist alliance tried to make the best of a bad bargain by insisting that it would conclude a ceasefire agreement only if the blockade of Dushanbe from the north were lifted. It was. A truce was signed on 25 November. But this proved to be a stop-gap affair.

With their political supremacy underwritten by the Supreme Soviet, the Communist forces now began finalizing their military plans, in conjunction with the Uzbek military high command, to wrest control of the capital from their adversaries. They got their go-ahead when a meeting of the defence ministers of Russia, Kazakhstan, Kyrgyzstan and Uzbekistan and the supreme commander of the CIS military, Marshal Shaposhnikov, endorsed the Tajik parliament's plan for a CIS peace-keeping force on 30 November. Significantly, the meeting took place in Termez, the centre of clandestine Uzbek military assistance to the Communist camp.

On the same day, the presentation by Premier Abdullajanov of a cabinet, dominated by Kulyabis and Hojandis, to the Supreme Soviet made the anti-Communist alliance realize that politically it was back to the period before the successful populist uprising of May 1992. All it was left with now was physical control of Dushanbe and its environs, which were under increasing pressure from refugees, estimated at nearly 120,000 in a city of over 540,000, resulting mainly from the continuing military successes of their adversaries. For the defence of the capital they had a few militias, now collectively called the Popular Democratic Army (PDA). Badly armed, poorly trained and lacking central command, the fighters of the anti-Communist PDA were none the less in high spirits. Also, this time it was obvious that the invaders would not have the advantage of surprise.

Dushanbe came under attack on 4 December. The Communist forces, including a brigade formed and trained at Termez, led by the new Tajik interior minister, Yakub Salimov, and equipped with machine-guns, artillery, tanks and armoured personnel carriers supplied largely by Uzbekistan, used Hissar as their staging-post to enter Dushanbe from the west. They failed. Fighting between the two sides erupted outside the capital on the western front on 7 December. Next day the authorities in Dushanbe handed out arms to the people to resist the attackers. Bitter combat broke out. The invaders gained an upper hand on 10 December only after their ranks had been reinforced with Popular Front contingents from Kulyab – who attempted to penetrate the capital from the south in a column of tanks – and Uzbek-owned fighter aircraft and helicopter gunships. The latter were introduced into the battle to overcome strong resistance from the anti-Communist defenders. According to local CIS sources, there were 'hundreds of burnt corpses' in the streets.[48] On 11 December Salimov entered the city, and began negotiating the surrender of the anti-Communist PDA, which did not materialize. Talks and fighting continued over the weekend of 12–13 December.

Having lost most of Dushanbe, anti-Communist partisans, especially Islamists, fanned out to the surrounding villages, with some of them regrouping in Kofarnihan, the home base of Haji Turajanzade and an Islamic stronghold, twenty kilometres (twelve miles) east of Dushanbe. But they were chased by Communist troops, and forced to retreat farther into the Pamir Mountains of Badakhshan when the town fell to their attackers on 21 December. A similar fate was to befall Islamic fighters in the province of Kurgan Tyube, thus leaving a few pockets of resistance in Kofarnihan and the Garm Valley for the next several weeks. For all practical purposes the civil war was over by the end of December 1992, with the Communists almost fully back in power and their opponents on the run.

While democratic and Islamist forces had enough popular support
to make them, singly or jointly, a substantial and effective opposition
in a democratic system, they faced insurmountable difficulties in
winning and keeping power, or even sharing it with Communists.
They had to operate within the republican constitution of 1978
which, like its predecessors, was based on the Leninist principle of
'All power to the Soviets'. The provision of an executive president,
inserted as an amendment by a Communist-dominated Supreme
Soviet, never really took root, primarily because the presidential
election in November 1991 threw up a viable alternative to the Communist candidate, something Communist deputies had not foreseen.
Whatever concessions the anti-Communist alliance won through
grass-roots politics – be it a share of cabinet posts or the appointment
of Iskanderov as the acting president of the republic – had to be
sanctified ultimately by the Supreme Soviet which was firmly in
Communist hands. The repeated failure of Iskanderov to convene
the Supreme Soviet owing to the lack of a quorum illustrated the
fatal weakness of the anti-Communist alliance. (For this reason the
plan to replace the Supreme Soviet with a National Assembly of
seventy members, composed of an equal number of pro- and anti-
Communist elements, agreed in May, remained still-born: a contrast
to what happened in Azerbaijan.) Had the anti-Communists overcome this hurdle by gaining majority support in the Supreme Soviet
to legitimize their power, they would have faced the problem of
maintaining the territorial integrity of the republic. For, as threatened, the authorities in the Hojand region would have seceded, and
then either declared the province independent or unified with Uzbekistan, thus intensifying the civil war as well as turning it into an
international crisis. The loss of a third of the republic's population
and over three-fifths of its industrial production would have played
havoc with the economy of the rest of Tajikistan. Any efforts by
the government in Dushanbe to regain Hojand would have made
matters worse. In short, the anti-Communist alliance was in a no-
win situation.

As it was, the economy was reeling from the impact of a year-long
civil war. The estimates of deaths varied from 'at least 20,000',
according to official sources, to 30,000, according to Uzbekistan's
foreign minister, Sadik Safayev.[49] The damage caused by the civil
conflict was put at R90 billion; and in a country short of housing,
600,000 square metres of living space was lost. The economy was
damaged further by the emergence of an army of 537,000 refugees,

forming one-tenth of the national population.[50] Industrial output shrank by twenty-three per cent and the national GDP by thirteen per cent; and rural unemployment rose to about seventy per cent.

In his New Year message, Rahmanov, the highest official of the republic, declared victory over the opposition. He blamed it for creating a 'real danger' of the Tajik people 'disappearing as a nation'. Those responsible for atrocities during the civil conflict would 'never be pardoned by history' while their leaders 'would be cursed for ever'. He then threatened that 'anyone who is against the government in Dushanbe could have charges brought against them and would stand to lose his job'. Naming specific leaders of the opposition and literary figures, he called on them to apologize to the nation for their activities over the past months. Soon the administration launched a campaign against leading oppositionists who had either fled or gone into hiding: Shodmon Yusuf of the Democratic Party; Muhammad Sharif Himmatzade and Usman Davlat of the IRP; and Haji Turajan-zade of the Kaziat (whose office was soon filled by Kazi Heidar Sharifzade, a government supporter). They were accused of conspir-ing to overthrow the government in May 1992. The government curtailed press freedom, and this measure caused the immediate demise of two independent newspapers. It threatened dissident jour-nalists who, taking the damage to their property that followed as an ominous sign, began leaving the capital for the provinces.

A far worse fate awaited those residents of Dushanbe who were born in the areas that offered the stiffest resistance to the Communist and Popular Front forces: Garm and Karategin Valleys, strongholds of Islamists, and Badakhshan Autonomous Region, a bastion of the Democratic Party and Lal-e Badakhshan. Those from Badakhshan, popularly known as Pamiris, were easy to spot since Pamiri and Tajik dialects are different. Starting with Dushanbe, death squads, operating with official approval or complicity, carried out political killings, which by early spring 1993 had amounted to between 300 and 1500. In the south, Popular Front activists went through local registers to hunt down all those who came from Badakhshan, Garm or Karategin. The bloody vendetta caused an exodus of an estimated 200,000 Pamiris and other persecuted groups to the mountainous Badakhshan Autonomous Region which, being largely inaccessible, continued to resist central control from Dushanbe. An anti-government leader in the regional capital, Khorog, claimed in late spring that there were 15,000 anti-Communist fighters in the area. The earlier efforts of the government in Dushanbe to recover unregistered weapons had failed, with the result that an estimated 18,000 to 35,000 arms were in circulation.[51]

Where the Tajik administration had succeeded unequivocally was in mustering diplomatic and economic backing from Russia and Central Asian members of the Collective Defence Treaty. They were quick to welcome publicly the restoration of the legitimate government in Dushanbe, and considered their Alma Ata plan fully implemented. The ten-member CIS summit in Minsk on 22–23 January 1993 decided to increase the CIS peace-keeping force by four motorized infantry battalions. More importantly, Tajikistan was one of the seven member-states which signed the CIS charter. Kazakhstan promised Tajikistan 400,000 tons of food grains, and Russia pledged food, fuel and medicines. These states encouraged Tajikistan to continue the economic reform initiated by Nabiyev, which included freeing prices, new banking and tax laws, encouragement to private enterprise, concessions to foreign investors, and plans for privatization.[52] Dushanbe initiated talks with Moscow to conclude a wide-ranging bilateral treaty. These came to fruition in June when the two countries signed a treaty on political, military, security, economic and cultural cooperation, following a similar set of treaties between Russia and Uzbekistan.

By early March the administration in Dushanbe had consolidated its hold over the country with the exception of Badakhshan. Since the only access to the region was through two mountain passes, it was comparatively easy for the regional government, which had sided with the Tajik opposition, to block the arrival by land of Tajik security forces. However, the two sides reached a compromise. Badakhshan's parliament recognized the supremacy of the Dushanbe government in exchange for the latter's promise not to despatch its forces into the autonomous region.[53] Dushanbe advised Khorog to raise its own defence force and begin disarming those of its citizens who possessed weapons. The normal population of 200,000 had been inflated by another 200,000 Badakhshani refugees from the rest of the republic and a further 100,000 Tajik opponents of the Rahmanov government. With the official ban on the Democratic Party, IRP, Lal-e Badakhshan and Rastakhiz, for violating the constitution by engaging in violent anti-state activities, imposed on 16 March and confirmed by the Supreme Court three months later, there was little chance of rapprochement between the government and the opposition. Indeed, the Tajik opposition had intensified its contacts with Islamists in Afghanistan, especially those led by Masoud and

Hikmatyar, who aided them with arms, cash and Afghan guerrilla experts.

Dushanbe and its CIS allies responded by strengthening the guard along the Tajik–Afghan border. In return the Islamic government in Kabul protested that the presence of Russian forces along the frontier threatened Afghanistan's security. Its prediction of tense relations with Tajikistan after the installation of a Communist regime in Dushanbe – which was accompanied by the arrival of tens of thousands of Tajiks crossing the Oxus River frontier into northern Afghanistan – proved correct. Indeed, relations between Dushanbe and Kabul deteriorated sharply, with each side accusing the other of violations of its land border and airspace.

In sum, while the old Communist nomenklatura had clawed back its power in Tajikistan after a bloody civil war, it found itself unable to restore stability in the republic, partly because control of the Badakhshan region still eluded it, and partly because Islamists were in power in Afghanistan, a country convulsed by coups and violence for a generation, and bristling with weapons.

EIGHT

Afghanistan: Islam Victorious

Afghanistan is one of the few Muslim countries that were not colonized by a European power. Contrary to what occurred in Turkey in 1924, Islamist forces overthrew a mildly reformist ruler, Amanullah, in January 1929, and promulgated a constitution with strong Islamic overtones two years later. But that did not inhibit the rise of a strong military leader, Muhammad Daoud Khan, in 1953, who made a break with orthodox Islamic elements and inadvertently paved the way for a coup by Marxist military officers a quarter of a century later. America perceived this as the first successful Soviet expansionist move since the Communist Party had monopolized power in Czechoslovakia in 1948. In the subsequent intensification of the Cold War, the US financed and trained Islamic forces to wage a long struggle against an alliance of a Marxist Afghanistan and the USSR. In Afghanistan, therefore, there emerged a fusion of nationalism with Islam, an alloy which finally triumphed in April 1992 against the background of the collapse of the Soviet system. Thus Afghanistan emerged as an Islamic state and society. Given its Tajik, Uzbek and Turkmen minorities inhabiting areas contiguous with Tajikistan, Uzbekistan and Turkmenistan, Afghanistan – land of Afghans, another term for Pushtuns – is certain to influence these Central Asian republics as they struggle to establish their political and cultural identities.

Earlier, Afghanistan was spared colonization because of the rivalry between Tsarist Russia and imperial Britain in Central Asia – the Great Game – with London determined to ensure that Russian expansion stopped well short of the borders of India, the most prized possession of its empire.

Competition between Britain and Russia led to two wars between Afghanistan and British India: in 1839–42 and 1878–80. The occupation of eastern Afghanistan which followed the First Anglo-Afghan War was resisted by the Afghans. In the wake of the second conflict the British left, but kept control of Afghanistan's foreign relations. The overall result of these wars was to isolate Afghanistan politically and diplomatically. Furthermore, the bloody experience made traditional tribal and Islamic leaders view all reform and modernization as Western innovations that had to be resisted.

It was against this backdrop that Abdur Rahman assumed power in 1880. Starting with firm control of Kabul and its environs, he staged several campaigns to subdue tribes in the south and south-east – and then Uzbek, Tajik and Turkmen tribes in the north. In 1888 when (Shia) Hazaras, who over the centuries had been pushed into the inhospitable Hazarajat mountains, rebelled, Abdur Rahman rallied Pushtun, Uzbek, Tajik and Turkmen tribes under the banner of Sunni Islam, and subdued the Hazaras in 1881. Four years later he seized Kafiristan, Land of the Infidel, to the east of Kabul, dotted with Christian missions, and converted its pagan inhabitants to Sunni Islam. This made Afghanistan ninety-nine per cent Muslim: eighty per cent Sunni of the Hanafi school, and the rest Shia of the Jaafari school, also known as Twelver Shia.[1] Overall, Abdur Rahman's victories created two Afghanistans, above and below the Hindu Kush Mountains – the northern region being dominated by Uzbeks, Tajiks and Turkmens, and the southern by Pushtuns, with the central highlands populated by Hazaras.

In foreign policy, Abdur Rahman conceived the idea of the Triple Alliance of the Ottoman empire, Iran and Afghanistan as a barrier to Russian expansion into the Middle East, something that appealed to the British. His successor, Habibullah (1901–19), pursued the concept actively. One of the results was the signing of the Anglo-Russian entente in 1907 which guaranteed Afghanistan's independence, but with Britain still controlling its foreign affairs. It was not until Amanullah (1919–29), who succeeded Habibullah, had waged a military campaign against the British in 1919, with mixed results, that Afghanistan regained the right to conduct its external relations. In March 1921 Amanullah concluded a treaty with Ottoman Turkey whereby Afghanistan recognized Turkey as the guide of Islam and custodian of the Islamic caliphate. Three months later he signed a treaty with Iran, thus moving towards Islamic solidarity along the lines mooted by Abdur Rahman, the founder of modern Afghanistan.

However, Amanullah was aware that his landlocked country, lacking financial resources of its own, needed to normalize relations with its powerful non-Muslim neighbours to the north and south-east. In the case of Russia, the need was all the more urgent in view of the success of the Bolshevik revolution there. Conscious of the might of Russia, and trusting its Bolshevik rulers' assurances forswearing any designs on Afghanistan, Amanullah became the first foreign ruler to recognize the revolutionary regime. By signing a comprehensive treaty in early February 1921 he sealed cordial relations with Soviet Russia.[2] However, this did not stop him from giving refuge to a fellow-Muslim, Said Alim Khan, the last emir of Bukhara, after the latter's forces were finally defeated by the Red Army.

The treaty with Afghanistan proved valuable to the Bolsheviks as they intensified their drive against the Basmachi rebels in Central Asia from late 1921 onwards, which culminated in a devastating attack on General Enver Pasha and his troops in August 1922.

Amanullah provided the nation with a written constitution in 1923. In it he declared Islam to be the official religion of Afghanistan, where the name of the ruler had to be mentioned in religious sermons. After returning home from a nine-month tour of India, the Middle East and Europe in July 1928, he offered a representative government to his subjects, to be based on votes for all adult males, and military conscription for men. Despite opposition from the mullahs, he issued decrees outlawing polygamy among civil servants, permitting women to discard the veil, and requiring all Afghan men residing in or visiting Kabul to wear Western dress complete with a European hat from March 1929 onwards. But before the dress order could be implemented he was overthrown in January 1929 by the Islamic forces led by Bacha-e Saqqao, a Tajik highwayman based in the Shamali plain north of Kabul, a stronghold of fundamentalism. On assuming power, Saqqao cancelled the decrees of Amanullah, and returned the task of running courts and schools to clerics.

Unlike Reza Khan Pahlavi, Shah of Iran, who rose to power as a military leader and built up a powerful army before challenging the clergy, Amanullah lacked a strong, secular force in the form of a properly trained, disciplined and, above all, loyal army. It was not until 1953 that the army came into its own in Afghanistan when, under the leadership of Muhammad Daoud Khan, it seized effective power.

In October 1929 Saqqao was overthrown by Muhammad Nadir Khan (later Shah), a third cousin of Amanullah. His brief four-year reign marked the zenith of Islamic fundamentalism in Afghanistan. Obligated to religious luminaries for his position, he set out to found a fully fledged Islamic state.

The constitution of 1931 formalized the dominant role of religion and religious leaders. The first four articles described Islam of the Hanafi school as the official religion, required that the king be a

Hanafi Muslim and that his name be mentioned in Friday sermons, and barred non-Muslims from becoming government ministers. Other articles institutionalized the powers that Nadir Shah had conferred on the clergy and Sharia courts, and recognized the supremacy and orthodoxy of the Hanafi school. The constitution incorporated the Quranic injunctions on popular consultation – 'Consult them on affairs' (3:153) and 'Their affairs are by consultation among them' (42:38) – by prescribing a consultative assembly based on votes for all adult male Afghans.

Nadir Shah inaugurated the first parliament in 1931, but did not live to address the second parliament three years later: he was assassinated in November 1933. The throne went to his son Muhammad Zahir Shah, a youth of nineteen. Power was exercised in his name by his three uncles, one of whom, Muhammad Hashim Khan, became prime minister, a position he held until 1946.

During these years, mirroring the debates in train in Russia's Muslim protectorates of Bukhara and Khiva, much thought was given to diagnosing the reasons for the backwardness of Afghanistan. A nationalist modernist minority held that social welfare and national defence demanded knowledge and science; that the Sharia provided guidance towards achieving public well-being, progress and justice; and that such principles could be learned by reason which could be cultivated only through education and learning. However, the majority view held firmly by most clerics and tribal leaders was that modernization was antithetical to Islamic and traditional values. With clerics and tribal chiefs wedded to the status quo, the monarchical regime became fossilized.

The Second World War, in which Afghanistan remained neutral, underlined the importance of science and technology. It made the ruling dynasty realize the pressing need for rapid socio-political reform and modernization as well as tackling rising socio-economic problems.

When Shah Mahmud became prime minister, he liberalized the system somewhat, giving comparative freedom to the press and to voters in parliamentary elections, the results of which in the past had been pre-determined by the royal family. But as elsewhere in the world, when the pent-up frustrations of a rising class – in this case an urban, educated modern middle class – were given a little opening, they burst forth, inducing repression in return. Prime Minister Mahmud arrested top opposition leaders before the 1952 parliamentary poll.

On the one hand the royal family, the ultimate arbiter of power, found Islamic and tribal leaders unrealistically conservative and a barrier to modernization. On the other it saw in the rival group of constitutional modernizers a threat to its unchallenged supremacy in the political arena. Mounting hostility between these competing polarities of religious tradition and secular modernization had left them both weak, thus creating an opportunity for a third force. The palace thus found the time ripe to introduce into the political drama its own active player: the military.

In September 1953 Muhammad Daoud Khan, commander of the Central Forces in Kabul, and a cousin of King Zahir Shah, mounted a coup against Premier Mahmud with the active consent of the palace, and became prime minister. His first priority was to modernize and strengthen the military. For this he relied heavily on the Soviet Union – a neighbour with which Kabul had built up a special relationship after the Bolshevik revolution – for historical and contemporary reasons. Following two serious border incidents in 1925 in the aftermath of a revival of the Basmachi movement, the Soviet Union and Afghanistan had concluded a Treaty of Neutrality and Non-aggression, which was reiterated and strengthened five years later. Good relations between the two neighbours were undisturbed by the Second World War owing to the neutrality that Afghans maintained in the conflict.

Oddly, the creation of Pakistan, a Muslim state, in August 1947 was badly received in Kabul. Britain's departure from the Indian sub-continent led to the revival of Afghan irredentist claims on the Pushtun lands in Pakistan, which had been kept in abeyance since 1893 when Abdur Rahman had signed an agreement with British India to delimit the border, which caused a division of various Pushtun tribes in the region. Now Afghanistan sponsored a movement for an independent Pushtunistan consisting of Pushtun tribes living east of its pre-1947 border with British India.

As Pakistan drifted towards the Western camp, formalizing its links with America with a Mutual Security Pact in 1954, Kabul tilted towards Moscow. In order not to upset its ally, Pakistan, the United States refused to sell arms to Afghanistan. Daoud Khan began attaching Soviet advisers to Afghan military academies and despatching Afghan officers to the Soviet Union for further training.

An autocratic personality, Daoud Khan wanted to centralize state authority through the military, and implement socio-economic reform through executive decrees rather than democratic debate and consensus. As he tried quietly to advance the emancipation of women by encouraging them to appear unveiled, he encountered clerical ire. Soon mullahs began preaching against the regime, arguing that Daoud Khan was an anti-Islamic leader who was letting atheistic Communists and Western Christians undermine the Islamic way of life. They were particularly apprehensive that Soviet advisers, military and civilian, would steer Afghans away from Islam, as they had the Muslim inhabitants of the USSR's Central Asian republics. But when the government arrested fifty clerical leaders and charged them with treason and heresy, the opposition to unveiled women died down. This was in marked contrast to what had happened under Amanullah: unlike Amanullah, Daoud Khan controlled a loyal, well-disciplined and modern army.

Daoud Khan's freshly revived Pushtunistan policy brought him into open conflict with Pakistan, and led to the severing of economic and transport links between Afghanistan and Pakistan, causing high inflation and acute fuel shortage in landlocked Afghanistan. Only after Daoud Khan had resigned as prime minister in March 1963 did Pakistan re-open the border. None the less the military continued to be the single most important centre of power, and it was ultimately loyal to King Zahir Shah.

The sovereign promulgated a new constitution in October 1964 which inaugurated constitutional monarchy, which was to prove to be the last chapter in the long history of monarchy in Afghanistan. This period witnessed an important change in the composition of Islamic forces and a growing antagonism between religious and Marxist camps.

At Kabul University, the Faculty of Theology emerged as a centre for Islamic thinking that presented Islam as a modern ideology – not an obscurantist faith associated with traditional clerics and village mullahs. The Organization of Young Muslims was the public face of Islamic fundamentalists who functioned secretly under the guidance of a council headed by Professor Ghulam Muhammad Niyazi. In 1970 the council decided to branch out of the university campus and establish cells in the army. Two years later they shifted their focus from spiritual revival of the community to acquiring political power. Following the adoption of a constitution by the fundamentalist council, its members elected Professor Borhanuddin Rabani, a Tajik, as president. They were as much opposed to the autocracy and corruption of the royal family as they were to the rising tide of Marxism both on the campus and outside, organized since 1965 under the banner of the People's Democratic Party of Afghanistan (PDPA). With unemployment among university graduates rising, the ranks of both fundamentalists and Marxists grew.

The palace found the Marxists particularly threatening since leftist students had taken to allying with industrial workers and their strikes. It ensured the defeat of all PDPA candidates in the 1969 parliamentary poll. It encouraged clerics and their followers to demonstrate against the PDPA. But once religious elements did so, they did not stop there. They argued that injecting large doses of non-traditional education into the system was fast eroding the morals of the young and undermining traditional social values. In 1972 the Kabul-based press reported famine in the provinces due to the failure of rains for two consecutive years, which reportedly claimed 100,000 lives in a country of fifteen million. Islamists staged demonstrations against food-grain hoarders and called for limits on personal wealth.

All in all, therefore, in the early 1970s there was a general sense of drift, decadence and turmoil in the country; and Islamists held the royal family responsible for it.

On 17 July 1973, while King Zahir Shah was in Italy for medical treatment, Daoud Khan seized power. This time he abolished the monarchy and set up a republic. He declared that he had assumed power in order to return Afghanistan to Islamic principles. But instead of ordering the application of the Sharia, he decreed land reform. For this he secured the backing of the moderate faction within the PDPA known as Parchamis (from Parcham – flag).

As before, Daoud Khan tried to monopolize authority. With Parchami Marxists supporting him, the only sizeable political force that hindered his path to total power was the Islamist camp. But it was divided between traditional and new fundamentalists. This helped Daoud Khan as he increased pressure on Islamists. In one swoop in June 1974 his government arrested 200 fundamentalists in Kabul as they gathered to discuss the blueprint of an Islamic republic where the Sharia was to be applied in its totality. Gulbuddin Hikmatyar, the leader of the Young Muslims at the university campus, fled to Pakistan. But Niyazi and Rabbani made one more attempt to persuade Daoud Khan to break with Parchamis. They failed. Rabbani, the leader of the Young Muslims' parent body, popularly known as Ikhwan (Brethren), fled to Pakistan; but Niyazi soon found himself in jail.

While in Pakistan, the exiled leaders made an attempt at an armed uprising in Afghanistan in July 1975. It failed. Hikmatyar and

Rabbani parted, forming their own parties. Hikmatyar, a lay Muslim, established Hizb-e Islami (Islamic Party), whose tenet was that the piety of a believer should be judged primarily on the basis of his political actions and only secondarily on his religious behaviour or knowledge. Rabbani, a graduate of the Cairo-based Al Azhar University, the leading Islamic centre of learning, was much respected by orthodox clerics as well as by the leaders of Sufi orders. He named his party Jamaat-e Islami (Islamic Society) of Afghanistan. A party by the same name, led by Sayid Abul Ala Maududi, existed in Pakistan.

Maududi believed that the character of a social order flowed from the top to the bottom, and therefore to change society one had first to change the theoretical thinking of its leaders. He founded his party to produce a cadre of sincere and disciplined Muslims capable of bringing about the victory of Islam in Pakistan. Unlike traditional clerics who spent their energies in tackling arcane and largely irrelevant matters, Maududi faced modern life armed with the Sharia.

What made Maududi particularly attractive to young, pious urban Afghans – caught in the web of Western cultural influences and Soviet military and economic links – was his argument that Islam was self-sufficient and, indeed, opposed to both Western and socialist ways of life. Describing the West as morally decadent and corrupt, he stated: 'Islam and western civilization are poles apart in their objectives as well as in their principles of social organization.'[3] He wanted Muslims to acquire scientific knowledge for the benefit of Islam.

While regarding the government under Prophet Muhammad as the model, Maududi gave it a democratic interpretation. He ruled that the Leader of an Islamic state today – heading the legislative, judiciary and executive organs – must be elected by the faithful; and so must the Consultative Council. Its members should be able to judge whether or not the Leader was following Islamic policies. Maududi had no objection to candidates contesting elections on party tickets, but ruled that once they had been elected they must give up party labels and vote on issues according to their individual judgement. On social and family issues, however, he showed a lack of innovation. He was for sexual segregation and the veil for women.

Overall, Maududi's thesis provided a modern interpretation of Islam as an alternative to the secular and atheistic ideologies that were being disseminated in Afghanistan.

Though Rabbani called his organization Jamaat-e Islami, he did not share Maududi's elitist views about the party. Aware that the structure of a modern political party was unsuited to the social conditions prevailing in a predominantly tribal Afghanistan, he wanted to adapt Jamaat-e Islami to tribal institutions.

In a different context, President Daoud Khan proved to be equally flexible. Having repressed Islamist elements, he turned against Parchamis, his erstwhile allies. He resorted to persecuting them as well as the radical Marxist group, Khalqis (from Khalq – people). This drove the two groupings to merge in July 1977, thus re-establishing the People's Democratic Party of Afghanistan. The persecution of Marxists soon took the form of assassinations. This aroused much disquiet in leftist ranks.

After the murder of Mir Akbar Khyber, a respected trade union leader, on 17 April 1978, the PDPA leadership organized massive anti-government demonstrations in Kabul. Daoud Khan ordered the arrest of all PDPA leaders. But Nur Muhammad Taraki, the party chief, escaped arrest. He activated the Marxist network in the military that had been built up over the years. The result was a coup by leftist military officers on 27 April 1978, an event officially described as the Saur (April) Revolution. Daoud Khan was killed in the fighting at the presidential palace, and his offices of president and prime minister went to Taraki. The new leader was assisted by Hafizullah Amin (of the Khalq faction) and Babrak Karmal (of the Parcham faction) as deputy premiers.

The coup was the culmination of Marxist efforts over the past many years to recruit military officers, and the policy of the Kabul regime, initiated by Daoud Khan in the mid-1950s, to send its officers for further training to the Soviet Union. Since they received their training at armed forces academies in Central Asian republics, often in Tashkent, they felt racially and culturally at home. More importantly, they could not avoid comparing the outstanding economic, social and educational progress of Central Asian Muslims with the backwardness of Afghans. These experiences made them pro-Soviet, and a suitable quarry for recruitment into the military network of Afghan Marxists.

THE 1978 MARXIST REVOLUTION AND AFTER

Once in power, differences between the PDPA's major constituents surfaced. Khalqi radicals, led by Taraki and Hafizullah Amin, wanted rapid changes, whereas the Parchami wing, headed by Babrak Karmal, advocated a gradualist approach.

As it was, Taraki described his regime not as socialist but as 'national democratic', based on an alliance of workers, peasants and national bourgeoisie in conflict with feudal lords and a comprador bourgeoisie subservient to foreign capital. Aware of national history and popular culture, revolutionary leaders reiterated their faith in Islam and began all their public utterances with '*Bismallah* (In the name of God)'. So too did all official statements and radio and television broadcasts. Taraki and other leaders offered Friday prayers in different mosques in the capital. They repeatedly assured the public that all reforms would be in line with the Sharia.

In May 1978, the government declared a jihad (campaign) against illiteracy, and prescribed compulsory education for both sexes. Only five per cent of girls were then attending school versus thirty per cent of boys.[4] The campaign went well in urban areas, but not in rural. Here, opposition to the mixing of sexes, particularly in adult education, was very strong. What made the situation even more tense was the fact that owing to the paucity of female teachers the task of teaching women fell on male teachers who had arrived from towns and cities, considered by rural folk as hotbeds of licentiousness. Also, the literacy drive completed the process, initiated by Daoud Khan, of expelling mullahs from the local education system, and swelled the ranks of anti-government clerics. The result was periodic murders of secular, revolutionary teachers by fundamentalists. The literacy campaign in villages reached a peak in early 1979 and then declined rapidly.

Decree 6 of July 1978 abolished all pre-1973 mortgages and debts, and drastically reduced the excess interest (often 100 per cent a year) on later loans. The revolutionary government estimated that this reform would benefit four out of five peasant families. In practice, in the absence of a socially committed bureaucracy, the decree created unprecedented problems for the new regime, and dulled its beneficial impact on rural communities, which formed eighty-five per cent of the national population. Village mullahs, often having blood ties with landlord-moneylenders, ruled that cancellation of debts amounted to stealing, and was therefore unIslamic. (On the other hand the pro-regime minority among clerics cited the Quranic verse against *riba* – usury.)

Many rural mullahs began delivering anti-government sermons in an environment where armed resistance against the regime took the form of murdering Marxist teachers and civil servants. The authorities responded by dismissing or arresting rebellious clerics. Indeed, in September 1978, encouraged by the ruling issued by a group of pro-regime mullahs in Kabul and elsewhere, the administration mounted a jihad against the Ikhwan, the generic term used for militant fundamentalists.

By then conflict within the ruling party had been resolved in favour of Khalqis, with the Parchami leader, Karmal, about to be eased out as Afghan ambassador to Czechoslovakia (in December 1978). So the pace of reform and secularization quickened. In mid-October the government replaced the national tricolour – black, red and green – with a red flag, flagrantly similar to the standards of the Soviet Central Asian republics. The disappearance of Islamic green from the national flag aroused popular suspicion that the state had taken the path of atheism. This view was reinforced when the practice of invoking God, 'In the name of Allah, the Merciful', at the beginning of broadcasting programmes or official statements, was dropped by the state media and political leaders. These two steps effectively undid all that had been achieved by months of official propaganda to the effect that the new regime believed in Islam and wanted to uphold it. They provided evidence to a rising number of clerics that the state was unIslamic: a sufficient basis for them to call on the faithful to resist it.

Such calls came around the time the government issued Decree 7 concerning marriage and family relations. Women were granted equal rights, forced marriage was banned, and the minimum age for marriage specified: sixteen for females and eighteen for males. The decree fixed the bride price at the equivalent of \$7, its going rate then being \$1000. This was meant to help poor prospective bridegrooms, but it was extremely hard to enforce in villages.

Finally, in late November 1978, came Decree 8 on the ownership of land, the primary source of income in a predominantly agrarian Afghanistan. Among peasants forty per cent were landless, and another forty per cent possessed only 1.5 to six acres per capita. In contrast, the top 2.2 per cent of landowners, holding thirty acres or more each, owned forty-two per cent of the total of twenty-five to twenty-nine million acres.[5] The new decree divided land into three categories, and fixed ceilings of thirty acres for first-class, perennially irrigated land and 300 acres for the dry variety. The government expected to secure 2.5 to three million acres of excess land for distribution to landless peasants.

To implement the reform, it set up land committees composed mainly of urban-based PDPA members. Beginning in January 1979, these committees, backed by radicalized, well-paid police, began visiting villages to hand over title deeds to the landless. This was a major means by which the leftist government planned to break the socio-economic power of the traditional-religious elite which had effectively ruled rural society for many centuries. Rich landlords protested while their religious allies, local mullahs, issued verdicts to the effect that taking somebody's land was tantamount to robbery, a crime, and that those receiving such property would be transgressing against the Sharia. This, and the fear of violent reprisals from landlords once the police had left the village, discouraged many landless peasants from accepting title deeds offered to them by the visiting committees. None the less, by March 1979, the government claimed to have distributed 512,000 acres to 104,000 families.[6]

Abroad, the Marxist administration strengthened its ties with the Soviet Union by signing a Treaty of Friendship and Cooperation with it in December 1978. The treaty, modelled on those Moscow had earlier concluded with Ethiopia, Angola and Vietnam, specified close military, political and economic links between the two neighbours. Article 4 of the Treaty stated that the signatories 'shall consult with each other and take, by agreement, appropriate measures to ensure security, independence and territorial integrity of the two countries'.[7] It was this provision that was later, purportedly, to be invoked by Kabul in extending an invitation to Soviet troops.

The cumulative effect of these developments was to polarize society, with the opposition gaining more supporters. Such Islamic luminaries as Muhammad Ibrahim Mujaddidi, the Hazrat of Shor Bazaar, condemned the recent socio-economic reforms as unIslamic and preached against the government. After a period of hesitation, the authorities moved against the religious opposition in January 1979. They seized the offices of the Hazrat of Shor Bazaar, arresting all adult male members of the Mujaddidi family. They executed some Islamic personages, but did not make this public. Their actions caused alarm in religious circles. Many Islamic and Sufi leaders fled the country, and joined the anti-government groups based in Peshawar.

Resistance against the Marxist regime hardened during the winter of 1978–9, with the (seasonally) inaccessible Nuristan slipping out of the control of the central government and falling into the hands of the (Islamic) Nuristan Front. A similar situation prevailed in the

Hazarajat highlands, now ruled by the Revolutionary Council of the Islamic Union of Afghanistan.

But the event that caused much worry in Kabul, and a shift in the balance of forces within the PDPA, was the uprising in Herat, situated 100 kilometres (sixty-five miles) from the Iranian border, in mid-March 1979.

Several dozen Afghan fundamentalists returned to Herat from Iran in the aftermath of the Islamic revolution there in early February. Some of them established contacts with pro-Islamic officers in the local garrison, while others mobilized the faithful in the surrounding villages on the issue of compulsory education for women being imparted by male teachers. On 16 March rural demonstrators murdered government teachers, and then converged on Herat in a series of armed marches. Here their ranks were bolstered by disaffected townsmen and defectors from the local garrison. Together they went on a rampage, killing PDPA cadres and military officers as well as Soviet advisers and their families. The insurgents took over Herat.

A few days later, when they found a column of armoured cars approaching from the direction of Qandhar, waving a green flag and a copy of the Quran, they thought that they were being joined by another contingent of rebels, and let the column pass. These were in fact government troops. Once they had entered Herat, and received air cover, they attacked the insurgents and recaptured the city. The five-day-long fighting caused some 5000 casualties, including several hundred loyalist troops and PDPA functionaries. Kabul blamed Tehran for having inspired and organized the insurgency. To meet the rising danger of counter-revolution, a government of 'national deliverance' was formed on 1 April, with Amin as the prime minister.

Amin was an uncompromising hardliner whose policy of purging the administration of Parchamis fell foul of President Taraki. In the ensuing power struggle Premier Amin gained ground and took over the defence ministry, and thus counter-insurgency operations. In mid-September 1979 there was a shoot-out between the aides of Amin and Taraki. On 6 October the official media announced that President Taraki had died after a 'serious illness'.

The Kremlin, which had provided refuge in Moscow to such leading Parchamis as Karmal, advised Amin to take conciliatory steps to allay rising public hostility towards the regime. Conscious of Kabul's dependence on Soviet aid, economic and military, Amin accepted the advice. He released several thousand political prisoners.

He re-introduced the invocation of Allah in official statements and broadcasts, and ordered repairs of mosques at state expense. While reiterating 'complete freedom of religion, and profound respect for and wholesale support for Islam', he vowed to combat 'religious fanaticism'.[8] He attempted to woo Sufi leaders, and instructed the committee drafting the new constitution to pay 'special attention to Islam'. Proclaiming an amnesty to a quarter of a million Afghan refugees in Pakistan, he invited them to return. This was a futile gesture. Anti-government sentiment among the refugees had risen to the point where activists of the Hizb-e Islami, a party popular among them, had taken to assassinating PDPA leaders in Kabul.

Such actions were symptomatic of the upsurge in anti-regime activities along the Afghanistan–Pakistan border. The eastern province of Paktiya became a hotbed of insurgency. Amin was obliged to call upon the Soviets to help him fight the rebels. Together, they defeated the insurgents in Paktiya.

Following this, Marshal Ivan Pavlovsky, head of Soviet ground forces, toured Afghanistan to prepare overall plans for countering insurgency. This was the beginning of a process that was to culminate in the arrival of tens of thousands of Soviet troops in Afghanistan.

From late October 1979 Soviet Central Asian contingents began taking over guard duties from Afghan troops to release the latter to fight the rebels. In mid-December two Soviet battalions arrived at Bagram air base near Kabul, which came increasingly under Soviet control. Following an attack on Assadullah Amin, head of the secret police, at the downtown headquarters of President Amin, the Afghan leader moved to Darulaman Palace on the outskirts of the capital. By 24 December there were some 12,000 Soviet troops and advisers in Afghanistan. The Kremlin also lent a large number of Tajik and Uzbek cadres to Kabul to take up crucial administrative and technical posts at different levels, thus strengthening the bureaucratic backbone of the new Afghan regime with experienced and ideologically reliable administrators. With Persian as the official language of Afghanistan, Soviet Tajiks were particularly at ease in their new environment.

Three days later, on 27 December, Soviet forces seized military installations in Kabul, and attacked Darulaman Palace. Amin was killed. Babrak Karmal, who had been in exile in Moscow for over a year, arrived to lead the new regime. Soon there were 50,000 Soviet troops, a sizeable proportion drawn from Tajikistan and Uzbekistan.

The strength of the Afghan military was then put at around 80,000.

The arrival of Soviet soldiers in such large numbers to bolster the Afghan state was an admission that the local Marxist regime had alienated large sections of society, and that its rulers had failed to assess the mood of their people correctly and calibrate the pace and nature of reform accordingly. For a long time thereafter the moderate PDPA leadership tried in various ways to undo the damage inflicted on the government's popular standing by the excesses committed by the over-zealous Khalqi faction, led by Amin, which exercised effective power from August 1978 to December 1979.

On assuming power, Karmal proclaimed the release of all political prisoners, abolition of 'all anti-democratic, anti-human regulations, and all arrests, arbitrary persecutions, house searches and inquisitions', respect for 'the sacred principles of Islam', protection of family life, and observance of 'legal and lawful private ownership'.[9] His actions had the full backing of Moscow whose despatch of Soviet troops to Afghanistan, stemming from Article 4 of the year-old Afghan–Soviet Friendship Treaty, was described by Karmal as heralding the 'second phase' of the Saur Revolution.

Moscow had soon to weigh the advantages of having Tajik and Uzbek soldiers in its units and parading them in public – which helped to give its action the semblance of a good-neighbourly act and to boost the morale of Afghan troops – with the disadvantages of not knowing exactly how Soviet Central Asians were developing relations with Afghan soldiers and civilians, and the risk of defections from their ranks to the Islamic resistance. When some desertions took place in early 1980 the opinion in the Kremlin swung sharply towards radically reducing the Central Asian proportion among the Soviet troops. This was accomplished by April 1980.

The USSR's military intervention also signalled the second phase of Afghan resistance. The arrival of Soviet troops was a severe blow to Afghan national pride, and resulted in thousands of nationalist-minded professional men leaving their homes either to join the resistance active in the countryside or to enrol with the anti-government parties based in Pakistan or Iran.

By the summer of 1979 there were six Pakistan-based (Sunni) Islamic parties of Afghans, and they had a vested interest in maintaining themselves as independent bodies: the Pakistan government had decided to channel Islamic charity to Afghan refugees through them rather than through its own bureaucracy. Three of these organizations were fundamentalist: the Hizb-e Islami (led by Hikmatyar), the Jamaat-e Islami (led by Rabbani), and the breakaway Hizb-e Islami (led by Maulavi Yunus Khalis). The rest were traditional religious parties: the National Islamic Front of Afghanistan (headed by Sayid Ahmed Gailani), the National Liberation Front of Afghanistan (headed by Sibghatullah Mujaddidi), and the Islamic Revolutionary Movement (headed by Maulavi Muhammad Nabi Muhammadi). The latter organizations wanted to return Afghanistan to its pre-1973 set-up with King Zahir Shah as the constitutional monarch; and they drew their support from village mullahs, tribal chiefs, landlords and Sufi leaders. If nothing else, the existence of these parties showed that within the Islamic spectrum there was much choice, and that a multi-party system could be sustained in an Islamic state.

In 1981 these organizations' active cadres totalled nearly 75,000, with the fundamentalists accounting for two-thirds, Hikmatyar's Hizb-e Islami contingent being by far the largest. In contrast the three traditional religious groupings were even in strength.[10]

It was little wonder, then, that the Karmal regime directed its fire, military and ideological, at the fundamentalist parties, especially Hikmatyar's Hizb-e Islami. Both the Hizb-e Islami and its predecessor, the Ikhwan, drew their inspiration from the ideology of the Muslim Brotherhood of Egypt, established in 1927 and led by a pious layman, Hassan al Banna, a teacher. Hikmatyar was unimpressed by the calibre of traditional Afghan mullahs who, according to him, had failed either to offer intellectual stimulation to the faithful or to constitute themselves into a strong independent force ready to confront an unIslamic ruler. He was equally scathing about Sufi leaders whom he often described as 'decadent, superstition-ridden self-seekers' who had corrupted Islam. Returning Afghanistan to the true path of Islam, he argued, meant having to reform the religious establishment, eradicate Sufism and Sufi orders, and implement the Sharia in its totality. The last requirement could only be achieved by abrogating the customary law among Pushtuns, the largest single ethnic group, known as Pushtunwali, which had monopolized political power.

Given Hikmatyar's negative attitude towards the traditional clergy, it was not long before he fell out with one of his colleagues in the party leadership, Yunus Khalis, a trained cleric who was also a tribal leader. The specific reason for the split was Khalis's insistence on an immediate armed struggle against the Kabul regime and his involvement with the uprising in the spring of 1979, something Hikmatyar opposed. He wanted to build up an extensive network inside Afghanistan before striking at the Marxist regime. Khalis lacked the organizational genius and charisma of Hikmatyar, and his breakaway faction, sharing the parent body's name, was only a fraction of its size.

Hikmatyar, who ran a very tightly knit party, was unwilling to adjust its structure in order to accommodate the peculiarly Afghan social reality of tribes, Sufi brotherhoods and a traditional rural elite. In contrast, Rabbani, the leader of the Jamaat-e Islami, swiftly abandoned the elitist nature of his organization to integrate supporters who were not fully committed to the party ideology, which was inspired by the works of Maudidi and Sayid Qutb, an Egyptian Islamic thinker. Rabbani's flexible attitude extended to Shias. Alone among Sunni leaders he conceded the Shia demand that the Jaafari school of Islam be recognized on a par with the Hanafi. He drew on the existing networks of clerics, Sufi orders and the newly emerging Islamists – leaving out only the tribal network – to strengthen his party. His weakness was that he was a Tajik, and not a Pushtun like Hikmatyar. Tajiks, forming nearly one-fifth of the national population of nineteen million, were about half as numerous as Pushtuns, constituting forty to forty-five per cent of the total, but more than Hazaras (at fifteen per cent) and Uzbeks (at ten per cent).[11]

While both Rabbani and Hikmatyar were committed to full implementation of the Sharia in a future Islamic state, Rabbani envisaged a multi-party system, as expounded by Maudidi. This was not the case with Hikmatyar. An authoritarian figure, he favoured a single-party Islamic state. He vehemently attacked his rivals, describing them variously as monarchists, religiously corrupt or deviant, or pro-Western. His party, he stressed, was a contrast to theirs: republican, religiously pure and committed to a 'Neither East nor West' policy.

Whereas the aim of other organizations was to bring about the withdrawal of Soviet troops from Afghanistan and restore Afghan independence, the Hizb-e Islami was more ambitious. It planned to carry guerrilla raids beyond the Oxus River into Soviet Central Asia and roll back Communism by freeing the 'Muslim lands of Bukhara, Khiva and Khorezm'.

Both Hikmatyar and Rabbani labelled the Kabul regime as infidel and exhorted believers to wage a holy war against it and die as martyrs if necessary. Hikmatyar's dogmatic ambition and exceptional organizational ability made the Hizb-e Islami by far the strongest party with a command structure that stretched as far as Herat, and a network of recruitment centres, training camps, medical facilities, warehouses and offices. His party claimed to have set up parallel government in the areas it controlled inside Afghanistan.

In the case of Rabbani, his ally Ahmed Shah Masoud in the Panjshir Valley near Kabul had proved to be one of the ablest guerrilla commanders. While successfully resisting central control, he had established a parallel political-administrative infrastructure in the valley. This bolstered the prestige and credibility of the Jamaat-e Islami.

Within Afghanistan, besides the areas controlled by the Peshawar-based parties, there were territories in the central Hazarajat highlands ruled by Shia organizations which maintained offices in Iranian cities as well as Quetta, Pakistan. The Revolutionary Council of the Islamic Union of Afghanistan, which set up its administration in the Hazarajat region in September 1979, consisted of moderate and radical Shia Islamists. In the spring of 1984 the coalition of the pro-Iranian Sazman-e Nasr (Organization of Victory) and Sejah-e Pasdran (Army of the Guards) overthrew the Revolutionary Council and assumed control of the region, thus strengthening Iran's role in the ultimate solution of the Afghanistan crisis.

Fundamentalist parties drew their recruits mainly from young college-educated men with rural or small-town backgrounds, from the families of civil servants, teachers or traders. They were often radical, dogmatic and intolerant – mirror images of the young cadres of the PDPA.

The traditional Islamic camp stemmed from the religious establishment of Afghanistan which had been close to King Zahir Shah. The leader of the National Liberation Front of Afghanistan (NLFA), Sibghatullah Mujaddidi, a graduate of Cairo's Al Azhar University and an Islamic teacher, was a nephew of the Hazrat of Shor Bazaar. Due to the cosy relations between the Mujaddidi family and the king, the NLFA attracted many monarchists. Indeed, the NLFA used the emblem of monarchy as a nationalist and Islamic symbol. Ahmed Gailani, leader of the National Islamic Front of Afghanistan and the head of the Qadiriya (Sufi) order, had been a close adviser to King Zahir Shah. He was the least religious of the Pakistan-based Afghan leaders. Nabi, leader of the Islamic Revolutionary Movement, was a cleric who had run an Islamic college in Logar, south of Kabul, and a leading figure in the Qadiriya order. His organization contained both traditional mullahs and young men with modern education. He was at ease with both religious and secular figures, modernistic or traditional, and was in a sense a bridge between traditionalist and fundamentalist camps.

The common denominator of these parties was that they were pan-Islamic and anti-Marxist, and used Islam as the exclusive, or at least a major, rallying cry to mobilize popular resistance against the leftist regime. To put it differently, Islam played a critical role in providing a sense of purpose to these organizations. Periodic efforts were made to bring them under one umbrella and one leader.

Attempts were made at the Islamic Conference Organization (ICO) foreign ministers' meetings in January and May 1980 to forge a united front of the exiled Afghan parties. These failed. What did happen, though, was that such leaders as Hikmatyar and Rabbani succeeded in soliciting funds from the oil-rich states of the Gulf. Strengthened by this aid, Hikmatyar's Hizb-e Islami tried to expand its turf into the regions where other parties and tribes were dominant. This worsened inter-party relations, and brought some 300 mullahs from Afghan provinces to Peshawar in April 1981 to foster unity. Under this pressure, Gailani, Mujaddidi and Muhammadi set up a joint council. The three fundamentalist parties formed an umbrella organization called the Islamic Alliance of Afghanistan under the chairmanship of Professor Abdul Rasul Sayyaf. Educated at Al Azhar and Medina universities, Sayyaf was fluent in Arabic, an asset that won him a warm reception in the Gulf capitals.

The establishment of these coalitions helped to coordinate the distribution of arms from America, Saudi Arabia and Egypt which in the summer of 1981 were arriving at the rate of two planeloads a week. Sayyaf used his exalted position to win over many floating Afghan groups with supplies of weapons, and transformed the Islamic Alliance of Afghanistan into a party of his own, a development that revived inter-party discord.

However, this did not discourage Saudi Arabia from pressuring various Islamic parties to unite. In early 1983, fearing that they would be excluded from the negotiations in progress under United Nations aegis between Kabul, Moscow, Islamabad and Tehran to solve the Afghanistan crisis, the Islamic parties tried hard to create an umbrella organization. The result in May 1983 was the seven-party Islamic Alliance of Afghan Mujahedin, popularly known simply as the Afghan Mujahedin, under the chairmanship of Sayyaf with Mujaddidi as his deputy.

Ignoring traditional Islamic forces, the Kabul regime concentrated its attacks on fundamentalist groups, particularly the Hizb-e Islami (both factions) and the Jamaat-e Islami. It combined this with a policy of projecting itself as a guardian of Islam. President Karmal took a lead in this. Having relegated the red flag to the PDPA in January 1980, he restored the national tricolour on the eve of the second anniversary of the Saur Revolution in April. Karmal prayed in public regularly and began his speeches with an invocation to Allah. The audience responded to his public addresses with intermittent cries of 'Allahu Akbar (God is Great)'. He instituted the Office of Islamic Teachings under his direct control, and radio and television re-introduced recitations of the Quran. In a speech in mid-June, he stressed that respect for Islam was part of official policy. Various steps were taken to illustrate this. A higher profile was given to the Ministry of Religious Affairs and Endowments whose activities were widely reported in the media. Among other things this ministry awarded hefty salary increases to clerics and gave them enhanced importance. In return the clergy became more willing to explain official policies and reforms to their congregations. The ministry initiated a well-advertised programme of building new mosques and religious schools.

It also introduced a programme designed to exchange Islamic del-egations with Soviet Central Asian republics. The purpose was to reassure Afghan Muslims that Islam and Islamic institutions con-tinued to exist in these constituents of the USSR. Radio broadcasts from these republics in the Persian, Tajik, Pushtu, Uzbek, Turkmen and Azeri languages stressed that Islam was safe in the Soviet system and that danger to it came from Zionist, American and Chinese imperialisms, which had been actively undermining the indepen-dence of various Muslim countries, including Afghanistan. Since such commentaries were delivered by the highest Islamic personali-ties in the Soviet Union, they had considerable impact on foreign, including Afghan, Muslims. After the Soviet intervention in Afghanistan, these broadcasts often called on their listeners in Afghanistan to oppose the aims of 'evil fanatics' exploiting the name of Islam and carrying out destructive acts against society.

As for Islamists, the government tried to challenge the monopoly over Islam they claimed, and took measures to block the movement of guerrillas to and from Pakistan. With the assistance of such promi-nent clerics as Sayid Bahauddin Jan Aqa, it mounted a campaign portraying the resistance as unIslamic. It attempted to win over the tribes along the Pakistan border with bribes and promises of regional autonomy.

Karmal's administration intensified its efforts to expand its popular base. In early 1981 it organized the founding of the National Father-land Front with due consideration to the composition, characteristics and qualities of various ethnic groups, tribes and clans which inhabited Afghanistan. Among the Front's components were the Jamaat-e Ulema (Society of Clerics) and numerous tribal *jirgas* (assemblies). The Front's major task was to publicize and explain official policies to the masses. By March 1981 the Front claimed to have 100,000 members affiliated to 400 local councils. The number of full and candidate members of the PDPA was officially put at 90,000, which was only a fraction of the 518,350 full and candidate members which the Communist Party of Uzbekistan, with a popu-lation of 15.5 million, could claim.[12] The activities of the Front and the PDPA were limited mainly to urban centres, since large parts of the countryside had slipped out of the control of the central authority, which in any case had been minimal before the 1978 Saur Revolution.

The extent of the resistance's activities could be judged by official statements in early 1983 to the effect that the counter-revolutionaries had destroyed or damaged nearly half of the schools and hospitals (1814 and thirty-one respectively), 111 basic health centres, three-quarters of communications lines, 800 heavy transport vehicles and 906 peasant cooperatives.[13] In a way the resistance offered by rural Afghans to the Kabul government was as much a rebellion against rapid socio-economic reform as it was against the increased role of the state.

Human casualties were mounting too. By early 1984 the number of dead or injured Afghan troops was put at 17,000 and among guerrillas at 30,000. The estimates of Soviet military casualties varied between 13,500 and 30,000.[14]

The two sides were now firmly divided. The Kabul regime, heavily dependent on 115,000 Soviet troops and generous military aid from Moscow, was committed to subduing the continuing resist-ance in rural Afghanistan. On the opposite side the Pakistan-based Afghan parties, receiving arms and cash from the US, Saudi Arabia, Egypt and China to an approximate value of $500 million in 1980 – twice the Afghan budget, including foreign aid, in that year – were equally determined to maintain the jihad against the Marxist govern-ment until they had achieved the expulsion of the Soviet forces and the collapse of the infidel regime.

It was against this backcloth that UN-sponsored talks between various parties proceeded, the points in dispute being the timetable for a Soviet pull-out, the cessation of foreign arms aid to Afghan groups, and the return of the refugees to their homes. The rate of Soviet withdrawal became the most intractable point. The Kabul–Moscow side offered a period of four years after a halt to foreign military assistance to the Afghan resistance. The Islamabad–Washington axis specified three to four months. The Afghan Mujahedin wanted an immediate and unconditional Soviet evacuation.

After Mikhail Gorbachev became First Secretary of the CPSU in March 1985, the Kremlin began to show flexibility toward Afghanistan. Gorbachev expressed his wish to scale down the Soviet commitment to Kabul. Consequently, in its talks with the Islamabad–Washington alliance the Kabul–Moscow axis offered to cut the period of Soviet withdrawal from forty-eight months to eighteen. The USSR wanted anti-Marxist leaders to negotiate with Karmal's government and reach an accord. When it realized that resistance leaders inside and outside the country were unwilling to deal with Karmal, it worked surreptitiously to ease him out in May 1986 in favour of Muhammad Najibullah.[15] Gorbachev opted for Najibullah (born 1947) partly because he had been a loyal party member for nineteen years, and partly because as the chief of Khad (*Khidmat-e Amniyat-e Dawlati* – State Security Service) for several years, he was considered adept at making underhand deals, a skill likely to be useful in ending the Afghan imbroglio. By announcing shortly afterwards that the USSR would pull out 6000 Soviet troops in October, Gorbachev underscored his seriousness about settling the Afghan crisis.

But that did not mean the cessation of military activities. In a joint operation in November, Afghan and Soviet forces seized Kama Dakka, a vital staging-post for Western and Chinese weapons from Pakistan. They also continued their campaign of exhorting and bribing the border tribes to impede the passage of arms and guerrillas into Afghanistan along its 2400-kilometre (1500-mile) border with Pakistan.

The Afghan Mujahedin and the Americans were not idle either. Having forced the Kabul–Moscow axis to adopt an openly compromising stance, they tried to raise the Soviet cost of continued presence in Afghanistan. They knew that whatever the strength of Islam's appeal to Afghans, the balance of forces could only be settled on the battlefield. There an extensive deployment of helicopter gunships by Afghan and Soviet troops gave them an overwhelming advantage over their Islamic adversaries. To neutralize Kabul's air superiority, Washington decided to arm the guerrillas with British-manufactured Blowpipe and US-made shoulder-held Stinger anti-aircraft missiles. About 150 Stingers were shipped to the area in the late spring of 1986, followed by 300 Blowpipes several months later. These were put to extensive use in the autumn, and proved more effective than the Soviet-made SAM-7s which had been in use before. Afghan sources in Peshawar claimed to have shot down sixty government helicopters in the last three months of 1986.[16]

Given this, resistance leaders had good reason to believe that the unilateral ceasefire for six months that Najibullah declared on 15 January 1987 stemmed from his growing weakness in the face of Islamist intransigence and perseverance. It was little wonder that the seven-party Islamic Alliance of Afghan Mujahedin rejected the truce offer, and decided to form an interim government to take over from the Najibullah administration.

Najibullah was undeterred. He established the Commission for National Reconciliation which in turn set up hundreds of branches in the country to encourage the opposition to give up its armed resistance and participate in normal political life. The media stopped calling guerrillas 'bandits' or 'counter-revolutionaries', and instead referred to them as 'misguided brothers' with whom the government was prepared to share power.

The Islamic resistance responded by assassinating provincial leaders of the Commission for National Reconciliation. By late March the ceasefire had practically collapsed. Whatever gains the government made were modest. It claimed that 44,000 refugees had returned and that 21,000 'misguided brothers' had abandoned their violent activities. Since, by official accounts, there were two million refugees and a quarter of a million (intermittently active) guerrillas,[17] the results of the unilateral truce were unimpressive.

With the consensus on the Soviet withdrawal informally settling around the period of eleven months, the main point to be tackled, outside the UN framework, was the composition of the government in Kabul that would be acceptable to the Islamic opposition and its backers. In June, Najibullah tried to lure the three traditional Islamic parties in the Afghan Mujahedin into sharing power with him, but failed.

Neither Kabul nor Moscow was prepared to cede the dominant position that the PDPA visualized for itself in any future coalition government. During its nine years of rule it had engendered its own constituencies: the peasants who had secured land; the emancipated women who dreaded the prospect of being returned to the four walls of home and the veil; and all those who had benefited, materially and otherwise, from the literacy campaign.

On the other side the traditional Islamic parties had managed merely to maintain the networks their leaders had headed before the 1978 Saur Revolution, when the state had made minimal inroads into the individual and social life of Afghans. It was the four fundamentalist parties that, like the PDPA, had created new constituencies inside and outside Afghanistan. Being the beneficiaries of foreign aid – running in 1987 at $640 million from America, matched by an equal amount from Saudi Arabia[18] – they had the means to sustain the vastly enlarged networks in order to promote the militant cause politically and militarily.

In short, the Marxist revolution backed by the USSR, and the resources and facilities provided by Pakistan, Iran, the Gulf states, Egypt and America, had been the main reasons for the upsurge in Islamic fundamentalism among Afghans.

Within the Islamist camp there were differences on such vital issues as the right of women to vote, and whether the future Islamic state of Afghanistan would be single- or multi-party. The traditionalists were monarchists whereas the fundamentalists regarded hereditary power as unIslamic. On the subject of co-existence with Moscow, such traditionalists as Gailani were ready to accept the exceptional interests that the USSR had in Afghanistan. In contrast, the fundamentalist Hikmatyar visualized the future Islamic state in Afghanistan as a springboard for exporting Islamic revolution to the Central Asian republics of the USSR. That this was not mere rhetoric became apparent when a Hizb-e Islami group tried to capture a frontier guard post near Pyanj in Soviet Tajikistan.[19]

The repeated failure of the Najibullah administration in the latter half of 1987 to persuade the rebels to join a government of national reconciliation did not stop the Afghan president from diluting the Marxist form and content of the political system. The new constitution adopted in December 1987 dropped the term 'Democratic' from the country's name, reducing it simply to the Republic of Afghanistan. More significantly, the constitution declared Islam to be the state religion, and allowed a multi-party system.

Indeed, the results of the parliamentary poll in April 1988 showed that the PDPA had secured only twenty-seven per cent of the seats, with the National Front, an umbrella body, gaining twenty-eight per cent, and the popular organizations, such as the Workers

Revolutionary Party, the Peasants Justice Party and the Islamic Party, together obtaining thirty-eight per cent. Premier Sultan Ali Keshtmand was replaced by a non-party politician, Muhammad Hassan Sharq.

Addressing the PDPA conference on 27 April 1988, the tenth anniversary of the Saur (April) Revolution, Najibullah criticized the party for not listening to the people and indulging in 'glib rhetoric' and 'deceitful verbiage' – and often mechanically applying models of advanced revolutions while ignoring the historical character of Afghan society. He urged the delegates not to underestimate the role of Islam and the prestige of the clergy, and declared that the objectives of the Afghan revolution could not, and should not, be realized by military means.[20]

He made these statements on the eve of the first stage of the withdrawal of 115,000 Soviet troops, starting on 15 May 1988 and ending on 15 February 1989. This was one of the four agreements signed by the Soviet Union, America and Pakistan under UN auspices in Geneva in February 1988. Following these signatures, the two superpowers exchanged secret letters that allowed them to continue military supplies to their allies. That is, Moscow agreed to let Washington give arms and ammunition to the guerrillas based in Pakistan. But since Pakistan had signed a document specifying non-interference it was required to bar transportation of military supplies into Afghanistan and close down the training camps for the Afghan rebels on its soil. In the event, to the chagrin of Kabul and Moscow, Islamabad openly breached this agreement.

The Afghan Mujahedin decided to intensify its political challenge to the Najibullah regime. Encouraged by the Pakistani Inter-Services Intelligence (ISI) Directorate – a military and internal security agency employing some 100,000 people[21] – it formed an interim government under the premiership of Ahmed Shah, a Wahhabi member of Sayyaf's Islamic Alliance of Afghanistan. This went down badly with the traditionalist parties, which had proposed holding immediate elections in the refugee camps in Pakistan, which held about three million Afghans. When they were overruled they ignored the newly formed interim government and its secretariat, funded exclusively by the Saudis. This, and the refusal of Pakistan and America to recognize the Ahmed Shah administration, led to its quiet demise some months later.

With the Soviet troops reduced by half by mid-August 1988, the Najibullah government decided to vacate many border posts and garrisons to consolidate its strategic position and encourage refugees to return. It slowed down its programmes of land reform and women's emancipation. In contrast, it raised its budget for the Ministry of Religious Affairs and Endowments, now employing 20,000 clerics, to the extent that it amounted to three times the budget for the foreign ministry. Addressing the PDPA's central committee in October, Najibullah said that the organization was prepared to put national reconciliation above party politics.

The resistance leaders rejected Najibullah's overture on the grounds that his government was a puppet of Moscow, and they would therefore only talk with the Soviets. This came about in December 1988 in Taif, Saudi Arabia, where Afghan Mujahedin leaders conferred with Yuli Voronstov, the Soviet ambassador in Kabul. But following their subsequent meetings with Voronstov in Islamabad, they rejected his proposal of a coalition with the PDPA. They also ignored Najibullah's offer of a unilateral truce from 1 January 1989.

As 15 February, the date of final Soviet withdrawal, approached, there were predictions that with the cement that held the Afghan Mujahedin together – the Soviet presence – gone, the coalition would disintegrate. But it did not. The chief reason was that America, under the new administration of President George Bush, pledged to continue supplying weapons to the Afghan Mujahedin to the tune of $500 million a year (with Saudi Arabia matching the American aid to the same extent). Any party breaking away from the Afghan Mujahedin would have lost its share of arms – and thus its followers in the field, whose loyalty rested largely on a steady supply of cash and arms.

Equally, on the other side, in the absence of a political settlement leading to a coalition government, the Soviets handed over their vast military stores to the Afghans, airlifted more arms and ammunition, and promised to honour their December 1978 Treaty of Friendship and Cooperation with Afghanistan, which specified mutual consultations about ensuring 'the security, independence and territorial integrity of the two countries'.

While the Afghan resistance could rightly claim that its jihad against Moscow had succeeded in ridding its country of foreign troops, it could not alter geography or international treaties. It had also failed to transform its essentially military alliance into a potential agency of civilian administration; and the divisions within it had proved unbridgeable.

AFTER THE SOVIET WITHDRAWAL

After several postponements the Afghan *shura* (consultative assembly), sponsored by the resistance groups, finally met in Rawalpindi, Pakistan, and began its session on 19 February 1989. Its 439 delegates decided to end the practice of rotating the chairmanship of the Afghan Mujahedin's Supreme Council every three months, and elect an interim government. In the elections that followed, Saudi officials and Pakistan's ISI operatives played crucial roles. As a result Mujaddidi and Sayyaf, securing the highest number of votes, emerged respectively as president and premier, with Hikmatyar, Khalis and Rabbani respectively as foreign, defence and interior ministers.

Aware of the Afghan Mujahedin's plan to infiltrate Kabul with men and weapons before besieging it, Najibullah grabbed the first opportunity to strike at his adversaries and prepare his followers for combat. Following the discovery on 18 February of weapons and explosive in the capital, the president declared a state of emergency, and suspended the constitutional rights pertaining to public assembly and labour strikes, and set up military courts to try those charged with breaking the law. He appointed a new twenty-member Supreme Council for the Defence of the Homeland consisting of military and party officials, with Sultan Ali Keshtmand, a Hazara, as its deputy head under him. He replaced Premier Sharq with Fazl Haq Khaliqyar, a non-party leader. But by replacing the other seven non-partisan ministers with PDPA members he increased the PDPA's proportion in the cabinet. The new government handed out 30,000 Kalashnikov assault rifles to the young Defenders of the Revolution, thus partially mobilizing PDPA members, aged between fourteen and fifty-eight, in Kabul. It recalled thousands of Afghans in schools and military academies in the USSR. It implemented its plan to raise the Special Guard Corps, with 30,000 of its personnel to be posted in Kabul, and another 15,000 in the provincial capitals, to replace the departed Soviet troops. In addition, there were interior ministry troops, 20,000–25,000 strong; and the armed State Security Service, Khad, numbering 15,000–20,000. This force of 80,000–90,000 out of an overall total of 140,000 regular troops and paramilitary personnel was regarded as the hard core of the Kabul regime, expected to fight to the bitter end the 70,000 full-time combatants in the opposite camp which lacked a central military authority.[22]

Thus, while curtailing his power base at the top, Najibullah enlarged the state machine as well as trade unions and professional syndicates. The media projected the image of the president as a nationalist struggling for Afghan independence (in contrast to the Mujahedin leaders operating under the influence of Pakistan, Saudi Arabia and America), a pious Muslim, and a leader committed to national reconciliation. An official source revealed that the authorities had been in contact with 575 groups representing 45,000 armed guerrillas inside the country, and that several local ceasefires were holding.[23]

On the other side, in March the forces of the Afghan Mujahedin's interim administration failed to capture Jalalabad – a city of 200,000 situated forty-five miles from the Pakistani border on the road to Kabul – with a view to establishing a secretariat there. The Kabul government's 15,000 troops, aided by the air force, successfully defended the city against an onslaught by 8000 armed rebels. About 1000 guerrillas were killed. The Mujahedin's interim government also failed to win the recognition either of Pakistan or America.[24]

In the aftermath of its defeat in Jalalabad, when its fighters found themselves exposed to severe air strikes, the morale of the Afghan Mujahedin fell. Its hopes of seeing the Kabul administration collapse evaporated. With the USSR keeping up military and civilian aid at the daily rate of twenty-five Ilyushin transport planes, each carrying twenty tons, the Najibullah regime was well supplied with arms, fuel and food. Though it had frustrated the Mujahedin offensive in Jalalabad, it continued to face resistance from many opposition field commanders, who had established an administrative infrastructure in the areas they controlled. However, overall unity among the constituents of the Afghan Mujahedin proved as elusive as before owing to deep personal and ethnic rivalries. Indeed, as spring gave way to summer, the simmering tension between Hikmatyar's Hizb-e Islami and Masoud's Jamaat-e Islami boiled over, with Hikmatyar's men killing thirty key lieutenants of Masoud in northern Afghanistan in July. In return Masoud's partisans sabotaged three attempts by Hikmatyar's guerrillas to attack Kabul during the summer and early autumn. None the less, Washington and Islamabad kept up their military and financial aid to the Afghan Mujahedin. They also ignored repeated proposals by Moscow and Kabul that arms supplies should be stopped on both sides: the US had decided to let Mujahedin fighters attempt to take over at least one prized Afghan city during the following spring or summer.

While the Najibullah regime without the prop of Soviet troops had proved to be more durable and better led than most Western observers had believed, it had its internal problems. The arrest of more than 100 Afghans, mainly military officers, in December 1989 for planning a coup showed that all was not well in the portals of power in Kabul. President Najibullah considered the time opportune to shed the last semblance of Marxism-Leninism and adopt nationalism, thus following the lead of the heads of Soviet Central Asian republics during the latter part of perestroika in the USSR. At his behest the People's Democratic Party of Afghanistan changed its name to Watan (i.e. Homeland) Party in January 1990, and began to distance itself from its Marxist past. But that did not make the Najibullah government immune to coups.

Indeed, the day after the trial of the military officers arrested in December opened in Kabul on 5 March 1990, a more serious attempt at a coup, led by the defence minister, General Shah Nawaz Tanai, was made. The rebels bombed the presidential palace as well as the defence and interior ministries, and briefly captured the major Bagram and Shindad air bases. Among those who were implicated in the plot were the interior minister, the air force chief, many generals and hundreds of other military officers and senior civil servants. Their intention was to replace the present administration with a view to facilitating reconciliation with Mujahedin leaders. The Najibullah government foiled the coup, but its prestige and credibility suffered. It alleged that Tanai had worked in collusion with Islamabad, and the fact that Tanai fled to Pakistan and Hikmatyar claimed that he had been in cahoots with him reinforced Kabul's charge. But the theory that Pakistan had deliberately launched a disinformation campaign about the Hikmatyar–Tanai link to highlight the Kabul regime's vulnerability seemed more plausible. What drove Tanai, a member of the Pushtun tribe of the same name, to his action was personal rivalry: his tribe came from the same Paktiya province as Najibullah's family, who belonged to the Ahmedzai tribe. He was a brilliant soldier. A graduate of a Soviet military academy, he became a commander of an elite commando unit brigade in 1983, and swiftly built up his reputation as an officer with combat experience. He rose fast to become chief of the army general staff, a position he held when Najibullah, lacking field experience, was promoted to the presidency in 1986. His own elevation to defence minister in August 1988 did not satisfy him. But so long as the Soviets were in Afghanistan, he could not move against Najibullah. Once they had left he began plotting against the president, winning support among fellow-officers by presenting himself as an Afghan nationalist.

Things were not going well in the Peshawar-based Mujahedin interim government either. Within a year of taking up his job as foreign minister, Hikmatyar had resigned his post. Inside Afghanistan, his men concentrated on attacking Jamaat-e Islami and other resistance groups in order to make them cooperate with their plan to attack Kabul. They refused, arguing that such an action would cause untold misery to civilians. In a sense, Hikmatyar's failure illustrated the bigger failure of the Mujahedin factions' inability to escalate their conflict from insurgency to a conventional war, as the failure of their offensive against Jalalabad had earlier shown. In the event, during the summer and early autumn all that happened was some fighting around Gardez, south of Kabul.

Concerned about the debilitating internecine conflict, local commanders inside Afghanistan began acting to dissipate it. Following meetings among local internal commanders in order to form a coordinating body in the eastern province of Paktiya in the spring of 1990, more such assemblies were held in different areas, culminating in a gathering of many important commanders in October in northeast Afghanistan. The result was the formation of the Council of Commanders under the leadership of Masoud. Later, this body was incorporated into a coalition of Mujahedin and tribal groups, named the Islamic Jihad Council, with Masoud as its chairman. In the coming months this organization came to compete with the Peshawar-based Afghan Mujahedin for external aid.

Nor was Najibullah inactive. Having proved his durability, he tried to weaken the Afghan Mujahedin. In October 1990 he held meetings in Geneva with some of the moderate Mujahedin leaders to discuss power-sharing, and also with the representatives of the former king, Zahir Shah, who supported the idea of setting up an interim government. On his way back home Najibullah met the Iran-based Afghan Shia leaders in Mashhad, with the Iranian government advising Afghan exile leaders to consider the advantages of a negotiated compromise with Kabul. To gain the loyalty of non-Pushtun minorities at home, the Najibullah government gave autonomy first to (Shia) Hazaras and then to Uzbeks. This won it the backing of a 10,000-strong Uzbek militia, led by Abdul Rashid Dostum, based in north-western Afghanistan, bordering Uzbekistan and Turkmenistan, which defected from the Mujahedin camp. The absence of Soviet troops lent credibility to Najibullah's claims that his government was now truly nationalist while his opponents were being propped up by such foreign powers as America, Pakistan, Saudi Arabia and Iran.

Sensing a general drift towards compromise, the US abandoned its plan to overthrow the Najibullah regime, and came around to accepting the idea that it could not be ignored in any future talks. This brought Washington's policy into line with Moscow's, which was to instal a broad-based transitional government including Watan Party leaders in Kabul as a means to securing permanent peace.

The USSR was quite determined to support Najibullah, if only to maintain stability around its southern border. Its policy-makers realized that since the alternative to Najibullah and his Watan Party was a regime dominated by Islamic fundamentalists, they really had no choice but to aid Najibullah and his secular colleagues. One of the leading proponents of this stance was General Boris Gromov, a veteran of Afghanistan, who, as deputy interior minister, was in charge of the ministry's Special Purpose Militia Units, Omon, which were used to suppress nationalists in the Baltic states and elsewhere. The actual cost of bolstering the regime in Kabul with weapons, food and 900,000 tonnes of oil annually was not as high as $250 million, as most Western observers estimated: a lot of military goods being supplied to Kabul were surplus from the Soviet stores being closed in Eastern Europe.

But the foundations on which the Soviet bloc rested were sinking as events in Eastern Europe showed. So Najibullah thought it prudent to espouse nationalism vehemently and strike a deal with the monarchist and Islamic opposition. In early 1991, to prove his peace-making intentions, he offered to step down if a credible interim government, which would guarantee that there would be no reprisals against the civilian and military members of the Watan Party, and which would provide safe passages for him and his close associates and their families, could be installed.[25]

Najibullah's overtures did not convince Mujahedin hardliners who dismissed them as a ruse by the much-hated former chief of the Afghan State Security Service, Khad, with a lot of blood on his hands. But Washington felt differently. It informed Islamabad in April 1991 that it had abandoned the military option and was prepared to accept a broad-based government in Kabul so long as it was not dominated by Hikmatyar's Hizb-e Islami. Earlier, to underline its policy of distancing itself from Hikmatyar – a long-time favourite of Pakistan's Inter-Services Intelligence, which channelled all outside assistance to the Mujahedin – the US had decided to funnel most of its aid through the Islamic Jihad Council headed by Masoud.

As a consequence of these diplomatic shifts, the UN was able in May 1991 to present a five-point peace plan to be implemented by an 'interim authority', which would facilitate dialogue among various Afghan parties in order to instal a broad-based government. The remaining points were: preservation of Afghanistan's independent, non-aligned Islamic character; the Afghan people's right to self-determination; an end to arms supplies from all sides; and external aid in repatriating refugees and reconstructing the country.

Inside Afghanistan, buoyed by assistance from external sources, the fighters under Masoud became more active, especially in their strongholds in north-east Afghanistan. They began nibbling away at the areas controlled by the Kabul government. They and other resistance groups, including Hikmatyar's Hizb-e Islami, resorted to crossing the fluvial border between Afghanistan and Tajikistan and Uzbekistan to incite anti-Communist feeling among Soviet Tajiks and Uzbeks, and aid such religious groupings as the Islamic Renaissance Party. They did so despite the argument offered by many Afghan nationalists that their actions would provide the hardliners in the Kremlin with a rationale for continuing to back the Najibullah administration as a means of preventing instability along the USSR's southern frontier.

But, with the defeat of diehards in Moscow and the collapse of the CPSU in the Soviet Union in the wake of the failure of the 19–21 August coup, the situation changed. The emergence of Russian power at the expense of Soviet power set the scene for a rapprochement between Russia and Afghan Mujahedin. In late August the Russian foreign minister, Andrei Kozyrev, said that 'the only obstacle to a settlement was Soviet support for the "extremists" led by Najibullah'. He argued that removing Najibullah from office would weaken his mirror images within the Afghan Mujahedin Alliance – that is, the fundamentalists – thus encouraging moderates within the Alliance to make peace with an equally moderate government in Kabul.[26] In any event, in the aftermath of the coup's failure, the USSR and the US signed an agreement in mid-September to cease arms supplies to their Afghan clients from 1 January.

In November 1991, in the thick of delicate negotiations about future relations between the constituent republics of the USSR, Soviet officials held meetings with Rabbani, the head of the Mujahedin's interim government. Their joint communiqué called for the creation of 'a transitional Islamic government' in Kabul. The statement later in the month by the Soviet border-guard commander in Tajikistan that most of the Tajik–Afghan border had fallen under the control of the Mujahedin showed that the internal balance of force was shifting away from Najibullah. These statements, coming on top of Moscow's decision to stop military aid to Kabul, further weakened the Afghan president's bargaining position.

The overall situation in Afghanistan at the end of 1991 was that Najibullah's government, claiming to have an armed force of 200,000 soldiers and paramilitary troops,[27] continued to hold major cities along the national highway that linked Mazar-e Sharif (in the northern Balkh province) with Kabul, Jalalabad, Qandhar and Herat. But in the countryside about three-quarters of the area was under the control of assorted elements of the opposition.

UN efforts to create a broad-based government became bogged down. Its plan to assemble the representatives of the seven factions of the Peshawar-based Afghan Mujahedin, the eight factions of the Tehran-based Hizb-e Wahadat-e Islami (Islamic Unity Party), the 'acceptable elements' of the Kabul government, as well as non-party religious and laymen leaders including the representative of the former king in a grand *jirga* (assembly), seemed to many Afghans to be unwieldy. Since radicals like Hikmatyar wanted to exclude all those who had not participated in the armed struggle against the Kabul regime, there was an unbridgeable division even within the Afghan Mujahedin.

The formal break-up of the USSR on 31 December 1991 brought about sharp policy changes in Islamabad and Kabul. Pakistan decided to develop trade with the newly independent Central Asian countries, and this necessitated a ceasefire in Afghanistan. It therefore resolved to back the UN peace plan. With economic aid from Moscow down to a trickle, Najibullah turned to Central Asian leaders for assistance. They supplied him with most of the six million barrels of fuel and half a million tons of wheat that Afghanistan needed to survive the winter months.[28] They did not want Najibullah to fall and give way to an Islamic regime, which would destabilize their own republics.

But at home the Watan Party, the core of Najibullah's support, began to divide between hardline Pushtun officers, advocating maintaining the status quo, and moderate Pushtuns backed by non-Pushtun officers, favouring political liberalization. In January 1992 there was a mutiny at the garrison in Hairatan on the Afghan–Uzbek border when the Uzbek and Tajik officers refused

Vladimir Lenin atop a pedestal decorated with tiled replicas of Turkmen carpets, an imaginative marriage of Soviet sculpture with local culture, in Ashqabat, Turkmenistan, October 1992.

The Communist-era personality cult continues with President Saparmurad Niyazov in Ashqabat, Turkmenistan.

The Islamic heritage of Samarkand, Uzbekistan, was preserved throughout the years of Communism.

Mullah Kyrgyz *madressa* (theological college) in Namangan, Uzbekistan, restored in 1992 after being used as a literary museum during the Soviet period.

Soviet-style symbol of reconstruction after the earthquake of April 1966 in Tashkent, Uzbekistan.

Below: A Muslim student at the Mir-e Arab *madressa* in Bukhara, Uzbekistan, one of only two such institutions in Central Asia which were kept open throughout the Soviet era.

A poster hailing cotton production in Uzbekistan,
October 1992.

A mural depicting the achievements of socialism
in industry, science, the arts, defence and sport, in
Tashkent, Uzbekistan, September 1992.

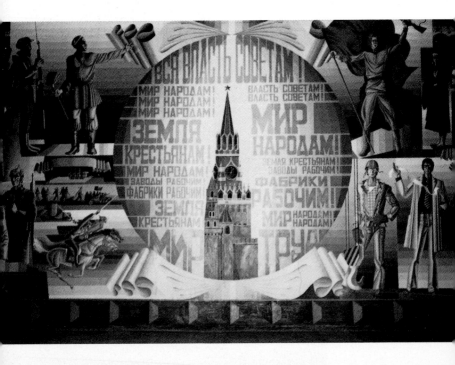

Believers outside a mosque in Samarkand, Uzbekistan, in traditional dress.

Right: A Muslim war veteran, wearing a Soviet military medal, in the compound of a mosque in Samarkand, Uzbekistan.

Former headquarters of the central committee of the Communist Party of Uzbekistan in Bukhara, now housing the local central committee of the People's Democratic Party (PDP) of Uzbekistan.

Below: Multi-ethnic students at the Institute of Foreign Languages, Samarkand, under the portraits of leading figures of English literature considered revolutionary by the Communist authorities: (from left) George Bernard Shaw, Ernest Hemingway, William Shakespeare and Ford Madox Ford.

PDP chief, President Islam Karimov of Uzbekistan (left), with President Turgat Ozal of Turkey, in Ankara a fortnight before the formal break-up of the Soviet Union on 31 December 1991. *Associated Press*

Despite over 70 years of Communism, and laws against under-age marriage and the veil, marriages of veiled teenage Tajik girls continue. *Steve Dupont/Katz*

Rahman Nabiyev, the Communist president of Tajikistan from November 1991 to November 1992, during whose tenure a civil war, resulting in at least 20,000 mainly civilian deaths, raged. *Popperfoto*

Imamali Rahmanov, a leading Communist, who succeeded Nabiyev as president of Tajikistan, rules a country which is heavily dependent on Russia for survival and has yet to return to normalcy. *A. Abbas/Magnum*

to surrender their jobs to the Pushtun officers sent from Kabul. It took some weeks for Kabul to suppress the mutiny and re-establish its authority; and this damaged its standing in the region. Also, with the end of Soviet largesse, Najibullah had great difficulty maintaining the loyalty of some 80,000 tribal militia, most of whom had earlier abandoned the Mujahedin camp owing to large offers of money, arms and food by his government.

These developments encouraged Benon Sevan, UN special envoy, to intensify his efforts to bring about a ceasefire in Afghanistan. During his four long meetings with President Najibullah in March 1992, Sevan told him that so long as he remained in office there would be no UN aid coming to Afghanistan. Under this pressure Najibullah told Sevan on 18 March that he would hand over power to 'an interim government' of fifteen neutral Afghans which the UN proposed to set up as a forerunner to a transitional, broad-based administration. The next day in a broadcast Najibullah made public his decision, saying that all executive power would be transferred to 'the interim government as of the first day of the transition period'.[29] He did this without consulting any of his fifty military generals or other leading civilian backers: a blunder that nearly cost him his life.

Najibullah's statement confused and demoralized his supporters, especially in the military and militia officer corps. In order to save their lives the commanders of garrisons and militias began striking deals with local Mujahedin leaders. Prominent among those who performed a *volte face* were General Dostum, whose Uzbek militiamen had established themselves as fierce fighters; General Abdul Momen, a Tajik; and General Mansur Naderi, an Ismaili (Shia). They now cut deals with local Mujahedin units, under the overall command of Masoud, and pro-Iranian Shia groups. Together they attacked Mazar-e Sharif, a major city fifty kilometres (thirty miles) from the Uzbek border, defended by the Afghan army's 18th division. They won after fierce street combat. By the end of March the city was under the control of the rebel military council. From here the rebel council extended its authority to the adjoining provinces as the Uzbek militia, led by Dostum, began advancing towards Kabul, bypassing the forces of Masoud whose headquarters were in Charikar, just north of the capital.

By the time Najibullah addressed a meeting of military leaders in Kabul on 12 April, appealing to them to stand by him, it was too late. The response was poor, and he knew that his time was up. When on 15 April he tried to escape via Kabul airport to join his family in Delhi, India, he was prevented from leaving by Dostum's militia, who controlled the airport. He then put himself into the hands of the United Nations mission in Kabul. It tried to get him out of Afghanistan, but in vain.

The commanders of major army garrisons began making deals with local Mujahedin commanders, starting with Charikar on 14 April, followed by Bagram air base on the 15th, Kunduz and Herat three days later, and Qandhar and Samangan a day after that. It was not until a week later that Vice-President Rahim Hatif, now heading the administration in the capital, was able to negotiate the entries of Masoud and Dostum's forces into the city, ignoring the ultimatum of Hikmatyar, entrenched in Charasyab to the south-east of Kabul, that they should surrender unconditionally to him by 26 April. The Mujahedin leadership meeting in Peshawar on 15 April decided to have the current chairman, Mujaddidi, as president of Afghanistan for two months, and established a Leadership Council of fifty-one members, including the chairman and deputy chairman, divided equally among seven constituent parties.

President Mujaddidi's arrival in Kabul, now under the military control of Dostum and Masoud, formally marked the end of the war between Afghan Marxists and Islamists that started in April 1978. Once the USSR had intervened militarily in December 1979, the civil conflict turned into a battle between two antagonistic super-powers. Washington's rising commitment to Afghan Islamists could be judged by the financial aid it provided them: up from $20 million in 1980 to $700 million in 1988, the last year of Ronald Reagan's presidency as well as of the Soviet military presence in Afghanistan. (The estimates of Soviet military aid to the Kabul regime varied from $1 million to $4 million a day, plus economic aid comprising food and fuel; but part of this was offset by the Afghan gas that Moscow bought at a giveaway price.) The withdrawal of USSR troops from Afghanistan in early 1989 loosened Soviet ties with the landlocked country, but did not end them. So the fate of Afghanistan continued to be linked with the performance of Moscow vis-à-vis Washington in their global Cold War. The bulldozing of the Berlin Wall in November 1989 foreshadowed the USSR's defeat in its struggle with the West which materialized, formally, in the break-up of the Soviet Union two years later. Though the combination of Afghan nationalism and Islam was a powerful force with which to confront the secular, leftist regime in Afghanistan, it was not enough to decimate the regime in Kabul. The ethnic and tribal differences among Afghans were so deep-seated and varied that the administration in power in Kabul would have successfully exploited these to weaken the insurgency and overcome it. In the final analysis, it was the lure of American and Saudi money and weapons that kept the seven recognized factions within the Mujahedin Alliance glued together. Thus the US emerged as the crucial player in bringing about the victory of Islamists over Marxists in Afghanistan. It is noteworthy that America achieved this outcome in Afghanistan while busily decrying Islamic fundamentalism in Iran.

THE ISLAMIC STATE OF AFGHANISTAN

One of the early decisions of the Islamist government in Kabul was to rename the country the Islamic State of Afghanistan. It was re-admitted to the Islamic Conference Organization from which it had been suspended twelve years before. The new regime's other decrees involved banning alcohol, gambling and nightclubs, prescribing the veil for women, transforming co-educational schools and colleges into single-sex institutions, and declaring the Sharia to be the sole source of Afghan law. This had a direct and immediate impact on life in urban centres, including Kabul, whose population had swollen to nearly two million, about a third of them Hazaras organized under the banner of the pro-Iranian Hizb-e Wahadat-e Islami, popularly known as Wahadat (Unity), based in the western part of the city.

Once the common enemy, the Najibullah regime, associated with the Soviet Union and its troops, had been overturned, the cement that had held the ethnically disparate groups within the Mujahedin Alliance together disintegrated. With this, long-standing rivalries between factional leaders and major ethnic groups came to the surface. Having enjoyed autonomy, stemming from access to large quantities of weapons and money, in their long struggle against the leftist government, the non-Pushtun minorities – especially Tajiks, Hazaras and Uzbeks – were not prepared to let the traditional Pushtun hegemony re-assert itself. As Islamic organizations, the Mujahedin parties remained open to members of all ethnic groups (though a few of them barred Shias on religious grounds). But it was widely known that Rabbani's Jamaat-e Islami was a Tajik-dominated party, and Hikmatyar's Hizb-e Islami an overwhelmingly Pushtun organization. There was of course little doubt about the militia led by Dostum: it was Uzbek. With Kabul now controlled by Tajik, Uzbek and Hazara fighters, and with Masoud as defence minister, the ethnic minorities were resolved all the more to frustrate any attempt by Pushtuns to re-impose their supremacy.

When Hikmatyar, based in Charasyab, thirty-two kilometres (twenty miles) to the south of Kabul, tried to muscle his way into the city by subjecting its residents to an unending barrage of shells and mortars from his enormous arsenal, built up over several years, he was resisted by the non-Pushtun forces entrenched in the capital. He called for the withdrawal of Dostum's militia, accusing him of being a Communist and a close aide of Najibullah. Dostum ignored the demand. The fighting, which went on for a few weeks, ended on 25 May, when the warring sides signed an accord. It included promises that Dostum's men would be made to leave Kabul, and that a presidential election would be held within six months. Hikmatyar agreed to join the government on condition that he would be allowed to name the premier. He named one of his leading commanders, Abdus Sabur Farid, as prime minister.

But the agreement proved still-born. Though Farid became prime minister, albeit without much executive authority, Dostum and his men stayed put in Kabul. Indeed, as head of the small National Liberation Front of Afghanistan, President Mujaddidi found it expedient to enlarge his support base by courting Dostum: he made him a four-star general before stepping down as president in late June. Mujaddidi was followed by Borhanuddin Rabbani, a Tajik, whose party included another Tajik leader, defence minister Masoud. This concentration of power in Tajik hands did not please Hikmatyar, who now began stressing Pushtun nationalism more than Islamic fundamentalism.

In early August, having assembled many units of his militia around Kabul, Hikmatyar resumed his attacks on the capital. These were so severe and indiscriminate that a meeting of the Leadership Council on 16 August declared Hikmatyar 'a criminal and an outlaw'. President Rabbani sacked Prime Minister Farid, a formality since he had left Kabul before Hikmatyar initiated the latest round of fighting. The Hazara-dominated Wahadat sided with Rabbani and Dostum in defending the city. But none of the three militia leaders contemplated offensives against Hikmatyar's forces as they were unwilling to accept the casualties that would involve. Consequently hostilities continued until 28 August, when a ceasefire was agreed. The latest bout of fighting was uncommonly severe. It caused 2500 deaths and injuries to many thousands, and displaced 500,000 people. Ironically, it was under an Islamic regime that civil war finally caught up with the residents of Kabul, a city that had remained comparatively peaceful during the previous fourteen years, when, it is estimated, up to three-quarters of a million people, including 15,000 Soviet soldiers, had died as direct or indirect casualties of the conflict – the former category including those who had been killed either in combat between the warring sides or among the varied constituents of each camp, or owing to acts of sabotage or the widespread drug trafficking in Afghanistan and Pakistan; and the latter, indirect category consisting largely of infants whose deaths could be linked to malnutrition or the breakdown of the health services caused by the hostilities, and those blown up by one of the millions of mines that had been scattered throughout the country.

Hikmatyar continued to make an issue of the presence in the capital of Dostum's militia. His hostility seemed to make the militia increasingly popular with an expanding body of Pushtuns and non-Pushtuns who disliked and feared Hikmatyar. Its initial size of 10,000 men had by now more than doubled. In August, Dostum undertook a few foreign trips to bolster his prestige and influence at home and abroad. He travelled to Ankara where he met Turkish and Western diplomats. In Tashkent he had several meetings with President Karimov, a fellow-Uzbek, who approved of his secular credentials and saw him as an effective brake on the regional ambitions of Islamist forces in Afghanistan. Indeed, Dostum began to visualize a separate, secular, Uzbek-dominated northern region of Afghanistan acting as a buffer for Central Asia against the spread of Islamic fundamentalism by Pushtuns in the south and Iran in the west. With a frustrated Hikmatyar increasingly thinking of establishing a Pushtun state in the Afghan areas adjoining Pakistan, an eventuality likely to destabilize Pakistan, with its own Pushtun minority, Islamabad began wooing Dostum as a counterweight to Hikmatyar's Pushtun nationalist scenario, likely to include the Pushtun tribes in Pakistan.

The continuing inroads that Islamists made in Tajikistan, capped by the resignation of President Nabiyev in early September, encouraged Hikmatyar to increase his assistance to the Islamic forces there. His policy had a dual purpose: to strengthen religious elements in Tajikistan, and to keep the political pot boiling in that republic, thus lessening any chances of ethnic Tajiks in Tajikistan and Afghanistan uniting.

Having acquired the presidency of Afghanistan by virtue of the rotation system used by the seven leaders of the Mujahedin Alliance,

Rabbani showed every sign of clinging on to power. When his four-month period finished in late October he managed to get himself an extension of two months by cajoling the Leadership Council, by now a fractured body. This angered Hikmatyar, who unleashed his shells and mortars on Kabul. The bombardments were so severe that all diplomatic missions, including the UN, but excluding those of Pakistan and Iran, left the city. But Rabbani was obdurate. As December approached, he floated the idea of an assembly (*jirga*) of traditional leaders to extend his term of office by two years, during which arrangements would be completed to provide Afghanistan with a new constitution and hold parliamentary elections. Hikmatyar and some other leaders of the Mujahedin Alliance objected. Ignoring this, Rabbani summoned the *jirga*, packed with his supporters, in early January 1993, and had it confirm him as president for two more years.

Events in Tajikistan in December 1992, which resulted in the defeat of the Islamist-led alliance and the creation of tens of thousands of refugees, indirectly raised the prestige and importance of Dostum, politically and diplomatically. 'We will never allow anyone to arm Tajik fundamentalists and send them back to Tajikistan [from the area under my control],' he declared in January.[30] In order to help Tajik refugees, such international organizations as the United Nations High Commissioner for Refugees (UNHCR) began dealing with Dostum, and using Mazar-e Sharif airport under his control.

The rising influence of his Tajik and Uzbek rivals made Hikmatyar hit out again. His major grievance was that Rabbani had hijacked the presidency; and in this he had the backing of some other constituents of the Mujahedin Alliance as well as the (Shia) Wahadat, which had boycotted the *jirga* convened by Rabbani. Therefore, during this bout of fighting, conducted as before with mortars and artillery shells, the Wahadat joined Hikmatyar in its attacks on that section of Kabul that was controlled by the forces of Rabbani and Masoud. And Dostum, having pulled his militia out of the city limits of Kabul but retaining control of the capital's airport as well as its north-eastern suburbs, stayed neutral in the latest confrontation which began in mid-January. As before, it was devastating in its impact on civilians and buildings, and resulted in a further reduction in the city's dwindled population. Despite repeated calls for a cease-fire by interested Afghan and foreign parties, the fighting continued well into February. The figure of 4000 wounded, based on hospital admissions, given by the International Committee of the Red Cross in mid-February, understated the extent of the carnage: it ignored the dead. 'In the south and west of the city, pounded mercilessly for weeks at a time, entire suburbs have been reduced to rubble,' reported Gerald Bourke in the *Guardian* in late February. 'Hundreds of thousands have fled to the provinces or to Pakistan . . . The destitutes tell harrowing tales of murder, mutilation, torture, abduction or rape at the hands of defence ministry or rebel forces. Their stories suggest not just a breakdown of law and order, but the disintegration of a society.'[31]

It was this state of affairs that persuaded Afghan leaders to accept the mediation offer by Pakistan's prime minister, Muhammad Nawaz Sharif. At the end of six days of talks in Islamabad in early March – in which the heads of eight Afghan parties, including the Wahadat, participated – the negotiating parties signed an accord in the presence of senior officials from Pakistan, Iran and Saudi Arabia. The latest agreement gave the premiership to the Hizb-e Islami led by Hikmatyar, describing the prime minister as 'the chief executive' who only had to 'consult' the president before appointing his cabinet, where each of the eight parties were to get an equal number of seats. To safeguard against too much power concentrating in the premier's hands, the defence and finance ministries were to be supervised by councils of sixteen members each, drawn equally from the eight governing parties. Masoud was required to step down as defence minister. Elections to the constituent assembly were to be held by the end of 1993 followed by a constitution and parliamentary elections before June 1994, when the terms of President Rabbani as well as the Hizb-e Islami premier (Hikmatyar) were to end. Yielding to Hikmatyar's vehement objections, Dostum was denied any role in the cabinet or the Leadership Council.

Political ostracism by the ruling groups in Kabul had little effect on the fortunes of Dostum who, calling himself the 'President of the Northern Alliance' and heading the National Islamic Movement (NIM), now controlled nine out of twenty-nine provinces, from the Central Asian borders to the outskirts of Kabul, and administered efficiently a state within a state, which had its own tax- and customs-collecting bureaucracy. The efficiency with which he ran Mazar-e Sharif, the capital of the 'Northern Alliance', ensuring that it had electricity, drinking water and public transport, contrasted with the bleak disorder and desolation that prevailed in Kabul whose population had been reduced to less than half a million. His military was the most powerful in Afghanistan. In the spring of 1993 it was

120,000 strong, his tank force between 1000 and 2000, and the size of his fleet of fighter aircraft, helicopter gunships and transport planes estimated at 100-plus. While manned chiefly by Uzbeks, Tajiks and Turkmens, the Northern Alliance military also contained former Communist Pushtun officers. Considered a stabilizing force, Dostum was courted and financed by a wide array of countries: Turkey (for espousing secularism), Russia (for acting as a counter-force to the Afghan fundamentalists), Uzbekistan (for being a secular Uzbek), Iran (for keeping Pushtun nationalism at bay), Saudi Arabia (as a counterweight to Iranian backing), and Pakistan (for frustrating Hikmatyar's excessive ambition, most likely to destabilize Afghanistan). In early 1993 Mazar-e Sharif was already home to an Iranian consulate, and a Turkish consulate was planned. Though containing two highly attractive attributes – Islam and nationalism – the name of the party which Dostum chose, the National Islamic Movement, was misleading. 'With Afghanistan's almost entire population being Muslim,' argued Dostum, 'it cannot be a non-Muslim state. And we also want democracy which the fundamentalists are opposed to. Further Islamic laws cannot be implemented. If the fundamentalists implemented these laws nobody would be able to live in Afghanistan.'[32]

Like its neighbour, Tajikistan, Afghanistan had developed a countervailing power inside its territory. Within Communist Tajikistan, Badakhshan had emerged as a counterpoint to the regime in Dushanbe, providing succour to its democratic and Islamist opponents as well as ethnic Badakhshanis. Similarly, in Islamic Afghanistan, the north-western region under Dostum had emerged as a counterpoint to the regime in Kabul, providing a haven for those who wanted to moderate the Islamic drive and also ensure that Pushtun hegemony did not return.

The problematic role of Dostum and his fiefdom remained after differences between Rabbani and Hikmatyar were supposedly resolved at a conference of Mujahedin factions in Jalalabad, which deliberated against the backdrop of another round of fighting that erupted on 10 May when, as before, Hikmatyar blocked the southern and eastern supply routes to Kabul from Pakistan while his lieutenant, Abdus Sabur Farid, controlled the Kohistan Valley, through which the highway to the north passes. The Jalalabad Accord, signed on 20 May, provided for the collection of all heavy weapons from various militias, and more importantly established commissions to run the ministries of defence (under Rabbani) and interior (under

Hikmatyar) for two months until two army commanders from each of the twenty-nine provinces gathered to elect ministers to these ministries. This time Masoud resigned, partly because the defence ministry came under the jurisdiction of a Tajik leader of his party. This paved the way for Hikmatyar to assume the office of prime minister and appoint his cabinet. He did so in early June from his headquarters in Charasyab, but his list did not include ministers of defence and the interior. Until and unless this issue was settled the rest of the cabinet could not be sworn in.

As if this were not enough, the Wahadat took to firing salvos at the Rabbani-controlled part of Kabul because it felt that its share in the cabinet was not commensurate with the proportion of Shias in the national population. Exact figures were unavailable. Estimates varied between ten per cent, claimed by Wahadat's adversaries, and twenty-five per cent, claimed by the Wahadat. But whatever the actual proportion of Shias in Afghanistan, the strength of the Shia militia lay in the fact that, as a surrogate of Iran, it was well supplied with arms and ammunition.

NINE

Iran: The Geopolitics of Islamic Revolution

With ninety per cent of its fifty-four million people being Shia, Iran has emerged as the foremost Shia nation. But it was not always so. Before the rule of the Safavids (1501–1722), Iran was a largely Sunni country. The founder of the dynasty, Shah Ismail, born in the Azeri-speaking part of present-day Iran, adopted Twelver Shia-ism[1] to appeal to the heterodox sentiments of the populace, particularly tribesmen, and to differentiate themselves from the competing Sunni Ottoman Turks who wanted to incorporate Iran into their empire. In his enthusiasm to spread Shiaism, Shah Ismail ordered all preachers to lead Friday prayers in the name of the Twelve Imams and curse the first three Sunni caliphs – Abu Bakr, Umar ibn Khattab and Uthman ibn Affan – for usurping the rightful place of Imam Ali ibn Abi Tabib, a son-in-law of Prophet Muhammad. This ideological uniformity aided Shah Ismail to secure territorial unity – as also did his competition and confrontation with the Sunni Ottoman empire.

In order to lessen the inter-sectarian gap, Nadir Shah Afshar (1736–47) banned public cursing of the first three caliphs. He renamed Shiaism as Jaafari school after Imam Jaafar ibn Sadiq, the sixth imam and the main codifier of Shia jurisprudence. But these moves proved inadequate to blur the sectarian divide which had by then become much too sharp and wide. The differences spanned doctrine, ritual, law, theology and religious organization.

Unlike Shias, Sunnis regard caliphs as fallible interpreters of the Quran and the Hadiths (Sayings and Doings of Prophet Muhammad), collectively called the Sharia (Islamic law). Shias insist that the ruler must be just, and refer to the appropriate verses in the Quran. Conversely, say Shia clerics, if the ruler is unjust he must be overthrown. According to Shias, the Quran bears a pledge of sovereignty of the earth to the oppressed. Rooted in this promise to reward the lowly and the suffering are the concepts of the return of the (Twelfth) Hidden Imam – the arrival of the Mahdi, the Messiah

– and the rehabilitation of society. In other words, according to Shias, Islamic history is moving towards a fixed goal, and the forces of injustice will ultimately be defeated. This acts as a spur towards radical activism. In contrast, Sunnis view Islamic history essentially as a drift away from the ideal *umma* (Islamic community) which existed under the rule of the four Rightly Guided Caliphs, including Imam Ali.

Sunnis and Shias differ on how to organize religion and religious activities. Sunnis regard religious activities as the exclusive domain of the (Muslim) state. As and when clerics act as judges, preachers or educators, they do so under the aegis of the state. There is no question of the clergy organizing religion on their own. This is not the case among Shias, as a study of Iran amply shows.

During the rule of the Qajars (1790–1921) clerics administered vast religious endowments, *waqf*s, and received ten per cent of the income as commission. Since they were regarded as trustees of the Hidden Imam they also collected Islamic taxes – *khums* and *zakat*. Though *khums* was originally one-fifth of the booty that the believers took from the conquered non-believers, to be handed over to the ruler of the Islamic *umma*, Shias interpreted it as a general income tax. The clergy used these funds to run educational, social and charitable institutions as well as theological colleges. They conducted Sharia courts which dealt with personal and family matters. In the process of enforcing court decisions, they resorted to leading private armies composed of their religious students and the fugitives they had sheltered. They enjoyed higher esteem among believers than local Friday prayer-leaders or judges appointed by the monarch to deal with crimes according to the customary law. Moreover, they felt uniquely independent since their superiors, living in the holy cities of Najaf and Karbala in Iraq, were outside the jurisdiction of the Qajars. Parallel to this ran the concept of religious sanctuary (*bast*). Since the clergy claimed that mosques, religious shrines and their homes were in principle territories of the Hidden Imam, the Qajar government had no right to enter them. As such these places came to provide sanctuary to all sorts of fugitives. More importantly, this tradition helped to make mosques physical centres of opposition to unjust Iranian monarchs.

As the nineteenth century progressed, the mujtahids (those clerics who practise interpretative reasoning in applying the Sharia) took to naming the most revered colleague as the *marja-e mutalaq* (i.e. absolute source), whose guidance they agreed to accept. All told, therefore, these developments gave the clergy much muscle – political, spiritual and ideological – and went a long way to spawning unity among them, and imparting coherence to their teachings.

Curiously, the practice of choosing the *marja-e mutalaq*, and the presence of senior clerical leadership outside Iran, meant that Iranian society developed a church–state divide along the lines witnessed earlier in Christian Europe. This was unlike the state of affairs in Sunni countries.

The emergence of an independent socio-economic base gave mullahs the potential for independent action. They exercised this power to protest against the erosion of Islamic tradition in society and against the economic penetration of Iran by European powers, particularly Britain and Tsarist Russia. The 1891–2 Tobacco Protest was a good example. The clergy allied with secular intellectuals and nationalists to protest against the concession given to Britain by Nasiruddin Shah (1848–96) for a monopoly over the production and sale of tobacco. Facing popular pressure, the ruler withdrew the concession. This episode was to prove to be the forerunner of something bigger: the Constitutional Revolution.

The constitutional movement was backed by the propertied classes as well as by religious and intellectual leaders. The former, consisting of landowners, administrators, merchants and artisans, wanted Iran to be free of European domination so that they could develop their own potential, unfettered by the Shah's practice of giving economic concessions to Europeans. Religious leaders felt, rightly, that a reduction in the monarch's authority would increase their power in manipulating tribal chiefs, feudal aristocrats and mullahs.

Though the clergy formed a majority in the assembly convened in October 1906 to produce a constitution, they failed to act as a bloc. Their training had not equipped them with a political theory, and they did not have a constitutional model in mind. On the crucial question of sovereignty, radical clerics argued that since sovereignty had been delegated by Allah to the Hidden Imam, and then on to mujtahids, it did not rest with the people. Their view was opposed by moderate clerics as well as by secular constitutionalists. They lost. 'Sovereignty is a trust confided (as a Divine gift) by the People to the person of the King,' stated Article 55. The final document, called the Fundamental Laws, modelled on the Belgian constitution, was a compromise between moderate and radical views, with the radical clergy winning a few points. With certain modifications, this constitution remained in force until the 1979 revolution.

It was framed within an Islamic context. Article 1 declared Jaafari or Twelver Shiaism to be the state religion. Only a Jaafari Shia could become the king, a minister or a judge. Article 39 enjoined upon the monarch to 'promote the Jaafari doctrine' and 'to seek the help of the holy spirits of the Saints of Islam to render service to the advancement of Iran'. Article 18 specified free education provided it did not contravene the Sharia. Article 27 confirmed the right of Sharia courts to exist.

In the following year came the longer Supplementary Fundamental Laws, which outlined a bill of rights for citizens, and a parliamentary form of government, with power concentrated in the legislature at the expense of the executive. Significantly, Article 2 specified that no bill passed by the Majlis (parliament) was valid until a committee of five mujtahids – elected by the Majlis from a list of twenty submitted by the clergy – had judged it to be in conformity with Islam. That is, though the mujtahids' committee possessed veto power, it could not act as a creative body in its own right as the radical clergy had wanted. In practice, however, this article was never implemented. The Qajars ignored it, and so did their successors, the Pahlavis.

In 1909 Muhammad Ali Shah mounted a royalist counter-revolution against the 1906–7 constitution. This was foiled, and the ruler was forced to abdicate in favour of his twelve-year-old son, Ahmed. But in order to forestall the occupation of Tehran by Russian troops at the behest of the Tsar, who wanted the constitution abrogated, the regent dissolved the Majlis in November 1911. This marked the end of clerical involvement in politics and the Constitutional Revolution, but not of the constitution itself.

Disregarding Tehran's neutrality in the First World War, the forces of Tsarist Russia, Britain and Ottoman Turkey invaded Iran. The Bolshevik revolution in Russia in October 1917 deprived the Iranian ruler of his major foreign patron, the Tsar. Two years later, Britain foisted a treaty on the Iranian regime which reduced Iran to a virtual protectorate of London. But, responding to the patriotic sentiment of the people, the Majlis refused to ratify it.

Iran was by now an important oil-producing state, with British capital and expertise playing a leading role. Britain thought it essential to have a strong administration in Iran to facilitate oil extraction among other things. It instigated Colonel Reza Khan of the Cossack Brigade (originally established by the Russian high command as the palace guard for the Shah) to depose the current government and instal himself as war minister. Having done so in February 1921, Reza Khan consolidated his position by suppressing internal rebellions. He took to cultivating the clerical leadership, and had its support when he deposed the Qajar ruler, Ahmed Shah, in December 1925, and appointed himself regent. Four months later, he crowned himself king. Later he chose as his surname the name of an ancient Iranian language, Pahlavi.

Having ascended the throne after consolidating his power as the head of the military, a secular power centre, Reza Pahlavi Shah set out to curtail the powers of the clergy. He brought the Sharia courts under government control, and then reduced their powers. His dress law of 1928 required all males to wear Western-style dress and a round peaked cap. The 1934 Law of Religious Endowments increased the power of the endowments department of the education ministry at the expense of the clergy. In 1935 he outlawed the veil – particularly the chador, an all-embracing shroud, commonly used by Iranian women. The clergy opposed this vehemently since the veil, to them, is sanctified by the Quran. But Reza Shah ignored their protest. He passed a decree to the effect that all men must replace round peaked caps with European felt hats. He took to rigging parliamentary elections. The result was dramatic. Whereas in the Sixth Majlis (1926–8) forty per cent of the deputies were clerics, in the Eleventh Majlis (1936–8) there was not a single well-known mullah. The cumulative effect of these changes was to divide society between religious masses and a secular elite. 'The upper and new middle classes became increasingly Westernized and scarcely understood the traditional or religious culture of their patriots,' noted Nikki R. Keddie, an American specialist on Iran. 'On the other hand, peasants and urban bazaar classes continued to follow the ulema [clergy], however politically cowed the ulema were . . . These classes associated "the way things should be" more with Islam than with the West.'[2]

When Reza Shah was forced by the British and Soviet forces to abdicate in favour of his twenty-three-year-old son, Muhammad Reza, in September 1941, the clergy were prominent among those who celebrated his departure. They had endured fifteen years of relentless pressure from the Shah who had considerably reduced their power and prestige.

Muhammad Reza Pahlavi Shah was too young and inexperienced to rule autocratically even if he wanted to. His kingdom was occupied by the USSR and Britain, and his government beset with acute problems stemming from the Second World War. He therefore tried to win the sympathy of the clergy, a group that was in daily touch with the masses.

So long as Ayatollah Muhammad Hussein Borujerdi – a moderate who directed clerics to keep away from politics – was the country's most senior mullah, the Shah had little problem with the mosque. But in the leadership vacuum that ensued following Borujerdi's death in 1960, a comparatively junior cleric, Ruhollah Khomeini, a radical who considered religion and politics as two sides of the same coin, came to the fore. He publicly challenged the Shah in June 1963, and was exiled.

After spending a year in Bursa, an Islamic centre in western Turkey, Khomeini moved to Najaf, Iraq, the burial place of Imam Ali, which was visited by thousands of Shia Iranian pilgrims. He stoked an anti-Shah movement which, growing slowly, culminated in a tidal wave. The revolutionary process passed through several steadily rising stages over a two-year period from February 1977 to 11 February 1979, which marked the end of the Pahlavi era.

Khomeini had the sagacity and charisma to unite disparate forces in the revolutionary movement behind the most radical demand: abolition of the monarchy. He kept the alliance together during a highly turbulent period by championing the cause of each of the groups in the anti-Shah coalition, and maintaining a studied silence on such controversial issues as democracy, agrarian reform, the clergy's role in the future Islamic republic, and the status of women.

He aroused hopes of deliverance and improvement in different strata of society. The traditional middle class of artisans, merchants and better-off farmers saw in Khomeini an upholder of private property, a partisan of the bazaar, and a believer in Islamic values. The modern middle class of professionals, businessmen and industrialists regarded Khomeini as a radical nationalist wedded to the programme of ending royal dictatorship and foreign influence in Iran. The urban working class backed Khomeini because of his repeated commitment to social justice which, it felt, could be achieved only by transferring power and wealth from the affluent to the needy. Finally, the rural poor saw the Ayatollah as their saviour: the one to provide them with arable land, irrigation facilities, roads, schools and electricity.

Actually Khomeini did more than hold the anti-Shah movement together. He helped to create a growing popular surge to propel it to greater strengths. He did so by making consistent use of the fortieth day of mourning of those killed by the Shah's security forces, by using the holy month of Ramadan to charge the nation with Islamic fervour, and by transforming the traditional Ashura (i.e. 10th of Muharram, the day Imam Hussein was killed) processions into demonstrations for the revolution. With the aid of the re-enactment of the passion plays of the early days of Islam, he helped to create a revolutionary play of modern times.

Khomeini's other outstanding contribution was to devise and implement an original set of strategy and tactics to neutralize the Shah's 440,000-strong military. He came up with the idea of a 'moral attack' on the army. 'We must fight from within the soldiers' hearts,' he said. 'Face the soldier with a flower. Fight through martyrdom, because the martyr is the essence of history. Let the army kill as many as it wants until the soldiers are shaken to their hearts by the massacres they have committed. Then the army will collapse, and you will have disarmed the army.'[3] Such advice appealed to the martyr complex that lies deeply embedded in the psyche of Shia Iranians. At the same time Khomeini tried to dissuade soldiers from firing by warning them that if they shot their brothers and sisters 'it is just as though you are firing at the Quran'.[4] Since these words came from a grand ayatollah, a *marja-e taqlid* (source of emulation), and since most of the troops were Shia, they were effective. In short, Khomeini devised revolutionary tactics that stemmed from the specific religio-cultural environment of Shia Iran, and therefore the Iranian people accepted them unhesitatingly and used them effectively.

The mosque played a crucial role in the revolution, both as an institution and as a place of prayer and congregation. Since it was impractical for the state regularly to suppress or disrupt activities in the mosque, it offered opportunities to the revolutionaries that no other place did or could. Khomeini knew this and made maximum use of it. He urged the clergy to base local Revolutionary Komitehs (i.e. Committees) in mosques. He thus spawned an institution that proved invaluable during the last, critical months of the revolutionary movement.

Of all the revolutionary bodies that sprouted during the final stages of the anti-Shah movement, the Revolutionary Komitehs proved to be the most broad-based and effective. They took over administrative and police powers once the Shah had departed on 16 January 1979, and consolidated their hold once Khomeini had overthrown the Shah's appointee, Prime Minister Shahpour Bakhtiar, on 11 February.

ISLAMIZATION OF STATE AND SOCIETY

On his return home from exile in Iraq and latterly France, Khomeini lost no time in dismantling the secular state he had inherited, and installing an Islamic one. He drew his own authority from the seventeen-point charter adopted by acclamation by the two-million-strong rally in Tehran on Ashura, 11 December 1978, which called for an end to monarchy, acceptance of Khomeini as leader, and the establishment of an Islamic government.

A popular referendum in March, based on universal adult franchise, opted overwhelmingly for an Islamic republic. In early August, voters were given the opportunity to elect a seventy-three-member Assembly of Experts, including three representatives of religious minorities (Christians, Jews and Zoroastrians). They drafted a constitution which was put to the vote in November and approved with near-unanimity.

Significantly, the constitution-makers conceded the demand of the predominantly Sunni Kurds, Baluchs, Turkmens and Arabs that the non-Shia schools of Islam – Hanafi, Hanbali, Maliki and Shafii – be recognized on a par with Twelver Shiaism. Article 5 was based on the Shia doctrine of the missing Twelfth Imam, Muhammad al Muntazar. Owing to his occultation, stated the article, 'the governance and leadership of the nation devolve upon the just and pious *faqih* [jurisprudent] who is acquainted with the circumstances of his age; courageous, resourceful, and possessed of administrative ability; and recognized and accepted as Leader by the majority of the people'. The Leader, who combined the role of head of state and chief justice, was Ayatollah Khomeini. He was to be succeeded by a Leader, or Leadership Council of three or five, to be appointed by a popularly elected Assembly of Experts.[5]

Sovereignty rested with the people. 'The affairs of the country must be administered on the basis of public opinion expressed by means of elections of the president of the republic, the representatives of the National Consultative Council [Majlis] and the members of councils, or by means of referendums in matters specified in the articles of the constitution,' stated Article 6.[6]

To ensure that parliament's decisions did not contradict 'the ordinances of Islam and the constitution', Article 91 specified the establishment of a twelve-member Council of Guardians, with six Islamic jurists selected by the Leader or Leadership Council, and six lawyers to be elected by the Majlis from a list submitted by the Supreme

Judicial Council. The Islamic jurist was required to be fully conversant with 'the issues of the day . . . the circumstances of his age'. That is, he must know how to apply and interpret basic Islamic precepts in the conditions prevalent in the late twentieth (Christian)/ early fifteenth (Islamic) century.[7]

By all accounts Iran's 1979 constitution was a pioneering effort. While it drew its inspiration from Islamic precepts, it was designed to serve the needs of a community in modern times, incorporating such concepts as the separation of legislative, executive and judicial powers, and basing the authority of the Leader and the president on popular will, expressed either directly, as in the president's case, or indirectly, through the Assembly of Experts to be convened to select the successor(s) to Khomeini.

Khomeini considered himself to be the final arbiter of who or what was Islamic, and who or what was not. He resolved that all non-Islamic elements had to be expelled from the government administration, military, judiciary, public and private enterprises and educational institutions. This was to be achieved by official decisions and popular actions. The other major task was to purify society, which had been corrupted by alien influences over the past few centuries, and Islamize it. Alcohol and gambling were banned immediately, and so were nightclubs, pornographic films and mixed bathing. Society needed to be Islamized in a positive sense. Therefore Friday noon prayers and sermons were made the focal point of the week. The sermons were used to inform and educate the faithful. All Friday prayer-leaders were appointed by Khomeini, and they were required to report to him.

Those who resisted the Islamic government were to be punished along the lines laid out in the Sharia. Such acts as raising arms against the Islamic state or spreading corruption in society were to be treated as capital offences.

This was the ideological framework which Khomeini laid out, and within which he operated during the various phases the Islamic revolution underwent.

With the takeover of the US embassy in Tehran by militant students on 4 November 1979, the Islamic revolution entered a virulently anti-American phase. The focus now was on expelling the remaining vestiges of American influence, which had dominated Iran since the CIA-backed coup in August 1953 that restored the Shah to the throne he had lost briefly in his tussle with a strongly nationalist prime minister, Muhammad Mussadiq, thus sharpening the anti-imperialist image of the Islamic regime. When this led to economic sanctions against Iran by the US and Western Europe, the USSR stepped in to aid Iran in its hour of need. But cordial feelings did not last long as Soviet troops marched into Afghanistan in late December 1979.

Iraq's invasion of Iran on 22 September 1980 heralded another phase of the revolution in which patriotism and Islam became inseparable. Traditional rivalry between Iraq and Iran worsened when, following the Islamic revolution, Iran's clerical leadership began appealing to the faithful in Iraq to overthrow the secular regime of President Saddam Hussein. In return, the Iraqi president encouraged Iranian Arabs in the oil-rich province of Khuzistan to rebel against the Khomeini regime. Finally, prompted by reports of low morale in the Iranian military and internecine fighting among Iranian leaders, Saddam Hussein attacked Iran.

In the spring of 1982 the tide began to turn in Iran's favour in the war. In a major offensive in May the Iranians recaptured most of the territory they had lost to Iraq at the beginning of the conflict. In June, Tehran rejected the Iraqi offer of an immediate ceasefire, and repeated its call for the overthrow of the Iraqi president, Saddam Hussein, the 'corrupt infidel', whom it held responsible for aggression against the Islamic regime of Iran. In early July it threatened that if Saddam Hussein were not punished for invading Iran, and $100 billion paid to it as war damages, it would carry the war into Iraq. Four days later it did so with a view to capturing the Iraqi port city of Basra. It failed to accomplish this. None the less, these events demonstrated that the armed conflict had entered a phase where the initiative lay with Tehran, a sign of the strength of Iran's Islamic revolution.

Against the background of war, the Iranian government kept up its Islamization drive. On 30 May 1982 the cabinet approved comprehensive plans to bring the existing penal and legal codes, civil law, trade law, and the registration of documents and land in line with the Sharia. Adherence to Islamic dress for women was enforced strictly. The parliament passed a law on moral offences in September. Two months later, Khomeini, the chief justice, issued a decree entitled 'Islamization of Judiciary'.

By early 1983, Islamic revolutionary organizations, which had sprung up in the wake of the Shah's downfall, covered all spheres of life: political, military, security, judicial, economic, social, cultural and religious. Some of these bodies functioned independently, others in tandem with government ministries. These organizations were so preponderant that one out of six Iranians above the age of fifteen belonged to one or more of them.[8]

With the Marxist Tudeh (Masses) Party banned in May 1983, all pre-revolution parties, which had existed clandestinely – excepting the liberal Liberation Movement headed by Mahdi Bazargan, the Islamic regime's first prime minister – were eliminated. Political life thus became the near-monopoly of the official Islamic Republican Party and its smaller allies.

In the military, the erstwhile bedrock of the Pahlavi monarchy, a series of purges resulted in the dismissal or retirement of all but a thousand officers of the pre-revolution period. Moreover, the regime took steps to inculcate Islamic values and ideas among military personnel. A political-ideological department was instituted in the military. It was often manned by young clerics, who were fiercely loyal to the Islamic Republic. They educated officers and ranks in Islamic history and ideology. The information and guidance department performed the general task of creating and sustaining support for the government's actions and policies, and the particular job of keeping an eye on potential dissidents or deviants. In addition, there were the Islamic Associations among military personnel – voluntary bodies which concerned themselves with raising the Islamic consciousness of their members and guarding the security of their units. Earlier the Islamic Revolutionary Guards Corps (IRGC) was created as a counter-force to the army commanded by officers of dubious loyalty to the new regime. Recruitment to the IRGC was strictly controlled. A recruit had to pass tests in the Quran, *Nahaj al Balaghe* (Fountain of Eloquence) by Imam Ali, and *Hukumat-e Islami* (The Islamic Government) by Khomeini.[9]

Schools underwent Islamization shortly after the revolution. New Islamic teaching materials were made available to primary schools within six months of the revolution. Similar speed was shown in furnishing secondary schools with Islamic textbooks. Special stress was put on the teaching of Arabic, the language of the Quran, with lessons in Arabic being offered on television. Universities and colleges were closed for two and a half years while new or modified textbooks were produced. Within three years of the revolution, all co-educational schools had been transformed into single-sex schools, and about 40,000 teachers purged.[10]

Efforts to Islamize such popular institutions as schools, colleges and the military went hand in hand with tackling specific moral ills like prostitution and drugs. The Family Protection Law of 1967/ 1975, which restricted polygamy and gave women the right to initiate divorce proceedings, was first suspended and then abolished. However, in late 1983, a woman's right to divorce her husband was restored. Contraceptives, considered unIslamic, were banned. There were hundreds of instances of public flogging or execution for adultery. There were also capital and other punishments for homosexuality. These were in accordance with the Quranic verses that describe allowable sexual relations and punishments for transgressing them.

Islamic principles were also applied increasingly to the economic aspects of life. The Majlis passed the interest-free banking bill in June 1983. It provided a transition period of eighteen months during which depositors were required to split their investments between their bank's two sections: interest-free and term deposit. Once this was done the interest-free section of the bank began lending funds to needy customers without interest; and the term deposit section advanced funds to commercial customers according to Islamic contracts. The profits earned, or losses incurred, by such loans were then shared by the depositors.[11] In short, the idea of a fixed interest rate was replaced by variable profit or loss margins by treating depositors as business partners.

While these changes were in train, efforts were being made continually to create an Islamic ambience in the street, the media and on the war front. One way to do this was by painting slogans and images on street walls. The mass media helped to create an Islamic environment by covering the proliferation of Islamic events throughout the year, not to mention the daily prayers which were strictly observed on radio and television. Besides the holy month of Ramadan, there were ten days of Muharram culminating in Ashura, the six-day-long hajj pilgrimage to Mecca, the birthdays of Prophet Muhammad and twelve Shia Imams, and the two joyous *eids* (religious festivals). To this had to be added the events of Iran's revolutionary Islam: ten days celebrating the revolution, a week commemorating the war with Iraq, and the founding days of the Islamic Republic, the IRGC, the Reconstruction Crusade, and so on.

A believer had an opportunity to involve himself in the Islamic process by joining the Islamic Association at work or in the neighbourhood. These associations performed many functions, including identifying unIslamic elements in society, aiding the war effort, strengthening Islamic culture, and encouraging voter participation in elections and referendums.

In all these activities the clergy were in the forefront. They were now more numerous than before. Estimates of qualified clerics varied from 90,000 to 120,000. In addition there were an unknown number of unqualified village preachers, prayer-leaders, theological school teachers and procession organizers. The number of theology students trebled from the pre-revolution figure of 10,000.[12]

Within two years of the revolution the number of mosques reached 22,000, with the urban mosques doubling their pre-revolution total of 5600.[13] Some of these were newly built while others were created out of old property. Besides being the place for religious activities, larger mosques became centres for food and fuel-rationing systems, consumer cooperative stores, recruitment for the IRGC and its auxiliary, the Basij, collections for the war effort, the teaching of Arabic, and offering interest-free loans to those in dire need. At the time of elections, mosques were often used as polling stations.

The Islamization process and the rise of revolutionary organizations affected the lives of all Iranians. Most of them either backed the change or went along with it. A minority, consisting largely of the upper-middle and upper classes, grumbled about the onset of Islamic values and behaviour. They were almost invariably related to the 1.5 million Iranian exiles settled in the West. They stayed behind not because they sympathized with the Islamic revolution but because they wanted to safeguard their valuable properties. As long as there was a brother or sister, or a son or daughter, present in Iran, the properties of the whole family were safe from the threat of confiscation. As it was, the Islamic regime upheld the right to property as inviolable, a policy rooted in the Sharia. Therefore the wealthy were free to enjoy their wealth through legitimate means.

In political science, revolution is defined by Webster's dictionary as 'the overthrow or renunciation of one government or ruler, and the substitution of another, by the governed'. The depth of revolution is determined by the degree to which the ruling elite of the *ancien régime* has been displaced from power, whether society has undergone a fundamental change in its perception of itself, and whether or not the revolution is inspired by a universalist ideology.

By these criteria the February 1979 revolution in Iran proved to be quite profound. It was inspired, in the main, by Islam, a divinely ordained system meant to end oppression and institute social justice nationally and internationally. The ruling elite of the monarchical regime was replaced totally. Following the success of the revolutionary movement, Iranians came to regard themselves more as part of a religious community, Islamic *umma*, than a nation-state.

IRAN'S REVOLUTIONARY ISLAMIC FOREIGN POLICY

Iran's foreign policy is guided by the principles outlined in three articles of the constitution, the first of which is pan-Islamic. 'In accordance with the [Quranic] verse "This your nation is a single nation, and I am your Lord, so worship Me", all Muslims form a single nation,' states Article 10. 'The government of the Islamic Republic of Iran has the duty of formulating its general policies with a view to the merging and union of all Muslim peoples, and it must constantly strive to bring about political, economic and cultural unity of the Islamic world.'[14]

Article 152 is more specific and states that the Republic's foreign policy is based *inter alia* on 'the defence of the rights of all Muslims' and 'non-alignment with respect to the hegemonist superpowers'. Article 154 implicitly sanctifies the concept of exporting revolution. 'The Islamic Republic of Iran considers the attainment of independence, freedom and just government to be the right of all peoples in the world,' states this article. '[It] therefore protects the just struggles of the oppressed and deprived in every corner of the globe.'

Several months before the promulgation of the constitution, Khomeini's regime had declared it to be its 'Islamic duty' to support the national liberation movements of the 'deprived peoples' of the world. Later, as numerous attempts were made by internal and external forces to overthrow the Islamic regime, Tehran concluded that the arguments for exporting the revolution were not merely ideological but also pragmatic: an effective way to defend the revolution was by going on the offensive, by extending the influence of the revolution abroad. As President Ali Khamanei put it in November 1983, 'If the revolution is kept within Iranian borders, it would become vulnerable.'[15]

There were obvious disadvantages in following this path. Tehran's attempts to bolster a revolutionary organization in a foreign country vitiated inter-governmental relations, and further increased Iran's isolation in the international community. So this course of action proved unpopular with many officials of the foreign ministry headed by Ali Akbar Velayati, a comparative moderate, from late 1980 onwards.

The conflict was resolved by setting up a separate department in the foreign ministry to deal with national liberation movements. Later the functions of this department were handed over to an independent body, the World Organization of Islamic Liberation Movements, led by Ayatollah Hussein Ali Montazeri, who was based in the holy city of Qom. Prominent among the affiliates of the World Organization were the Party of the Islamic Call active in Iraq and Kuwait; the Party of Allah, Hizbollah, in Lebanon; and the Army of the Guards, Sejah-e Pasdaran, and the Organization of Victory, Sazman-e Nasr, in Afghanistan, later to be banded together under the Islamic Unity Party, Hizb-e Wahdat-e Islami.

As for the leftist regime in Kabul, it welcomed the Shah's downfall in early 1979, which held the promise of improved ties with Tehran. But the revolutionary government soon began deporting Afghan workers, who had been attracted to Iran because of its booming economy, alleging that they were criminals. This soured relations between Kabul and Tehran. On 18 March Iran closed its borders with Afghanistan. When fighting broke out in Herat between the security forces and Islamic rebels, the Kabul government expelled the Iranian consul in Herat, alleging an Iranian hand in fomenting trouble.[16]

As guerrilla activity in Afghanistan increased, President Taraki blamed it on Pakistan, Iran and the US. When Taraki was overthrown by his prime minister, Amin, the government pursued counter-insurgency measures with greater vigour than before. This cooled Kabul–Tehran relations further.

Iran vehemently condemned the Soviet Union's military intervention in Afghanistan, a neighbour and a fellow-Muslim country, in December 1979. 'Because Afghanistan is a Muslim country and a neighbour of Iran,' said Sadiq Qutbzadeh, the Iranian foreign minister, 'the military intervention of the government of the Soviet Union . . . is considered a hostile measure not only against the people of that country but against all Muslims of the world.'[17] The conciliatory steps towards the mosque taken by the new Afghan president, Karmal, at home made little difference to Tehran. At the Islamic Conference Organization foreign ministers' meeting in Islamabad in January 1980, it worked closely with Pakistan to rally sentiment against the leftist regime in Kabul. The ICO suspended Afghanistan's membership.

Karmal addressed a letter to Khomeini suggesting 'consolidation of fraternal and friendly Islamic relations between the Afghan and Iranian peoples', with the objective of delivering 'an ultimate rebuke to the world-craving imperialism and Zionism'.[18] Khomeini was unmoved, and his government continued its policy of non-recognition of the Kabul regime.

At the next ICO foreign ministers' conference in May, the Iranian delegation included two Afghan rebel leaders. Qutbzadeh was appointed to the three-member ICO commission charged with uniting various Afghan rebel parties. But the differences among them proved to be irreconcilable. In the summer of 1981 the Karmal administration tried to implement its conscription law. This led to an exodus of young men to Pakistan and Iran. As a result the number of Afghan refugees in Iran – which stood at 900,000 in early 1981 – rose sharply.[19] Anti-government activities in Afghanistan were high in the areas adjoining Iran and Pakistan. The effectiveness of the Islamic guerrillas inside Afghanistan depended on how well they had coordinated their activities with those outside the country.

In due course the CIA became the coordinator of the foreign aid, in cash and weapons, that flowed to Afghan rebels from the US, Saudi Arabia, Pakistan, Egypt and China; and the CIA then used Pakistan's Inter-Services Intelligence to distribute the aid to various Afghan factions. This applied to the activities of the rebels on the Pakistani side. Being on the opposite side of the Pakistani frontier, the Iranians kept well clear of the CIA and its activities, independently assisting the guerrillas belonging mainly to the Sejah-e Pasdaran and Sazman-e Nasr, both being Shia and drawing their support from the Hazaras in the central highlands.

In late July 1982, working in conjunction with Pakistan, Iran helped to create the United Front for the Liberation of Afghanistan, headed by Gulbuddin Hikmatyar. The Front committed itself to expelling the Soviets from Afghanistan and establishing an Islamic regime there.

In the spring of 1983 Iran agreed to hold talks with the Afghan government under the UN aegis in order to create conditions conducive to Soviet withdrawal. However, Iran stated that it would not take part until 'the real representatives of the Afghan people' participated in these negotiations. So the stalemate continued, as did Iran's policy of aiding Afghan Shias to fight the Communist regime. During the winter of 1985–6, for instance, Tehran despatched 1000 camel-loads of light arms and ammunition to the Hazarajat highlands in central Afghanistan.[20]

The Soviet presence in Afghanistan continued to cast a shadow over friendly ties between Tehran and Moscow. In the early days of the Iranian revolution it had seemed to Moscow that once Iran had quit the Western-dominated Central Treaty Organization and joined the Non-Aligned Movement in March 1979, relations between the USSR and Iran would blossom. However, on the eve of the Iranian New Year (on the spring equinox) in 1980 Khomeini stated: 'We are the enemies of international Communism in the same way we are against the world predators of the West, headed by the United States.'[21]

Indeed, within a couple of months of the revolution, Tehran had started beaming radio broadcasts at the Soviet Central Asian republics in Tajik, Uzbek, Turkmen and Azeri. The intention was to revive religious feeling among the Muslim inhabitants of these republics. Clearly Tehran wanted to launch Islam as a supra-national ideology to rally Muslims everywhere, starting with the neighbouring regions.

Despite ups and downs in mutual relations, the Soviets continued to have strong economic links with Iran, which involved them in 140 industrial and other projects, accounting for ninety per cent of Iran's coal output, eighty-seven per cent of its iron ore production, and seventy per cent of its steel output.[22]

In his survey of world developments before the Twenty-sixth Congress of the CPSU in February 1981, Leonid Brezhnev referred to the Iranian revolution as 'a major event in the international scene in recent years'. He added, 'However complex and contradictory, it is essentially an anti-imperialist revolution, though reaction at home and abroad is seeking to change this feature.'[23] In other words, the Kremlin was committed to forging its policy towards Iran on the basis of the latter's actions rather than its slogans.

When Iran refused to accept a ceasefire in its conflict with Iraq in June 1982, and tried to seize Iraqi territory, the Soviet Union was disappointed, and reversed its earlier decision to stop supplying arms and spares to Iraq, its long-term ally. This soured relations between Moscow and Tehran. A year later, when Iraq began using the newly supplied Soviet weapons, especially Scud ground-to-ground missiles, Khomeini responded by banning the Tudeh Party and launching a campaign on behalf of 'the oppressed Muslims of the USSR'. Propaganda posters depicted the Kremlin as the capital of the Devil. The move was directed towards sharply rekindling interest in Islam among the Muslims of the southern republics of the USSR. This was the first time that any neighbour of the Soviet Union had initiated a propaganda campaign of this kind. The Kremlin was used to radio broadcasts of an Islamic nature – originating in Iran, the Gulf monarchies, Egypt or from Radio Liberty and Radio Free Europe – being beamed at the Muslim regions of the Soviet Union, but none of the countries involved had tried to drum up support for Soviet Muslims within their own boundaries.

The efforts of Iran and other Muslim states began to bear fruit. One of the manifestations was the rise in the number of unofficial clerics. In late 1983 Turkmenistan, with a population of 2.8 million, was reported to have 300 such clerics. Following his visit to the Soviet Union, Fakhruddin Hejazi, an Iranian parliamentarian, said that he had been told by Muslims in Soviet Azerbaijan that during Ramadan they listened to Radio Ardebil (based in northern Iran) to find out the correct times for breaking the fast.[24] Such statements tallied with the assessment of the situation by the other side. Soviet officials agreed that Azerbaijan and Tajikistan had proved susceptible to Iran's propaganda. Like their counterparts in Iranian Azerbaijan, a large majority of Muslims in Soviet Azerbaijan were Shia. The fact that Iran had a consulate in Baku was also a contributory factor. With their language akin to Persian, Tajiks had always been close to Iranians. In these republics there was a growing demand for mosques and religious schools, and more and more women were adopting Islamic dress.[25] These developments were viewed with disapproval by the Soviet authorities, and created ill-will towards Iran.

Along with this came Tehran's ban on the Tudeh and intensified persecution of its members and sympathizers. The state-run Soviet media turned decidedly anti-Iran. A study by the Iranians of the Soviet broadcasts in Persian on Iran showed that of the 370 commentaries by Soviet radio stations between 23 August 1983 and 5 January 1984, two-thirds focused on the Tudeh and were critical of the Iranian government.[26] Others probably referred to Iran's behaviour in its war with Iraq. Moscow blamed Tehran for its refusal to end the conflict. In April 1984, following a meeting between the Soviet premier, Nikolai Tikhnov, and the Iraqi vice-president, Taha Yassin Ramadan, a joint communiqué publicly blamed Iran for not ending hostilities.[27]

It was not until two years later that owing to the steep fall in oil prices, caused by the deliberate flooding of the oil market by

Saudi Arabia and Kuwait, Iran's financial capacity to wage war was irrevocably damaged. But it took two more years for Iran to reach a point where it realized the futility of further hostilities. The result was a ceasefire in August 1988 under UN auspices.

By then Moscow had withdrawn half of its 115,000 troops from Afghanistan, thus considerably easing the strain on its relations with Tehran. In mid-November, Alexander Besvernikh, the first deputy foreign minister of the Soviet Union, arrived in Tehran to strengthen bilateral ties.

Soon after there were popular demonstrations against the Communist authorities in Soviet Azerbaijan to express dissatisfaction with the government's handling of the festering Nagorno Karabakh crisis. At these protests posters of Khomeini and the green flags of Islam began appearing, as well as chanting of Islamic slogans. This unprecedented phenomenon was widely noted and reported. It was the first sign that the Iranian government's broadcasts in Azeri and Turkish over the past decade, calling on the Muslims in the region to unite and resist the superpowers, including the USSR, had begun to pay off. Taking note of the news agency reports of the display of religious symbols and the shouting of Islamic slogans, Radio Tehran reported on 25 November that the 'political movement' in Soviet Azerbaijan had 'religious aspects' as well. 'Posters of Khomeini and slogans demanding "reunification with our brothers" have started to appear in Soviet Azerbaijan, according to the reports from the region,' noted Hugh Pope, the regional correspondent of the *Independent*, on 1 December 1988. 'There is no evidence that Iran is involved in the unrest. It seems that the Azeris have latched on to Khomeini as the nearest figure they have to a national hero in their dispute with their Armenian neighbours [about Nagorno Karabakh].' When the Soviet ambassador in Tehran was asked to comment on the subject by a local newspaper, *Resalat* (Mission), he said, 'Demonstrations in Soviet Azerbaijan were the consequences of some mistakes in the USSR's nationalities policy as well as economic and social shortcomings. There was nothing wrong with a Soviet demonstrator carrying the portrait of a leader of a neighbouring friendly country.'[28]

As it was, that particular leader, Khomeini, had been monitoring the progress of his counterpart in the Soviet Union, Gorbachev, with much interest. Once the hurdles of Iran's war with Iraq and the Soviet military presence in Afghanistan had been overcome, Khomeini took the initiative of addressing a long epistle, written in the form of a Friday sermon, to Gorbachev.

In it, Khomeini noted that since assuming power Gorbachev had embarked on 'a new round of revision, development and facing realities of the world' with '[praiseworthy] courage, boldness and bravery'. This, he predicted, was 'quite likely to disrupt the dominant balance of interests across the world.' However, he added: 'It is clear to all that henceforth Communism would be sought in the world's political history museums. It is not possible to save humanity from the crisis of lack of conviction in spirituality through materialism, a crisis which is the most fundamental ailment in eastern and western societies.' He then offered his advice. 'The first issue, which would definitely bring you success, would be to revise the policy of your predecessors on eradication of [faith in] God and religion in society, which has doubtless dealt the heaviest blow to the Soviet people. You must realize that only by doing so, you could really face up to world issues.' Then came the reference to economic stagnation in the Soviet Union. 'If you wish to put an end to the economic woes of socialism and Communism by simply resorting to the core of western capitalism you will not ease the pains prevalent in Soviet society,' he warned Gorbachev. 'The main problem facing your country is neither that of ownership and economics nor of [lack of] freedom. Rather your problem is lack of faith in God. It is the same lack of faith which has driven, or will drive, the West towards decadence and stalemate. Your main problem is the long and futile struggle against God, the source of [all] creation and life.' He stressed the tenacity and power of religious belief. 'When recently after 70 years one heard from the minarets of some mosques in your [Soviet] republics the cry of *Allahu Akbar* [God is Great], and the confession of the faith in the prophethood of the Last of the Prophets [Muhammad], all the followers of genuine Muhammadan Islam cried with joy,' he wrote. In conclusion he offered the Soviet leader practical advice. 'I call on Your Excellency to inquire seriously about Islam . . . because the exalted and universal values of Islam can give comfort and save nations, and Islam can also resolve the basic problems confronting humanity.'[29]

Khomeini's letter was carried by a personal emissary, Ayatollah Javadi Amoli, and delivered to Gorbachev in the Kremlin on 3 January 1989, and given much prominence in the Iranian media. 'Relations between Iran and the Soviet Union have been upgraded to the highest level,' said Muhammad Javed Larijani, deputy foreign minister of Iran, who had accompanied Amoli to Moscow. 'It is unprecedented for the Imam [Khomeini] to make direct communication with the head of another regime.'[30]

Protocol required that Gorbachev should deliver his response in the same way he had received the letter: through a personal emissary. On 26 February, the Soviet foreign minister, Eduard Shevardnadze, read out Gorbachev's letter to Khomeini during a meeting with him. 'We agree with many major points – but there are many major points with which we disagree, too,' wrote Gorbachev. While Moscow respected freedom of choice for all nations and recognized the Islamic revolution in Iran, it defended the Soviet system as the right choice for its people in spite of 'the gross errors' made in the past, he continued. On a more practical plane, Gorbachev referred to the Soviet Union's 'conviction that conditions are ripe for relations between our two countries to enter a qualitatively new stage of cooperation in all fields'. This was welcomed by Khomeini who had in his letter emphasized the importance of 'expanding strong ties in various fields so as to confront the devilish acts of the West'.[31] This was all the more pertinent since with the departure of the Soviet troops from Afghanistan there was now no barrier to close ties between the two neighbours.

Its war with Iraq now over, Iran could afford to channel a larger share of its considerable military and diplomatic resources into aiding the Tehran-based eight-party alliance of Afghan parties, the Hizb-e Wahadat-e Islami, popularly known as Wahadat, led by Muhammad Karim Khalili, a Hazara from central Afghanistan. Since Iran sheltered and fed some two million Afghan refugees (in contrast to over three million in Pakistan), with a substantial number of them being Sunni rather than Shia, it was an important player in the Afghan drama.

In mid-January 1989 the Iranian foreign ministry sponsored a conference on the future of Afghanistan in Tehran in which the leaders of the three moderate Mujahedin parties participated. Later, Hikmatyar undertook an official visit to Tehran, his first since 1984. But that did not ensure unqualified support by the Wahadat of the Afghan assembly called by the Mujahedin leadership in Rawalpindi, Pakistan, in mid-February. The Wahadat refused to take its allotted sixty seats in the assembly of 519 members, insisting on 100 seats, commensurate with the estimated proportion of Shias in the national population.

Overall, on Afghanistan both Tehran and Moscow had a common aim, spelled out by Ayatollah Montazeri, head of the World

Organization of Islamic Liberation Movements, thus: 'Now that the Soviet forces have left Afghanistan, the Americans and their agents must not be allowed to interfere in that country.'[32] Having seen the Wahadat shabbily treated by the Sunni conveners of the Afghan assembly in Rawalpindi, Iran had refused to recognize the pro-Saudi, pro-American Mujahedin interim government that emerged. This left open the possibility that the Wahadat would cut a deal with the Najibullah regime in Kabul, something that went down well in Moscow.

Before he died on 3 June 1989, Khomeini was said to have offered his aides last-minute advice to improve relations with the 'Northern neighbour', meaning the USSR. Within three weeks of Khomeini's death, Ali Akbar Hashemi Rafsanjani, the powerful speaker of Iran's parliament, flew to Moscow. Here he had a series of long, friendly meetings with Gorbachev. The two leaders signed diplomatic, economic and military protocols, and topped them with a Good Neighbourly and Cooperation Agreement. Referring to 'the new thinking in the Soviet Union on one hand and the victory of the Islamic revolution on the other', the Agreement specifically called for 'more contacts and exchanges between Iranian and Soviet religious leaders', a suggestion originally made by Khomeini in his letter to Gorbachev. Being himself a religious figure, Rafsanjani visited Baku, a city with an Iranian consulate, where he delivered a sermon in one of the two official mosques. In return Gorbachev obtained a promise from Rafsanjani to cease fanning the flames of Islamic fundamentalism among the Muslims of Soviet Central Asia. This meant stopping Iranian radio broadcasts beamed at these republics. Since Rafsanjani's brother, Muhammad, was the director-general of Iranian radio and television, this proved to be a fairly simple act.[33] From the standpoint of the Gorbachev administration, the wide-ranging agreements with Iran were useful in demonstrating to the world that its policy was now pragmatic, not ideological, and that it was able to have cordial relations with regimes of any political colour. In any case, the USSR was eager for rapprochement with a country with which it shared its second longest border, 2000 kilometres (1200 miles), and which had undergone a revolution a decade ago.

Moreover, the Kremlin was also deeply troubled by the continued crisis in Afghanistan, another state along its southern border; and it needed Iran's assistance in resolving it. But however willing Tehran was to help, its leaders made it clear that they could not do so at the cost of their abiding loyalty to Islam. That was why, at his press conference in Moscow after his talks with Gorbachev, Rafsanjani publicly praised the leaders of the Afghan Mujahedin and the Wahadat, calling them 'really heroic resisters, the defenders of Islam'.[34]

Having thus established the religious credentials of the Iranian government, its leadership proved amenable to a suggestion from the Soviet foreign minister, Shevardnadze, during his visit to Tehran in early August, that it stop arming the Wahadat and encourage it to talk to President Najibullah, who was willing to consider offering autonomy to the Shia region in the Hazarajat highlands.

During the autumn the political situation in Azerbaijan deteriorated, with the opposition Popular Front making spectacular gains, and Azeris turning increasingly nationalist, looking southwards to fellow-Azeris in Iran, and some PF leaders openly demanding secession from the USSR and re-unification with Iran. From early December 1989, hundreds of Azeris took to demonstrating across the Aras River which formed the frontier between Soviet Azerbaijan and Iran. Their ethnic kinsmen on the Iranian side responded by demonstrating on the other bank of the river. What brought the two peoples to this stage was shared nationalism and religion – as well as plain family ties in many cases (the separation having occurred around the 1918–20 Civil War following the Bolshevik revolution). On 31 December, protesting demonstrators attacked the fence and border posts along the frontier in the Nakhichevan enclave of Azerbaijan with tractors, and demolished them. Noting the strong nationalist feelings that had come to the fore, and unwilling to cause bloodshed, the Soviet authorities did not intervene, a step appreciated by the Iranian media and government. The Soviets seemed quite willing, in the light of the tourist agreement made with Iran six months earlier, to facilitate officially sanctioned travel across the border.[35]

However, when the Popular Front raised the ante in Azerbaijan on 18 January 1990 by demanding the government's resignation and calling a general strike, Moscow responded with an iron fist, with Gorbachev justifying the despatch of troops to Baku on the ground that the 'secessionists' had planned to set up an Islamic republic in Soviet Azerbaijan. He exaggerated the Islamic threat in order to muster a unified response from the rest of the USSR. None the less, there was a grain of truth in it. Had the separatists succeeded in breaking away, the only direction in which they would have moved was that of Iran – and therefore Islam.

Iran's leaders were divided on how to respond. 'The Soviet leadership should know that resort to violence is not the solution to the problem in Azerbaijan,' said Mahdi Karrubi, the speaker of Iran's parliament. 'Violence against the people will entail [negative] consequences.'[36] He represented hardliners in Tehran who were in favour of offering moral and material aid to the agitating Azeris across the fluvial frontier in order to enhance their chance of seceding from Moscow and declaring an independent Azerbaijan. He was opposed by pragmatists, led by Rafsanjani who, elected the republic's president in July with a ninety-five per cent vote, maintained the earlier policy of combining sympathy for Muslim Azeris with increased human contacts between Azeris across the border – nothing more. At the United Nations the Iranian ambassador described the emerging Azeri nationalist movement as an internal problem for the USSR. Rafsanjani thus ensured that Iran did not get diverted from its post-war reconstruction policy by getting involved in revolutionary upsurges in the region, be they Islamic or nationalist. He also wanted to protect the agreements he had signed in Moscow, especially the military protocols, which included the purchase of advanced Soviet weaponry, as well as the economic ones, which involved boosting Iran's electricity generating capacity.

Unlike his radical colleagues, Rafsanjani realized that in the long run Azeri nationalism would prove as problematic for the Islamic regime in Tehran as it was proving then for the Communist administration in Moscow. In addition to six million Azeris living in Soviet Azerbaijan, there were about eight million Azeris living in the Iranian provinces bordering the southern Soviet frontier. Their language, Azeri, akin to Turkish, is quite distinct from Persian. The emergence of a strong, independent Azerbaijani republic – whether Islamic or not – would fan the flames of Azeri nationalism within Iran. To counter it, Iranian leaders would argue that Islam, a creed that recognizes only believers and non-believers, was above ethnic differences, just as Communist leaders in Moscow and elsewhere had argued that class differences overrode ethnic distinctions. But just as Communist arguments seemed to have lost their effectiveness, there was reason to believe that Tehran's arguments would also fail. It was this prospect of ethnicity and nationalism successfully challenging the universality of Islamic ideology that made Rafsanjani wary of fishing in troubled Azeri waters.

As it was, Azerbaijan figured prominently in the economic protocols Iran had concluded with the USSR, starting with that relating to joint exploration for oil and gas in the Caspian Sea, signed in the autumn of 1988. Once Ayaz Mutalibov, the newly installed First Secretary of the Communist Party of Azerbaijan, had consolidated his power in the summer of 1990, he tried to strengthen economic links with Iran, partly to palliate the Popular Front, and partly to strengthen Azerbaijan's hands in its bargaining with the centre. The signing of agreements by the Russian president, Yeltsin, with other Soviet republics during the following summer, as if they were all independent states, emboldened Mutalibov in his dealings with Iran.

Indeed, Mutalibov was in Tehran negotiating closer ties with Iran in August 1991 when the anti-Gorbachev coup was mounted in Moscow. His impromptu remark about it there was taken to mean that he supported the coup, something he later denied vociferously.

Once the Soviet Union had broken up in December 1991, and Azerbaijan and Armenia had become independent countries, thus freer to settle their dispute over Nagorno Karabakh, differences between Mutalibov and the opposition Popular Front, led by Abulfaz Elchibey, became unbridgeable, with Mutalibov tilting towards Iran and Elchibey towards Turkey.

In ethnic and religious terms there was enough ground for the pro-Iranian and pro-Turkish partisans to build up their strength. With three-quarters of Azeris belonging to the Shia sect, there was much that was attractive about Iran, which had by now demonstrated that Islam was a viable socio-political ideology for a modern state and society. On the other hand, as members of the Turkic race, and speakers of a language akin to Turkish, Azeris felt ethnically and culturally close to Turks. Having discarded the Arabic script first for Latin and then Cyrillic, they seemed more inclined to back the PF demand for reversion to the Latin alphabet currently used by Turks than the Arabic script used by Iranians. An orientalist and an Arabic scholar, who had worked as an Arabic interpreter in Egypt for a team of Soviet engineers constructing a dam on the Nile, Elchibey was a leading proponent of a changeover to the Roman script. When he was told by an Iranian clergyman that acceptance of a Roman alphabet amounted to acceptance of Christianity, and that Azeris ought to return to Arabic, 'the alphabet of Islam', Elchibey replied: 'Arabic is a step-child of Aramaic and Hebrew, and goes all the way back to Phoenicians, and can in no sense be described as an inherently "holy" or "Islamic" alphabet.'[37] Such a viewpoint illustrated a widening gap between the Popular Front and Iran. Later, when the Azeri Supreme Soviet opted for the Latin script, the pro-Iranian elements could do no more than mount a feeble demonstration outside the parliament building. However, they could draw comfort from the fact that the Azeri government had by now introduced a weekly hour-long programme on Islam on television, along with more frequent programmes on radio.

In any case, geopolitics favoured Iran more than Turkey. Both Azerbaijan and its enclave, Nakhichevan, shared long land and sea borders with Iran, with a rail link connecting Nakhichevan with the Persian Gulf. In contrast, physical contact with Turkey was limited to a short common frontier between it and Nakhichevan. This factor was important when it came to aiding Azerbaijan materially in its struggle with Armenia over Nagorno Karabakh. Iran also shared its frontier with Armenia. This placed it in a stronger position vis-à-vis Turkey.

Iran under President Rafsanjani continued to follow a pragmatic policy towards Azerbaijan, whether ruled directly by Gorbachev in Moscow, or by Mutalibov or Elchibey in Baku. In Azerbaijan's dispute with Armenia over Nagorno Karabakh, Tehran did not automatically opt for the purely Islamic stance of siding with Muslim Azerbaijan against Christian Armenia. Instead, treating its national interest as paramount, it weighed up the attitude of the Baku government towards Iran in particular and the concept of an Islamic state in general, and the prospects of a strong, nationalist, independent Azerbaijan fostering irredentist tendencies among Iranian Azeris. Since Armenia and Armenians were deeply antipathetic towards Turkey and Turks, rivals of Iran in the region, Tehran found a common denominator with Yerevan in undermining the influence of Ankara. It therefore concluded that so long as the ruling Azeri PF was dominated by such leaders as Elchibey – who had combined his pro-Turkish tendencies with admiration not only for the West but also for Israel – it was in its interests to keep Azerbaijan weak. A by-product of Iran's stance was that it became acceptable as a mediator between Azerbaijan and Armenia. Indeed, it had succeeded in negotiating a ceasefire in mid-March 1992 after Mutalibov had been forced to resign as president.

Knowing Tehran's preference for Mutalibov over Elchibey and the PF, it was not surprising that pro-Iranian demonstrators should side with Mutalibov when he tried to regain power, unsuccessfully, on 14–15 May 1992.

During the run-up to the presidential election on 7 June, Elchibey presented himself as an Azeri nationalist, wary of both the Russian-dominated Commonwealth of Independent States and the Islamic

Republic of Iran. His views on the Islamic set-up in Iran, and his analysis of Iran as an empire made up of different nations, including Azeris, were deeply abhorrent to Tehran. 'Iran is as much a heterogeneous empire as Russia and is thus doomed to fall apart if democratic reform and voluntary confederation do not occur,' Elchibey said. 'Religion cannot hold a state together for long. Nationalism spelled the end for the Christian empire-states of the West, and it will now spell the end for the Muslim states of the East.'[38] In the opinion of Elchibey and most Azeris, independent Azerbaijan had found the right balance between nationalism, democracy and Islam, and this was well conveyed by its flag: the green band in the tricolour signifying Islam, the blue, democratic values, and the middle red band with a crescent and star, pan-Turkism.

Iran's political weakness in Azerbaijan was apparent from the fact that none of the five candidates for the presidency was known for his pro-Iranian or pro-Islamic views. Indeed, the Islamic Progress Party – one of the two religious groups established in September 1991 and led by Haji Sabir, (Sunni) deputy to Shaikh-al-Islam Allah Shukr Pashazade, (Shia) head of the Trans-Caucasian Muslim Spiritual Directorate – backed Elchibey. It did so because Elchibey had been a long-time dissident under Communist rule when he had been imprisoned for eighteen months during 1973–4, and he had a 'democratic vision'. What the party wanted were longer and more frequent Islamic programmes on radio and television, and religious education in the state-run schools of Azerbaijan. 'There is compulsory Islamic education in Turkey which is a secular state by constitution,' said Sabir. 'So why should we lag behind?'[39]

Once Elchibey had become president he looked increasingly to Turkey and further west, and accused Iran of meddling in his country's affairs. His charges against Iran were based on reports that, taking advantage of relaxed cross-border travel, many Iranian mullahs, fluent in Azeri and Persian, had taken to delivering sermons in the mosques in the area. There was little evidence that by so doing these Iranian clerics were acting as agents of the Tehran government. On the other hand, disregarding diplomatic norms, President Elchibey openly continued to stoke nationalist feelings among Iranian Azeris. 'If the Azerbaijanis in Iran struggle for their independence,' he said, 'they deserve to be supported.'[40] It was small wonder that Elchibey remained deeply unpopular with the leadership in Iran, where the media had taken to calling him 'a Godless Zionist'.

Following the unravelling of the Soviet Union, Tehran had

devised an overall policy towards Central Asia as well as the Caucasian republics of Azerbaijan and Armenia. Of these seven states, it needed to concentrate on those with which it had common land frontiers – Azerbaijan, Armenia and Turkmenistan – and Tajikistan, because of the affinity of Tajik with Persian and the common cultural heritage that Tajiks and Iranians shared. (In addition, Iran had common borders with Kazakhstan and Russia in the Caspian Sea.)

Iran's position was to be articulated publicly, later, by its foreign minister, Ali Akbar Velayati. 'Given the role of the Islamic Republic of Iran in the region our responsibilities are manifold,' he stated. 'Iran shares the Islamic heritage with her neighbouring countries and in view of the recent urge for independence in Central Asia, it has to fill the existing cultural and economic vacuum. Hence all countries that seek Iran's assistance in these realms [of culture and economics] will be welcomed.'[41] In short, contrary to what America and, to a lesser extent, Turkey had been saying, Tehran's agenda was limited to culture and economics, and fell well short of exporting Islamic revolution to these countries.

Iran seemed to have realized early on that with the possible exception of Tajikistan, conditions for such a revolution did not exist. Muslims in these countries had been deprived of religion and religious education for more than three generations, and they needed at least a decade to familiarize themselves with the basics of Islam and its rituals, and engender a sufficient body of clerics to provide religious education and guidance to the faithful before any serious attempt could be made to create a social order based on the Sharia. Iran was also aware that given major differences in the way Shia and Sunni sects are organized religiously, and the preponderance of the Sunni sect's Hanafi school in the region, its direct contribution to training clerics in these countries could only be marginal – the bulk of this task falling willy-nilly on the Sunni religious establishment in Turkey, which was Hanafi, and to a far lesser extent on the Islamic establishments of Egypt and Saudi Arabia.

Iran's strong geopolitical position was underscored by the fact that while all Central Asian republics as well as Azerbaijan and Armenia were landlocked, Iran's seashore line covered not only all of the 1450-kilometre- (900-mile-) long Persian Gulf but also 480 kilometres (300 miles) of the Arabian Sea. That is, Iran held the key in providing access to warm-weather seaports to these landlocked former Soviet republics. It wanted to assist them partly out of a feeling of Islamic solidarity, and partly to frustrate what it perceived as the avaricious ambitions of Western multi-national companies keen to exploit their vast natural resources while depriving them of high technology. 'Azerbaijan and Central Asia could be turned into a raw materials store for the West,' said President Rafsanjani, addressing the seventeenth session of the Islamic Development Bank in Tehran. 'To enable these countries to avoid this trap they need to be given large-scale economic aid.'[42]

Actually, Iran had begun acting along these lines soon after the break-up of the USSR. In February 1992 a regional body, the Economic Cooperation Organization (ECO), consisting of Pakistan, Iran and Turkey, was expanded to take in Azerbaijan and all the Central Asian republics, except Kazakhstan, which was given observer status. The first summit of the expanded ECO was held in Tehran; and the different emphasis made by the presidents of Turkey and Iran was illustrative. President Turgut Ozal hoped ECO would emerge like the European Community, whereas President Rafsanjani hailed the enlarged body, with an Iranian, Ali Reza Salari, as its secretary-general, as 'one great Muslim family of 300 million'.[43]

Tehran lost little time in offering $50 million to Turkmenistan in March to enable it to buy Iranian food, and promised assistance in the construction of a gas pipeline to carry Turkmen gas to Turkey and Western Europe through Iran, thus bypassing any other CIS member. The idea of such a pipeline, costing $3 billion, dependent for its operation on the continued goodwill of Iran, went down badly in Washington, which tried to sabotage the plan. It succeeded. In July it was announced that the plan was being held in abeyance since international bankers were unwilling to finance a project involving Iran which could, for political reasons, turn off energy supplies to Turkey and Europe.

But the one project where neither Iran nor Turkmenistan was dependent on Western funds or expertise was the 150-kilometre (ninety-mile) rail link between the eastern Iranian city of Mashhad and the border town of Sarakhs to link up with the Central Asian rail network at Tejand, Turkmenistan. Work started on it in June 1992, and was expected to end three years later.

Border restrictions between the two neighbours, which were at the front line of the Cold War until the fall of the Shah, Muhammad Reza Pahlavi, in early 1979 – a fact still marked by a fenced border running along the entire 1000 kilometres (620 miles) – were eased, allowing increased trade and human contacts.

In late August, President Saparmurad Niyazov of Turkmenistan visited Tehran where he signed economic, technical, cultural and scientific agreements. Three months later the two neighbours concluded further protocols on cooperation and collaboration. Iran mounted its second trade fair in Ashqabat which attracted representatives from other Central Asian republics. It was little wonder that Iranian–Turkmenistan trade in 1992 was two and a half times the figure for the previous year. After meeting a visiting Iranian minister in January, Niyazov said: 'All possible measures will be taken to expand and consolidate ties with Iran.'[44]

As elsewhere, there has been a rapid increase in the number of mosques in Turkmenistan. But the foreign money for their construction has come largely from the Mecca-based World Muslim League funded by Saudi Arabia. Among both Turkmen officials and intellectuals there is little or no fear of contacts with Iran and Iranians. The main reason is that Turkmens are Sunni. Also, as a Turkic people who until recently led a nomadic or semi-nomadic existence, Turkmens do not find much in common with the way of life of sedentary Iranians. Furthermore, their unrelated languages, Turkmen and Persian, set them apart. Unlike the (Shia) Azeris in Iran who, as a substantial minority often engaged in trade, are scattered throughout the country and integrated into Iranian society at all levels, the (Sunni) Turkmens in Iran, less than one million strong and confined to a small border area, are not as fully integrated into the Iranian system. Hence their potential as propagandists for their Islamic regime abroad is limited.[45]

Conversely, Iran had no trouble in spreading its message among Tajiks, given the linguistic and racial affinity between Iranians and Tajiks. Long before the turmoil of the late 1980s, culminating in the disintegration of the USSR, there were signs that interest in Islam was growing in Tajikistan.

With the anti-Communist movement rising in Tajikistan in late 1991 and early 1992, Iranian interest in the republic increased. Tehran expressed its approval when the Tajik Supreme Soviet decided to change the Cyrillic script of the Tajik language to Arabic, albeit from 1995. It was equally pleased to note that many Tajik intellectuals felt that people should learn to write Persian, which they considered an integral part of Tajik culture. It felt, rightly, that the victory of the Afghan Mujahedin in April 1992, which it welcomed, would fuel Islamic feeling in Tajikistan. The Iranian media gave wide coverage to the popular protest in Dushanbe, in which Islamic elements played a leading role. Commenting on the decision of President Rahman Nabiyev in May to include members of the opposition, secular and religious, in his administration, Radio Tehran hailed it as a triumph of 'the Muslim people of Tajikistan' who were engaged most importantly in 'renovation' of their 'Islamic, national identity'.[46]

Having incorporated Islamist forces, Nabiyev thought it prudent to win the sympathy of Iran. In July he flew to Tehran, where he signed a treaty of friendship and cooperation covering culture, trade, science and banking. Soon after, Iran began broadcasting television programmes in Persian to Tajikistan. It helped the Tajik authorities to rehabilitate Persian culture and language by supplying them with Persian-language school textbooks. As the economic situation deteriorated in Tajikistan, Tehran came to its assistance. In early September it offered Tajikistan oil worth $40 million as grant aid to ease its energy crisis,[47] a gesture much appreciated in the republic, especially by the mayor of Dushanbe, who was friendly with Iran, and who was able to keep public transport running owing to Iran's generosity.

In late September, following the forced resignation of President Nabiyev, the Iranian foreign minister, Velayati, told the visiting Tajik culture minister, Zakirjan Vazirov, that Iran was ready to help devise a peaceful settlement to the civil war. But this offer was not taken up because, unlike in the Azerbaijan–Armenian conflict, Iran was not regarded as truly neutral. Indeed, there were reports in the early autumn, attributed to Asian diplomats in Moscow, that Iran had supplied arms to a pro-Tehran Islamic faction in southern Tajikistan, and that the Russian foreign ministry had admitted that its relations with Iran were undergoing 'some problems at present'.[48] But given the logistical hurdles faced by Iran, the paucity of Shia Tajiks, and the comparative ease with which the Afghan Mujahedin, bristling with weapons, could and did arm Tajikistan's Islamic fighters to a far greater extent, the impact of weapons supplied by Tehran could only have been marginal. Both Moscow and Washington had their own reasons for exaggerating the Iranian input, ideological and military, into the civil war in Tajikistan. Russia wanted to do so in order to justify the supply of arms and ammunition to the pro-Nabiyev forces, and the United States was only too willing to paint its long-term adversary, Iran, as hell-bent on destabilization everywhere in the Muslim world. In the end, when Islamist partisans in Tajikistan were defeated and butchered by pro-Nabiyev forces in December 1992, there was very little Iran did, or could, do.

Equally, on the American–Turkish side, there was a limit to what Washington could do to discourage the Central Asian republics from having cordial relations with Tehran. Whatever else diplomatic and economic power can do, it cannot suppress the imperatives of geopolitics for long. Even the president of Kazakhstan, Nursultan Nazarbayev, who had publicly declared in early 1992 that Kazakhstan and Russia had a 'special responsibility' for steering Central Asia away from Islamic fundamentalism and Iranian influence, concluded that there was no alternative to having normal, friendly relations with Iran. He paid an official visit to Tehran on 1 November 1992, and signed protocols of mutual cooperation. In between, in August, the Iranian oil minister, Ghulam Aqazadeh, had visited Alma Ata to discuss the proposal that Kazakhstan should supply its oil to north Iran through a short pipeline, with Tehran exporting an equivalent amount of Iranian crude through its Gulf ports. Once again this project underlined the importance of Iran as the lynchpin of the Central Asian republics' plans to integrate themselves into the world economy through trade, a point Tehran was keen to emphasize.

Last but not least, the president of Uzbekistan, Islam Karimov, an ardent opponent of Islamic fundamentalism, made his peace with Iran after his government had repeatedly warned it to refrain from exporting its revolution to Uzbekistan. Given the strained relations, Iran, one of the first countries to recognize Uzbekistan, was quite late in opening its embassy in Tashkent: it did so in October 1992.

Normalization of relations between the two countries had to wait until Karimov's surprise decision to visit Tehran on 24 November. Once there, he had friendly meetings with President Rafsanjani when, among other things, they discussed the rail link between Tejand and Mashhad, to be completed by 1995, which would provide the shortest route for Uzbekistan's trade in the international market. The two leaders signed a series of economic and cultural agreements, areas that Iran had singled out for cooperation with the regional states.

As a member of ECO, which had established a Trade and Development Bank to finance joint ventures, Uzbekistan, being the most populous Central Asian state, expected to attract a large number of such projects. As a major contributor to the bank's capital funds of $400 million, Iran had pinned its hopes on ECO, whereas Turkey was focusing on the Black Sea Cooperation Council (BSCC). As the second-largest oil producer in the Gulf, and an exporter of oil,

Iran had more hard currency to spare than any other members of ECO or the BSCC.

Even Azerbaijan under Elchibey could not afford to ignore the economic significance of Iran. In January 1993 the Islamic Republic News Agency reported that during the six-month period of July 1992–January 1993, Azerbaijan's trade with Iran had grown to $500 million. It was the largest segment apart from its trade with CIS members, far ahead of its trade with Turkey. Negotiations were afoot for Azerbaijan to deliver 100,000 barrels of oil per day to the refinery in the Iranian city of Tabriz, with Iran delivering the same amount to Azeri customers from its oil ports.[49] More importantly, Azerbaijan's long-term prosperity, dependent on speedy exploitation of its proven petroleum reserves of between five and eight billion barrels by a consortium of Western oil companies, seemed to rest on Iran. Unwilling to route its petroleum pipeline either through overbearing Russia or adversarial Armenia, and pay transit charges to Moscow or Yerevan, the state-owned Azeri oil company insisted, much to the disapproval of the Western consortium, that the pipeline should go through Iran.[50] Apparently realism had triumphed over ideology in Baku.

The Azeri state oil company's stance reflected the change in the attitude of the Elchibey administration towards Tehran after the Armenians had occupied 3900 square kilometres (1500 square miles) of Azerbaijani territory in a major offensive in April, and Turkey, its erstwhile Big Brother, had failed to provide either military or effective diplomatic backing for it. A nervous Elchibey despatched his prime minister, Panah Husseinov, to Tehran where he described Iran as Azerbaijan's 'closest friend', and pleaded with President Rafsanjani for urgent aid. Having seen Elchibey thus humble himself publicly, the Iranian leader was at best non-committal, saying his government would take 'a serious view' of the matter if the Armenians continued their offensive. He was not certain that Elchibey had given up his pro-Ankara and pro-Washington proclivities: his sudden respect for Iran seemed more expeditious than real.

By May Elchibey became dangerously isolated. He had alienated Russia by pulling Azerbaijan out of the CIS; he had angered Iran to such an extent that his latest gesture of friendship failed to mollify it; and he found Ankara singularly incapable of delivering material aid to his country in its hour of need. This encouraged Colonel Suret Husseinov to rebel in early June, and bring about the downfall of Elchibey, an event that was heartily welcomed in Iran.

The elevation of Geidar Aliyev to acting president of Azerbaijan pleased Tehran. It had dealt with him as the leader of Nakhichevan and found him a pragmatic, level-headed statesman. With the ousting of Elchibey, who besides being extremely pro-Turkic had been cooperating with Washington to destabilize Iran by stoking up an irredentist movement among Iranian Azeris, Tehran had good reason to celebrate.

But Iran too had had its disappointments. Having made strides in establishing influence in a Tajikistan ruled jointly by Islamic forces for seven months, Iran eventually lost out there. And having become the foremost foreign friend of the Azeri regime under Elchibey for a year, Turkey lost its prime position. Judging by the way in which Aliyev had conducted his external affairs as the effective ruler of Nakhichevan, in his new role as leader of Azerbaijan he was going to follow an even-handed policy towards Turkey and Iran. Given all the complex factors of ethnicity, language, religion, nationalism, geopolitics and the imperatives of economic development, adopting such a stance seemed to be a sensible course for Azerbaijan to follow, especially when it had the merit of being sustainable in the long term.

Overall, therefore, in the summer of 1993, the score between the regional rivals, Turkey and Iran, was even.

TEN

Summary and Conclusions

The preceding narrative can broadly be divided into two sections: the first dealing with the former Soviet republics of Central Asia and Azerbaijan; and the second their Muslim neighbours – Afghanistan, Iran and Turkey. The driving forces behind the histories of the latter category are: religion, relations between state and mosque, secularism, nationalism, anti-imperialism, the jihad against foreign military intervention, the struggle against feudalism and for modernization, capitalist development, and Islamic fundamentalism. As for Central Asia and Azerbaijan, the pre-eminent dynamics of their histories are: Tsarist imperialism; territorial loyalty; Islam; pan-Turkism; Bolshevik revolution; Marxism-Leninism; a highly centralized CPSU; Stalin's theory of nations; socialist development in economics and culture, including scientific atheism; the Stalinist purges; the Great Patriotic War; deStalinization; glasnost and perestroika; the defeat of the Soviet bloc in the Cold War; ethnic nationalism; religious revival; Islamic fundamentalism; the market economy; and multi-party politics.

Today's Central Asian states owe their existence to the policies pursued by Joseph Stalin, a Bolshevik specialist on nationalities, from the mid-1910s onwards. He built his theory of nations on the premises defined by Vladimir Lenin, who perceived nationalism as a response to national-social oppression caused by the emergence of early capitalism, and therefore bound to disappear in the course of building socialism, which would foster proletarian internationalism. For the present, as a practical politician, Lenin recognized the particularist nationalisms that had arisen in the wake of Tsarist expansion, and supported the right to national self-determination vis-à-vis Great Russian imperialism, a concept that he later extended to include 'the right to free secession'.

But what constituted a nation? Stalin defined a nation as a 'stable and historically developed community' based on four criteria: a common language, a unified territory, a shared economic life, and a common culture. The national delimitation, implemented in the

USSR during 1924–5, which created Union republics as well as autonomous regions within these republics, signified implementation of the policy of national self-determination in Stalinist terms, providing each of the major nations in Central Asia and elsewhere in the USSR with 'a united territory'. Since a nation also had to have its own language, this was achieved in Central Asia by exaggerating differences between several Central Asian languages which were written in the Arabic script and were members of the Turkic group. It was thus that distinctions were sharpened between Kazakhs and Kyrgyzs, so paving the ground first for separate autonomous regions for them within the Russian Soviet Federation, and then for Union republics. A break with the Arabic script, favoured by many local intellectuals before the Bolshevik revolution, was recommended by the CPSU: it highlighted the onset of the revolution. Between the Cyrillic and Roman scripts, the latter was chosen because Cyrillic smacked too much of Great Russian chauvinism.

It was some years after the 1924–5 national delimitation, which created the Turkmen SSR and the Uzbek SSR (containing the Tajik ASSR) in Central Asia, that Stalin decided to upgrade the Tajik ASSR to a Union republic. This had as much to do with respecting the distinction of Tajik – akin to Persian – from the Turkic-based languages of the region as with Stalin's decision to create a socialist showpiece on the doorsteps of Afghanistan and India. At the same time, aware of the affinity of the Tajik language and culture with its Persian counterparts, he ensured that the Tajik SSR did not share its border with Iran (then called Persia).

Geopolitical factors also figured in Stalin's demarcation of the borders of Azerbaijan and Armenia. By allocating the Zangezur strip to Armenia and thus hiving off Nakhichevan from mainland Azerbaijan, he broke the territorial continuity of Turkic lands from the Balkans to China, and eliminated a potential bridgehead for a regional enemy. He tried to compensate Azerbaijan for this loss by giving it control over the Armenian-majority enclave of Nagorno Karabakh. This was also his way of rewarding the Baku Soviet for its unflinching loyalty to the Bolshevik revolution during the grim period of the 1918–20 civil war.

The overall result of the demarcation of the Central Asian and Caucasian regions along ethnic-linguistic lines was to destroy any potential for the unification of Central Asia and Azerbaijan around the twin banners of pan-Turkism and pan-Islamism, with Jagatai, a Turkic language, as the *lingua franca* – a concept that was popular among local intelligentsia before the Bolshevik revolution, and which to this day continues to inspire many among the regional population of Turkic origin, especially in Azerbaijan, which had experienced two years of independence during the civil war as the Democratic Republic of Azerbaijan. (The DRA had failed to win Allied recognition as an independent state partly because of its disputes with Armenia over Nagorno Karabakh and Zangezur.)

Once the danger of pan-Turkism and pan-Islamism destabilizing the region had been tackled, the central planners in Moscow pressed ahead with a rapid socio-economic transformation of this predominantly rural region heavily dependent on agriculture and cattle-breeding. Their main instrument was the all-pervasive Communist Party of the Soviet Union – formerly the All Russian Communist Party, renamed in 1925 – with its affiliates in the constituent Union republics, all committed to cementing republican divisions into an ideologically and administratively centralized USSR. Since Central Asia and Azerbaijan largely lacked the engine of the Bolshevik revolution – the industrial working class – except in such industrial centres as Baku, there was an under-representation of locals in the membership and hierarchy of the republican Communist parties. Therefore the task of destroying feudalism in production and social relations fell disproportionately on the Russian members and officials of the party.

The general thrust of Communist agrarian reform and the accompanying propaganda was to redistribute land and deprive landlords of their traditional political, economic and social power, and release the peasantry from the oppression of the past. The economic and political beneficiaries of this campaign were the landless, poor and middle-income peasants, the bulk of the populace. They also benefited from the literacy drives which reduced illiteracy from anywhere up to ninety-eight per cent in 1926 to almost nil within two generations.

Since Islam was seen as an integral part of a feudal order resting on the troika of the landlord, the mullah and the rich trader – and since the Sharia impinged on every facet of life, individual and social, viewed the state and mosque as two sides of the same coin, and considered the right to private property sacrosanct – periodic campaigns against Islam (as well as Christianity and Judaism) were conducted. Religious superstitions and archaic customs associated with Islam – polygamy, bride purchase, child marriage, the veil for women, the segregation of sexes in public places, circumcision for male children, fasting during Ramadan, and self-flagellation by Shias during Ashura ceremonies – were derided. Islamic art, architecture and literature, rooted in feudal times and ambience, were portrayed as fossilized, having failed to keep pace with changing times. Since it sanctified discrimination against women and enjoined excessive reverence for male elders, Islam was portrayed as a conservative faith. Finally, by insisting on dividing the world between believers and non-believers, Islam ruled out fraternization among different peoples of the USSR as equals, thus hindering the creation of the New Socialist Person, who transcended his/her religious, ethnic and racial background, to build a socialist order.

Initially, the party and the state conducted anti-Islamic education and propaganda, coordinated with literacy drives and re-organized socio-economic activities of the masses, with considerable caution, concentrating on winning a few converts to scientific atheism in each village with a view to using them as models of rationalism and modern thinking. Anti-religious propaganda and education went hand in hand with measures to weaken and destroy both the extensive religious networks of mosques and theological institutions, and more importantly their financial support – the religious trust properties – which was nationalized. (In Turkey, Mustafa Kemal Ataturk followed a similar path, except that there were no parallel literacy campaigns and no ideological ballast of historical materialism or scientific atheism: it had more to do with destroying the possibility of the return of the Sultan-Caliph on the backs of revived Islamic institutions and clerics.) When popular protest erupted in 1926 in the USSR's Muslim regions in the wake of the promulgation of the socialist family code, according equality to men and women, Stalin temporized by exempting them from the code. But this proved to be an expeditious move. During the next two years the governments in the Muslim-majority Union and Autonomous republics and regions abrogated the practices of polygamy, bride purchase and the veil, and shut the Sharia and *Adat* courts. Furthermore, they prohibited religious propaganda as well as religious education to minors in groups larger than three. As in Turkey, the proscription of the Arabic script in 1929 struck at the root of Islamic scriptures and commentaries, making the surviving clergy totally dependent on the religious material that the Soviet authorities deemed fit to be published in the Cyrillic or Roman script.

In the early 1930s, towards the end of the First Five Year Plan (1929–33), Stalin launched a concerted five-year anti-religious campaign. The control of all places of worship was transferred to the

Union of Atheists: it transformed them into museums, places of entertainment or factories. The authorities banned the Muslim customs of going on a pilgrimage to Mecca and paying a religious tax (*zakat*) to provide funds to the needy and for maintaining mosques and religious monuments. They forbade the printing and distribution of the Quran. They banned some 3500 books on the ground of propagation of Islamic superstition. And they encouraged Muslim women to burn their veils in public, which they did in their thousands. They suppressed protest demonstrations by the believers and arrested thousands of mullahs.

The anti-religious drive (1932–6) ran almost parallel to the more important anti-kulak (rich farmer) campaign that Stalin mounted from 1930 to 1934. As soon as Stalin had consolidated his power in 1925, he argued that since the nationalist movements drew the bulk of their militant members from the peasantry, the 'national problem' could not be resolved without tackling the 'peasant problem'. He labelled kulaks as the foremost class enemies because they combined their socio-economic power with being the repositories and propagators of national consciousness which was antithetical to proletarian internationalism. The solution lay in destroying kulaks by collectivizing farmland. When Stalin's campaign for voluntary collectivization in 1927 proved patchy, he initiated compulsory collectivization in early 1930. He aimed to destroy the authority not merely of kulaks but also of tribal and clan chiefs and village elders, and make the new order prevail in the rural USSR, which contained a majority of Soviet citizens.

For nomadic Kazakhs, Kyrgyzs and Uzbeks, mainly engaged in cattle-breeding, collectivization proved traumatic. It involved settling down and giving up their herds. The result was a migration of whole clans from Kazakhstan, Kyrgyzstan and Uzbekistan into neighbouring China, Afghanistan and Iran. This and the subsequent depletion in the local population due to collectivization and the ensuing famine in the mid-1930s reduced the size of the indigenous populace, especially in Kazakhstan and Kyrgyzstan. Among other things it turned the majority Kazakhs and Kyrgyzs into minorities in their autonomous regions, which were upgraded to Union republics in 1936 at the time of a new USSR constitution. The centre overcame the opposition of local kulaks, peasants and livestock breeders by combining force, large-scale deportations and propaganda with the despatch of Slav-dominated Communist Party contingents from the European USSR to Central Asia to furnish the newly established collective farms with manpower and technical and managerial skills. This explains the present-day demographic composition of Kazakhstan, where Kazakhs are still a minority, and that of Kyrgyzstan, where Kyrgyzs became a bare majority only in 1989.

In due course collective farms – called *kolkhozes* – possessing land and farm machinery, and managing schools, clubs, libraries, cinemas and agro-based industries, engendered their own milieu. While being under the supervision of the local Communist Party's central committee, they enjoyed substantial freedom. Since a typical collective farm in Central Asia was established around a long-established village, it drew extended families and even whole clans, thus grafting feudal social relations onto socialist production relations, and engendering strange distortions. This was particularly true of the cotton-growing areas of Uzbekistan, which became a major source of supply of the commodity in the USSR – as well as the centre of a huge corruption scandal in the Union in the mid-1980s.

Unsurprisingly, as the most populous and strategic republic in Central Asia, Uzbekistan emerged as one of the important centres of the 'nationalist conspiracy' during the Stalinist purges of 1937–8. The leading conspirators were Akmal Ikramov, the party chief, and Faizullah Khojayev, the prime minister (accused more specifically of having accorded an Islamic burial to his brother). Later they were tried in Moscow as members of the 'bloc of Rightists and Trostkyites', found guilty of various charges, and executed. The party and government positions of the purged leaders went to younger cadres whose lives had been moulded completely by the Bolshevik order. The disappearance of rural property in the wake of the nationalization of land, water and forests, followed by collectivization, destroyed the power and influence of the traditional elite, and created opportunities for young party activists imbued with Marxism-Leninism.

As Stalin became obsessed with creating a highly centralized Soviet Union, party and government leaders increasingly ignored local traditions and interests, thus deviating from one of the principal Leninist guidelines on nationalities, and inadvertently sowing the seeds of disintegration in the future. Unquestioned loyalty to Moscow from republican capitals became highly prized; and the Russian party members either domiciled in a Central Asian republic or Azerbaijan, being immune to local influences, rose fast in the republican hierarchy, thus creating (unexpressed) disaffection among native party ranks. In this environment Moscow's decision in 1938 to make

Russian compulsory in all non-Russian schools in the Union came as no surprise. During the next two years the script of Azeri, Kazakh, Kyrgyz, Tajik, Turkmen and Uzbek was changed from Latin to Cyrillic. By depriving the regional peoples of their ability to read foreign publications in the Roman script, the Moscow authorities controlled further their reading material. With a large body of literate citizens in the region, this decision had a far greater impact than the earlier one to change the Arabic script to the Latin when illiteracy was rampant. The switch-over came at a time when major road and rail projects in the region, as well as the ambitious Fergana Canal, had been accomplished. This enabled the centre further to tighten its control over Central Asia.

All in all, on the eve of the Second World War, Central Asia and Azerbaijan had undergone much greater socio-economic and administrative changes in a decade and a half under Stalin than they had over the past century and a half. Among other things, due to the fast rising literacy rate and the practice of mentioning nationality on a citizen's identity card, there was now greater ethnic-linguistic awareness among the numerous nationalities in the region and elsewhere than ever before. This was to prove a lasting legacy.

The Great Patriotic War, which began with Germany's invasion of the USSR in June 1941, had a profound effect on the country. It resulted in immense human and material damage to the Soviet Union. But it also allowed the Moscow regime to engender symbiosis between patriotism and socialism, thereby enabling the Bolshevik revolution to be absorbed into the popular psyche. Aware of the crucial importance of the Russian Soviet Federation's geographical and demographic size, Stalin encouraged a revival of Russian nationalism to mobilize the people to resist the mighty invader. Reversing his militant atheism, he co-opted the Russian Orthodox Church for the purpose. In September 1943 he permitted its followers to elect a new synod and patriarch. He performed a similar *volte face* with respect to the Islamic leadership which had seen the number of functioning mosques in the Soviet Union decline by ninety-five per cent from the pre-revolution total of over 26,000. The result was the establishment in October 1943 of the Official Islamic Administration. It operated through regional Muslim Spiritual Directorates, including one in Tashkent for the Muslims of Middle Asia and Kazakhstan, and another in Baku for the Muslims of Trans-Caucasia. In return for serving the political interests of the Soviet regime at home and abroad, the directorates were authorized to manage functioning mosques through registered clerics and religious communities. Having uprooted the powerful Islamic tree, Stalin could now afford to allow a sapling to grow under strictly controlled conditions. Overall, though, this concordat between mosque and state had a healing effect in the Muslim-majority Central Asian republics and Azerbaijan.

When it came to supporting the war effort, the region's Muslim citizens proved second to none. The uninterrupted operation of the Ashqabat railway and the Caspian port of Krasnovodsk, Turkmenistan – connecting the southern fronts and the Trans-Caucasian republics with Central Russia under German occupation – during the winter of 1941–2, enabled the Soviet military to expel the Germans from the Volga region and the foothills of the Caucasus, and finally break the German siege of Volgograd (Stalingrad). The Baku region produced more than two-thirds of the total Soviet oil output.

Moscow's policy of transferring industrial enterprises from front-line zones in the European USSR to peripheral regions benefited Central Asia, with Kazakhstan, Kyrgyzstan and Uzbekistan gaining 270 factories. With warfare creating unprecedented employment opportunities for women, further progress was made towards their emancipation. The cumulative effect of wartime developments was to bring together numerous nationalities living in Union republics. In the process of working with Russian troops, hundreds of thousands of indigenous Central Asians and Azeris improved their Russian, and this reinforced the politico-economic unity of the USSR. The victory in the war was the zenith of the Soviet system under Stalin.

The tasks of rapid economic development and cultural sovietization began in earnest after the war because the pre-conditions for their success had now been met. Citizens had been exposed to political education, and leading party cadres had been trained both ideologically (to engender unity between the Russian core and the non-Slavic periphery) and professionally (to perform managerial and executive jobs). Indeed, a new generation of such Soviet-educated, war-hardened party cadres had begun coming up the hierarchical ladder in the Central Asian republics and Azerbaijan. As before, to prove their loyalty to Moscow, they initiated purges in 1951–2, although these were not as severe as those carried out by Stalin in 1937–8. The victims in Central Asia and Azerbaijan were those party activists who had allegedly displayed one or more of the failings of 'local favouritism', 'bourgeois nationalism', and 'archaic [i.e. Islamic] customs'.

In the jockeying for power that followed Stalin's death in March 1953, Nikita Khrushchev unveiled a plan in late 1953 to make the USSR self-sufficient in food grains, meat, cotton and tobacco by the early 1980s by transforming underused land in the Urals, the Volga region, North Caucasus, southern Siberia and Kazakhstan into fertile agricultural fields, with the last two areas contributing the most. The adoption of the Virgin Land programme by respective Communist parties at the republican and regional levels reinforced Khrushchev's hand in Moscow. He then initiated a deStalinization programme in the party, quietly removing diehard Stalinists from power.

For a wholesale attack on Stalin, however, Khrushchev had to wait for the next CPSU congress which met in February 1956. Here, in a long, unpublished speech, he exposed the numerous misdeeds of Stalin, including trampling upon socialist legality, fostering a personality cult, and committing gross violations of basic Leninist principles in his nationalities policy by banishing entire ethnic groups to the far corners of the USSR on the unsubstantiated grounds of being pro-German during the Great Patriotic War. Among those who had suffered this fate were the Inguish, Crimean Tartars, Khemshins (Armenian Muslims), Kurds and Meskhetian Turks (Georgian Muslims).

While Khrushchev was serious about ending the state terror institutionalized by Stalin, his militant atheism allowed no compromise with religion and religious practices. At his behest, Communist Youth League activists launched an anti-veil campaign in 1955 and concluded it in 1959, marking the official end of the practice in the Soviet Union. The newly revived Union of Atheists focused on closing down places of worship as well as religious schools and monuments. During the next five years the number of functioning churches, mosques and synagogues fell sharply.

In his report on domestic developments to the Twenty-second CPSU congress in 1961, Khrushchev declared that the Soviet Union had entered 'mature socialism', and that during this phase of socialism the dialectics of national relations would follow the line of 'blooming, rapprochement and amalgamation': the twin processes of blooming (i.e. the fullest self-realization of each Soviet nation) and rapprochement (i.e. the coming together of nations, through cross-fertilization and the sharing of a common socialist economy and social formations) resulting in rapid progress towards ultimate amalgamation.

His successor, Leonid Brezhnev, was not so sanguine. Reassessing the 'national question', he concluded that Khrushchev's scenario of the merger of all Soviet nations was too idealistic,[1] and would have to await the global triumph of socialism over capitalism. At the Twenty-third CPSU congress in March 1966, therefore, he took a realistic stand, declaring that the party would continue to show 'solicitude' for the interests and characteristics of each of the 123 nationalities that constituted the USSR.

Reflecting a similar realism on the 'religious question', Brezhnev ended the excesses of Khrushchev's anti-religious propaganda, and tried to placate the Official Islamic Administration by allowing the restoration of religious monuments. The reconstruction of all the mosques destroyed by the 1966 earthquake in Tashkent showed his policy at work. Allowing the Muslim Spiritual Directorate in Tashkent to publish a magazine in Uzbek, Arabic, Persian, English and French was a further example of the new stance on Islam. In 1970, encouraged by the government, Ziauddin Babakhan, the Tashkent-based mufti, convened an international Islamic conference in the Uzbek capital, the first such assembly in Russian or Soviet history. Mullahs justified their cooperation with the Soviet state by arguing that Marxism-Leninism was primarily concerned with managing the economy and administration whereas Islam dealt essentially with spiritual and ethical matters.

Officially registered clerics now operated in an environment that had spawned a new generation of Central Asians and Azeris. Reared on Soviet education and the welfare state, which guaranteed the basic needs of food and housing and provided free social services, it possessed the kind of confidence that its parents had lacked. Many young Uzbek and other Central Asian intellectuals tried to rediscover their national-cultural origins; and because these were intertwined with Islamic heritage, their quest led them to Islam. But their newly discovered interest in religion could not be properly satisfied by the registered clerics working under government supervision. This led to the growth of unregistered clerics, collectively called 'unofficial' or 'parallel' Islam. Their existence was soon to be acknowledged by officials of the Union of Atheists and others.

In Azerbaijan repeated anti-religious campaigns had diverted the feelings of Muslim and Christian believers into ethnic channels, reviving animosity between (Muslim) Azeris and (Christian)

Armenians, encapsulated in their dispute over Nagorno Karabakh, which had been quiescent since the mid-1920s. In a pattern that was to become familiar later, the Armenians petitioned Moscow (unsuccessfully) in 1963 to incorporate the enclave into Armenia or the Russian Soviet Federation, thus infuriating the Azeris, who responded by attacking the Armenian minority in their midst. There was a repeat of this cycle in 1968 and again in 1973.

By then Brezhnev had lost his impetus for reforming the system, to which he had committed himself in 1966. He had become obsessed by production targets; and achieving these had become an end in itself. Also, the expensive arms race with the West distorted the Soviet economy, siphoning off a hefty twenty-five per cent of the GDP on defence and defence-related industry, as well as the major part of the first-rate scientific and intellectual talent. Under Brezhnev's leadership the party arrogated greater powers to itself and fostered a ruling elite: it cosseted itself with ever-rising privileges, thus distancing itself further from ordinary citizens and party members. This demoralized workers and peasants. Many of them lost their motivation for hard work. Attitudes towards public property – which is all that existed – deteriorated. Many employees took to pilfering from their work-places while managers resorted to underhand practices to procure raw or intermediate materials and other needs to meet their production targets. In agriculture the practice of doctoring output, especially in cotton, took root. Bribery and corruption thrived. So too did the mafia, men in sharp suits who, for a price, got things done in a highly bureaucratic set-up. The resulting parallel economy thrived to the detriment of its legitimate counterpart. By the late 1970s the system was in deep trouble, and needed drastic corrective measures from a vibrant leadership. But Brezhnev was then quite ill, and totally dependent on the information and advice he received from his close aides. Being sycophantic, they had no interest in alarming him by providing him with a true picture of the fast deteriorating situation. They humoured him. Despite his failing powers, he hung on to supreme power until his death in November 1982. He passed on to his successor a Soviet Union that was in urgent need of radical reform.

Yuri Andropov launched a campaign to improve labour discipline and productivity, and to eliminate corruption. With the graft being more common in Central Asia, especially in Uzbekistan, than elsewhere, the anti-corruption drive had more impact on this region than others. But it made headway in Uzbekistan only after Sharaf

Rashidov, the long-serving party leader who had become extremely influential during the Brezhnev era, had died in October 1983. The charges against him and his aides included not merely widespread bribery and nepotism but also large-scale embezzlement of funds, stemming from fraudulent cotton output figures, and general economic mismanagement. As Uzbekistan produced nearly two-thirds of Soviet cotton, this was a serious matter.

But before Andropov's campaign could gather momentum, and before he could stamp his imprint on the administration, he died in early 1984. Konstantin Chernenko, his successor, was by all accounts a failure. Luckily for the Soviet Union, he lasted about a year.

Mikhail Gorbachev, the youngest leader of the Soviet Union so far, was determined to put things right. Within a year of assuming supreme office, he had launched glasnost and perestroika. These were well-meaning moves, but Gorbachev, a leader cast in the CPSU mould, had not thought through the consequences of his actions. He failed to realize the basic contradiction in his strategy: democracy *and* centralized power as embodied by the CPSU. Indeed, he counted on using the CPSU to usher in a democratic set-up. He never seriously considered allowing a multi-party system – either by letting the existing monolith, the CPSU, break up into three parties embodying the existing conservative, radical and centrist trends, or allowing genuine non-Communist groupings to emerge and grow.

When the dictatorial state and party loosened its iron grip, long-suppressed feelings and views exploded, pushing to the fore not only the economic problems stemming from decades of highly centralized planning, including party and administrative corruption, but also the unresolved or partially resolved problems of inter-ethnic relations. In Central Asia and Azerbaijan, the 'national question' manifested itself in different forms: (a) relations between Slavs and non-Slavs, most prominently in Kazakhstan; (b) relations between ethnic groups with different religious backgrounds, e.g. Azeris and Armenians; and (c) relations between ethnic groups sharing the same religious background, e.g. Uzbeks and Tajiks in Uzbekistan.

To highlight the heralding of a new era with his assumption of power, Gorbachev resolved to get rid of old party stalwarts in the central party Politburo as well as the republican ones. The most notable example of this policy was the removal in mid-December 1986 of Dinmuhammad Kunayev as First Secretary of the Communist Party of Kazakhstan, and his replacement by an ethnic Russian, Gennadi Kolbin. By so doing, Gorbachev, inadvertently or otherwise, sharpened the contradiction that had existed all along between the centre (Moscow) and the periphery (Alma Ata), and reinforced Kazakh nationalism even within the CPK's Kazakh members.

What made matters worse was the authorities' dismissal of the young protesters as hooligans and extremists, and their use of police force to disperse the pro-Kunayev demonstrators, causing up to a score of deaths. It was not until eighteen months later that the Soviet government's newspaper, *Izvestia*, begrudgingly conceded that the removal of Kunayev had been viewed by 'certain young people' as 'a blow against national esteem and pride . . . [and] as the eclipse of their hopes'.

A similar insensitivity was shown towards Uzbeks and Uzbekistan on the issue of corruption by both republican and central Communist leaders. Inamjan Usmankhojayev, who succeeded Rashidov, never let past an opportunity to lambast his predecessor, only to find himself arrested for corruption, found guilty and convicted. The conclusions of a comprehensive investigation into corrupt practices in Uzbekistan, published in 1987 at a time when press censorship was lax, showed a cumulative loss to the public exchequer over a quarter-century of $2 billion for inflated cotton production figures, the fraud involving over 2600 officials in Uzbekistan and Moscow, including a son-in-law of Brezhnev.

Contrary to Gorbachev's expectations, instead of restoring popular faith in the system now purportedly cleansed of corrupt elements, the unprecedented scandal and the subsequent party and governmental purges left the populace confused and cynical, with their trust in the system at an all-time low. Ethnic Uzbeks felt offended by the way officials and the media in Moscow began to treat the 'Uzbek Affair' and corruption as two sides of the same coin. This feeling soon became transformed into a resolve to resist Moscow. It created a milieu favourable to the emergence of opposition groups, nationalist and Islamist.

Housing two-thirds of the 230 working mosques in Muslim Central Asia in the mid-1980s, Uzbekistan was the single most important Soviet republic in terms of Islam. Developments in this field were therefore of great interest not only to the republic-level leadership but also to the centre. The hard line taken by party leaders on participation in Islamic rituals collapsed when during the run-up to the millennium celebrations in 1988, the Russian Orthodox Church was accorded an honoured place in the Russian Soviet Federation. The Soviet media waxed eloquent on the inextricable bond between the

Russian Church and culture, and the significance of religion in the history of Russia. These celebrations came in the wake of a survey of Tashkent University undergraduates with a Muslim background published in 1987: it showed sixty per cent describing themselves as 'Muslim' and only seven per cent calling themselves 'atheist'. These findings were a contrast to what had been discovered by a Soviet survey of 'formerly Muslim peoples' eight years earlier: only thirty per cent had called themselves 'believers' whereas fifty per cent had described themselves as 'unbelievers'. Unlike the Tashkent University sample, the believers had been mainly rural, old and semi-literate. The new survey results jolted party bosses.

Several factors explained the change. The relaxed atmosphere engendered by perestroika and glasnost made people less afraid of expressing their true feelings than before. Secondly, the events in Iran and Afghanistan made Islam a living socio-political ideology rather than a fossilized creed of feudal times, as Soviet ideologues portrayed it. Thirdly, in the absence of familiarity with any other non-Marxist creed, people with Muslim backgrounds fell back on Islam as an all-embracing saviour: it helped them to counter the influence of the Slavic Big Brother and assisted them in re-asserting their own ethnic-cultural identity which, stretching back many centuries, stood apart from Christianity and Europe.

It was thus little wonder that new mosques built with private contributions began opening every week, and enrolment in existing theological colleges soared. So long as the Central Asian republics and Azerbaijan were part of the USSR, opposition nationalist parties and their ideologues frequently used Islam and Islamic symbols to rally support. But once these republics became sovereign independent states in the aftermath of the collapse of the Communist Party, the situation changed somewhat.

The collapse of Marxism-Leninism created an ideological vacuum, which only nationalism or Islam could satisfactorily fill. Since the population and politicians had no experience of Western-style democracy or of private enterprise, neither had any chance of providing ideological ballast for the ruling parties in these newly independent countries. In any event, since all these states were committed to a multi-party system and a market economy, there was no point in setting up a grouping with the aim of achieving these objectives. As for nationalism and Islam, each of them offered two gradings: either ethnic nationalism per se, or within the overall context of pan-Turkism; Islam as a font of ethics and spirituality, part of Central Asian culture, or Islam as a socio-political ideology, informing and guiding society and government at large – Islamic fundamentalism.

There was no dispute between the ruling parties and the opposition about reviving Islam. So there were no limitations on religious activity by citizens, and no barriers on the expansion of mosques and theological institutions. The Central Asian republics and Azerbaijan were quick to declare two Islamic *eids* as public holidays. State-run radio and television were allowed to transmit Islamic programmes. The presidents in the region made a point of undertaking *umra*, a short hajj to Mecca, during their trips to Saudi Arabia. In Tashkent, President Karimov took his oath of office on the Quran. And like Muhammad Najibullah in Kabul, the head of the ruling People's Democratic Party of Afghanistan, Karimov, now leader of the governing People's Democratic Party of Uzbekistan, the renamed Communist Party, had no difficulty prefacing his public speeches with '*Bismallah al Rahman al Rahim* (In the name of God, the Merciful and the Compassionate)'. But Karimov and his PDP were determined to preserve the secular basis of the state by maintaining a strict division between religion and government.

In the changed climate of the former Muslim-majority Soviet republics functioning as independent states, the Islamic Renaissance Party – established originally in 1990 as an all-Union organization to secure the same religious rights for Muslims as were then enjoyed by Christians – turned radical. The IRP in Tajikistan, accorded legal status in September 1992, declared as its objective the setting up of an Islamic state, to be achieved only through the ballot. The IRP in Uzbekistan, operating clandestinely, also had the same aim. The Wahhabi activists in the Fergana Valley made no secret of their commitment to establishing an Islamic republic in Uzbekistan to replace 'the Communist government in Tashkent'. But by concentrating on providing mosques and religious schools to the faithful, they had managed to avoid repression by the Karimov administration which feared that any action against them would be portrayed as 'crushing Islam'.

In the secular arena in Uzbekistan, ethnic nationalism had been appropriated by Birlik and Erk opposition groupings. With Birlik denied the status of a recognized political party, the role of fostering Uzbek nationalism fell on Erk, which emphasized its nationalist, anti-Communist credentials by adopting the flag of the Kokand Autonomous Government of 1917–18 as its own. With no immediate chance of gaining power, Erk could afford to be as nationalist as it wanted, thus pre-empting any lurch towards nationalism that the ruling PDP might find expeditious. On the other hand, with non-Uzbeks forming a third of the republic's population, any party propounding militant nationalism was unlikely to win power through the ballot box.

On the whole the existence of recognized and unrecognized Islamic and nationalist organizations in Uzbekistan reduced the PDP's choice of a coherent ideology – a severe handicap for a ruling party which, in desperation, had fallen back on the slogans of 'Discipline and Order' and 'nation-building'. The governing Democrat Party in Turkmenistan, the renamed Communists, had turned its commitment to raise living standards into some sort of ideology, and imposed a virtual ban on oppositional activities until its economic objective has been achieved.

The one Central Asian state where ethnic arithmetic precluded any prospect of local nationalism holding sway was Kazakhstan. The impact of the presence of a large body of Slav settlers there was reinforced by the long, unguarded Kazakh–Russian border. President Nazarbayev understood this; and so too did the drafters of the new constitution. Unsurprisingly, it required a registered public association to be open to every and any citizen, irrespective of his/her ethnic origins, mother tongue or 'attitudes towards religion' (which included being irreligious or atheistic). And by letting any citizen who was 'fluent in Kazakh' become president, the 1993 constitution held out the possibility of an ethnic Slav winning supreme office, a setback for militant Kazakh nationalists.

At the other end was Azerbaijan. There, ethnic arithmetic did not militate against local nationalism. With the departure of the Armenians by mid-1990, the only substantial minority left was the Russians, who constituted about nine per cent of the republic's population. Unsurprisingly, the opposition Popular Front went all out to foster Azeri nationalism and won the presidential election in mid-1992 on that platform. Given the cultural-linguistic affinity that Azeris – categorized as Turks in the 1926 census of the USSR – have with the Turks of Turkey, there was little doubt that the Azeri nationalism propounded by the PF had its place within the larger framework of pan-Turkism.

As a governing party, therefore, the PF had no problem rooting itself firmly in an ideology that had a long and appealing history, and a possibly bright future. The fact that Turkey was a secular state, part of NATO and an associate member of the European Community, made the idea all the more attractive. Using Turkey's assistance and Western contacts, the new Azerbaijan, overflowing with oil and gas, would soon transform itself into another affluent state like Kuwait. So a likely scenario seemed destined to unroll – but the Armenians in Armenia and Nagorno Karabakh were determined to spoil it. As a large majority in the Karabakh enclave, the Armenians had logic and equity on their side in their call for incorporation into Armenia. But there were many other such anomalies in the former USSR. After the free-for-all following the independence of Azerbaijan and Armenia, the Armenians performed well on the battlefield, partly because they had the advantage of surreptitious military advice and supplies from the locally stationed Russian/CIS troops, and partly because, nursing the memory of a million Armenians who, according to them, had been killed or deported from Turkey by the Turks in 1915, they were strongly motivated to decimate Azeri Turks (since they could not possibly get even with the original perpetrator of the 1915 Armenian massacres, Turkey).

But by extending Azeri nationalism to the extent of pulling out of the CIS, the PF leader, Elchibey, upset Moscow: its withdrawal broke the geographical continuity of the CIS. Russia's subsequent undercover assistance to the Armenians in their efforts to capture Azeri territory in April 1993, which, thanks to the entente between Moscow and Washington, went unpunished by the UN Security Council, illustrated the limitations of ethnic nationalism in the former Soviet republics. What reinforced these limitations was the failure of Turkey, the Azeris' freely chosen Big Brother, to come to the aid of Elchibey in reversing the Armenian aggression. Aware that its military intervention in the Azerbaijani–Armenian conflict would result in a Western embargo, and unwilling to upset its newly emergent business class, linked closely with the West, the Turkish government failed its Turkic cousins over the border, in the process inadvertently proving that its assets of close ties with the West had proved in this instance to be its liabilities.

However, militant ethnic nationalism in Azerbaijan was not the only ideology to fail in the region. Earlier, militant Islam allied with anti-Communist democratic forces had failed in Tajikistan, with a bloody civil war, causing 20,000–30,000 mainly civilian deaths, ending in its defeat at the hands of the local Communists, who had been helped actively by Uzbekistan and tacitly by Russia. The reasons for its failure went beyond its comparative military weakness: they embraced constitutional provisions as well as geopolitics.

The events in Tajikistan from May to October 1992 demonstrated that whereas the Islamist–Democratic alliance enjoyed enough popular support to make it an effective opposition in a multi-party system, it faced insurmountable problems in winning and retaining power, or even sharing it with Communists. It had to function within the republican constitution of 1978 which, like its predecessors, rested on a Leninist principle: 'All power to the Soviets'. The provision of an executive president, inserted as an amendment to the constitution, failed to take root, mainly because the presidential election that followed threw up a serious rival to the official candidate, Nabiyev, something Communist deputies had not bargained for. Whatever concessions the Islamist-led alliance obtained through demonstrations and sit-ins – cabinet posts or the appointment of Akbarsho Iskanderov as the republic's acting president – needed to be ratified by the Communist-dominated parliament. Iskanderov's failure to convene the Supreme Soviet owing to the lack of a quorum highlighted the fatal weakness of the Islamist-led coalition. (This was the main reason why the plan to replace the Supreme Soviet with a National Assembly of seventy members, composed of an equal number of pro- and anti-Communist elements, agreed in May 1992, remained still-born.)

As if this were not enough, there would have been further hurdles in store for the Islamist-led coalition if it had managed to legitimize its power by obtaining the necessary vote in parliament. The authorities in Hojand, which had taken to defying the Iskanderov administration, would have carried out their threat of seceding and returned to Uzbekistan, thus re-creating the situation that had existed before 1929, and depriving Dushanbe of a third of the republic's population and three-fifths of its industrial production. Any efforts by the government in Dushanbe to regain Hojand would have exacerbated the situation.

Instead of being satisfied with their military victory and acting in a humanitarian way towards their adversaries, the Communists carried out a bloody vendetta against their enemies, thus sowing the seeds of future conflict through endless feuding. They made matters worse by seeking and getting increased Russian military aid to patrol the Tajik–Afghan border. The large-scale fighting that erupted along the frontier in July 1993 demonstrated that relations between Communist Dushanbe and Islamist Kabul had worsened considerably.

What had become clear in the course of the civil conflict in Tajikistan was that the regional country that had had most impact on the hostilities was Afghanistan – not Iran, which had long been portrayed by the West, particularly America, as the Islamic demon in the area. On the eve of the break-up of the Soviet Union, US officials and media, working in conjunction with their Turkish counterparts, had made it appear that the Muslim-majority republics faced a stark choice between secular, democratic, pro-Western Turkey and fanatical, theocratic, anti-Western Iran. US Secretary of State James Baker publicly warned the newly independent states of Central Asia and Azerbaijan to keep well clear of Iranian influence. Within months, the Turkish media had announced that Turkey had won the race for influence in the region, leaving Iran behind, sulking.

However, by the spring of 1993 it had become clear that the presentation and analysis that Washington had vociferously retailed – along with its dire warnings of an 'Islamic atom bomb' materializing due to the emergence of Kazakhstan as a nuclear power – was heavily flawed. Part of the reason why the US went into overdrive in its campaign against Islamic influence was that it had come to believe its own propaganda: since 1980, following the Soviet military intervention in Afghanistan, it had mounted a broadcasting campaign (in conjunction with Saudi Arabia and Egypt) designed to increase Islamic consciousness in Central Asia and Azerbaijan, and ally it with local nationalism in order to undermine the Moscow-directed Soviet system.

It is obvious that, as a Shia country with a Shia system of religious organization and an Islamic code, Iran can have only limited impact on the Muslim citizens of these countries – except in Azerbaijan, where most Azeris are Shia. As stated earlier, religious organizations in the predominantly Sunni Central Asia are sending their students to theological institutions in Turkey.

The analysis of Turkey in Chapter 1 shows that over the past several decades Islam has recovered the place in society it had lost under the militant secularism of Mustafa Kemal Ataturk, who died in 1938. There have been unmistakable signs of Islamization in Turkey. The prediction of Professor Serif (Sherif) Mardin in 1981, during the period of military rule in Turkey, that if 'parliamentary institutions are placed back in operation, then an Islamic revival would take the form of a slow infiltration of Islamic world-views in Turkish society without much change in the legal system and in the present legal implementation of secularism'[2] has come to pass.

In a sense, underneath the shell of secular law, Turkey has moved closer to its historical Islamic roots. Hence presenting Turkey and Iran as antagonistic choices to Central Asia and Azerbaijan is to distort reality.

Iran is perceived as a threat to Western interests (especially by Washington) merely because it exists as a viable state. But as the earlier account in this book shows, Tehran is more interested in exploiting the geopolitical advantages it has and in encouraging its newly acquired Muslim neighbours to integrate their economies with its own, especially in the communications sphere, rather than in urging them to run society according to the Sharia. In any case, given the hiatus of seventy years when religion was actively suppressed, it would take the Muslims of Central Asia and Azerbaijan at least a decade to familiarize themselves with the basics of Islam and create a religious infrastructure. Only then would there be an environment in which to instal and sustain a social system based on the Sharia. Meanwhile, Iran will continue to manifest a tendency to act in its national interest rather than take an ideological position. Its stance in the Azeri–Armenian dispute over Karabakh is a case in point. It did not side unequivocally with Muslim Azerbaijan. Rather it acted as a mediator between the warring parties. Sharing borders with Armenia, it has signed agreements with the republic to supply it with oil and gas. It has so far given no cause for Turkmenistan's leader, Niyazov, to dampen his enthusiasm for economic co-operation with it.

The key geopolitical card that Iran holds is that it has several hundred miles of shoreline in warm waters. It thus provides Central Asian countries with the shortest route to international markets. And, as the most suitable transit country for Azeri oil exports to Europe, Iran is proving almost indispensable to the planners in Baku.

Tehran is currently more interested in integrating the economies of these six Muslim-majority states into its own than in aiding Islamic movements or groups in these countries. Tajikistan, the one republic that still has the potential for an Islamic movement, is closer to and more interlinked with Afghanistan than with Iran, even though its cultural ties with Iran are of long standing.

In a sense, Tehran and Ankara are more complementary than competitive – with Turkey concentrating more on developing the Black Sea Cooperation Council, which includes Azerbaijan, and Iran focusing on the Caspian Sea Cooperation Council – both of them being founder-members of the Economic Cooperation Organization, which in its enlarged form has admitted the Central Asian republics, Azerbaijan and Afghanistan. In the expanded ECO, Iran is offering geopolitical advantages to Central Asia and Azerbaijan, and Turkey economic and administrative expertise as well as Islamic education and training, both an amalgam of pan-Turkism and pan-Islamism together assisting the newly emergent Muslim-majority countries to move away from the legacy of the socialist red star and towards the green crescent (the official Turkish symbol, but in green, the colour of Islam).

But above and beyond the regional powers, Iran and Turkey, stands Russia. It is the leader of the CIS to which these countries, excepting Azerbaijan, belong. It has multilateral and bilateral cooperation treaties in culture, economics, military and security matters with these states. Russia, the Russian language, and the Russian minorities in these republics are important and will remain so. This is most obvious in Kazakhstan owing to the sheer size of its Slavic population. But even in Tajikistan, where, at about a quarter of a million, the Russian population is now less than five per cent of the total, Moscow has decided to take a strong stand in the context of its bilateral and multilateral military agreements with Dushanbe, and to safeguard the country from the advance of Islamists from adjoining Afghanistan: an enterprise in which it has the full backing of Washington. Kyrgyzstan is economically so weak that it continues to rely on hand-outs from Russia. For many years to come, Russian will continue to be the inter-ethnic language in all Central Asian republics – as well as the inter-state language in the region.

In any event, the legacy of seven decades, which brought to the region universal literacy and health care, full employment, women's emancipation, extensive transport and communications networks, advanced agricultural methods and industrialization, cannot be wiped clean within a matter of years. Despite the vast distance, physical and cultural, that separates India and Britain, it took the former British colony more than two decades to move from under the shadow of its ex-imperial master and find its own feet in the world community.

Present signs indicate that relations between Russia and its erstwhile partners in the USSR will follow the same path as those between the United States and the countries of Central and South America. Just as Washington, exercising its military and economic power now and in the past, treats the nations south of its border as virtual client states, Russia will do the same. Running individual Soviet republics from the centre for nearly three-quarters of a century has left Moscow with a leverage more powerful than that possessed by Washington vis-à-vis Latin American countries. Already an understanding seems to have been reached between the US and Russia that the disputes arising out of the break-up of the USSR should be kept out of the UN, giving Moscow the chance to act as the regional policeman. The repeated failure of the UN Security Council to act against Armenia for its flagrant aggression against Azerbaijan is a case in point.

In sum, Russia will continue to be a powerful force so far as Central Asia and Azerbaijan are concerned, with their Muslim neighbours to the south and west – Afghanistan, Iran and Turkey – finding that they can only increase their influence in these countries gradually, and that in the limited diplomatic space they have there is not much room for mutual antagonism and rivalry.

EPILOGUE

'No one and nothing can relieve Russia of its political and moral responsibility for the fate of the countries and peoples which for centuries went together with the Russian state.'

Boris Yeltsin, President of Russia, 28 June 1994[1]

The installation in June 1993 of Geidar Aliyev as acting President of Azerbaijan, with Colonel Suret Husseinov as prime minister, did little to improve the military capability of the republic, shaken by political upheavals and armed conflict. In early July the Armenians struck at Agdam, arguing that its surrounding hills were being used by the Azeris to rain artillery shells on Nagorno Karabakh, and captured it. Following this, there was a ceasefire. But, as before, it proved temporary. To demonstrate his fighting prowess, Husseinov ordered an offensive in mid-August to regain recently lost land. This provided the Armenians with a rationale to mount an ambitious campaign to seize the rest of south-western Azerbaijan.

After capturing Jebrail on 18 August, the Armenians besieged Fizuli, only 24 kms (15 miles) from the Iranian border. Baku protested at the Armenian conquest of undisputed Azeri territory. On 19 August at the UN Security Council its current president, Madeleine Albright of the United States, issued a statement demanding 'an immediate, full and unconditional withdrawal from the Fizuli district, Kelbajar, Agdam and other newly-occupied areas of Azerbaijan, and for an end to the supply of weapons'. But, despite the widely-known involvement of Armenia – which enabled 'volunteers' from among its nationals and the Armenian diaspora to attack Azerbaijan, and provided them with arms, ammunition, fuel and sanctuary – the Council once again failed to name Yerevan as the aggressor. Instead, it called on Armenia to use 'all its influence to secure a withdrawal'.[2]

The Azeri rout continued, with Fizuli falling to the Armenians on

23 August, followed by further withdrawals by Baku's forces. This gave the Armenians control of nearly twenty per cent of Azerbaijan - three-quarters of it outside Nagorno Karabakh - with an Azeri population of a quarter of a million, 100,000 of whom had fled and become refugees.

With Tehran facing the prospect of sheltering these refugees in a region where its own ethnic Azeris were predominant, it condemned the Armenian aggression against Azerbaijan. It was relieved when it was asked by Aliyev to help establish a refugee camp inside the republic near the Azeri-Iranian frontier after the border settlement of Goradiz had fallen in early September. By seeking Tehran's assistance on the eve of his visit to Moscow, Aliyev handed himself the 'Iran card', and then strengthened it by leaking to 'diplomatic circles' in Baku that he had promised a 20-km (13-mile) wide security zone for Iran inside Azerbaijan.[3] This was his ploy to extract concessions from the Kremlin, which detested the prospect of Iran gaining a foothold inside the frontiers of the former Soviet Union.

Russia was equally determined to keep Ankara out of the Azeri sphere, a far easier aim to achieve: Turkey lacked a common border with mainland Azerbaijan, and there was lack of trust between Ankara and Aliyev. Also by now even the most ardent pan-Turkists in Turkey had realized that Azerbaijan was too weak and corrupt to be backed. Having accepted the demise of its vision of a truly independent, pro-Ankara Azerbaijan, Turkey felt chastened.

In contrast the Armenian camp felt bullish. When a team of diplomats from fifteen member-states of the UN Security Council arrived in Baku to conduct talks in line with the Council statement, the Armenian delegation did not turn up for a meeting. The UN's failure, in the wake of the earlier collapse of CSCE efforts, to resolve the Azeri-Armenian conflict, which had so far claimed nearly 10,000 lives,[4] led the warring sides to look elsewhere: to Russia. The Azeri parliament authorized Aliyev to negotiate with Russia and Armenia to settle the Karabakh dispute. This came soon after a referendum on 29 August when 97 per cent of the voters expressed lack of confidence in the presidency of Elchibey, thus legitimizing Aliyev's position.

During his meeting in early September with Yeltsin, who had once been his colleague on the CPSU's Politburo, Aliyev asked for Russian involvement in settling the dispute. Yeltsin reportedly told him that was possible only if Azerbaijan rejoined the CIS, which would also benefit it economically by restoring raw-material supplies to its factories. Aliyev agreed.[5]

The fulsome coverage by the state-controlled Azeri media of Aliyev's visit to Moscow, especially his virtuoso performance at the Kremlin – where he had wielded power for sixteen years – re-established his reputation as a shrewd political operator among Azeris, who had been downhearted by a series of military defeats. Aliyev was thus assured of election as president on 3 October. In the event, he overdid the exercise, securing 98.8 per cent of the votes cast, with his two rivals picking up the niggardly rest.[6]

On 20 September the Azeri parliament voted to rejoin the CIS, ending not only the Baku–Moscow rift but also the geographical discontinuity of the CIS caused by Azerbaijan's withdrawal. All was set for Azerbaijan's attendance at the next CIS summit in Minsk on 24–25 September. But the venue was changed to Moscow when Yeltsin precipitated a crisis by dissolving the Congress of People's Deputies on 21 September, an action which was challenged by the CPD's chairman Ruslan Khasbulatov and Vice-President Alexander Rutskoi.

On the eve of the CIS summit, Aliyev signed a security pact with Russia, thus putting Azerbaijan on the same footing as Armenia. Following his meeting with Armenian President Petrossian, the ceasefire, which had been holding, was extended to 5 November. Earlier, Aliyev had recognized Russia's economic interests by suspending Baku's impending $7 bn agreement with a consortium of Western oil companies, which Elchibey had planned to sign on 30 June 1993 during his visit to London. In the re-negotiations that followed, the Russian state conglomerate, Lukoil, was included.

All in all, therefore, after a year of decline in its influence over Azerbaijan, Russia succeeded in re-integrating this Caucasian republic into its orbit by using militarily and political means. Indeed, Russia now recouped something that the CIS did not possess at its formation: Georgia. By military aiding the separatist rebels from the Abkhazian province, the Russian defence ministry enabled them to defeat the central government in Tbilisi led by Eduard Shevardnadze, thus raising the prospect of the republic's disintegration. To abort this prospect, during his visit to Moscow on 8 October Shevardnadze offered to take Georgia into the CIS.

By then Yeltsin had emerged as the undisputed ruler of Russia, thanks largely to the backing the Russian military gave him in crushing the revolt by parliament on 4 October, resulting in nearly 150 fatalities.

Reacting to a minor effort by the Azeris in the last week of October to regain their recently lost territory, the Armenians mounted a vigorous campaign which gave them complete control of south-western Azerbaijan, including the 100-km (60-mile) long border with Iran. Despite Azerbaijan's membership of the CIS and its mutual security pact with Russia, Moscow did nothing. This shocked Aliyev into rethinking his strategy. He devised a three-pronged plan to recover the lost Azeri land: build up the military, make use of Moscow's influence over Armenia without succumbing to its pressures to station Russian troops in Azerbaijan, and cultivate leading Western powers. As a start, in December he paid a visit to France, a bastion of pro-Armenian opinion.

In January 1994 the Azeri military, trained by instructors from Turkey, Iran, Russia and America, went on the offensive to regain the lost land. It succeeded in retaking villages in the plains, but, despite repeated attempts, failed to dislodge the Armenians entrenched in the surrounding mountains. With a death toll of 6–10,000, its human losses were high. Yet, during his visit to Ankara in February, Aliyev declared that Azerbaijan would fight on. He rejected Moscow's offer to post Russian troops along the Armenian front lines in Azerbaijan as peacekeepers, seeing in it a ploy to deploy Russian troops inside Azerbaijan, something Moscow had achieved in Armenia and Georgia through security pacts. None the less, thanks to mediation by Russia, a truce between the Azeris and Armenians went into effect on 1 March. At the CIS summit in mid-April, Moscow sought and won CIS endorsement for the use of Russian troops to separate Azeri and Armenian troops in Karabakh. Aliyev, who attended the summit, prevaricated, saying he was not yet ready to sign the order.

In early May the CIS-mediated talks between the two parties in Bishkek broke down when Azerbaijan refused to sign a peace accord, insisting that it would discuss the future of Karabakh only after the Armenians had evacuated the occupied Azeri land. Fighting in north-east Karabakh, which flared in late April, continued until mid-May when the defence ministers of Azerbaijan and Armenia, and the commander of Karabakh's army, met in Moscow to sign a truce. But the talks to build on the ceasefire collapsed amidst mutual accusations of bad faith. The truce held until late July when Azerbaijan and Karabakh signed an official ceasefire as a prelude to negotiating a political agreement. The talks between Azerbaijan and Armenia broke down in mid-August because of a disagreement on the composition of the peacekeeping forces, with Baku insisting that the Russians should not exceed 30 per cent of the total peacekeepers posted under CSCE aegis. Fresh efforts to bridge the differences were made in Moscow, with Aliyev and Petrossian meeting on 8 September. Among the major hurdles to an agreement was the Armenian refusal to vacate the Lachin corridor connecting Karabakh with Armenia.[7]

However, the numerous problems besetting Azerbaijan's talks with the Western oil consortium were finally overcome. On 20 September the State Oil Company of Azerbaijan Republic (SOCAR) signed a $7 bn deal to develop two offshore oilfields. It gave a 70 per cent stake to the Western oil consortium, 20 per cent to SOCAR, and the remainder to Lukoil, a Russian company. Lukoil was also granted a primary role in developing a third, adjacent oilfield.[8] Russia was able to extract this concession because, being landlocked, Azerbaijan could not export oil without its cooperation.

Moscow enjoyed a similar advantage in the case of petroleum exports from Kazakhstan, which had signed a contract with a Western consortium, led by Chevron, for its Tengiz oilfield. Russia used its ownership of the pipeline to its Black Sea port of Novorossiysk to demand 20 per cent of Kazakhstan's takings from its deal with Chevron. It also wanted priority for Russian petroleum companies in exploration and their admission into the consortium. In May 1994 Moscow cut off almost all of Kazakhstan's petroleum exports by blocking its only pipeline, thus causing a severe drop in its oil output.[9]

This was part of the Greater Russia policy, which included classifying former Soviet republics as 'Near Abroad', and which the Yeltsin government had adopted wholeheartedly following the success in December 1993 of the Liberal Democratic Party (LDP), led by Vladimir Zhirinovsky. After winning 25 per cent of the popular vote, the LDP emerged as the largest single group in parliament.[10] The ultra-nationalist LDP called for bringing back into Russia's orbit the republics in Central Asia, the Caucasus and the Baltics. It also demanded the protection of ethnic Russians living outside Russia. (Significantly, this concept was incorporated in the draft of the Russian military doctrine, which stated: 'It is our special mission to protect the rights and interests of Russian citizens and persons abroad connected with [Russia] ethnically and culturally'.[11]

Among other things, this encouraged the Russians living in Kazakhstan to protest against Kazakhization that had been in train since 1989: the growing role of the Kazakh language; increasing domination of Kazakhs in the political, economic and administrative spheres; pauperization of the Slavic-controlled enterprises and collective farms in the north to facilitate their privatization by Kazakhs; and manipulation of the parliamentary poll in March 1994 which had raised the Kazakh proportion far above their size of population.

The respective ethnic breakdown of the new parliament and the national population was: Kazakh 60 per cent (43 per cent); and Russian-Ukrainian 34 per cent (42 per cent). Because of the high proportion of children and adolescents among Kazakhs, their percentage among the voters was only about thirty. In other words, they had managed to secure twice as many parliamentary seats as their proportion among the electorate warranted. This was achieved by President Nursultan Nazarbayev issuing an electoral decree after the parliament had been dissolved in December 1993. Of the 176 seats, he allocated only 75 to public associations – i.e. political parties and mass movements – dividing the rest into the 'state list' of 42, nominated by him, and the 'general list' of 59, open to the electors contesting as individuals. In the last category, the local election commissions, composed of government officials, tried to dissuade potential opponents of the president from running. When this failed, the election commissions disqualified them arbitrarily. There were also instances where the male head of a household was allowed to vote for the whole family. The parties and individuals backing Nazarbayev were given maximum coverage by the state-run radio and television.[12] As a result, the pro-Nazarbayev parties, the Society for National Unity of Kazakhstan (SNUK) and the People's Congress Party of Kazakhstan (PCPK) won more than two-thirds of the seats on the party list. The pan-Turkic Azat Movement and Republican Party together secured only four seats – as few as the Republican Slavic Movement (RSM), which demanded dual nationality for the Slav settlers and protested against increasing discrimination against them in housing, education and government jobs.

Though the parties at the core of the Kazakh–Slav tension were virtually excluded from the parliament, relations between the two groups remained fraught. Pursuing its Greater Russia policy, Moscow pressured Nazarbayev to grant dual nationality to the Slav settlers, a demand which he resisted, arguing that such a step would divide the population between 'us' and 'them', and proposing instead easier naturalization laws in all CIS countries. On the other hand, realizing the handicap that Slav citizens, unfamiliar with Kazakh, suffered, he called on the newly-elected parliament to amend the language law. In order to reassure his Kazakh constituency that no territorial compromise was in the offing, he had the parliament pass a law in July 1994 to transfer the capital over the next six years from Alma Ata (now Almaty) in the extreme south-east to the north-central city of Akmola, capital of Akmola province with 58 per cent Slav population. By immediately moving his office to Akmola, he underlined his resolve to retain the Slav-majority northern provinces inside Kazakhstan.

The future of inter-ethnic relations depends partly on how the Kazakh economy fares in the medium term. The signs so far have been unpromising. When Alma Ata could not meet Moscow's strict conditions on continued membership of the rouble zone, it launched its own currency, tenge, in November 1993 at the official exchange rate of 4.5 tenges to 1 US dollar. Due to high inflation, running at 75 per cent in December, and the drop of 17 per cent in the GDP in 1993, the tenge lost nine-tenths of its value by mid-1994.

To counter the continuing decline, in January 1994 Nazarbayev entered into an economic union with Uzbekistan, starting with the abolition of customs duties. Three months later Kyrgyzstan joined the union. A summit meeting in July established committees to coordinate foreign and defence policies of the three member-states and standardize their laws.

As it was, the citizenship law of Uzbekistan was not dissimilar to that of Kazakhstan. It excluded dual nationality. Like his Kazakh counterpart, Uzbek president Islam Karimov had rejected Moscow's demand for dual citizenship, arguing that such a measure would create inequality between the native population of Uzbekistan and the ethnic groups having the nationality of two countries.[13] Like Kazakhstan, Uzbekistan had been forced to launch its own currency, sum, in November 1993.

Unlike his Kazakh and Kyrgyz counterparts, Karimov had continued his repression of opposition. Indeed, official harassment of Erk, deprived of its licence in late 1993, had increased, resulting in a split in the party in January 1994, with the breakaway faction, led by Shodi Karimov, calling itself Istiqlal Yoli (Independent Path), and promising 'positive' opposition by seeking consultation, not confrontation, with the government.

In the previous month, the Uzbek authorities had successfully prevented human rights activists from attending a regional conference on the subject in Bishkek, where a Congress of Non-Governmental Human Rights Organizations was founded under the leadership of Tursunbai Akhunov, a Kyrgyz. Bishkek thus continued to maintain its position as the freest Central Asian capital.

Yet fundamental freedoms were by no means fully secure in Kyrgyzstan. Nervous about the rising exodus of Russians, much valued for their technical and managerial expertise, and growing tension between Kyrgyzs and Slavs, President Askar Akayev, reputed to be committed to democracy, criticized the press for behaving irresponsibly, and called for a ban on the Russian-language *Svobodnie Gory* (Free Mountains).[14]

On the economic front, though, Akayev could rightly claim that inflation at 40 per cent a month in May 1993 – the date when the new currency, som, was introduced – was reduced to 5 per cent a month within a year due to the central bank's strict monetary policy. He could also claim that Kyrgyzstan was the only Central Asian republic to have effected the transition to the market economy in accordance with IMF and World Bank criteria.

But, as elsewhere in the world, following the IMF's strict prescriptions had created much popular resentment, and this was reflected in the disenchantment of law-makers with the regime. As a result, parliamentarians disregarded Akayev's proposal to give 'temporary' dual nationality to ethnic Slavs. More seriously, they came into conflict with the administration, which led to the dismissal of two cabinets in the first nine months of 1994 – a bad omen for foreign investors.

By contrast, Turkmenistan had proved to be extraordinarily stable. Its president, Saparmurad Niyazov, felt confident enough to end the monopoly of his Democrat Party by letting the Peasants' Party register in January 1994, even though it lacked the legal requirement of having a thousand members. Earlier, in December, he had signed an agreement with President Yeltsin permitting dual nationality for ethnic Russians in Turkmenistan, something that was allowed by the republic's constitution.[15]

Turkmenistan strengthened its links with Moscow without compromising its overall independence of action in foreign policy. In May 1994 it became the first Central Asian republic to be accepted by NATO in its Partnership for Peace programme. The next month Niyazov visited Ankara, which offered further credits to Turkmenistan for trade. In early July he acted as host to Israeli foreign minister Shimon Peres.

But all along Niyazov actively followed his policy of reinforcing ties with Tehran. Between January and August 1994 he visited Iran thrice, each time signing several cooperation agreements, capping these with his decision to go ahead with building a pipeline through Iran to supply gas to Europe. The project, worth $7 bn, with Iraq agreeing to meet half the cost of $3.5 bn for the pipeline in its territory, was expected to be finished by 2001. The committee dealing with the plan consisted not only of Turkmenistan and Iran but also Turkey, Russia and Kazakhstan. Ashqabat also discussed the possibility of combining the electrical grids of the two neighbours: Turkmenistan had electricity to spare, and Iran was deficient. By so doing Niyazov disregarded Washington's public warnings not to get too close to Iran. His confidence derived from the country's gas reserves, the fifth largest in the world. And his free hand in economic affairs allowed him to deal self-assuredly with Iran, Turkey, Russia, Israel and the West.

At the other end of the spectrum was Tajikistan. Dependent on Moscow for its economic survival and security, it could not act independently in its external or internal policies. An agreement signed in November 1993 between Tajikistan and Russia subordinated the former's finances to the latter's. As for security, there was an element of inter-dependence between Dushanbe and Moscow. 'If we remove Russian troops [from Tajikistan], then our next problem will be Uzbekistan,' said Captain Viktor Grankin, commander of Border Post 11 on the Tajik–Afghan frontier, in September. 'Next, the way we stand here, we would be standing at our own doorstep [in Russia].'[16]

Several months before the formal adoption of the Greater Russia policy by Moscow in January 1994, the events in Tajikistan had led President Yeltsin to assert Russian hegemony in the region. In mid-July an attack on Border Post 14 on the Tajik–Afghan frontier by Tajik Islamists operating from Afghanistan led to the deaths of twenty-five Russian border guards as well as scores of Tajik attackers. In retaliation, the Russians bombarded border villages in Afghanistan, killing more than a hundred people. Reflecting national outrage in Russia at the deaths of its border guards, Yeltsin asked:

'Why did we not have a plan to protect this border, which everyone must understand is effectively Russia's, not Tajikistan's, border?'[17] He reinforced the Russian presence along the Tajik–Afghan frontier, and pressured Tajikistan's Central Asian neighbours to send troops to safeguard what he called 'the CIS border', raising the total frontier guard force to some 15,000. Actually the military top brass in Moscow had taken to regarding the Tajik—Afghan frontier as an 'advance Russian base' to protect Russia from the infiltration of guns, narcotics and Islamic fundamentalism from Afghanistan much earlier. 'By guarding the Tajik section of the [CIS] border we defend the strategic backbone of Russia,' said Viktor Barranikov, the security minister. 'If we lost our [Central Asian] allies there, we will have to defend a [Russian] border which is far longer, absolutely transparent and most likely aggressive.'[18]

Among those who disagreed with the views of Barranikov and Yeltsin were senior foreign ministry officials. They remembered the eleven-year Soviet military involvement in Afghanistan, which *inter alia* cost 15,000 Soviet lives and billions of roubles. They advocated a political solution in Tajikistan which, they argued, lay with Dushanbe. After all, one-third of the electorate, which had voted for the candidate of the Democrat–Islamist alliance in the November 1991 presidential poll, could not be wished away. To pacify the foreign ministry, Yeltsin pressured the Tajik head of state, Imamali Rahmanov, to conciliate the regime's opponents. Rahmanov agreed to talk to 'responsible' elements within the opposition. But, given his administration's banning of important opposition parties, confirmed by the Supreme Court in June 1993, it was hard to see where such adversaries could be found.

It was not until early December that an official delegation from Dushanbe met the leadership of the Moscow-based Coordinating Council of the Democratic Forces (CCDF), which hitherto had questioned the legitimacy of the Rahmanov administration, based on the parliamentary elections held in March 1990, when Tajikistan was part of the former Soviet Union. (Unlike other Central Asian states, Tajikistan had not passed a new constitution, and continued to operate according to the one adopted in 1978). The dialogue between the two sides, resumed in Moscow in early April 1994, focused on hammering out an agenda, but failed. A fortnight later the government in Dushanbe published a draft of the new constitution which specified the executive presidency that had been abolished in December 1992. This was the background against which the opposing sides met in June in Tehran, the base of the Islamic Nationalist Movement (INM) of Tajikistan, led by Haji Akbar Turajanzade. The talks were also attended by Russia, Iran and Pakistan. The Tajik government demanded unilateral disarmament of the opposition; but the latter proposed bilateral disarmament under the joint supervision of the UN, CSCE, Russia, Iran, Afghanistan and Kazakhstan. It also specified the release of political prisoners, freedom of the press, and legalization of political parties as preconditions for a ceasefire. The government proposed a four-month timetable for freeing political prisoners and amnesty for opposition leaders. At home the Tajik administration, having adopted the new constitution, settled on late September as the date for presidential elections. This angered the opposition; and it decided to escalate its armed campaign inside Tajikistan. In late July there were large-scale clashes between rebels and government troops near Tavil Dara, east of Dushanbe, and in the Tajikabad and Garm Valley regions,[19] reviving memories of the 1992 civil war, whose death toll was now revised upwards to 60,000. When talks between the opposing sides resumed in Tehran, the Iranian government advised the Tajik Islamists to negotiate a ceasefire with the authorities in order to participate in the forthcoming polls. By postponing the presidential election from 27 September to 6 November, the Tajik parliament paved the way for an agreement. Signed on 18 September in Tehran by Turajanzade and Abdul Majid Dostiyev, deputy chairman of parliament, it specified a 'temporary' ceasefire until the holding of a referendum on the new constitution and an election for president, and supervision of a truce by the UN observers.[20]

In a general sense, the agreement stemmed from the conclusion that the warring parties had reluctantly reached: neither of them was strong enough to overpower the other. For the future, much would depend on the fairness of the polls, and whether or not the main loser accepted the results. No matter what the outcome of the electoral exercise, Badakhshan Autonomous Region would continue to be a stronghold of the Islamist–Democrat alliance. The Dushanbe government's campaign in early August 1993 to regain the region had failed. The oppositionists gathered there had consolidated their hold since the regional administration was sympathetic to their cause. Sharing its borders with the mountainous north Afghanistan, Badakshan remained inaccessible, and therefore difficult to pacify if the government in Dushanbe was politically at odds with the Badakshani populace.

★　　★　　★

Equally, in Afghanistan most of the country was outside the control of President Borhanuddin Rabbani. Even in the capital there was no unified authority. The duality of power, with Rabbani exercising control in central Kabul and Prime Minister Gulbuddin Hikmatyar in Charasyab, continued. Rabbani went on overseeing the defence ministry and Hikmatyar the interior. In the forty-member Constitutional Committee, composed of an equal number of the eight major Islamic parties, a controversy emerged on the question of allowing the Jaafri code of the Shia minority the same status as the Hanafi code of the Sunni majority in the constitution. Three of the Mujahedin parties, especially the Islamic Alliance led by Saudi-backed Abdul Rasul Sayyaf, opposed including the Jaafri code in the constitution, with the Wahadat insisting on it. As a result the Wahadat, headed by Abdul Ali Mazari and based in western Kabul, took to exchanging fire with the Islamic Alliance forces based elsewhere in the capital, causing more than 200 deaths by mid-October 1993 and throwing into disarray the timetable for elections following the adoption of the constitution. The fact that the Constitutional Committee lacked any representatives from the camp of General Abdul Rashid Dostum, the president of the 'Northern Alliance' of Afghanistan, was a source of potential crisis. The other troubling factor was the failure of Rabbani to reward Dostum for his assistance with the post of deputy defence minister, which led to intermittent fighting between the two sides in north Afghanistan from late September onwards.

Two months later there were clashes between Rabbani and Hikmatyar, in which Dostum remained neutral. When the battling sides suspended fighting in late December in order to replenish their ammunition stocks, Dostum attacked Rabbani's forces in central Kabul on 1 January 1994. Hikmatyar, entrenched in the south-eastern suburbs of Kabul, entered the fray on the side of Dostum, whom he had until then described as a foe. Deaths of 1400 people and injuries to 13,000 in the following two months illustrated the severity of the fighting.[21] More than a quarter of a million people were made homeless. Rabbani's term as president ended on 28 June, but he refused to step down. This gave further impetus to the civil war despite the fact that Hikmatyar's forces in Kabul's suburbs had been routed. Fighting also spread to such provincial centres as Doshi in Baghlan, and Herat.

Unlike in the past, the efforts of neither the regional powers nor the UN had any success in ending violence in Afghanistan. The various Afghan factions, originally fostered by foreign powers, had become autonomous. Now neither Saudi Arabia, nor Pakistan nor Iran had meaningful influence over its favoured group in Afghanistan. There was no concerted effort by the UN to bring peace to the war-ravaged country. This was so because both Russia and America were content to see Afghans continue their internecine violence. The alternative of a stable Islamic Afghanistan did not suit them, as they saw it actively aiding Islamic forces in Tajikistan.

Interestingly, addressing the foreign ministers of the ten-member Economic Cooperation Organisation (ECO), including Afghanistan, in Tehran in late January 1994 the Iranian president, Ali Akbar Hashemi Rafsanjani, urged his audience to distance themselves from the West as the US and Europe were 'uninterested in resolving conflicts in the new countries in the region which do not affect their interests, and might even encourage such conflicts'.[22]

Rafsanjani's audience included the foreign minister of Turkey, a country much chastened by the collapse of its plan to hold a pan-Turkic summit in Baku earlier in the month due to lack of interest. With Moscow forging ahead with the implementation of its Greater Russia policy as 1994 progressed – the appearance of Russian troops on the Turkish–Georgian and Turkish–Armenian borders, and the call in April by Russian defence minister General Pavel Grachev to CIS members to unite their forces (under Russian leadership) – the mood in Ankara had turned downbeat. Among other things this dampened Turkey's rivalry with Iran over gaining influence in Central Asia and Azerbaijan.

There was also a domestic reason for this change. The countrywide local elections in March revealed rising support for the pro-Islamic Welfare Party. By more than doubling its vote since the last such poll to 19 per cent, the Welfare Party now vied with the mainstream True Path (at 21.5 per cent) and Motherland (at 20 per cent). Its capture of the town halls in Ankara *and* Istanbul surprised many. Rising corruption of the ruling coalition partners was one reason for the Welfare's victory. Another factor was 100 per cent inflation. Still another was the secular government's failure to do anything about Azerbaijan and Bosnia. By concentrating on curbing corruption and improving local services, Welfare Party mayors will widen the popular base of their party. They will also control zealots within their ranks so as not to frighten the Westernized middle class, which has virtual monopoly over the media. If the two leading parties – the

True Path and Motherland – enjoying 40 per cent electoral support, were to combine, the status of the chief opposition, now resting with the Motherland, would pass to the Welfare. This would enhance its power to set the political agenda and polarize society into two opposing camps, secular and religious. The chances are that in the next general election, expected in 1995, the Welfare will emerge as the power-broker. Such a prospect has already resulted in Turkey improving its relations with Iran. In late July President Demirel signed a host of agreements in Tehran on transport, communications, energy and other economic fields, and reaffirmed continued cooperation on a crackdown on each other's opposition groups.[23]

This is not to the liking of Washington. But it and other Western capitals need to focus on devising an overall policy towards the Greater Russia doctrine, and the plans of Moscow to transform the unified CIS forces into a variant of NATO. So far the West has allowed Russia a free hand in acting as the Big Brother to stabilise the Caucasus and Central Asia on its terms partly because the West sees no threat to its direct interests, partly because it lacks expert knowledge of the region, and partly because its hands are full in tackling civil and other conflicts in the rest of the world. But the subsystems of the projected unified CIS military command – as outlined by Leonid Ivashov, secretary of the CIS defence ministers council – include not only (a) the Central Asian theatre controlled from Tashkent by the Uzbek president against the Tajik Islamic rebels from Afghanistan; (b) Kazakhstan and the Ural theatre under the Kazakh president against China; and (c) the Caucasus and north Caucasus theatre controlled from Rostov-on-Don by a Russian general against conflicts in the region; but also (d) the Belarus and Kaliningrad region under the Belarusian president against Germany.[24]

Thus the Greater Russian doctrine runs counter not only to genuine independence of the fledgling Central Asian and Caucasian states but also to the interests of such leading Western nations as Germany.

CHRONOLOGY: CENTRAL ASIA AND AZERBAIJAN

Before the Bolshevik revolution

1731–1854	Russia conquers the Kazakh/Kyrgyz steppes
1805	Russia conquers the Caucasus
1828	Border between Russia and Iran is delineated
1865–81	Russia completes its takeover of Central Asia, and names the region Turkestan
1883	Trans-Caucasian railway links Baku with Black Sea coast
1888–9	Trans-Caspian railway is extended to Samarkand and Tashkent
1901	Baku becomes the leading oil centre
1904	Socialist study circle is formed in Baku
1905	Constitutional reform in Russia Alliance of Muslims is founded in Nizhniy Novgorod (later Gorkiy)
1906	Rail link between Tashkent and Orenburg is established Alliance of Muslims is transformed into the Muslims Party Himmat Party is formed in Baku
1912	Himmat Party is banned; Musavat Party is established in Baku

1914	First World War erupts

1916	
July	Muslim insurrection in Turkestan is crushed

1917	
February	Abdication of Tsar Nicholas II. Provisional government of Alexander Kerensky is formed
April	Russian Social Democratic Labour Party declares right of self-determination for 'all nations forming Russia'
September	Second All Muslim Conference in Tashkent calls for autonomy of Turkestan within Russian Federation

The 1917 Bolshevik revolution and after

(Julian and Gregorian calendar dates stipulated until 1 February 1918)

1917	
24–25 October/ 7–8 November	Bolsheviks overthrow Kerensky government
1 November/ 14 November	Bolsheviks take over in Tashkent
15 November/ 28 November	Third All Muslim Conference in Tashkent demands autonomy for Turkestan and opposes the Bolshevik revolution
25 November/ 8 December	Fourth Regional Muslim Conference forms Kokand Autonomous Government in Kokand
3 December/ 16 December	Vladimir Lenin and Joseph Stalin declare religious and cultural freedom for all minorities
mid-December	Third All Kazakh National Congress forms Provisional People's Council of Alash Orda in Orenburg

1918

January	Turkmen Regional Congress forms a nationalist government in Ashqabat
February	Bolshevik forces defeat the Kokand Autonomous Government
March	Russian Bolshevik government moves from St Petersburg to Moscow
April	Turkestan Autonomous Soviet Socialist Republic is formed in Tashkent
May	Azeri members of the Trans-Caucasian Assembly declare independence of the Democratic Republic of Azerbaijan with Ganja as its capital
June	Kazakh Autonomous Region is established with Orenburg as its capital
October	First World War ends in victory for the Allies
November	First Congress of the Russian Party of Muslim Communists is held
	Azeri parliament is elected on the basis of universal suffrage for both sexes

1919

May	First Congress of Muslim Organizations in Tashkent demands formation of the Soviet Republic of United Turkestan including Turkic-populated parts of Russia and the Caucasus
July	Soviet forces capture Ashqabat
September	Second Congress of Muslim Organizations reiterates its demand for the formation of the Soviet Republic of United Turkestan
October	Moscow appoints the Commission for Turkestan

1920

January	Basmachi movement emerges in Central Asia
	Red Army marches into Khiva
April	Khiva is renamed Khorezm People's Soviet Republic

	With the Red Army poised along the DRA's border, the Azeri parliament hands over power to the Baku Bureau of the Caucasian Regional Committee of the RCP. The latter establishes Azerbaijan SSR
August	Following the Red Army's capture of the Kyrgyz-Kazakh region, Kyrgyz Autonomous Province is formed within the RSFSR
September	Following the Red Army's advance into Bukhara and the ruler's flight, the Bukhara People's Soviet Republic is constituted
	Azerbaijan SSR forms a military and economic union with the RSFSR
Autumn	Hand-over of Russian colonizers' land to local peasants in Central Asia begins

1921	Moscow ends 'war communism' and launches the New Economic Policy
	Turkmen language is created out of two tribal dialects, to be written in Arabic script
March	Treaty between Soviet Russia and Turkey specifies that Nakhichevan must remain part of Azerbaijan
July	The Caucasian Regional Committee of the RCP decides to keep the Armenian-majority Nagorno Karabakh enclave within Azerbaijan

1922	Kyrgyz to be written in Arabic alphabet
	Switch-over of Azeri from the Arabic script to Latin
March	Azerbaijan SSR joins Armenia SSR and Georgia SSR to form the Trans-Caucasian SFSR
May	Basmachi commander, Enver Pasha, gives ultimatum to Moscow to withdraw from Turkestan
August	Enver Pasha is killed in an ambush
December	Union of Soviet Socialist Republics is formed

1924

January	Lenin dies
October	First USSR constitution is proclaimed
	National delimitation creates Uzbek SSR
	(including Tajik ASSR) and Turkmen SSR – as
	well as Kara-Kyrgyz Autonomous Province and
	Kyrgyz Autonomous Province within the
	RSFSR. In May 1925 Kyrgyz Autonomous
	Province is given its ethnically correct name of
	Kazakh Autonomous Province

1925 Russian Communist Party is renamed the
Communist Party of the Soviet Union with
branches in the constituent SSRs except in the
RSFSR
Agrarian reform, including land ceilings, is
introduced, and literacy campaign is launched. State
takeover of religious trust properties

1926 Official end of the Basmachi rebellion in Tajikistan
First post-revolution census is conducted
First All Union Conference of Atheists is held
All Union socialist family code, giving *inter alia*
equality to men and women, is withdrawn from
Muslim-majority areas of the USSR after popular
protest

1927–8 Decrees abolishing polygamy, bride purchase, the
veil for women, and the Sharia and *Adat* courts
are issued at republican and regional levels
Voluntary collectivization of land is initiated (in
1927). Latin script for Kyrgyz is adopted (in 1928)

1929 Union-wide ban on Arabic alphabet
Latin script for Kazakh and Turkmen is adopted.
First Five Year Plan is launched

1930	Latin script for Tajik and Uzbek is adopted
	Five-year plan for compulsory collectivization of land and cattle is launched. The hardship and famine caused by the campaign reduce the populations of Kazakhs and Kyrgyzs by more than a third due to starvation and migration into the adjoining countries
1932	Launch of five-year anti-religious campaign, involving takeover of religious places by the Union of Atheists; and banning of hajj pilgrimage, religious taxes, the veil, printing and distribution of scriptures and religious education. Resulting protest is suppressed
1934	Collectivization of land and cattle is completed
1936	Kazakh ASSR and Kyrgyz ASSR are upgraded to SSRs
	Trans-Caucasian Soviet Federated Socialist Republic is broken up into Azerbaijani SSR, Armenian SSR and Georgian SSR
December	Second USSR constitution is promulgated
1937–8	Central Asian and Azerbaijani SSRs adopt their own republican constitutions
	Large-scale purges in the Communist Party and government in the USSR
	Russian is made compulsory in schools throughout the USSR (in 1938)
1939	Changeover from Latin script to Cyrillic for Azeri
	Census reveals literacy rates of seventy to eighty per cent in Central Asia and Azerbaijan
September	Second World War erupts

1940	Changeover from Latin to Cyrillic script for Kazakh, Kyrgyz, Tajik, Turkmen and Uzbek
1941	
June	With the German invasion of the USSR, the Great Patriotic War begins. Muslim-majority areas of the Soviet Union back the war effort
1942	All Union Islamic Conference in Ufa calls on Muslims at home and abroad to support the Allies Transfer of a few hundred industrial plants from the European war zones to Central Asia
1943	
September	Stalin allows the Russian Orthodox Church hierarchy to elect a new synod and patriarch
October	Stalin allows the establishment of the Official Islamic Administration with three regional directorates
1945	
May	Second World War/Great Patriotic War ends with Allied victory
1946	Post-war reconstruction begins
1948	
6 October	Earthquake in Turkmenistan destroys much of Ashqabat
1950–51	Small-scale purges in the party and government

1953

| March | Stalin dies |
| November/ December | Nikita Khrushchev unveils plan to increase output of food, meat, cotton and tobacco |

1954

| February | Communist parties of Kazakhstan and Kyrgyzstan back Khrushchev's Virgin Land programme |
| Winter | DeStalinization begins with low-key purges of diehard Stalinists |

1955 Khrushchev launches anti-religion drive, including an anti-veil campaign

1956 Purges of Stalinists are intensified. Tursunbai Ulaajabayev becomes First Secretary of the Tajik Communist Party, replacing Babajan Gafurov

| February | At the Twentieth CPSU congress, Khrushchev denounces Stalin for socialist illegality, personality cult and gross violations of Leninist nationality guidelines |
| October | Nuritdin Mukhitdinov, First Secretary of the Communist Party of Uzbekistan, urges party delegates to develop national culture |

1959 Sharaf Rashidov becomes First Secretary of the Communist Party of Uzbekistan. Balish Ovezov replaces Suhan Babayev as First Secretary of the Communist Party of Turkmenistan

Official end of veil-wearing for women in the USSR

1960 Dinmuhammad Kunayev becomes First Secretary of the Communist Party of Kazakhstan, and

Turdahun Usubaliyev First Secretary of the Communist Party of Kyrgyzstan

1961

September   Jabar Rasulov becomes First Secretary of the Tajik Communist Party

October   Khrushchev tells the Twenty-second CPSU Congress that during the current phase of 'mature socialism' in the USSR national relations would follow the path of 'blooming, rapprochement and amalgamation'

1963

February   Middle/Central Asian Economic region is formed

May/June   The Armenians of Nagorno Karabakh petition Moscow for incorporation into Armenia or Russian Federation. Anti-Armenian riots in Baku and Sumagit

December   Kunayev is replaced as the CPK's First Secretary by I. Yusupov

1964

October   Khrushchev is replaced by Leonid Brezhnev as First Secretary of the CPSU

December   Kunayev is elected the CPK's First Secretary Middle/Central Asian Economic region is disbanded

1966

March   At the Twenty-third CPSU congress Brezhnev downgrades Khrushchev's thesis on nationalities getting amalgamated, and promises 'solicitude' for all nationalities
                  Kunayev is elected a candidate member of the CPSU's Politburo

26 April	Earthquake in Uzbekistan destroys much of Tashkent
1967	530 miles of Karakum Canal completed in Karakum desert of Turkmenistan
1968	Founding of *The Muslims of the Soviet Union*, a magazine published in Uzbek, Arabic, Persian, English and French by the Muslim Spiritual Directorate of Central Asia Riots in Nagorno Karabakh's capital, Stepankert
1969	
February	Geidar Aliyev is elected First Secretary of the Communist Party of Azerbaijan
May	Anti-Russian demonstrations in Tashkent
1971	Kunayev is elected a full member of the twelve-strong CPSU Politburo Turkmenistan's gas production reaches seventeen billion cubic metres a year Muhammad Nazar Gapusov is elected First Secretary of the Communist Party of Turkmenistan
1973	Rahman Nabiyev becomes chairman of the Council of Ministers in Tajikistan
July	After overthrowing King Zahir Shah, his cousin Muhammad Daoud Khan declares Afghanistan a republic
1976	Aliyev is elected a candidate member of the CPSU's Politburo

1977

October — Third USSR constitution is adopted

1978 — Central Asian and Azerbaijani SSRs promulgate their own republican constitutions

April — Successful coup in Afghanistan by leftist military officers, most of them trained at Soviet military academies in Central Asia

1979 — An official Soviet survey shows fifty per cent of 'formerly Muslim peoples' describing themselves as 'unbelievers' and thirty per cent as 'believers'

An international symposium on the Soviet Muslims' contribution to Islamic thought is held in Dushanbe

February — Islamic revolution under the leadership of Ayatollah Ruhollah Khomeini triumphs in Iran

December — Soviet military intervention in Afghanistan with active involvement of units stationed in Central Asia

1981 — Addressing the Sixteenth Congress of the CPK, Kunayev states that Islam is gaining acceptance even among party members

1982

November — Aliyev is elected a full member of the CPSU's Politburo. Brezhnev dies. Yuri Andropov becomes First Secretary of the CPSU

1983 — Andropov launches a campaign against corruption and for improved labour productivity

October — Following Rashidov's death, Inamjan Usmankhojayev becomes First Secretary of the Communist Party of Uzbekistan

December	Geidar Aliyev is elected deputy chairman of the USSR Council of Ministers. He gives up his job as First Secretary of the CPA

1984

February	Andropov dies, and is succeeded by Konstantin Chernenko

1985

March	Chernenko dies, and is succeeded by Mikhail Gorbachev
October/ December	Absamat Musaliyev replaces Usubaliyev as the Party's First Secretary in Kyrgyzstan; Saparmurad Niyazov replaces Gapusov in Turkmenistan; and Kakhar Mahkamov replaces Nabiyev in Tajikistan

1986

January	At the CPU congress in Tashkent, ten of the twelve members of the Politburo are replaced
February	At the Twenty-seventh CPSU congress, Gorbachev launches glasnost and perestroika, and intensifies earlier anti-corruption drive
December	Kunayev is replaced as First Secretary of the CPK by Gennadi Kolbin, an ethnic Russian. Suppression of protest demonstrations results in between two and twenty deaths and injuries to over 2200

1987

	Final report on corruption in Uzbekistan reveals loss of $2 billion to the public treasury over twenty-four years owing to doctored cotton output figures, involving 2600 officials
August	A survey in Tajikistan shows forty-five per cent of 'formerly Muslim peoples' describing

	themselves as 'believers', the highest figure yet anywhere in the USSR during the Soviet era
September	Aliyev loses his membership of the CPSU Politburo
November	Abel Aghanbegian, Gorbachev's chief economic adviser, recommends return of Nagorno Karabakh to Armenia

1988	Celebrations of a millennium of Christianity in Russia
	A survey of Tashkent University undergraduates shows sixty per cent describing themselves as 'Muslim' and only seven per cent as 'atheist'
January	Rafiq Nishanov replaces Usmankhojayev as First Secretary of the Communist Party of Uzbekistan
February	Gorbachev signs an agreement with Kabul to withdraw all 115,000 Soviet troops from Afghanistan within a year
	Nagorno Karabakh Soviet demands transfer of enclave to Armenia
	Demonstrations in Yerevan trigger two-day anti-Armenian riots in Baku and Sumagit in which between twenty-six and 300 lives are lost
June	Tajiks in Samarkand and Bukhara demonstrate for the incorporation of the cities into Tajikistan
	Purges in the Communist Party of Uzbekistan affect 58,000 members
October	Gorbachev is elected chairman of the Presidium of the USSR Supreme Soviet
7 December	Earthquake in Armenia

1989	
January	USSR Supreme Soviet Presidium makes Nagorno Karabakh a centrally administered area
	Demonstration against Mufti Shamsuddin Babakhan in Tashkent leads to his resignation as head of the regional Muslim Spiritual Directorate

March	Muhammad Sadiq Muhammad Yusuf is elected head of the regional Muslim Spiritual Directorate in Tashkent
	Elections are held for the 2250-member USSR Congress of People's Deputies
May	The Birlik Popular Front is founded in Tashkent
June/July	Nursultan Nazarbayev replaces Kolbin as First Secretary of the Communist Party of Kazakhstan
	Rioting between Uzbeks and Meskhetian Turks in Uzbekistan's Fergana Valley leaves 200 dead
	Islam Karimov replaces Nishanov as First Secretary of the CPU
September	Azeri Popular Front paralyses Baku with a general strike
October	New constitution of Azerbaijan reiterates its right to secede from the USSR if so decided by a referendum
November	USSR Supreme Soviet Presidium ends centrally administered status of Nagorno Karabakh
	Kyrgyzstan Supreme Soviet declares Kyrgyz as the official language to be so adopted over eight years
December	Muslim Congress in Alma Ata secedes from the regional Muslim Spiritual Directorate in Tashkent, and elects Radbek Nisanbayev as its mufti

1990

January	Anti-Armenian riots in Baku and Sumagit. Popular Front combines its demand for the resignation of the Communist government with a call for a general strike. Moscow sends troops and tanks to Baku to restore order; 131 people are killed.
February	Ayaz Mutalibov replaces Abdul Rahman Vazirov as First Secretary of the Communist Party of Azerbaijan
	Disregarding the July 1921 document, placing Nagorno Karabakh under Azeri jurisdiction, Armenia demands return of the enclave

Riots triggered in Dushanbe by news of housing given to refugees from the anti-Armenian riots in Baku turn anti-European. Before security forces restore order eighteen people are killed

March

USSR Supreme Soviet amends the 1977 constitution to create a new post of executive president, and elects Gorbachev to that position

In republican Supreme Soviet elections Communists win eighty-five per cent of 350 seats in Kyrgyzstan, ninety per cent of 500 seats in Uzbekistan, ninety-three per cent of 310 seats in Tajikistan, ninety-four per cent of 360 places in Kazakhstan, and almost all 330 seats in Turkmenistan

April

Democratic Party of Erk is founded in Uzbekistan

May

Democratic Kyrgyzstan Movement is formed in Bishkek

June

Boris Yeltsin is elected chairman of the 1041-member Supreme Soviet of the Russian Federation

Kyrgyz–Uzbek rioting in Osh leaves 300 dead

Supreme Soviet in Uzbekistan declares Uzbek as the official language, to be so adopted in seven years

Islamic Republican Party is established as an All-Union organization at its founding convention in Astrakhan, Russia

Russian Supreme Soviet declares superiority of Russian laws to Soviet laws

July

Islamic Republican Party becomes (surreptitiously) active in Tajikistan and Uzbekistan

At the Twenty-eighth CPSU congress Yeltsin resigns his membership of the CPSU

August

The Turkmen Supreme Soviet declares superiority of Turkmen laws to Soviet laws

September

In Azeri Supreme Soviet elections the Communists gain ninety-one per cent of 360 seats. The Popular Front boycotts the poll

The Kazakh Supreme Soviet declares the superiority of Kazakh laws to Soviet laws. It makes Kazakh the official language, to be so adopted over the next five years

October	Turkmenistan becomes the first Soviet republic to hold a popular election for the executive presidency. Niyazov, the sole candidate, wins with a 98.3 per cent vote
	The Uzbek Supreme Soviet declares the superiority of Uzbek laws over Soviet laws
	After amending the republican constitution the Uzbek Supreme Soviet elects Karimov executive president
November	The Kyrgyz Supreme Soviet deputies elect Askar Akayev executive president. Musaliyev becomes First Secretary of the Communist Party of Kyrgyzstan

1991

March	All Union referendum on renewed federation of Soviet states is boycotted by Armenia, the Baltic states, Georgia and Moldova. Of those participating, two-thirds vote Yes
May	Democratic Congress of Central Asia and Kazakhstan is formed in Bishkek
June	Yeltsin wins popular presidential election in the Russian Federation
19–21 August	Coup by conservative centralists, including five of the eight-member USSR Security Council, against Gorbachev fails. Russian Supreme Soviet and President Yeltsin oppose the coup.
	Nazarbayev and Akayev oppose the coup; Niyazov remains neutral; Karimov changes his mind swiftly after supporting the coup initially; Mutalibov says his informal remarks about the coup (passed during his visit to Tehran) had been misunderstood as support for it; and Nabiyev denies the charge that he had backed the coup surreptitiously
23–31 August	Yeltsin suspends the CPSU within the Russian Federation
	Karimov challenges Yeltsin's right to do so
	Nazarbayev resigns from the Communist Party

Akayev resigns from the Party, and suspends it in Kyrgyzstan

The Supreme Soviets in Tajikistan, Turkmenistan, Azerbaijan, Kyrgyzstan and Uzbekistan declare their respective countries independent states

The Baltic states of Estonia, Latvia and Lithuania are recognized as independent countries by the West

September
In a popular presidential poll in Azerbaijan, Mutalibov, the sole candidate, wins ninety-eight per cent of the vote

In Tajikistan the Supreme Soviet replaces its chairman, Kadriddin Aslonov, with Nabiyev, after refusing to pass his proposal to ban the Communist Party. Nabiyev grants the IRP legal status

The Communist Party of Azerbaijan dissolves itself

Following its dissolution the Communist Party of Uzbekistan re-emerges as the People's Democratic Party

A non-stop anti-government demonstration and sit-ins start in Dushanbe

Azerbaijan and Armenia agree a ceasefire until 1 January 1992

October
Under popular pressure the Tajik Supreme Soviet bans the Communist Party of Tajikistan, and introduces a popularly elected executive presidency

In a popular presidential poll in Kyrgyzstan, Akayev, the sole candidate, wins 98.5 per cent of the vote

Following dissolution of the Communist Party of Kazakhstan, the Socialist Party of Kazakhstan is formed

November
In a Tajik presidential poll, Nabiyev wins fifty-seven per cent of the vote, and Davlat Khudanazarov, backed by Islamists and Democrats, thirty-four per cent

1 December
In a Kazakh presidential poll, Nazarbayev, the sole candidate, gains ninety-eight per cent of the vote

Ukrainian voters opt for independence, thus dashing Gorbachev's plans for a new federation of sovereign states

8 December	Russia, Ukraine and Belarus decide to form the Commonwealth of Independent States
13 December	Five Central Asian republics decide to join the CIS
16 December	The Kazakh Supreme Soviet declares Kazakhstan independent
	Turkey recognizes all five Central Asian republics and Azerbaijan
20 December	Following dissolution of the Communist Party of Turkmenistan, the Democratic Party of Turkmenistan is formed
	President Karimov visits Ankara
21 December	Leaders of all Soviet republics, except Georgia, form the eleven-member CIS at a meeting in Tashkent
29 December	In an Uzbek presidential poll, Karimov wins eighty-six per cent of the vote, and his rival, Muhammad Salih, thirteen per cent
31 December	The USSR officially ends, with its permanent seat at the United Nations Security Council going to the Russian Federation

The post-Soviet era

1992

February	A preliminary meeting of the Black Sea Cooperation Council, including Azerbaijan, is held in Ankara
	A meeting of the expanded Economic Cooperation Organization (consisting of Pakistan, Iran and Turkey), including Azerbaijan, Turkmenistan, Uzbekistan, Tajikistan and Kyrgyzstan, is held in Tehran
	Under popular pressure President Mutalibov replaces the Azeri Supreme Soviet with a fifty-member National Council composed equally of pro-PF democrats and former Communists
March	Mutalibov resigns following Azeri military defeats in Nagorno Karabakh and a massacre of Azeris

	in Hojali. Yakub Mahmedov is elected acting president by the Supreme Soviet
	Congress of the Supporters of Turkestan is held in Tashkent
	Arrests of Islamic leaders on eve of Karimov's visit to Namangan
April	Gorno-Badakhshan Autonomous Region parliament declares the territory Pamir-Badakhshan Autonomous Republic, and backs the opposition in Dushanbe
	Islamic Mujahedin forces win in the civil war in Afghanistan
	During his visit to Saudi Arabia, President Niyazov undertakes short pilgrimage to Mecca
	Iran offers Turkmenistan $50 million aid
	The Turkish premier, Suleiman Demirel, offers $1,200 million aid during tour of Central Asian republics (except Tajikistan) and Azerbaijan
May	Caspian Sea Cooperation Council is established in Tehran
	During his visit to Saudi Arabia, President Karimov undertakes short pilgrimage to Mecca
11 May	After fifty-one days of protest, the Tajik opposition allows Nabiyev to stay as president, and secures eight out of twenty-four cabinet seats
14 May	Mutalibov, re-installed as president by the Azeri Supreme Soviet, fails to consolidate his power and flees to Moscow. Isa Gambarov becomes acting president
15 May	At a CIS summit in Tashkent a Collective Defence Treaty is signed by Russia, Armenia and the Central Asian countries excepting Turkmenistan
18 May	A new Turkmen constitution is ratified by a referendum
23 May	Kazakhstan agrees to despatch its tactical nuclear weapons to Russia
25 May	Kazakhstan and Russia sign a treaty of friendship and cooperation
28 May	The Azeri government celebrates the seventy-fourth anniversary of the Democratic Republic of Azerbaijan

June	Work on a rail link between Iran and Turkmenistan starts
	Uzbekistan and Russia sign a treaty of political, economic and cultural cooperation, followed by a similar treaty on military and security matters two months later
7 June	The Popular Front leader, Abulfaz Elchibey, wins the Azeri presidential election, obtaining fifty-nine per cent of the vote, and Nizami Suleimanov, an independent, thirty per cent
8 June	A three-year military cooperation agreement between Turkmenistan and Russia is signed
17 June	Turkmenistan joins the Islamic Conference Organization
21 June	Niyazov is re-elected president of Turkmenistan under a new constitution, winning 99.5 per cent of the vote
July	Nabiyev of Tajikistan signs cooperation protocols with Iran in Tehran
August	Niyazov signs cooperation protocols with Iran in Tehran
September	Iran gives $40 million worth of free oil to Tajikistan
2 September	Under pressure the Tajik Supreme Soviet presidium states that President Nabiyev had been removed from power owing to his failure to solve the country's political crisis
3 September	The presidents of Kazakhstan, Kyrgyzstan and Uzbekistan warn that civil war in Tajikistan is a danger to the CIS
7 September	Nabiyev hands over power to Supreme Soviet chairman Akbarsho Iskanderov and flees to Hojand
October	Azerbaijan withdraws from the CIS
	First World Congress of Kazakhs is held in Alma Ata
9 October	A CIS summit in Bishkek decides on a peace-keeping mission in the Tajik civil war and wants CIS/Russian troops to remain in Tajikistan
23–26 October	Pro-Communist forces fail to retain strategic buildings in Dushanbe, and retreat. Total fatalities in the Tajik civil war put at 18,500

29 October	Summit of Central Asian countries (except Tajikistan) and Azerbaijan in Ankara is hosted by Turkey
November	Nazarbayev and Karimov in Tehran sign cooperation agreements
4 November	Leaders of Kazakhstan, Kyrgyzstan, Uzbekistan and Russia meeting in Alma Ata send a peace-making committee to Tajikistan
10 November	Tajik cabinet and Supreme Soviet presidium resign
16–23 November	Iskanderov resigns as chairman of the Supreme Soviet and acting president. The Supreme Soviet elects Imamali Rahmanov as chairman. Following Nabiyev's (proper) resignation as executive president, the Supreme Soviet abolishes 'presidential rule' and declares Tajikistan a 'parliamentary republic'
December	The Democratic Congress of Central Asia and Kazakhstan holds second conference in Bishkek
4–13 December	Pro-Communist forces attack Dushanbe, and capture it after fierce fighting. Civil war ends, with estimated death toll of 20,000–30,000, mainly civilians; 537,000 Tajiks become refugees
8–10 December	Following promulgation of a new constitution in Uzbekistan, the Supreme Soviet revokes the registration of Birlik as a public movement

1993

3–4 January	Summit of Central Asian countries in Tashkent discusses Central Asian common market
23 January	Four out of five Central Asian members sign the CIS charter at the CIS summit in Minsk. Turkmenistan signs another generally worded document that allows it to stay in the CIS
28 January	The Kazakh Supreme Soviet ratifies a new constitution
April	Following a two-week offensive in mid-March, the Armenians set up a second corridor through Azeri territory to link Nagorno Karabakh with Armenia. Elchibey declares state of emergency

	300 to 1500 murders of opposition supporters in Dushanbe. Badakhshan Region's population swells to 500,000 from 200,000
May	Kyrgyzstan's new constitution, adopted by the Supreme Soviet, renames the country as the Kyrgyz Republic
June	The rebel forces of Colonel Suret Husseinov advance from Ganja to Baku
	President Elchibey flees to his home town in the Nakhichevan enclave. The Supreme Soviet elects Geidar Aliyev acting president; he appoints Husseinov prime minister
	The Tajik Supreme Court upholds a government ban on opposition parties
	Tajikistan signs a bilateral treaty with Russia on political, economic, security and military cooperation

ETHNIC COMPOSITION OF CENTRAL ASIA AND AZERBAIJAN, 1989*

Figures in thousands

	Azerbaijan	Kazakhstan	Kyrgyzstan	Tajikistan	Turkmenistan	Uzbekistan
Total Population	7,005	16,464	4,258	5,092	3,552	19,810
Armenians	391 (5.6%)	–	–	–	–	–
Azeris	5,806 (82.9%)	–	–	–	–	–
Kazakhs	–	6,535 (39.7%)	–	–	88 (2.5%)	808 (4.1%)
Kyrgyz	–	–	2,230 (52.4%)	–	–	–
Russians and Other Europeans	423 (6.0%)	8,263 (50.2%)	1,126 (26.4%)	412 (8.1%)	370 (10.4%)	2,204 (11.1%)
Tajiks	–	–	–	3,172 (62.3%)	–	934 (4.7%)
Turkmens	–	–	–	–	2,536 (71.4%)	–
Uzbeks	–	332 (2.0%)	550 (12.9%)	1,198 (23.5%)	317 (8.9%)	14,142 (71.4%)
Others†	385 (5.5%)	1,334 (8.1%)	352 (8.3%)	310 (6.1%)	241 (6.8%)	1,722 (8.7%)

* Source: *Vestinik Statistiki* 11 and 12, 1990; 4, 5 and 6, 1991
† Mostly non-Europeans

SELECT BIBLIOGRAPHY

Abrahamian, Ervand, *Iran Between Two Revolutions*, Princeton University Press, Princeton, NJ, and Guildford, 1982

Akchurin, Marat, *Red Odyssey: A Journey Through the Soviet Republics*, Secker and Warburg, London, and HarperCollins, New York, 1992

Akiner, Shirin, *Islamic Peoples of the Soviet Union*, Kegan Paul International, London and Boston, 1983

Allworth, Edward, *Central Asia: A Century of Russian Rule*, Columbia University Press, New York and London, 1967

Arnold, Anthony, *Afghanistan: The Soviet Invasion in Perspective*, Hoover Institution Press, Stanford, Ca, 1985

Benningsen, Alexandre and Broxup, Marie, *The Islamic Threat to the Soviet State*, Croom Helm, London and Canberra, 1983

Benningsen, Alexandre and Lemercier-Quelquejay, Chantal, *Islam in the Soviet Union*, Columbia University Press, New York and London, 1967

Caroe, Olaf, *The Soviet Empire: The Turks of Central Asia and Stalinism*, Macmillan, London, and St Martin's Press, New York, 1953

Crawshaw, Steve, *Goodbye to the USSR: The Collapse of Soviet Power*, Bloomsbury, London, 1992

Critchlow, James, *Nationalism in Uzbekistan: A Soviet Republic's Road to Sovereignty*, Westview Press, Boulder, Col, and Oxford, 1992

d'Encausse, Hélène Carrère, *The Great Challenge: Nationalities and the Bolshevik State 1917–1930*, Holmes & Meier, New York and London, 1992

Fierman, William (ed.), *Soviet Central Asia: The Failed Transformation*, Westview Press, Boulder, Col, and Oxford, 1992

Gorbachev, Mikhail, *Perestroika: New Thinking for Our Country and the World*, Fontana, London, 1988

Great Soviet Encyclopedia, Vols 1 to 26, Third Edition, Macmillan, New York, and Collier Macmillan, London, 1973 to 1981

Great Soviet Encyclopedia (in Russian), Fourth Edition, Moscow, 1989

Haji-Zadeh, A., *Soviet Azerbaijan*, Progress Publishers, Moscow, 1965

Hiro, Dilip, *Iran Under the Ayatollahs*, Routledge and Kegan Paul, London and Boston, Mass, 1985

——, *Islamic Fundamentalism/Holy Wars: The Rise of Islamic Fundamentalism*, Paladin, London/Routledge, New York, 1989

Hyman, Anthony, *Afghanistan under Soviet Domination, 1964–83*, Macmillan, London, 1984

Karimov, I. A., *Uzbekistan: Its Own Road to Renewal and Progress* (in Russian), Izdatyelsto Uzbekistan, Tashkent, 1992

Kaushik, Devendra, *Central Asia in Modern Times: A History from the Early 19th Century*, Progress Publishers, Moscow, 1970

Kazemzadeh, Firuz, *The Struggle for Transcaucasia (1917–1921)*, Philosophical Library, New York, 1951

Keddie, Nikki R., *Roots of Revolution: an Interpretative History of Modern Iran*, Yale University Press, Yale, Ct, and London, 1981

Kolarz, Walter, *Russia and Her Colonies*, Frederick A. Praeger, New York, 1952

Lewis, Bernard, *The Emergence of Modern Turkey*, Oxford University Press, Oxford and New York, 1961

Lewis, Richard A. (ed.), *Geographic Perspectives on Soviet Central Asia*, Routledge, London and New York, 1992

Mortimer, Edward, *Faith and Power: The Politics of Islam*, Faber, London, 1982

Nahaylo, Bohdan and Swoboda, Victor, *Soviet Disunion: A History of the Nationalities Problem in the USSR*, Hamish Hamilton, London, 1990

Olcott, Martha Brill, *The Kazakhs*, Hoover Institution Press, Stanford, Ca, 1987

Park, Alexander G., *Bolshevism in Turkestan 1917–1927*, Columbia University Press, New York, 1957

Piscatori, James P. (ed.), *Islam in the Political Process*, Cambridge University Press, Cambridge and New York, 1982

Rakowska-Harmstone, Teresa, *Russia and Nationalism in Central Asia: The Case of Tadzhikistan*, Johns Hopkins University, Baltimore, Md, and London, 1970

Roy, Olivier, *Islam and Resistance in Afghanistan*, Cambridge University Press, Cambridge and New York, 1986

Safarov, Georgy I., *The Colonial Revolution (The Case of Turkestan)*, Society for Central Asian Studies, Oxford, 1985

Taheri, Amir, *Crescent in a Red Sky: The Future of Islam in the Soviet Union*, Hutchinson, London, 1989

Walker, Christopher J., *Armenia and Karabagh: The Struggle for Unity*, Minority Rights Publications, London, 1991

Wheeler, Geoffrey, *The Modern History of Soviet Central Asia*, Weidenfeld and Nicolson, London, 1964

Yazkuliyev, Bally, *Turkmenia*, Novosti Press Publishing House, Moscow, 1987

NEWSPAPERS AND PERIODICALS

Ashqabat Vecherni (Ashqabat)
Azat (Alma Ata)
BBC World Service: Central Asia Report Digest (London)
BBC Summary of World Broadcasts (Reading)
Central Asia and Caucasus in World Affairs Newsletter (Hastings)
Central Asia Monitor (Amherst)
Central Asia Newsfile (London)

Daily Telegraph (London)
Echo of Iran (Tehran)
The Economist (London)
Far Eastern Economic Review (Hong Kong)
Financial Times (London and New York)
Foreign Broadcast Information Service (Washington)
Guardian (London)
In These Times (Chicago)
Independent (London)
Independent Magazine (London)
Islam i Natsiya (Moscow)
Islam i Obshchestvo (Moscow)
Izvestia (Moscow)
Kabul New Times (Kabul)
Kommunist Uzbekistana (Tashkent)
Krasnaya Zvezda (Moscow)
Literaturnaya Gazeta (Moscow)
Mainstream (New Delhi)
MERIP Middle East Report (Washington)
The Middle East (London)
Middle East International (London)
Moscow News (Moscow)
Nation (New York)
Nauka i Religia (Moscow)
New York Times (New York)
Observer (London)
Pravda (Moscow)
Pravda Vostoka (Tashkent)
Radio Free Europe Daily Report (Munich)
Radio Liberty Report on the USSR (Hamburg)
Slovo Kyrgyzstan (Bishkek)
Sunday Times (London)
Tehran Times (Tehran)
The Times (London)
Trud (Moscow)
Turkish Daily News (Ankara)
Turkmeniskaya Iskra (Ashqabat)
Uzbekistan Adabiyati va Sanaati (Tashkent)
Wall Street Journal (New York and Brussels)

NOTES

Introduction

1. This meant one mosque for every 700 Muslims compared to one church for every 11,000 Christians. V. Monteil, *Les Mussulmans Soviétiques*, Paris, 1982, p. 21.

2. Vasiliy V. Barthold, *Istoriya Kulaturnoy Zhizni Turkestan* (History of the Civilization of Turkestan), Leningradski Institute Zhivykh Vostochnykh Iazykov, Leningrad, 1927, p. 78.

3. By 1916 there were 5000 reformed schools in the Muslim-populated parts of the Tsarist empire.

4. The only non-Tatar member was Ali Mardan Topchibashev, an Azeri newspaper baron based in Baku.

5. Cited in Alexandre A. Benningsen and Chantal Lemercier-Quelquejay, *Islam in the Soviet Union*, Columbia University Press, New York and London, 1967, pp. 41–42.

6. Sunni means one who follows *sunna*, custom. Sunnis are the majority sect in Islam; and Shias – derivative of Shiat Ali, Partisans of Ali – are a minority. See further Dilip Hiro, *Islamic Fundamentalism/Holy Wars: The Rise of Islamic Fundamentalism*, Paladin, London/ Routledge, New York, 1989, pp. 17– 24.

7. The decree would have applied to 120,000 men in the area now comprising Uzbekistan. *Great Soviet Encyclopedia*, Vol. 26, Macmillan, New York, and Collier Macmillan, London, 1981, p. 658.

8. Firuz Kazemzadeh, *The Struggle for Transcaucasia (1917–1921)*, Philosophical Library, New York, 1951, pp. 15–16.

9. A. Haji-Zadeh, *Soviet Azerbaijan*, Progress Publishers, Moscow, 1965, p. 40.

10. Cited in Kazemzadeh, op. cit., p. 16.

11. Hence the 'Great October Revolution' came to be celebrated on 7 November in the Soviet Union.

12. This was to reflect the backing that Muslim peasants and workers, mainly in the construction and leather industries, organized under the Unions of the Toiling Muslims, had provided to the Soviets in Tashkent, Samarkand and the Fergana Valley, leading finally to the creation of the Soviet of Muslim Workers' and Soldiers' Deputies. See Alexander G. Park, *Bolshevism in Turkestan 1917–1927*, Columbia University Press, New York, 1957, p. 19.

13. Though the term 'Sart' meant 'trader', it was used to describe all those settled in valleys and oases. Thus 'Kyrgyz and Sarts of Siberia and of Turkestan' covered both the nomadic and settled inhabitants of these regions.

14. V. I. Lenin, *Collected Works*, Vol. VI, Progress Publishers, Moscow, 1962, p. 213.

15. Georgy I. Safarov, *The Colonial Revolution (The Case of Turkestan)*, Society for Central Asian Studies, Oxford, 1985, pp. 121–2.

16. The Commissariat of Nationalities consisted of eight sections, including one for Muslims.

17. Until the mid-1920s the Bolsheviks continued the Tsarist practice of calling Kazhaks Kyrgyz, and Kyrgyz Kara-Kyrgyz.

18. Geoffrey Wheeler, *The Modern History of Soviet Central Asia*, Weidenfeld and Nicolson, London, 1964, p. 135.

19. *Great Soviet Encyclopedia*, Vol. 26, Third Edition, Macmillan, New York, and Collier Macmillan, London, 1981, pp. 659–60.

20. By late 1922 the sole source of armed resistance to Soviet rule in the region was Qurban Muhammad, a Turkmen leader. After he had been overthrown as the self-declared Khan of independent Khiva by the Red Army in 1920, he proclaimed himself the Khan of Karakum (literally Black Sands) in Trans-Caspia, and kept on fighting the Soviets until 1928.

21. Cited in Alexander G. Park, op. cit., pp. 77 and 81.

22. This figure excluded the population of the Leninabad Province, then estimatedly 350,000, which was to be transferred from the Uzbek SSR to the Tajik SSR in October 1929. Teresa Rakowska-Harmstone, *Russia and Nationalism in Central Asia: The Case of Tadzhikistan*, Johns Hopkins University, Baltimore, Md, and London, 1970, p. 48. In 1925 the Pamir region gained formal autonomy as the Gorno-Badakhshan Autonomous Province.

23. V. I. Lenin, *Collected Works*, Vol. 26, Progress Publishers, Moscow, 1965, p. 175.

24. J. V. Stalin, *Collected Works*, Vol. II, Progress Publishers, Moscow, 1946, p. 296. Among others, pan-Turkists found this definition deficient since it did not take into account the reality of a single nation living in different territories.

25. In another sense this was seen as compensation to Tajikistan for its loss of the Tajik cultural centres of Samarkand and Bukhara to the Uzbek SSR.

26. Rakowska-Harmstone, op. cit., p. 34.

27. Park, op. cit, p. 247. Judged by the Stalinist criteria of a 'nation', only a certain proportion of the 123 nationalities in the USSR qualified as nations.

28. See Alexandre A. Benningsen and Marie Broxup, *The Islamic Threat to the Soviet State*, Croom Helm, London and Canberra, 1983, p. 48.

29. What sustained this anomaly was the fact that seventy-two per cent of the party members in 1922 were Russians then forming 52.9 per cent of the population of the USSR. Five years later their party membership percentage fell to sixty-five. Hélène Carrère d'Encausse, *The Great Challenge: Nationalities and the Bolshevik State 1917–1930*, Holmes & Meier, New York and London, 1992, p. 153.

30. Rakowska-Harmstone, op. cit., p. 40. The purge of the 'bourgeois nationalists' that followed the second congress of the party in January 1934 included Abdul Rahim Hojibayev (Hajibai), chairman of the Council of People's Commissars, for trying to create Greater Tajikistan at the expense of other republics.

31. Bohdan Nahaylo and Victor Swoboda, *Soviet Disunion: A History of the Nationalities Problem in the USSR*, Hamish Hamilton, London, 1990, p. 67. During the early 1930s an average of 32,000 kulak families were put through the collectivization pro-cess in the Kazakh and Kyrgyz ASSRs. Amir Taheri, *Crescent in a Red Sky: The Future of Islam in the Soviet Union*, Hutchinson, London, 1989, p. 106.

32. Walter Kolarz, *Russia and Her Colonies*, Frederick A. Praeger, New York, 1952, p. 14.

33. In 1953 the Voroshilov *kolkhoz* in the Issyk Kul province of Kyrgyzstan, with 2588 workers, living in the villages of Darkhan and Chichkhan, and possessing a flour mill, a club, a library and schools, was typical. Geoffrey Wheeler, *The Modern History of Soviet Central Asia*, Weidenfeld and Nicolson, London, 1964, p. 168.

34. *Constitution of the Tajik Soviet Socialist Republic of 1 March 1937*, American-Russian Institute, New York, 1950, p. 21.

35. Shirin Akiner, *Islamic Peoples of the Soviet Union*, Kegan Paul International, London and Boston, Mass., 1983, pp. 296 and 334.

36. Shirin Akiner, op. cit., pp. 296 and 309; and Frank Lorimer, *The Population of the Soviet Union*, League of Nations, Geneva, 1946, p. 199.

37. Alexandre A. Benningsen and Marie Broxup, op. cit., p. 48.

38. Donald S. Carlisle, 'Power and Politics in Soviet Uzbekistan: From Stalin to Gorbachev', in William Fierman (ed.), *Soviet Central Asia: The Failed Transformation*, Westview Press, Boulder, Col., and Oxford, 1992, p. 99.

39. *Great Soviet Encyclopedia*, Vol. 1, 1973, p. 557.

40. Ibid., Vol. 11, p. 511; Vol. 12, p. 487; and Vol. 26, pp. 660 and 661.

41. Ibid., Vol. 11, p. 511; Vol. 12, p. 487; Vol. 25, p. 292; and Uzbekistan: Vol. 26, p. 660.

42. Kazemzadeh, op. cit., p. 143.

43. Cited in Amir Taheri, op. cit., p. 165.

44. Cited in Kazemzadeh, op. cit., p 284.

45. Cited in Christopher J. Walker, *Armenia and Karabagh: The Struggle for Unity*, Minority Rights Publications, London, 1991, p. 108.

46. A. Haji-Zadeh, *Soviet Azerbaijan*, Progress Publishers, Moscow, 1965, pp. 23–4 and 60; and *Great Soviet Encyclopedia*, Vol. 1, Third Edition, 1973, p. 556.

47. Haji-Zadeh, op. cit., p. 40.

48. The Armenians and Russians constituted about twelve per cent each.

49. *Great Soviet Encyclopedia*, Vol. 1, Third Edition, 1973, p. 556.

Chapter 1: Turkey

1. Kazemzadeh, op. cit., p. 91; see also Introduction, pp. 42–3

2. Cited in Edward Mortimer, *Faith and Power: The Politics of Islam*, Faber and Faber, London, 1982, p. 135.

3. After the formal end of the Greek–Turkish War in 1923 there was an official exchange of population, with Greeks and other Christians exchanged for Turks and Greek-speaking Muslims, numbering two million each.

4. Cited in Mortimer, op. cit., p. 137.

5. Cited in Bernard Lewis, *The Emergence of Modern Turkey*, Oxford University Press, London and New York, 1961, p. 263.

6. Serif Mardin, 'Religion and

Politics in Modern Turkey', in James P. Piscatori (ed.), *Islam in the Political Process*, Cambridge University Press, Cambridge and New York, 1982, pp. 156–7.

7. For this infringement of the constitution, Adnan Menderes was executed in September 1961.

8. Cited by Feroz Ahmad, 'The Islamic Assertion in Turkey: Pressures and State Response', paper at the First International Seminar, Institute of Arab Studies, 5–6 June 1981.

9. Serif Mardin, op. cit., p. 154.

10. Cited in *The Middle East*, May 1978, p. 10.

11. *Middle East Report*, July/ August 1988, p. 15.

12. Serif Mardin, op. cit., p. 153.

13. According to the pan-Turkic legend of bozkurt (steppe-wolf, often called grey wolf), it was always a grey wolf which led their ancestors on their various migrations from their legendary place of origin, Turan, consisting of the Altai Mountains and the Gobi Desert.

14. *The Middle East*, November 1980, p. 25.

15. While leftist and Islamist activities ceased in Turkey, these continued unabated in West Germany, home to more than one million Turkish 'guest workers'.

16. During the three years of military rule the number of divinity faculties at universities went up from two to eight. Interviews in Istanbul, May 1992.

17. *The Times*, 29 January 1982.

18. *Nation*, 28 June 1986, pp. 882 and 883. See Chapter 1, note 1.

19. *Nation*, 28 June 1986, p. 883.

20. *Inquiry*, February 1986, p. 30; and *Nation*, 28 June 1986, p. 883.

21. *The Middle East*, March 1990, p. 8; and *Financial Times*, 20 May 1991.

22. *Financial Times*, 20 May 1991; and *Turkish Daily News*, 9 April 1992. In Europe there were large Turkish communities in Germany and France.

23. See further Chapter 2, p. 88.

24. Cited in *Middle East International*, 17 May 1991, p. 18. To be fair to Ozal, he was following Kemalist principles in diplomacy: develop and maintain relations with neighbours, and avoid involvement in disputes that do not concern Turkey directly and affect its security.

25. *Financial Times*, 20 May 1991.

26. Also gone were the penal code's Article 141, outlawing the organizations that aimed to establish the domination of one social class (used successfully against Marxist organizations), and Article 142 pertaining to undermining 'national morale'.

27. Cited in *Middle East International*, 10 January 1992, p. 19.

28. With 350,000 on their rolls, these religious schools had become an alternative to the secular school system, especially when their graduates were allowed to enrol at universities – but not at military academies. *The Middle East*, August 1992, p. 13.

29. *Financial Times*, 20 May 1991.

30. Interview in Ankara, May 1992.

31. *Middle East International*, 21 February 1992, p. 13.

32. *Turkish Daily News*, 9 April 1992. This was a modest beginning of a much more ambitious project. Interviews in Alma Ata and Ashqabat, October 1992.

33. Interview in Ankara, May 1992.

34. Cited in *Middle East International*, 15 May 1992, p. 12.

35. These sanctions were imposed

even though Turkey was entitled under a 1959 treaty to safeguard the interests of the Turkish minority in an independent Cyprus dominated by Greek Cypriots.

36. *Turkish Daily News*, 21 May 1992.

37. *Observer*, 4 April 1993.

38. *Guardian*, 8 April 1993.

39. BBC World Service, 14 April 1993. In the end nothing came of Ozal's offer because Elchibey had not asked for such a pact in the first place.

40. The irony of the statement – coming from a country with a recent history of three military coups, one of which led to the execution of the elected prime minister – made by the Acting Prime Minister of Turkey, Erdal Inonu, was probably lost on him.

41. *Independent*, 3 July 1993.

Chapter 2: Azerbaijan

1. *Great Soviet Encyclopedia*, Vol. 1, Third Edition, 1973, p. 559.

2. 108,800 included 7500 candidate members, and 143,700 included 8700 such members. Ibid.

3. *Nauka i Religia*, Vol. VII, December 1986, p. 19.

4. According to the 1979 census, the population of Nagorno Karabakh was 160,000.

5. In 1979 there were 352,000 Armenians in Azerbaijan outside of Karabakh among a total population of six million in the republic, and 161,000 Azeris in Armenia with a population of three million. Shirin Akiner, *Islamic Peoples of the Soviet Union*, op. cit., pp. 114–15; and Christopher J. Walker (ed.), *Armenia and Karabagh*, op. cit., p. 63.

6. *Pravda*, 19 January 1989.

7. On 10 Muharram 61

A.H.(After Hijra)/8 May 681, Imam Hussein and his small band of warriors were killed by their adversary, Yazid, commanding 4000 troops, near Karbala in southern Iraq. See further Dilip Hiro, *Islamic Fundamentalism/Holy Wars: The Rise of Islamic Fundamentalism*, op. cit., pp. 18–19.

8. See further Chapter 9, p. 288.

9. Tass, 12 November 1988.

10. These figures were published by a committee of inquiry appointed by the Azerbaijan Supreme Soviet. It described Moscow's move as 'a criminal act' and 'one of the shameful pages in Soviet history'. *Observer*, 8 March 1992.

11. Cited in Steve Crawshaw, *Goodbye to the USSR: The Collapse of Soviet Power*, Bloomsbury, London, 1992, p. 109.

12. At the history department of the State University of Azerbaijan in Baku, all of the twenty-one teaching staff, except one, left the party. Interview with Professor Jamil Hassanov on 25 May 1992.

13. Yet Yeltsin's support amounted to only forty-three per cent of the total electorate.

14. See Introduction, p. 27.

15. In the Soviet Union the term 'mafia' – originally applied to those men who, unlike the apparatchiks, looked dapper in their well-cut suits – was later extended to those who could get all kinds of jobs done through underhand means – Mr Fix-its.

16. *Turkish Daily News*, 21 May 1992.

17. *Guardian*, 9 June 1992.

18. *Turkish Daily News*, 27 May 1992.

19. These promises were based on the fact that Azerbaijan's oil reserves under its land and its waters in the

Caspian Sea totalled 7.5 billion barrels, a fraction of the ninety-five billion barrels possessed by Kuwait with a population of around 1.6 million.

20. Interview in Baku, May 1992.

21. *Independent*, 20 June 1992.

22. *New York Times*, 8 April 1993. The 'Republic of Nagorno Karabakh' had started issuing its passport stamps in February 1993.

23. *Guardian*, 13 April 1993. President Yeltsin also played a role in getting Armenia to halt its offensives on all fronts. *Middle East International*, 14 April 1993, p. 15.

24. *Observer*, 11 April 1993.

25. *Guardian*, 1 July 1993.

26. Acting President Aliyev, who inherited the problem, managed to fudge the issue by stating that 'I'm poorly informed about this creation [CIS]'. *Guardian*, 1 July 1993.

Chapter 3: Kazakhstan

1. Shirin Akiner, *Islamic Peoples of the Soviet Union*, op. cit., p. 294.

2. Martha Brill Olcott, *The Kazakhs*, Hoover Institution Press, Stanford, Ca, 1987, p. 239.

3. In contrast there were only 418 cooperative farms, each one having about 500 households. Ibid., p. 239.

4. Between 1951 and 1961 the CPK membership rose by nearly two-thirds, from 194,714 to 317,700. *Great Soviet Encyclopedia*, Vol. 11, Third Edition, 1976, p. 513.

5. Between 1950 and 1979 milk output grew by 264 per cent, meat by 318 per cent, and eggs by 536 per cent. Olcott, op. cit., p. 240.

6. After the USSR–US ban on atmospheric nuclear tests in 1963, the site near Semipalatinsk continued to be used for underground tests.

7. In Kazakh legend Alash (or Alach) is depicted as the progenitor of the Kazakh people whose three sons founded the three Kazakh hordes: Small, Middle and Great. Alash Orda was originally formed in 1905 to contest parliamentary elections.

8. Cited in K. B. Beisembiev, *Ideino-politicheski Techeniia Kazakh-stane* Kontsa XIX–Nachala XX veka, Alma Ata, 1961, pp. 113–14.

9. *Islam i Natsiya*, Moscow, 1975, p. 48.

10. *Islam i Obshchestvo*, Moscow, 1978, pp. 180–90.

11. The lower figure for the deaths was given by Nursultan Nazarbayev, then chairman of the Council of Ministers, in February 1987. The higher figure for the fatalities, including seven guards, based on eye-witness accounts, was published in the *Guardian*, 30 December 1986. The statistics for the injured and the arrested were released by a Supreme Soviet committee on 24 September 1990. Interviews in Alma Ata, October 1992.

12. Interview with Anvar Alimjanov, president of the Socialist Party of Kazakhstan, and chairman of the influential Writers Union at the time of the rioting, in Alma Ata, October 1992.

13. *Izvestia*, 7 June 1988.

14. *Literaturnaya Gazeta*, 21 May 1987, p. 13.

15. Amir Taheri, *Crescent in a Red Sky*, op. cit., p. 192.

16. Like other senior party leaders, Nazarbayev had backed Kolbin in December 1986, a fact overlooked by most Kazakhs in mid-1989.

17. Interveiw with Haji Radbek Nisanbayev in Alma Ata, October 1992. In the first five months of 1990 the new directorate had re-opened twenty-seven old mosques with voluntary donations. *Far Eastern*

Economic Review, 12 July 1990, p. 25.

18. Mukhtar Shahanov, Chairman of the Presidium of the Supreme Soviet of Kazakh SSR, *About Conclusions and Recommendations Concerning the Final Assessment of Events on 17 Dec 1986 in Alma Ata*, issued by Y. Asanbayev, President of the Supreme Soviet of Kazakh SSR, Alma Ata, 24 September 1990, p. 3.

19. The tablet reads: 'On this square on 17 December 1986 took place an expression of the democratic will against the diktats of the command administrative system. Let the memory of this event bring forth unity of nationalities.'

20. Later, when the authorities in Moscow began harassing him, he sought refuge at the Azerbaijani embassy. He then moved to Baku. *Asia Weekly*, 14 October 1992.

21. *Far Eastern Economic Review*, 1 August 1991.

22. But the issue was far from over. Listing the regions of territorial conflict, *Moscow News* in early January 1992 showed a large part of northern Kazakhstan claimed by local Cossacks to be Russian territory.

23. Cited in *Central Asia Monitor*, No. 2, 1992, pp. 13–14.

24. *Krasnaya Zvezda* (Red Star), 10 December 1991.

25. *Radio Free Europe Daily Report*, 4 February 1992.

26. Washington was particularly disturbed by intelligence reports that Kazakhstan had test-fired SS-19 intercontinental ballistic missiles on 20 December 1991, just a few days after a visit to Alma Ata by the US Secretary of State, James Baker, when he reportedly expressed American concern about nuclear weapons in the republic. *Far Eastern Economic Review*, 30 January 1992, pp. 20–21.

27. Earlier, Nazarbayev had demanded that Kazakhstan should monitor the Moscow-controlled Baikonur Space Centre, used mainly for missile launching.

28. Nothing came of it because the Kazakh prosecutor announced that it was unlawful for public associations to form any military or paramilitary organization.

29. Interview with Saida Sultanat Ermakova, an Alash Orda leader, in Alma Ata, October 1992.

30. Interview with Haji Nisanbayev in Alma Ata, October 1992.

31. *New York Times*, 24 May 1992.

32. Interviews in Alma Ata, October 1992; and *Central Asia Monitor*, No. 6, 1992, p. 7.

33. *Azat*, 16 June 1992.

34. *Central Asia Monitor*, No. 4, 1992, p. 4; and *The Economist*, 8 August 1992, p. 56.

35. Of the sixteen members of the CPK's Politburo, only two, including Nazarbayev, were in power. Interviews in Alma Ata, October 1992; and *Great Soviet Encyclopedia*, 1989, Fourth Edition, Moscow, p. 119.

36. *Central Asia Newsfile*, No. 2, December 1992, p. 1.

37. *BBC World Service: Central Asia Report Digest*, No. 1, 1993, p. 2; and *Central Asia Monitor*, No. 1, 1993, p. 1.

38. Cited in the *Independent*, 27 February 1993.

39. Since less than one per cent of Russians spoke Kazakh, the chance of an ethnic Russian becoming the republic's president was almost nil.

Chapter 4: Kyrgyzstan

1. In 1926, a census year, Kyrgyzs constituted sixty-seven per cent of the population of 990,000. But owing to collectivization and famine during the 1930s their number fell so that in 1959 they constituted only forty-one per cent of the total population of a little over two million, and about as numerous as Russians (thirty per cent), Ukrainians (seven per cent) and Germans (two per cent) combined. Shirin Akiner, *The Islamic Peoples of the Soviet Union*, op. cit., p. 332.

2. Interview in Bishkek, October 1992.

3. Nancy Lubin, 'Implications of Ethnic and Demographic Trends', in William Fierman (ed.), *Soviet Central Asia: The Failed Transformation*, op. cit., p. 41.

4. According to an Uzbek journalist in Tashkent, Kyrgyz interior ministry forces, wearing red bands, went from house to house in Osh, killing Uzbeks. He put the number of dead at 5000 – a figure considered grossly exaggerated by non-Uzbeks, and more likely to be under 1000. Cited in the *Independent Magazine*, 5 October 1991, p. 28.

5. *The Economist*, 19 October 1991.

6. Interview in Bishkek, October 1992.

7. Azade-Ayse Rorlich, 'Islam and Atheism: Dynamic Tension in Soviet Central Asia', in William Fierman (ed.), op. cit., p. 188.

8. Cited in ibid., p. 192.

9. *Central Asia Monitor*, No. 4, 1992, p. 16.

10. *Great Soviet Encyclopedia Annual*, Moscow, 1990, p. 124.

11. Interviews in Bishkek, October 1992.

12. *The Economist*, 19 October 1991.

13. Interviews in Bishkek, October 1992.

14. See later, Chapter 7, pp. 206ff passim, and Chapter 8, pp. 263ff passim.

15. *Central Asia Monitor*, No. 5, 1992, p. 2.

16. Interview in Bishkek, October 1992.

17. On 10 May, backed by the International Monetary Fund, Kyrgyzstan launched its own currency, Som, the first Central Asian republic to do so.

Chapter 5: Turkmenistan

1. *Great Soviet Encyclopedia*, Vol. 26, 1981, p. 491, and *Turkmeniskaya Sotsialisticheskaya Respublika*, Ashqabat, 1984, p. 214.

2. *Turkmen Soviet Socialist Republic*, Novosti Press Agency Publishing House, 1972, p. 36; and *Great Soviet Encyclopedia*, Vol. 26, 1981, p. 492.

3. Cited in the *Independent Magazine*, 5 October 1991, p. 27.

4. *Trud* (Labour), 1 October 1988.

5. Bally Yazkuliyev, *Turkmenia*, Novosti Press Agency Publishing House, Moscow, 1987, pp. 28 and 41.

6. The relative strengths of the important tribes in the early twentieth century were: Tekke, 39.2 per cent; Yomut, 13.2 per cent; Salory, 5.2 per cent; and Sariki, 4.8 per cent. Marat Durdyev and Shokhrat Kadyrov, *The Turkmens of the World*, Kharp, Ashqabat, 1989, p 14.

7. At the Academy of Sciences in Ashqabat, the Communist Party had 300 members, but the Democrat Party membership was about 100. Interviews in Ashqabat, October 1992.

8. *Turkmeniskaya Iskra* (Spark of Turkmenistan), 24 February 1992.

9. *Ashqabat Vecherni* (Ashqabat Evening), 19 May 1992.

10. Interview in Ashqabat, October 1992.

11. *Central Asia Monitor*, No. 3, 1992, pp. 4–5. The agreement allowed the two parties to rename the (nominally) CIS troops as Russian forces. The three-year plan was to reduce the troops stationed in Turkmenistan in stages, from 120,000 to 60,000, when ninety per cent of them would be ethnic Turkmen and would be commanded by Turkmen officers. Interviews in Ashqabat, October 1992.

12. Interviews in Ashqabat, October 1992.

13. The World Turkmen Humanitarian Association was set up after representatives of Turkmens from ten countries gathered under the leadership of Saparmurad Niyazov in May 1991. Of the five million Turkmens worldwide, 2.1 million lived outside Turkmenistan. Durdyev and Kadyrov, op. cit., p. 45.

14. Reuters, 26 March 1993.

15. Interviews in Ashqabat, October 1992.

16. Interview with Durdimurad Khojamuhammad, *Central Asia Monitor*, No. 4, 1992, p. 16.

17. Ibid., p. 14.

18. *Ashqabat Vecherni*, 20 October 1992.

19. Interviews in Ashqabat, October 1992.

20. Cited in *Central Asia Monitor*, No. 4, 1992, p. 4.

Chapter 6: Uzbekistan

1. Of the two million residents of Tashkent in autumn 1992, ethnic Russians were estimated to form thirty to forty per cent of the aggregate, as against ten per cent of the republican total. Interviews in Tashkent, September 1992.

2. See Introduction, p. 16.

3. Bohdan Nahaylo and Victor Swoboda, *Soviet Disunion: A History of the Nationalities Problem in the USSR*, op. cit., p. 159.

4. The normal role of the Council of Ulemas was to discuss religious issues and deliver fatwas (religious decrees) if necessary.

5. When asked if 'parallel Islam' existed, the muftis would say: 'Islam is where believers are'. Amir Taheri, *Crescent in a Red Sky*, op. cit., p. 134.

6. Cited by H. Alleg, *Etoile Rouge et Croissant Vert*, Paris, 1983, p. 231.

7. Cited in Edward Mortimer, *Faith and Power: The Politics of Islam*, op. cit., p. 371.

8. Cited in Dilip Hiro, *Iran Under the Ayatollahs*, Routledge and Kegan Paul, London and Boston, 1985, p. 288.

9. As for Iran, it had embarked on such radio transmissions as early as March 1979.

10. Cited in Nahaylo and Swoboda, op. cit., p. 217.

11. The extent of the purges could be judged by the fact that in January 1985 forty of the sixty-five oblast party secretaries were removed, and ninety new officials were brought into the top echelons of the civil administration. Donald S. Carlisle, 'Power and Politics in Soviet Uzbekistan: From Stalin to Gorbachev' in William Fierman (ed.), *Soviet Central Asia: The Failed Transformation*, op. cit., p. 114.

12. *Pravda Vostoka* (Truth of the East), 31 January 1986.

13. *Die Presse* (Vienna), 1 September 1986, and the *Independent Magazine*, 5 October 1991, p. 24.

14. *Far Eastern Economic Review*, 26 November 1992, p. 40.

15. Carlisle, op. cit., p. 116.

16. *Pravda Vostoka*, 25 November 1986.

17. *Literaturnaya Gazeta*, 20 May 1986.

18. *Pravda Vostoka*, 12 August 1987. In mid-1987 the membership of the CPU at 582,000 was down from 640,000 at the time of the party congress in January 1986. Carlisle, op. cit., p. 154, note 17.

19. Cited in Nahaylo and Swoboda, op. cit., p. 248.

20. *Pravda Vostoka*, 10 April 1988.

21. Cited in Amir Taheri, op. cit., p. 141.

22. *Kommunist Uzbekistana*, No. 5, 1988, p. 83.

23. A similar suggestion had been made a year earlier regarding the 1800 'unofficial' mosques in existence in the Muslim regions, by Yegor Baliyev, an orientalist and a former Tass correspondent in the Middle East. He recommended a similar course for mosque construction. 'Would it not be wiser to authorize the construction of mosques where there is a need for them?' he asked. 'Things would be much clearer for the faithful and the local authorities.' *Literaturnaya Gazeta*, 13 May 1987, pp. 12–13.

24. *Kommunist Uzbekistana*, No. 6, 1988, pp. 58–65. Most of the 751 registered 'Muslim communities' were based in Central Asia. In addition, there were 1800 unregistered Muslim communities, each having a mosque. Azade-Ayse Rorlich, 'Islam and Atheism: Dynamic Tension in Soviet Central Asia', in Fierman (ed.), op. cit., p. 188.

25. Cited in the *Independent*, 2 October 1991; and the *Independent Magazine*, 5 October 1991, p. 28.

26. A movement, political or non-political, concerned itself with one or more general issues: environment, language, welfare of soldiers, etc.; whereas a political party was expected to have an overall programme for society covering its various facets.

27. Nahaylo and Swoboda, op. cit., p. 337. Actually, an earlier report had stated that the average per capita income of forty-five per cent of Uzbekistan's population from all sources was R75 a month, which was only marginally below the official subsistence level of R78 a month. And the figure of one million unemployed had been given earlier by Nishanov at the CPU Central Committee's plenum in January 1988. Radio Liberty *Report on the USSR*, 23 June 1989; and *Pravda Vostoka*, 31 January 1988.

28. *Kommunist Uzbekistana*, June 1989, pp. 47–8.

29. *Pravda Vostoka*, 7 December 1989. Italics in the original.

30. James Critchlow, *Nationalism in Uzbekistan: A Soviet Republic's Sovereignty*, Westview Press, Boulder, Col., and Oxford, 1992, pp. 63, 64 and 66.

31. The next year an important road in Tashkent was renamed after Sharaf Rashidov in an effort to rehabilitate him. And in November 1992 the leader's seventy-fifth birthday was celebrated in his home town of Jizk with full official honours.

32. A proviso in the decree gave the right to the conscript and his family to agree specifically to a posting outside the Turkestan Military District.

33. *Pravda Vostoka*, 29 November 1990.

34. As for the mufti, he initiated a programme of Islamic education in January 1990 with a series of sermons published in the Uzbek cultural weekly *Ozbekistan Adabiyati va Sanaati.*

35. When Anvar Usmanov, a journalist, reported the event on Radio Liberty, he was arrested for stirring up ethnic hatred. *Independent Magazine*, 5 October 1991, p. 30.

36. *Independent*, 18 September 1991.

37. Later, Karimov attacked the 'witch hunt' in Moscow against those alleged to have participated in the coup, comparing it to the Stalinist purges of 1937–8. *Independent*, 18 September 1991.

38. *Independent Magazine*, 5 October 1991, pp. 24–5.

39. *Independent*, 21 December 1991.

40. In late November the electoral commission required the opposition groups to submit 100,000 voter signatures for their candidate within three days to qualify for the contest. Birlik reportedly managed this, but by the time its representatives reached the commission's office on the afternoon of the deadline, a Friday, they found the office closed. Interviews in Tashkent, September 1992.

41. Interview with Muhammad Salih in Tashkent, September 1992.

42. I. A. Karimov, *Uzbekistan: Its Own Road to Renewal and Progress*, Izdatyelsto Uzbekistan, Tashkent, 1992, p. 50.

43. Interviews in Namangan, November 1992.

44. *Foreign Broadcast Information Service*, 24 March 1992; and *Far Eastern Economic Review*, 19

November 1992, p. 24. The IRP was comparatively weak in Tashkent, with a clandestine membership of about 5000 in a city of two million. *The Economist*, 21 September 1991.

45. *Central Asia Monitor*, No. 4, 1992, p. 27. The situation deteriorated steadily so that in July the party decided to suspend its publication. Interview with Muhammad Salih, September 1992.

46. Interview with Muhammad Salih in Tashkent, September 1992. In August 1992, Anwar Usmanov, a journalist working for Radio Liberty, was attacked by unknown persons in Tashkent. To recover from the injuries he went to Istanbul. While away, his unoccupied house was burnt down on 2 September.

47. Karimov, op. cit., pp. 39, 48 and 49. After December 1991, according to the law on land ownership, a citizen could lease land from the government but could not sell or inherit it. The reasons were both ideological and practical: to prevent speculation in land which could play havoc with prices and distort production; also, if land were privatized, then there would be no way of ensuring that a certain percentage of land was used for growing cotton. The new owners would decide on the general basis of supply and demand.

48. Ibid., p. 26.

49. Ibid., pp. 37, 40 and 43.

50. Ibid., p. 10.

51. Ibid., p. 31.

52. *Far Eastern Economic Review*, 19 November 1992, p. 23.

53. Ibid., p. 24. A number of Wahhabis had reportedly joined the police and other security agencies. Ibid., p. 26.

54. Interviews in Namangan, November 1992.

55. *Slovo Kyrgyzstan* (Word of Kyrgyzstan), 10 October 1992.

56. See further Chapter 7, pp. 223ff.

57. *Guardian*, 12 December 1992; and *Central Asia Monitor*, No. 1, 1993, p. 3.

58. According to a senior American diplomat in Tashkent, while the Islamic forces were not currently strong in Uzbekistan, they could become so rapidly because the infrastructure of mosques and religious organizations already existed. Interview, September 1992.

59. Interviews in Tashkent, September 1992; and *Great Soviet Encyclopedia Annual*, 1990, p. 175.

60. *Independent*, 2 January 1993. On 5 May 1993 Shukrat Ismatulayev (Ismatullah), co-chairman of the Birlik Popular Front, was attacked with brass knuckles by unknown assailants in Tashkent, and hospitalized. *Central Asia Newsfile*, No. 6, May 1993, p. 1.

61. Interview in Tashkent, September 1992.

Chapter 7: Tajikistan

1. Teresa Rakowska-Harmstone, *Russia and Nationalism in Central Asia: The Case of Tadzhikistan*, op. cit., pp. 57 and 58.

2. *Pravda*, 23 May 1963.

3. Dilip Hiro, *Islamic Fundamentalism/Holy Wars: The Rise of Islamic Fundamentalism*, op. cit., p. 256; and Alexandre Benningsen and Marie Broxup, *The Islamic Threat to the Soviet State*, op. cit., p. 113.

4. In return the Soviet authorities agreed to moderate their atheist propaganda and allow the re-opening of some old mosques.

5. Dilip Hiro, op. cit., p. 257.

6. Amir Taheri, *Crescent in a Red Sky*, op. cit., p. 197.

7. The problem continued: the Tajik press reported in early 1988 that the arrest and trial of two underground mullahs, one of them advocating an Islamic state, had led to disorder in Kurgan Tyube. Ibid., p. 215.

8. *Volksstimme* (Voice of the People), Vienna, 9 May 1987.

9. *Central Asian Newsletter*, May 1988, p. 14.

10. Radio Dushanbe, 13 November 1988.

11. *Observer*, 15 May 1988.

12. The number of Russians in Tajikistan was 395,000 in 1979 and 388,000 in 1989. Cited in Nancy Lubin, 'Implications of Ethnic and Demographic Trends', in William Fierman (ed.), *Soviet Central Asia: The Failed Transformation*, op. cit., p. 40.

13. *Great Soviet Encyclopedia Annual*, 1990, p. 167.

14. Shirin Akiner, *Islamic Peoples of the Soviet Union*, op. cit., p. 308.

15. *The Economist*, 21 September 1991.

16. *Central Asia Monitor*, No. 1, 1992, p. 17.

17. Cited in ibid., p. 10.

18. Ismailis are a sub-sect within Shia Islam. See Dilip Hiro, op. cit., p. 22.

19. *Far Eastern Economic Review*, 9 January 1992, p. 18.

20. The regional parliament acted on a petition, calling for the political-administrative upgrading of Badakhshan, signed by 15,000 supporters of Lal-e Badakhshan, a party formed in 1989.

21. The statement was taken seriously, with the deputy commander of the Central Asian Border Guard District announcing

that he was tightening border patrols.

22. *Financial Times*, 7 May 1992.

23. *Moscow News*, No. 20, 1992, p. 4.

24. *Central Asia Monitor*, No. 3, 1992, p. 6.

25. Safarali Kenjayev fled to Hojand and then to Uzbekistan. *Central Asia and Caucasus in World Affairs Newsletter*, No. 4, p. 3.

26. With the rise of Tajik nationalism over the past few years, the role of the Russian-language media and schools had declined sharply.

27. *Turkish Daily News*, 2 September 1992.

28. *Central Asia Monitor*, No. 5, 1992, p. 5.

29. Ibid. According to another version, Nabiyev was lured from CIS headquarters to Dushanbe airport's VIP lounge by some of the men occupying the presidential palace. Then members of the Tajikistan Youth, a pro-Islamic militia, led by Juma Khan, encircled the lounge with tanks and armoured personnel carriers, and threatened to fire unless Nabiyev resigned. He did. *Financial Times*, 9 October 1992. A third version, a mixture of the above two, had Nabiyev 'kidnapped by an armed opposition group at Dushanbe airport' as he was escaping to Hojand. *Middle East International*, 9 October 1992, p. 15.

30. According to the *Far Eastern Economic Review* of 9 January 1992, there were 2870 mosques in Tajikistan. This figure, probably provided by the Kaziat in Dushanbe, seemed to include tea-houses and halls used for prayers since there was no evidence that there were that many proper mosques in the republic. Dushanbe, a metropolis of 608,000, had only five mosques.

31. *Pravda*, 10 October 1992.

32. *Central Asia Monitor*, No. 5, 1992, p. 9.

33. Ibid., p. 6.

34. Ibid., p. 7.

35. While the provincial capital had reverted to its pre-Bolshevik revolution name of Hojand, the province was still called Leninabad.

36. *Pravda*, 10 October 1992.

37. Moscow Radio, 10 and 11 October 1992; and *Slovo Kyrgyzstan*, 10 October 1992.

38. *Central Asia Monitor*, No. 5, 1992, p. 9.

39. Cited in *In These Times*, 23–30 June 1992, p. 9, and the *Independent*, 27 June 1992.

40. Cited in *Central Asia Monitor*, No. 5, 1992, p. 9.

41. *Central Asia and Caucasus in World Affairs Newsletter*, No. 4, p. 4.

42. Tajikistan Radio, 31 October 1992, cited in *Central Asia Monitor*, No. 6, 1992, p. 2; *Middle East International*, 6 November 1992, p. 15; and *Financial Times*, 26 November 1992.

43. *Guardian*, 30 October 1992; and *Central Asia Monitor*, No. 6, 1992, p. 2.

44. *Far Eastern Economic Review*, 5 November 1992, p. 19.

45. *Central Asia Monitor*, No. 6, 1992, p. 3.

46. Nabiyev died on 10 April 1993.

47. *Guardian*, 26 November 1992.

48. *Guardian*, 10 December 1992, and *Observer*, 3 January 1993. The use of Uzbek fighter aircraft and helicopter gunships against the Islamic forces offering strong resistance in Dushanbe was confirmed by Russian officers of the 201st motorized division. *Central Asia Newsfile*, No. 3, January 1993, p. 1.

49. *Independent*, 27 March 1992.

The figure of 30,000 probably included up to 10,000 'disappearances'.

50. *Central Asia and Caucasus in World Affairs Newsletter*, No. 4, 29 February 1993, pp. 10 and 11.

51. BBC World Service Radio, 10 June 1993; and *Central Asia Monitor*, No. 1, 1993, p. 7.

52. *Central Asia and Caucasus in World Affairs Newsletter*, No. 3, 11 January 1993, p. 14. This must have been the most unique programme implemented by the leader of a Communist party anywhere in the world.

53. *Central Asia Newsfile*, No. 5, March 1993, p. 2.

Chapter 8: Afghanistan

1. See further Dilip Hiro, *Islamic Fundamentalism/Holy Wars: The Rise of Islamic Fundamentalism*, op. cit., pp. 22 and 27.

2. Nine months later, in November 1921, Amanullah signed a similar treaty with Britain.

3. Sayid Abul Ala Maududi, *Purdah and the Status of Women in Islam*, Islamic Publications, Lahore, 1979, p. 23.

4. Olivier Roy, *Islam and Resistance in Afghanistan*, Cambridge University Press, Cambridge and New York, 1986, p. 83.

5. *The Area Handbook of Afghanistan*, Kabul, 1973.

6. Anthony Hyman, *Afghanistan under Soviet Domination, 1964-83*, Macmillan, London, 1984, p. 90.

7. *Kabul Times*, 9 December 1978.

8. Ibid., 11 October 1979.

9. *Kabul New Times*, 1 January 1980. (After the Soviet intervention the *Kabul Times* became the *Kabul New Times*.)

10. Tahir Amin, *Afghanistan Crisis: Implications and Options for the Muslim World, Iran and Pakistan*, Institute of Policy Studies, Lahore, 1982, pp. 96-7.

11. Since, unlike in Soviet Central Asia, citizens of Afghanistan did not carry identity cards specifying their nationality/ethnic group, an exact ethnic breakdown of Afghanistan was not available. Even the figure of nineteen million for total Afghan citizens at home and abroad (mostly in refugee camps) was approximate.

12. Anthony Hyman, op. cit., pp. 203 and 204; and *Great Soviet Encyclopedia*, Vol. 26, Third Edition, p. 662.

13. Anthony Hyman, op. cit., p. 204.

14. Anthony Arnold, *Afghanistan: The Soviet Invasion in Perspective*, Hoover Institution Press, Stanford, Ca, 1985, p. 100. Soviet deaths probably amounted to 6000-8000.

15. Another major reason for Karmal's replacement was his alcoholism: it had reached a stage where his work suffered.

16. *Sunday Times*, 8 February 1987.

17. *New York Times*, 28 April 1987.

18. *Observer*, 10 May 1987; and *Independent*, 26 May 1987.

19. *Washington Times*, 23 April 1987.

20. *Observer*, 15 May 1988.

21. *Sunday Times*, 26 February 1989.

22. *The Times*, 15 February 1989; and *Guardian*, 16 February 1989. The loyalty to the Najibullah regime of many of the 45,000-50,000 men in the army and air force was questionable.

23. *Guardian*, 25 and 27 February 1989.

24. The only countries to

recognize the Afghan Mujahedin's interim government were Saudi Arabia, Bahrain, Sudan and Malaysia.

25. *The Middle East*, February 1991, p. 15.

26. Cited in *Far Eastern Economic Review*, 16 January 1992, p. 21.

27. *Far Eastern Economic Review*, 31 October 1991, p. 28.

28. *The Economist*, 1 February 1992, p. 66.

29. *Far Eastern Economic Review*, 2 April 1992, p. 18; and *Mainstream*, 25 April 1992.

30. However, Dostum added that he did not control 'the border to the east and north-east of Afghanistan'. *Far Eastern Economic Review*, 28 January 1993, p. 19.

31. *Guardian*, 26 February 1993.

32. *Far Eastern Economic Review*, 18 February 1993, p. 26; and *Middle East International*, 28 May 1993, p. 18.

Chapter 9: Iran

1. The twelve Shia Imams are: Ali, Hassan, Hussein, Zain al Abidin, Muhammad al Baqir, Jaafar al Sadiq, Musa al Kazim, Ali al Rida, Muhammad al Taqi Javad, Ali al Naqi, Hassan al Askri, and Muhammad al Muntazar (who disappeared in infancy, and is therefore known as the Hidden Imam).

2. Nikki R. Keddie, *Roots of Revolution: an Interpretative History of Modern Iran*, Yale University Press, Yale, Ct, and London, 1981, p. 111.

3. Cited in the *Sunday Times*, 13 April 1980.

4. Ibid.

5. *Constitution of the Islamic Republic of Iran* (trans. Hamid Algar), Mizan Press, Berkeley, Ca, 1980, pp. 29–30. The wording of the constitution is either from Algar or the *Constitution of the Islamic Republic of Iran*, published in the *Middle East Journal*, spring 1980, Washington, DC, pp. 184–202.

6. Ibid., p. 30.

7. Ibid., p. 60.

8. *Sunday Times*, 11 April 1982.

9. Sepehr Zabih, *Iran since the Revolution*, Croom Helm, London, 1982, p. 99.

10. *The Middle East*, February 1982, p. 30.

11. Dilip Hiro, *Islamic Fundamentalism/Holy Wars: The Rise of Islamic Fundamentalism*, op. cit., pp. 202–3.

12. Ervand Abrahamian, *Iran between Two Revolutions*, Princeton University Press, Princeton, NJ, and Guildford, 1982, p. 433; and *Sunday Times*, 4 April 1982.

13. Dilip Hiro, op. cit., p. 204.

14. *Constitution of the Islamic Republic of Iran* (trans. Hamid Algar), op. cit., p. 30.

15. Islamic Republic News Agency, 2 November 1983.

16. *Sunday Times*, 5 June 1983. See also Chapter 8, p. 240.

17. *Kayhan International*, 29 December 1979.

18. *8 Days*, 16 February 1980, p. 6.

19. Dilip Hiro, *Iran Under the Ayatollahs*, op. cit., p. 354.

20. *MERIP Reports*, January 1983, p. 22; and *Guardian*, 31 January 1986.

21. *Daily Telegraph*, 22 March 1980.

22. *Events*, 6 October 1979, p. 21.

23. *Report of the Central Committee of the CPSU to the XXVI Congress of the Communist Party of the Soviet Union, 23 February 1981*, Novosti Press Agency Publishing House, Moscow, 1981, p. 23.

24. Radio Tehran, 8 December 1983.

25. *MERIP Reports*, January 1983, p. 22.

26. *BBC Summary of World Broadcasts*, 21 January 1984.

27. *Guardian*, 26 April 1984.

28. Cited in *Echo of Iran*, 15 December 1988, p. 8.

29. Cited in ibid., 12 January 1989, p. 24, and *The Middle East*, April 1989, p. 11. Lest eyebrows be raised in the Muslim world at the concept of an Islamic personality like Khomeini addressing epistles to the head of an atheist state, his special emissary, Ayatollah Javadi Amoli, pointed out that Khomeini was merely following in the footsteps of Prophet Muhammad. After assuming power, Muhammad had called on both the Byzantine and Sassanian kings to embrace Islam.

30. *Tehran Times*, 8 January 1989.

31. Cited in *The Middle East*, April 1989, p. 12.

32. *Echo of Iran*, 23 March 1989, p. 5.

33. *Wall Street Journal*, 7 July 1989. If criticized, Rafsanjani and his brother could have argued that continued broadcasts might jeopardize the prospect of further contacts be-tween the peoples of Iran and Soviet Azerbaijan.

34. Cited in *Wall Street Journal*, 7 July 1989.

35. Later, a forty-five-kilometre (twenty-seven-mile) passport-free travel zone was to be opened up to facilitate visits between Azeri families split by the Bolshevik revolution and its aftermath.

36. Cited in *The Middle East*, February 1990. p. 11.

37. Cited in *Nation*, 14 September 1992, p. 243.

38. Cited in ibid. p. 242.

39. Interview in Baku, May 1992.

40. Elchibey referred to an 'unwritten law' in America according to which people 'fighting for liberation' should be encouraged. *American Spectator*, April 1993, p. 25.

41. Cited in *Financial Times*, 23 June 1992.

42. *Central Asia and Caucasus in World Affairs Newsletter*, No. 3, 11 January 1993, pp. 1–2.

43. Cited in *Financial Times*, 23 June 1992. The figure of 300 million Muslims was somewhat inflated. The total estimated population of the member-states of the enlarged ECO was about 280 million, including some twenty-four million non-Muslims.

44. *Central Asia Newsfile*, No. 2, December 1992, p. 7, and No. 3, January 1993, p. 3.

45. Interviews in Ashqabat, October 1992.

46. Cited in *Financial Times*, 23 June 92.

47. *Turkish Daily News*, 2 September 1992.

48. *Far Eastern Economic Review*, 15 October 1992, p. 22.

49. Islamic Republic News Agency, 16 January 1993; and *Central Asia and Caucasus in World Affairs Newsletter*, No. 2, 1 December 1992, p. 6.

50. *Sunday Times*, 27 January 1993.

Chapter 10: Summary and Conclusions

1. Viewed against the background of mixed-nationality marriages, Khrushchev's scenario did not appear overly optimistic. The figures for mixed-nationality marriages in Azerbaijan and Central Asia in 1959 and 1970 expressed as percentages were: Azerbaijan, 11.8 (12.8); Kazakhstan, 17.5 (23.8); Kyrgyzstan,

18.1 (20.9); Tajikistan, 16.7 (22.3); Turkmenistan, 14.9 (20); and Uzbekistan, 14.7 (18.4). Shirin Akiner, *Islamic Peoples of the Soviet Union*, pp. 115, 295, 333, 308, 320 and 378.

2. Serif Mardin, 'Religion and Politics in Modern Turkey', in James Piscatori (ed.), *Islam in the Political Process*, op. cit., p. 157.

Epilogue

1. *Guardian*, 29 June 1994.
2. Ibid. 20 August 1993.
3. *Middle East International*, 10 September 1993, p. 13.
4. *Independent*, 20 August 1993.
5. Barely two months earlier, Aliyev had described the CIS as 'a creation' about which he was 'poorly informed'. *The Times*, 1 July 1993.
6. The official claims of 90 per cent turn-out were disputed by foreign diplomats who put the figure at 50 per cent, a realistic estimate since three opposition parties boycotted the poll. *Independent*, 9 October 1993.
7. *Financial Times*, 9 September 1994; and *Turkish Daily News*, 12 September 1994.
8. *Financial Times*, 19 September 1994; and *Turkish Daily News*, 20 September 1994. The British Petroleum-led consortium included Statoil (of Norway), Turkish Petroleum, and five American oil companies.
9. *Wall Street Journal*, 9 May 1994; and *Financial Times*, 28 June 1994.
10. *The Times*, 14 December 1993.
11. *The Middle East*, January 1994, p. 14.

12. *Middle East International*, 1 April 1994, p. 14.
13. One solution being suggested is that, emulating Israel, Russia should pass a Law of Return, guaranteeing citizenship to the Russians returning home from the diaspora.
14. *Central Asia Monitor*, No. 4, 1994, p. 8.
15. *Financial Times*, 24 December 1993.
16. *Guardian*, 6 September 1993.
17. Cited in *Observer*, 22 August 1993. Yeltsin's statement was apparently based on the bilateral security and military cooperation treaty that Russia and Tajikistan had signed in June 1993.
18. Cited in *Middle East International*, 6 August 1993, p. 15. By the following August, while the total of Slav settlers in Tajikistan had dwindled to about 100,000, the number of Russian troops there had risen to 25,000.
19. *Central Asia Monitor*, No. 4, 1994, p. 5.
20. *Turkish Daily News*, 19 September 1994.
21. *Guardian*, 9 March 1994. Since the fall of Muhammad Najibullah in April 1992 some 15,000 Afghans had been killed in the civil conflict. *Turkish Daily News*, 10 September 1994.
22. *Central Asia Monitor*, No. 1, 1994, p. 1.
23. Ibid., No. 4, 1994, p. 2.
24. *Guardian*, 29 June 1994.

INDEX

For a name starting with Al, Der or El, see its second part. Individuals' religious or secular titles have been omitted.